The Chinese Cornerstone of Modern Banking

Legal History Library

VOLUME 14

Studies in the History of Private Law

VOLUME 6

The titles published in this series are listed at *brill.com/shpl*

The Chinese Cornerstone of Modern Banking

The Canton Guaranty System and the Origins of Bank Deposit Insurance 1780–1933

By

Frederic Delano Grant, Jr.

BRILL
NIJHOFF

LEIDEN | BOSTON

Cover Illustration: Howqua II (Wu Bingjian), 1769-1843. Oil portrait by Lamqua (Guan Qiaochang), ca. 1840. (Private collection. Photograph by permission.)

Library of Congress Cataloging-in-Publication Data

Grant, Frederic Delano, Jr. author.
The Chinese cornerstone of modern banking : the Canton guaranty system and the origins of bank deposit insurance 1780-1933 / By Frederic Delano Grant, Jr.
p. cm. — (Legal history library ; v. 10) (Studies in the history of private law)
Includes bibliographical references and index.
ISBN 978-90-04-27655-0 (hardback : alk. paper)—ISBN 978-90-04-27656-7 (e-book) 1. Deposit insurance—China—Guangzhou—History. 2. Suretyship and guaranty—China—Guangzhou—History. 3. Banks and banking—China—History. I. Title.

HG1662.C5G73 2014
368.8'5400951—dc23

2014027748

This publication has been typeset in the multilingual 'Brill' typeface. With over 5,100 characters covering Latin, IPA, Greek, and Cyrillic, this typeface is especially suitable for use in the humanities. For more information, please see brill.com/brill-typeface.

ISSN 1874-1793
ISBN 978-90-04-27655-0 (hardback)
ISBN 978-90-04-27656-7 (e-book)

This book is printed on acid-free paper.

Printed by Printforce, the Netherlands

Dedicated to Barbara
who made it possible

Contents

Acknowledgements IX
List of Illustrations XII
List of Tables and Charts XIV
Note on Spelling XV
Glossary XVI

1 **Introduction** 1
 1 Subject and Framework 3
 2 Previous Research 8
 3 The 1829 Crisis in the State of New York 13
 4 The Crisis in the Chinese Port of Canton: 1829 15
 5 The 1829 Crises as Prologue 16

2 **Sources of the Canton Guaranty System** 18
 1 Conquest and Pacification 18
 2 The Organization of Merchants Engaged in Maritime Trade 31
 3 Official Roots of Collective Responsibility 39
 4 Collective Responsibility in Chinese Tradition 47

3 **Evolution of the Canton Guaranty System** 54
 1 Official Management of Maritime Foreign Trade 54
 2 The Security Merchant System and Origins of Collective Responsibility 60
 3 The Formal Regulation of Maritime Foreign Trade 71
 4 Debt Collection Under the Canton System 93
 5 The 1780 Crisis and Imposition of the Collective Guaranty 111

4 **The Fund is Drained, 1780–1799** 126
 1 The Hong Merchants, 1780–1799 127
 2 The Demands of Government, 1780–1799 129
 3 Trading Conditions, 1780–1799 132
 4 The Collective Guaranty of Debt, 1780–1799 138

5 **Three Plagues: War, Piracy and Litigation, 1800–1814** 146
 1 The Hong Merchants, 1800–1814 148
 2 The Demands of Government, 1800–1814 151
 3 Trading Conditions, 1800–1814 154
 4 The Collective Guaranty of Debt, 1800–1814 157

5 The Abortive 1810 Receivership of Gnewqua II and Ponqua 159
6 The 1813 Receivership of the Junior Hong Merchants 163

6 Years of Rebound and Opium, 1815–1828 166
1 The Hong Merchants, 1815–1828 166
2 The Demands of Government, 1815–1828 170
3 Trading Conditions, 1815–1828 171
4 The Experience of Conseequa, 1796–1823 173
5 The Collective Guaranty of Debt, 1815–1828 184

7 The Last Years of the Canton System, 1829–1842 192
1 The Hong Merchants, 1829–1842 194
2 Trading Conditions, 1829–1842 202
3 The Collective Guaranty of Debt, 1829–1842 207

8 From Safety Fund to Bank Deposit Insurance 218
1 Joshua Forman 221
2 The Power of Suggestion 224
3 The Banking Crisis in the State of New York 226
4 The 1829 New York Safety Fund Statute 230
5 Early State Bank Guaranty Programs 237
6 Implementation of National Deposit Insurance in the United States 240

9 Eighty Years of Bank Deposit Insurance 252
1 Federal Deposit Insurance in the United States 253
2 The International Progress of Bank Deposit Insurance 257

10 Epilogue 263

Appendices
Appendix 1. The Original Five Regulations (1760) 283
Appendix 2. The Original Five Regulations (1760) 286
Appendix 3. The Eight Regulations (1831) 291
Appendix 4. The Eight Regulations (1835) 301
Appendix 5. The Eight Regulations (Per W.C. Hunter) 312

Bibliography 315
Index 333

Acknowledgements

The gratitude that I feel for all of the assistance that I have received on this project reaches back many years. The seed was planted when I was a student at Boston College Law School, from which I graduated in 1983. My law classmate, Max Kumin, who worked with Carter Golembe, brought Mr. Golembe's work on the Chinese origins of American bank deposit insurance to my attention while we were in school. I am very grateful to Max for that direction. My college professor Geoffrey Suess Law (1944–1980), a gifted teacher who ignited the interest in Chinese economic and institutional history that I carry to this day, had given me the skills I needed to start to analyze this information when I finally made time for it. I shall always be grateful to Geoff Law.

This account of the travel of an idea would not have been written without the travel of an individual. Early in 2006 I met Dr. Johan Leonard Blussé van Oud-Alblas, then a visiting professor at Harvard University, who was preparing the Reischauer Lectures that he delivered in April 2006. My travels to the Netherlands began soon thereafter, and the scheme of this work gradually began to take shape with the guidance and encouragement of Dr. Blussé.

The first steps toward this book were presented as a paper at the China Business Seminar at the John King Fairbank Center for Chinese Studies of Harvard University in February 2007. Comments made then helped focus my work. My initial research on guarantee process at Canton was presented at the conference "Americans, Macao and China 1784–1950: Historical Relations, Interactions and Connections" at the University of Macao (December 2008), and specific study on legal release from debt at Canton was presented in a talk at the East Asian Legal Studies Program at Harvard Law School (October 2009). The collegiality and the intellectual support that I have received from the officers, staff and others who now are or have been associated with the Fairbank Center and the East Asian Legal Studies Program have proven helpful in so many ways. In particular, I wish to thank: William C. Kirby, William P. Alford, Regina Abrami, Peter K. Bol, Lydia Chen, Jerome Alan Cohen, Mark Elliott, James R. Fichter, Jonathan Goldstein, Elisbeth Kaske, Nelson Y.S. Kiang, Linda Kluz, Elisabeth Köll, Philip A. Kuhn, Raymond Lum, John Schrecker, Elizabeth Sinn, Joanna F. Handlin Smith, Ronald Suleski, Michael Szonyi, Ross Terrill, Wen-hao Tien, Rudolph Wagner, Jeffrey R. Williams, Winnie Wong and Silas Wu.

The project was advanced with my admission to the doctoral program at Leiden University in 2007. The manuscript went through a series of iterations with the assistance of the always enthusiastic, ever questioning and constantly demanding Professor Leonard Blussé. Having him as my Leiden promotor, and guide through the historical thicket of the China coast during the turbulent years 1644–1842, was an extraordinary blessing. This good fortune was compounded when Dr. Egbert Koops agreed to join Leonard Blussé as doctoral co-promotor. A specialist in law, legal history, and comparative law, Dr. Koops brought powerful legal discipline to his review of my work as it slowly advanced. Egbert Koops and Leonard Blussé devoted extraordinary amounts of time to this project, often at great inconvenience to them. My debt to them is profound. While this book has advanced much from its final dissertation form, I hope that it will be found equal to the high standards that Drs. Koops and Blussé each set as a scholar.

I have had much additional assistance. I am deeply indebted to my friend and mentor Jacques M. Downs (1925-2006), a scholar of the early American trade with China who was unfailingly generous in sharing his knowledge with me and with many others. Special thanks go to Robert A. Falk, David A. Moss, Lincoln P. Paine, Winton Rossiter, James M. Stone, Cathleen Douglas Stone, Marijke van Wissen-van Staden and Paul A. Van Dyke, each of whom provided help at crucial moments. For their assistance, I am grateful as well to Wayne Altree, Dilip Kumar Basu, Robert A. Brink, Richard Capurso, Kuo-tung Ch'en, Patrick Conner, Carl Crossman, Peter Drummey, David Faure, H.A. Crosby Forbes, Robert Gardella, Martyn Gregory, Brian Harkins, Koos Kuiper, Richard Milhender, Diane Charipar Milhender, Stephen Z. Nonack, Vincent Smith, Christine Sullivan, Puk Wing-kin and Conrad E. Wright. I am indebted to Jayson Brooks, James Kadlick, Jeff Lajoie, Mary McClay, Leonid Monisov, Peter and Elizabeth Shattuck, and Shawn J. Smith, each of whom made this work possible as well.

There is simply no way to adequately express my gratitude to my entire family for their confidence and their support over the years that this study was prepared. My wife Barbara Lemperly Grant and my daughter Eva Taylor Grant have weathered much and have been helpful through all. My mother in law Bertha Lemperly has helped in many ways and I am grateful to her too. The support of my mother Madeleine Grant, and my siblings, also helped bring this work to fruition. I am sure that my late father Frederic D. Grant would enjoy this study. For whatever ability I have to bring the past to life, I owe much to him.

Many interesting people introduced themselves to me as I worked on this study. My favorite is the anonymous Buddhist monk who was jeered at by Shang Kexi for his solitary efforts to bury the dead in the chaos after the city of

Canton was taken by the Manchus in November 1650. “The priest replied that he did not look at the magnitude of the task or attempt to calculate its possibility; he merely did what was in his power and left the rest to Heaven.”

It is proper to emphasize that the errors in this work are mine alone. It is my hope that whatever errors I have made will not themselves be transplanted.

Milton, Massachusetts
9 June 2014

List of Illustrations

PLATE	CAPTION
1	The Kangxi Emperor, reigned 1661 to 1722, architect of the "open door" foreign trade policies implemented in 1683. Hanging scroll, ink and color on silk, artist unknown 24
2	Shang Kexi, 1604–1676, Prince Pacifier of the South. Engraving, 1666 55
3	A singsong: mechanical clock with a writing figure, gilded copper, made in England by Timothy Williamson, about 1770 66
4	A singsong: mechanical clock supported by four goats, gilded copper, agate and glass, made in England by William Hughes, about 1770 67
5	A singsong: mechanical clock with a peacock and a timekeeping figure, gilded copper and enamel, made in England by Timothy Williamson, eighteenth century 68
6	A singsong: automaton in the form of a chariot pushed by a Chinese attendant and set with a clock, gold, with diamonds and paste jewels set in silver, and pearls, white enamel, brass and steel, made in London, England by James Cox, 1766 69
7	Chinese people reading notices posted on a wall. Sketch by George Chinnery, October 1841 80
8	View of Mingqua's hong and Old China Street, showing a large number of notices posted on the wall, Canton, 28 November 1838. Pen, ink and watercolor sketch by Warner Varnham 80
9	The trial of the Neptune sailors. Painting by an unknown Chinese artist, ca. 1807 104
10	View of the foreign factories at Canton. Gouache on silk, 1780 117
11	View of the foreign factories at Canton. Oil on glass painting, ca. 1782–1784 133
12	The Spanish dollar, the primary currency of China's maritime foreign trade during the period 1780–1842, as hard currency and as a work of porcelain art 136
13	A hong merchant. Oil portrait by Spoilum, ca. 1800 149
14	Too big to fail 'with Chinese characteristics.' The senior hong merchant Howqua II (Wu Bingjian), 1769–1843. Oil portrait by Lamqua, ca. 1840 168

15 The foreign factories at Canton. Oil painting, ca. 1825–1835 193
16 The hong merchant Mowqua II (Lu Wenjin). Oil portrait by Lamqua, 1830s 204
17 "The Broken Hong Merchant or the Empty Tea Chest." British satirical print, November 1838 216
18 Joshua Forman, 1777–1848, the father of bank deposit insurance. Oil portrait by an unknown artist 222
19 Cover of the pamphlet containing Joshua Forman's proposal for the adoption of bank liability insurance, as presented to the New York legislature on 26 January 1829 232
20 The page of the Safety Fund Act proposal, in which Joshua Forman states that inspiration for this banking reform came from "the regulation of the Hong merchants in Canton" 233
21 Franklin Roosevelt with Warren Delano II—a China trader who did business with Howqua II and was in Canton during the Opium War—and twelve of his Delano first cousins. Photograph, September 1897 243
22 President Franklin Delano Roosevelt signing the Banking Act of 1933. Photograph, 16 June 1933 248
23 Portrait of a hong merchant who traded with the Philadelphia merchant Stephen Girard, ca. 1787–1824. Oil on canvas, by an unknown Chinese artist 264

List of Tables and Charts

TABLE	CAPTION	
1	List of the Assets of the Eryi hong, and their values	141
2	Payments from the Consoo Fund, 1806–1813	153
3	Increase in collective liability burden, 1780–1828	184
4	Hong Merchant Collective Guaranty Liability for Foreign Debt, 1780–1842	206
5	Increase in collective liability burden, 1780–1842	207

CHART	CAPTION	
1	Collective Guaranty Liability, 1780–1842, By Year	209

Note on Spelling

The *pinyin* system of romanization is used throughout the text of this study. However, certain proper names and titles of publications, where they are normally written in other forms of romanization, have not been uniformly changed to the *pinyin* system. Exceptions have also been made in the cases of some historical names of places, such as Peking, Canton, Macao and Amoy.

Glossary

British EIC	The British East India Company.
Canton Customs	The Guangdong Province Maritime Customs (*yuehai-guan*), headquartered at Canton (Guangzhou), which was headed from 1700–1842 by an official Western merchants called the Hoppo.
Canton Guaranty System	The system under which members of the hong merchant guild were subject to unlimited liability on a collective basis for the debts of failed members of the guild, enforced from 1780 until 1842.
Canton System	The set of rules under which the Chinese government managed the monopolized maritime trade between Canton and the West between 1684 and 1842.
Chop	An official stamp or permit, and by extension any official document bearing the impression of a seal or stamp. From Hindi *chhäp*.
Cohong	The hong merchant guild (*gonghang*). An informal organization during much of the period of the Canton System, it enjoyed official recognition and independent powers in 1720–1721 (the Cohong of 1720) and also from 1760–1771 (the Cohong of 1760).
Comprador	A Chinese citizen employed by a Western merchant to serve as an agent to supply provisions.
Consoo Fund	The fund through which the hong merchant guild paid its collective responsibility liability for unpaid debts of guild members to foreign traders and certain common obligations to the Chinese government. The fund took its name from the guild hall (*gongsuo*) in which it was originally kept in a chest or chests.
Country trader	A private merchant trading between ports in Asia, principally between India and China. The term usually refers to private British merchants.
Deposit insurance	A program under which claims of depositors or certain other creditors of banks or depository institutions are paid in whole or in part from a fund maintained with regular contributions from such institutions, if a given insured institution fails or becomes insolvent.

Foreign factories	The business premises and residences of the foreign traders at Canton during the period 1700 to 1842.
Governor	The Governor (*fuyuan*) of the province of Guangdong, with his official office at Canton (Guangzhou).
Governor-General	The Governor-General (*zongdu*) of the provinces of Guangdong and Guangxi, with his official office at Canton (Guangzhou). Western merchants also called this official the "Viceroy."
Hangyong tax	The tax collected from the Western trade of Canton from 1780 to 1842, to be used to pay obligations of the hong merchant guild from the Consoo Fund.
Hong merchant	A member of the group of Chinese merchants who were licensed by the Qing government to trade with Western merchants at Canton on a monopoly basis.
Hoppo	Commissioner of the Guangdong Province Maritime Customs. The term is a Western corruption of part of his Chinese language title: *Duli Guangdongsheng Yanhaidengqu Maoyishuiwu Hubufensi* (Commissioner of the Board of Revenue [*Hu Bu*], in Charge of the Customs Duties on the Trade of the Maritime Area of the Province of Guangdong).
Ili	A region in Xinjiang Province, to which the Qing state banished hong merchants who failed to pay debts.
Imperial Household Department	The ethnic Manchu Imperial Household Department (*neiwufu*) managed operations of the Imperial Court and administered businesses monopolized for the benefit of the Emperor, including the salt and ginseng administrations and the Canton Customs.
Ladrone	A pirate.
Liang	See "Tael."
Moral hazard	Excessive risks taken when insurance coverage shields parties from the economic consequences of their actions.
Outer seas merchants	Chinese merchants (*waiyang hang* or *yang hang*) who specialized in and were licensed by the Qing state to do business with Western merchants.
Outside shopman	Chinese merchants who did business with Western merchants outside of the official trade monopoly. The "outside shopmen" often specialized in non-staple trade commodities such as porcelain.

Security merchant	One of the hong merchants who secured foreign vessels and were held responsible by the Chinese government for the conduct of the crew of such vessels and for the customs duties that were owed.
Shroff	Private Chinese money changer, frequently involved in transactions to confirm the weight and quality of the silver used as currency.
Singsongs	Pidgin English term used to describe European luxury objects such as musical boxes, mechanical toys, clocks and watches which were purchased from Europeans at Canton and sent as official gifts to the Court in Beijing.
Tael	Chinese unit of account for silver, equivalent to a Chinese ounce (*liang*). On its accounts, the British East India Company treated the Spanish dollar as equal to 0.72 tael.
Thirteen hongs	Common reference to the group of licensed hong merchants, and to their business premises at Canton.
Truck	The British EIC practice of directly tying the sale of its woolen imports to its export purchases of tea from the hong merchants.
Viceroy	See "Governor-General."
Weiyuan	A military official who served as deputy to the Hoppo.
Whampoa	The outer port or anchorage of Canton (Guangzhou), in the Pearl River, located approximately 15 kilometers to the southeast of the city.
Yamen	The office or residence compound of a Chinese official.
Yi ben yi li	Rule of Chinese law barring the collection of interest in excess of the principal amount of a claim.

CHAPTER 1

Introduction

Transfers of goods and ideas at ever increasing speed are hallmarks of the modern globalized economy. Goods originally brought cultures in contact. By land and by sea, in orderly exchanges and through deception and violence, products moved about the world. This process connected societies in the pre-modern East and West. Across the globe, people gradually became aware of the existence of different material cultures, foods and traditions. The movements of goods, and their bearers, affected imaginations and altered societies. Initially a trickle, the traffic was diverse in scope, ranging from the humble potato carried from colonial Peru to fine porcelain exported from imperial China. Over centuries it grew into the torrent that is modern international trade. The transcultural effects of this movement of goods are well known and have received much scholarly attention.[1]

The flow of ideas has received less attention. The economic significance of ideas is well recognized in the modern world, shrunken as it has been through improvements in the speed of communications, travel, and the shipment of goods. Rights in ideas are challenging physical goods for primacy in market valuation. "Intellectual property" constitutes a great part of the value of leading companies in many nations today. Ideas developed elsewhere have profound influence worldwide, in disparate fields such as medicine, telecommunications, entertainment, manufacturing, computers, law and banking. The flow of ideas is now comparable in importance to the flow of goods.

Great debates have been joined concerning innovation and the movement of ideas, especially from West to East. Specific conditions which favored scientific and technological development in the West in and after the fifteenth century have been noted,[2] as has the failure of Eastern science to continue

1 See, for example, Alfred Crosby, *The Columbian Exchange: Biological and Cultural Consequences of 1492* (Westport, Conn.: Praeger, 2003); Stewart Gordon, *When Asia was the World* (Philadelphia: Da Capo Press, 2008); John Keay, *The Spice Route: A History* (Berkeley: Univ. of California Press, 2006); Donald F. Lach and Edwin J. Van Kley, *Asia in the Making of Europe*, published in three volumes and nine books (Chicago: Univ. of Chicago Press, 1965–1993); and Michael Pollan, *The Botany of Desire: A Plant's Eye View of the World* (New York: Random House, 2001).

2 Daniel Chirot, "The Rise of the West," American Sociological Review, Vol. 50, pp. 181–195 (1985), p. 192.

 | DOI 10.1163/9789004276567_002

the strong creative pace it demonstrated through the fourteenth and fifteenth centuries.[3] Some of the facts that figure in these debates provided intellectual cover for nineteenth century imperialism, and as such the subject matter is sensitive. Western pretensions to innovative superiority have proven especially controversial in the areas of business and finance. The stern treatment of Asian nations by Western creditors in the 1997 Asian financial crisis sparked anger, and the apparent unraveling of parts of the Western financial model in the cycle of international economic crises that began in 2007 has left that model much discredited in the East.[4]

Some of these sharply contrasted and simply expressed notions of the spread and influence of ideas may simply reflect the present inadequate state of study of the subject matter. Our understanding of the transit of ideas between East and West is limited,[5] in contrast to the abundant attention that has been paid to the movement of physical goods, both practical and artistic in character.

3 Kent G. Deng, "Development and Its Deadlock in Imperial China, 221 b.c.–1840 a.d.," Economic Development and Cultural Change, Vol. 51, pp. 479–522 (2003); David S. Landes, "Why Europe and the West? Why Not China?," The Journal of Economic Perspectives, Vol. 20, pp. 3–22 (2006), p. 21; Justin Yifu Lin, "The Needham Puzzle: Why the Industrial Revolution Did Not Originate in China," Economic Development and Cultural Change, Vol. 43, pp. 269–292 (1995), p. 282.

4 See, for example, Reg Little, "Confucian Reconstruction of Global Economics and Finance," Culture Mandala: Bulletin of the Centre for East-West Cultural & Economic Studies, Vol. 8, pp. 62–73 (2009) ("the high risk character of American financial innovation").

5 The flow of ideas has received some treatment, in works such as Lach and Van Kley's *Asia in the Making of Europe*, Gordon's *When Asia was the World*, A. Owen Aldridge, *The Dragon and the Eagle: The Presence of China in the American Enlightenment* (Detroit: Wayne State University Press, 1993) and Joanna Waley-Cohen, *The Sextants of Beijing: Global Currents in Chinese History* (New York: W. W. Norton & Co., 1999). There have also been a few studies of specific transits, such as the transmission of Chinese concepts of collective responsibility to Russia by the Mongols in the thirteenth century, Horace W. Dewey, "Russia's Debt to the Mongols in Suretyship and Collective Responsibility," *Comparative Studies in Society and History, Vol. 30*, pp. 249–270 (1988), and the influence of traditional Chinese programs for the warehousing of agricultural surpluses on agricultural reform in the United States in the 1930s. Derk Bodde, "Henry A. Wallace and the Ever-Normal Granary," Far Eastern Quarterly, Vol. 5, pp. 411–426 (1946), p. 422 ("Thus the American Ever-Normal Granary may fairly be said to have taken not only its name and part of its practice from its ancient Chinese prototype, but to share with the latter much of its underlying philosophy."). Bodde, who received his Leiden doctorate in 1938 and was a leading scholar of Chinese law, closed the cited article with an "Additional Note" concerning a similar surplus program that was instituted in Prussia in the early 1700s, which he thought might reflect a Chinese influence born of the enthusiasm for China shared among certain German thinkers of the era. The author is grateful to Jonathan Goldstein for bringing the Bodde article to his attention.

While the tangible is by its nature more obvious than the intangible, it was not solid goods alone that traveled in the past.

1 Subject and Framework

This study examines one example of the international flow of ideas. It considers a Chinese idea that came to New York State at a moment of banking and currency crisis in the early nineteenth century. A practice used by the Qing government to regulate monopolized business inspired the first American bank deposit insurance statute, the Safety Fund Act of 1829. Joshua Forman, a respected former judge and legislator, told the New York legislature that:

> The propriety of making the banks liable for each other was suggested by the regulation of the Hong merchants in Canton, where a number of men, each acting separately, have by the grant of the government the exclusive right of trading with foreigners, and are all made liable for the debts of each in case of failure. The case of our banks is very similar; they enjoy in common the exclusive right of making a paper currency for the people of the state, and by the same rule should in common be answerable for that paper. This abstractly just principle, which has stood the test of experience for seventy years, and under which the bond of a Hong merchant has acquired a credit over the whole world, not exceeded by that of any other security, modified and adapted to the milder features of our republican institutions, constitutes the basis of the system.[6]

The New York statute became the basis in turn for national bank deposit insurance in the United States, implemented in 1933. Bank deposit insurance has since spread worldwide, and is now found in about one hundred nations. The progress of this "American" innovation was notably slow in Asia until very recent years, having been adopted, for example, by Taiwan but still not in China.

While this early transplant of a Chinese idea to the United States of America has received slight attention as a footnote to U.S. banking history, its full history has never previously been examined. This work is the first study of the origins and experience of the Chinese idea of collective financial responsibility at

6 Martin Van Buren, *The Message of His Excellency Gov. Van Buren on the Subject of Banks; with the Plan Suggested to Place them Under Proper Regulations, Secure the Public from Loss by Failure, and Furnish a Sound, Well Regulated Currency; Made to the Assembly, January 26, 1829* (Albany, N.Y.: Croswell & Van Benthuysen, 1829), p. 23.

Canton and of its adoption and transplantation in the United States during the years through 1933. It seeks to answer several questions about this transplant. First, was the Chinese idea of collective legal responsibility for debt accurately transmitted to the New York legislature in 1829? Second, was the actual experience of the guaranty system at Canton accurately transmitted to the New York legislature in 1829? Third, do either the Chinese idea of collective legal responsibility for debt or the experience of the guaranty system that was enforced at Canton offer lessons for contemporary bank deposit insurance? In addition, with respect to the history of collective guaranty at Canton during the years 1780–1842, it asks: Who won, who lost, and why?

Consideration of the foregoing questions has required analysis of certain topics which have not previously been considered on their own. This is the first study of the collective guaranty of debt that was enforced at Canton between 1780 and 1842. It is the first study of the development and implementation of the regulations that constituted the Canton System from 1684 to 1842, and also the first study to set that system in the national Chinese context and to consider it as an operating system. Also new is the analysis of the debt collection rules that were made available to foreigners under the Canton System, and how they worked. The methodology of this study required the analysis of every instance in which hong failure resulted in a call on the collective guaranty, both as to the circumstances of the original underlying debt and creditor interests and as to the draw on the guaranty fund and its consequences.

Debt, and various modes of guaranty of debt, individual and collective, are concepts of ancient origin. Guaranty systems, collective guarantees and early forms of proto-insurance are not exclusive to imperial China. They have existed in numerous places around the world at various points at time, sometimes with long pedigrees, as for example in ancient Rome and the Middle East. This study simply examines the course of one such idea as it traveled and was transformed as it went from China to the United States and then across the world. Other similar ideas have existed at other places and times and may indeed be relevant to certain adoptions of deposit insurance in providing a historical, cultural and legal context to such adoptions. These are nevertheless outside the scope of this work.

This first chapter introduces the reception of a Chinese idea by the State of New York in the context of parallel financial crises which occurred in the year 1829. Chapters Two and Three address, respectively, why and then how the system of collective financial guaranty that was enforced at Canton was developed. Chapters Four through Seven examine the Chinese system of unlimited financial guaranty as it operated at Canton during the eventful years 1780 to 1842. Chapter Eight traces the development of the idea in the United

States, as it progressed from a state law guaranty program to national deposit insurance during the years 1829 to 1933. Chapter Nine provides a brief sketch of the international history of bank deposit insurance since 1933,[7] and is followed by an Epilogue, numbered as Chapter Ten.

The "hong merchants" were the small group of Chinese merchants who were licensed by the Qing government to trade with Western merchants at Canton on a monopoly basis. The system of enforced unlimited collective guaranty of individual private debt is referred to in this study as the "Canton Guaranty System." This concept is distinct from, but also was a key part of, the "Canton System," a term which refers to the rules by which the Qing government managed the monopolized maritime trade between Canton and the West. The Canton System evolved gradually through rules set down starting in the early 1700s, first formalized on imperial approval in 1760. The Canton Guaranty System began in 1780 as an amendment, imposed over hong merchant resistance, to trading rules that were otherwise long in existence.

The experience of bank deposit insurance is relatively young, and so is its history. There is an enormous literature on various aspects of the sometimes troubled history of deposit insurance in the United States, but no full length history as of yet. While the quality of this material is typically quite high, a great part of it has been written as part of a debate that has run for over eighty years about the propriety of and reforms to the deposit insurance system of the United States. Much of the rest is framed as technical analysis of banking issues, presenting history in tandem with mathematical formulae. Generally speaking, this is a banking literature, written by people concerned about banking for consideration by others with comparable interests. The Chinese origin of bank deposit insurance is well recognized in this literature, but the topic has received almost no further comment. To the extent the idea has been addressed, a complete accuracy of transmission to New York State has been assumed, as well as a total success in operation at Canton. Writing in 1957, during what is now recognized to have been a period of calm in the American history of bank deposit insurance, banking historian Bray Hammond stated that "[t]he sorry consummation of the [New York Safety] Fund was not the fault of

7 The analysis contained in Chapter Eight merely dips an oar into this complicated history. Its purpose is simply to establish the context for parallels between historical guaranty experience and post-1933 deposit insurance experience which are noted in Chapter Nine. The histories of bank deposit insurance in each of the hundred plus nations which have implemented such programs to date, some fascinating, merit full studies in their own right. It is hoped that the present work, by exploring the Sino-American prehistory of all modern bank deposit insurance, may prove useful to the authors of such studies when they are prepared.

the principle underlying it, which the Chinese had applied with so much more success than the hasty New Yorkers."[8]

This lack of attention may reflect, in part, objective difficulties in accessing source materials. Much of the Chinese history and experience of collective financial liability was kept hidden from contemporaries.[9] The ethnic Manchu Imperial Household Department (*neiwufu*), the employer of the Hoppo who directly supervised the Canton trade, the manager of several highly profitable businesses monopolized by the Chinese state for the benefit of the imperial court, and the recipient of a large part of the receipts of the Canton maritime customs, was largely invisible to the Chinese people. In the words of Chang Te-ch'ang, its affairs were kept secret, "almost a shrouded mystery."[10] Our knowledge of this and other key Manchu administrative institutions has been and continues to be greatly advanced by modern work with Chinese archival sources by scholars such as Chang, Preston Torbert,[11] Mark Elliott,[12] and others, but much remains to be known.

The Western experience of the Canton trade and the operation of the collective guaranty was also largely kept secret from contemporaries. The foreign traders were engaged in a high value, long-distance intensely competitive trade. They were compulsive diarists of the business they did, maintaining detailed current records and reporting to and corresponding with others about such affairs. These records were proprietary and highly confidential when they were made. They were never shared with competitors, and the China traders certainly avoided public attention. Edward Delano, a clerk with the American firm of Russell & Co., thus wrote his brother in 1841: "If you think of 'putting into print'—my remarks &c. upon men and things in general and China in particular, I may be under the disagreeable necessity of discontinuing my remarks relative thereto—for be it known unto you that the Americans who write

8 Bray Hammond, *Banks and Politics in America from the Revolution to the Civil War* (Princeton: Princeton Univ. Press, 1957), p. 563.

9 R. Randle Edwards, "Ch'ing Legal Jurisdiction Over Foreigners," pp. 222–269 in Jerome A. Cohen, R. Randle Edwards and Fu-mei Chang Chen, eds., *Essays on China's Legal Tradition* (Princeton: Princeton Univ. Press, 1980), p. 244 (although many Chinese regulations and edicts were translated and known to the foreign traders, there were still many edicts "which were for official eyes only and were not transmitted to the foreigners.").

10 Chang Te-ch'ang, "The Economic Role of the Imperial Household in the Ch'ing Dynasty," Journal of Asian Studies, Vol. 31, pp. 243–74 (1972), p. 243.

11 Preston M. Torbert, *The Ch'ing Imperial Household Department: A Study of its Organization and Principal Functions, 1662–1796* (Cambridge: Harvard Univ. Press, 1977).

12 Mark C. Elliott, *The Manchu Way: The Eight Banners and Ethnic Identity in Late Imperial China* (Stanford: Stanford Univ. Press, 2001).

home and have their letters published—are severely—(I mean their letters) criticized—and the small community of true blooded Yankees resident here, enabling them to discern the author without much difficulty."[13]

In addition, the passage of centuries has exacted a heavy toll on the trade records that were kept. Private Chinese records of the Canton trade have been almost entirely lost, along with the great part of the records kept by Qing officials, casualties of fires, wars and domestic disruption.[14] As a consequence, the history of hong merchants is written primarily with information drawn from Western records. While much of the Western records have also been lost, staggering amounts yet survive, in repositories scattered across the world. The volume and diffusion of these records, the many languages in which they were kept, and the now antique form (and handwriting) of this material, all pose challenges to scholarship.[15] One consequence of the state of surviving primary source material is that our knowledge of the activities of the hong merchants is fragmentary. They are seen as if in freeze frame photography, caught at given moments in particular transactions about which little else may be known. They are also seen from the standpoint of the records themselves, that is to say, in the light of the purpose for which records were required to be kept and maintained. Much information survives about crisis points, such as demands for the payment of defaulted debt and the exercise of guaranty rights, and less about the precise circumstances under which the obligations at issue in a given crisis had come to exist.

As many of these records are devoted to problems arising in the trade, such as loans past due or failures to perform as agreed, our knowledge of the hong merchants therefore focuses primarily on the expense side of the hong merchant ledgers. No hong firm records have been found. With not a great deal more than fragments of transaction records from which inferences may be drawn, scholars have been left to make rough estimates of hong firm profit.[16] This understanding is at least two steps removed from the trade in which these

13 Letter from Edward Delano to Franklin Hughes Delano, dated Canton 24 September 1841. Edward Delano Correspondence, Delano Family Papers, Franklin Roosevelt Library, Hyde Park, New York.

14 Gang Zhao, "Shaping the Asian Trade Network: The Conception and Implementation of the Chinese Open Trade Policy, 1684–1840" (Ph.D. diss., The Johns Hopkins University, 2007), p. 232 ("very few materials about the Qing regulation of Chinese private trade have survived").

15 See, for example, Lyman H. Butterfield, "Bostonians and their Neighbors as Pack Rats," The American Archivist, Vol. 24, pp. 141–159 (1961).

16 See Kuo-tung Anthony Ch'en, *The Insolvency of the Chinese Hong Merchants 1760–1843* (Nankang: Institute of Economics, Academia Sinica, 1990), pp. 152, 43–88, 102–3 and 251.

Chinese merchants were engaged—both by the passage of time and by the fact that it typically comes from non-Chinese sources. As a result, in this study, care has been taken to distinguish between sources which show specific experiences and sources which just say that things happened or are otherwise conclusory. The transactions and obligations at issue under the Canton Guaranty System were accounted for in the silver currency in which the trade was done, i.e., dollars (Spanish) or taels (Chinese ounce). There was inflation during the period of this study, but it was at a modest level.[17]

2 Previous Research

Generations of scholars have accepted the challenge posed by all of the scattered source materials left by the participants in the Canton trade. Patient research and the responsible reporting of that work has begun to dispel the nostalgic and often counterfactual fog that has too long obscured the history of Western trade with China. Hosea Ballou Morse opened up the records of the British East India Company (the "British EIC" or "EIC") in his *Chronicles of the East India Company Trading to China, 1635–1834*, published in five vol-

17 Robert B. Marks, "Rice Prices, Food Supply, and Market Structure in Eighteenth-Century South China," Late Imperial China, Vol. 12, pp. 64–116 (1991), p. 72 ("mild inflationary pressures" evident in the price of rice during the entire Qianlong period, 1735–1796); Madeline Zelin, *The Magistrate's Tael: Rationalizing Fiscal Reform in Eighteenth-Century Qing China* (Berkeley: Univ. of California Press, 1984), pp. 293–4, 298 and 307 (inflationary pressure, notably in the prices of rice and of land, linked to population growth); Paul A. Van Dyke, *The Canton Trade: Life and Enterprise on the China Coast, 1700–1845* (Hong Kong: Hong Kong Univ. Press, 2005), p. 57; Paul A. Van Dyke, unpublished paper, "Description of Price and Wage Data from Canton and Macao 1704–1833" (4 March 2008), p. 5, see: "http://www.iisg.nl/hpw/canton.pdf" (accessed 9 September 2012). The calculation of inflation over the period of this study is an extremely complicated subject, made the more difficult by occasional sharp year to year changes in domestic Chinese and imported agricultural and other commodity prices, and by shifts in the value of metal currency itself, notably copper. Marks, "Rice Prices," p. 68 ("The difficulty that the Chinese practice of converting copper prices into silver introduces is that the exchange ratio between copper and silver was constantly changing, although a complete time series is not available. While the official exchange rate was pegged at 1000 copper cash to one ounce of silver, during the eighteenth century the exchange rate ranged from about 700 to 1200 copper cash per ounce. What this meant is that if copper depreciated relative to silver, the copper price of one unit of rice increased while the silver price remained constant.").

umes between 1926 and 1929.[18] Louis Dermigny delved into French sources, producing the equally monumental *La Chine et L'Occident: Le Commerce A Canton Au XVIIIe Siècle 1719–1833*, published in four volumes in 1964.[19] Jack Wills and Leonard Blussé have both brought forward large amounts of information from Dutch records, in numerous published works. Jacques M. Downs, who examined the scattered and bulky records of China traders from the United States, published his invaluable *The Golden Ghetto: The American Commercial Community at Canton and the Shaping of American China Policy, 1784–1844* in 1997.[20] The work of these and many other scholars has improved our understanding of the actual conduct of the Western side of the trade.

The history of the Chinese side of the trade has also been transformed through the work of generations of scholars. This process has been especially arduous, as so many of the original Chinese records have been lost. The work began with Henri Cordier, a French academic whose career started as a clerk with Russell & Co. in Shanghai. Cordier's pioneering article, "Les Marchands Hanistes de Canton," was published in 1902.[21] Liang Jiabin, a Chinese scholar whose grandfather had been a hong merchant, devoted much of his career to disentangling their history. Liang wrote the *History of the Thirteen Hongs of Canton* (*Guangdong Shisan Hang Kao*), an important source which was published in two editions in Chinese, the first in 1937 and a revised edition in 1960.[22] Ann Bolbach White produced the first history of the hong merchants in a Western language, "The Hong Merchants of Canton," her 1967 University of Pennsylvania doctoral dissertation. White synthesized Western and Chinese source material, including records of the imperial court in Beijing. Her work

18 Hosea B. Morse, *The Chronicles of the East India Company Trading to China, 1635–1834* (Oxford: Oxford Univ. Press, 1926–1929), 5 Vols.

19 Louis Dermigny, *La Chine et L'Occident: Le Commerce A Canton Au XVIIIe Siècle 1719–1833* (Paris: Service de Vente des Publications Officielles de l'Education Nationale, 1964), 4 Vols. See also Philippe Haudrère, *La Compagnie française des Indes au XVIIIe siècle* (Paris: Les Indes Savantes, 2005), 2 vols.

20 Jacques M. Downs, *The Golden Ghetto: The American Commercial Community at Canton and the Shaping of American China Policy, 1784–1844* (Bethlehem: Lehigh Univ. Press, 1997).

21 Henri Cordier, "Les Marchands Hanistes de Canton," T'oung pao (2d ser.), Vol. 3, pp. 282–315 (1902).

22 Liang Jiabin, *Guangdong Shisan Hang Kao* (Shanghai: Commercial Press for the State Institute of Compilations and Translations, 1937; revised edition, Taipei, 1960). A partial English language translation of this important work was produced in 1958. An-yun Sung, "A study of the Thirteen Hongs of Kuangtung; A Translation of Parts of the Kuangtung Shih-San-Hang Kao of Liang Chia-Pin" (M.A. thesis, Univ. of Chicago, 1958).

stands as a useful introduction to hong merchant history.[23] Dilip Kumar Basu followed with "Asian Merchants and Western Trade: A Comparative Study of Calcutta and Canton 1800–1840," a doctoral dissertation completed at the University of California, Berkeley, in 1975. Basu's work remains the leading analysis of the vital trade that was conducted between Calcutta and Canton. It is also a key hong merchant work, both for the archival materials Basu brought to the topic and his understanding of the business problems the hong merchants faced.[24]

Hong merchant scholarship has taken enormous strides since these works were prepared. Two studies, published in the 1990s, began the process of opening up hong merchant history in such a manner that events that occurred between 1683 and 1843 can begin to be understood in meaningful individual detail. Kuo-tung Anthony Ch'en completed *The Insolvency of the Chinese Hong Merchants 1760–1843* as his Yale University doctoral dissertation in December 1989, and the work was published in 1990. Noting that prior studies had been particularly weak on this topic, Ch'en examined hong merchant insolvency, which he called "the characteristic phenomenon of the history of the Hong merchants."[25] Ch'en's work includes individual histories of many but not all of the hong firms. The year 1997 saw the publication of Weng Eang Cheong's *Hong Merchants of Canton: Chinese Merchants in Sino-Western Trade 1684–1798*.[26] The fact-rich Cheong volume is a historical study of the evolution of the hong merchant guild between 1683 and 1798. With the appearance of the Ch'en and Cheong works, hong merchant scholarship had generated studies comparable in depth and quality to the work produced by leading scholars of the Western side of the trade. Neither study attempts a regulatory or legal analysis of the Canton System, or of the collective guaranty of debt that was enforced at Canton between 1780 and 1842. The two works ask different questions about distinct but overlapping historical periods. While they contain considerable information about the subject matter of this study, that information is found in varied contexts throughout the pages of these volumes.

---

23 Ann Bolbach White, "The Hong Merchants of Canton" (Ph.D. diss., Univ. of Pennsylvania, 1967).

24 Dilip K. Basu, "Asian Merchants and Western Trade : A Comparative Study of Calcutta and Canton 1800-1840" (Ph.D. diss., Univ. of Calif., Berkeley, 1975).

25 Kuo-tung Anthony Ch'en, *The Insolvency of the Chinese Hong Merchants 1760-1843* (Nankang: Institute of Economics, Academia Sinica, 1990), p. v.

26 Weng Eang Cheong, *The Hong Merchants of Canton: Chinese Merchants in Sino-Western Trade 1684–1798* (Richmond, Surrey: Curzon Press, 1997), © Nordic Institute of Asian Studies.

Like computer science, modern hong merchant scholarship has shown an ability to process large amounts of data at substantially higher levels of detail at regular intervals. The knowledge of the 1970s was greatly improved upon in the 1990s, and this process is recurring. The hackneyed old notion of unitary hongs doing a strictly individualized business under exotic trading names in accordance with the dictates of all-powerful Western firms is falling away. The work of Paul A. Van Dyke, notably *The Canton Trade: Life and Enterprise on the China Coast, 1700–1845* (2005)[27] and *Merchants of Canton and Macao: Politics and Strategies in Eighteenth-Century Chinese Trade* (2011),[28] offers a view of a more complicated hong merchant world. This understanding shows hong merchants conducting substantial trade unconnected with their business with the West, illuminates shifting alliances among and competition between hong merchant families, and shows that the hong merchants traded variously on their own, in joint ventures, and in partnerships. Each of these elements can be found in the work of Ch'en and Cheong, and in some of the earlier studies as well, but an integrated picture is now coming together. As a result, the hong merchants are coming to be seen less as idiosyncratic curiosities of "Old Canton" and instead to be understood in the context of the larger Chinese trading world in which they did business. The present study seeks to continue these trends in recent scholarship by examining the regulatory and business experience of the regime of collective liability for foreign debt at Canton and placing it in an international context.

This study also seeks to place the regulation of the hong merchants in the overall context of Qing regulation of businesses monopolized for the benefit of the imperial court. Hints of the importance of national regulation appear in the literature. Liang Jiabin quotes his grandfather—the hong merchant Kinqua—as having told him that "The licensed merchants of the hong system were much like the Salt Merchants."[29] Liang—and Kinqua—are correct. The system under which the hong merchants were licensed and regulated is notably similar to the systems under which the Manchu Imperial Household Department (*neiwufu*) managed the monopolized salt and ginseng businesses

27 Paul A. Van Dyke, *The Canton Trade: Life and Enterprise on the China Coast, 1700–1845* (Hong Kong: Hong Kong Univ. Press, 2005).

28 Paul A. Van Dyke, *Merchants of Canton and Macao: Politics and Strategies in Eighteenth-Century Chinese Trade* (Hong Kong: Hong Kong Univ. Press, 2011).

29 Sung, "Study of the Thirteen Hongs," pp. 5, 78–9 and 31 ("the monopoly system of the Hong Merchants in fact also followed the monopoly system of the Salt Merchants.").

for the benefit of the imperial Court in Beijing.[30] Indeed, the subject matter of this study—collective financial responsibility among merchants for debt—itself appears to have been a *neiwufu* transplant to Canton. It was first imposed on the head merchants of the ginseng monopoly in Manchuria in 1739, as a mutual liability to pay the state the value of any deficiency in the quality or quantity of collected ginseng. The practice then continued, presumably having been judged a success. A little over a decade later, collective liability was introduced in a preliminary manner in three aspects of the Canton maritime customs during the 1752–59 administration of Hoppo Li Yongbiao, a *neiwufu* bondservant.

The 1829 reception of a Chinese idea by the American State of New York was thus one stage in a long chain of transplants. Traditional Chinese concepts of collective responsibility had been employed by the Imperial Household Department as part of its regulation of several businesses monopolized for the benefit of the Emperor. After having been tested in the ginseng administration, and applied in certain aspects of the administration of the hong merchants in the 1750s, collective liability for the foreign debt of individual hong merchants was imposed on the guild on a general basis in 1780. The idea traveled to New York State in 1829 where it was adapted and used as a basis of the first bank deposit insurance program, which operated from 1829 to 1866. Various American states subsequently adopted guaranty fund bank deposit insurance, inspired by the New York example, which existed for different periods and with uniformly poor success over the following century. In 1933, bank deposit insurance was implemented on a national level in the United States, under a system that adopted from and improved upon the guaranty fund model that was introduced in New York in 1829. Explicit bank deposit insurance programs have since been adopted in over one hundred countries worldwide, all based upon but varying in degrees from the "American" model of 1933.

This originally Chinese idea has traveled far, through Manchu, American and other hands. It has been repeatedly adapted to local situations, and has been used by many different societies at different times and places. Its reception in the West was as part of a contemporary trend of interest in Chinese ideas. This trend has been described by scholars such as Donald Lach and Edwin Van Kley,

30 The significance of the Mongols, of which the Manchu were a part, in the transmission of ideas has received some scholarly attention, and deserves further study. See Jack Weatherford, *Genghis Khan and the Making of the Modern World* (New York: Three Rivers Press, 2004); Bertold Spuler, *The Mongols in History* (New York: Praeger Publishers, 1971); Dewey, "Russia's Debt to the Mongols."

in *Asia in the Making of Europe* (1993)[31] and A. Owen Aldridge, in *The Dragon and the Eagle: The Presence of China in the American Enlightenment* (1993).[32] This international chain of uses and adaptations of a legal idea also conforms with the concept of "legal transplants" that was introduced by the scholar Alan Watson in his 1974 book under that title.[33] Drawing principally from his substantial knowledge of Roman law, Watson showed the wide influence and diffusion of transplanted legal ideas. Moved from one place to another, in whole or in part, understood or misunderstood, transplanted legal ideas have often thrived in their new home. Watson tells us that "A successful legal transplant—like that of a human organ—will grow in its new body, and become part of that new body just as the rule or institution would have continued to develop in its parent system." Under this criterion, this series of transplants achieved technical success at any number of stages of its journey across time and cultures.

The idea arrived in the United States in the context of parallel financial crises that occurred in the year 1829. At Canton, in China, the group of hong merchants who were licensed to conduct China's maritime foreign trade was depleted in number, deep in debt, and experiencing difficulty recruiting new members. In the State of New York, in the United States of America, a series of bank failures had raised concerns about the trustworthiness of the paper currency the state permitted private banks to print and circulate. Each crisis was different, and each was addressed by the responsible local authorities. Although the world was closely bound by ties of international trade in 1829 and information was moving with increasing speed between East and West, news of these crises did not travel. Just as the crisis in New York was unknown in Canton, the crisis in Canton was likewise unknown in New York.

3 The 1829 Crisis in the State of New York

The New York crisis was primarily about currency. As the early United States lacked domestic sources of silver, the nation depended on private bank notes and on imported silver coins for its money supply. The bulk of the money in circulation in 1829 was paper banknotes issued by private banks. There were no national banknotes, and would not be until 1863. Bank failures, which became more common as banks themselves became more common, caused

---

31 Lach and Van Kley, *Asia in the Making of Europe, Vol. III*, pp. 1605–6.

32 Aldridge, *The Dragon and the Eagle*, p. 268.

33 Alan Watson, *Legal Transplants: An Approach to Comparative Law (2d ed.)* (Athens, Ga.: Univ. of Georgia Press, 1993), p. 27.

immediate pain on the street. When a bank failed its banknotes failed as well. New York had experienced multiple bank failures in the late 1820s, despite various attempted reforms including the imposition of double liability on the shareholders of failed banks. While some muttered against the use of paper banknotes at all, they were a practical necessity given the shortage of silver and the rapidly developing nation's voracious appetite for money. The critical issue became keeping the paper currency sound, i.e., assuring the ready convertibility of banknotes into coined silver or gold.

Individual states licensed private banks which in turn issued banknotes. Tested by early bank failures, the states developed differing approaches to supervision of the proliferating banks and their circulating paper. The leading states recognized both that a sound currency supported commerce, and that it would spur economic development. In the nineteenth century much of the business of America was focused on development—of land, infrastructure, trade and manufacturing. That development required an adequate supply of sound money.

A banking crisis was looming when Martin Van Buren was sworn into office as Governor of the State of New York on 1 January 1829. Alarmed about the condition of the state's banks, the legislature had denied all applications for either the issuance or renewal of bank charters in 1827 and again in 1828. The charters of the majority of New York's banks were up for renewal within the next two or three years, and there was deep concern that some of these banks were in an unsafe condition.

At this juncture, Governor Van Buren was approached by Joshua Forman with a proposal for a bank deposit insurance program. Forman was a respected public figure with financial experience developed as a lawyer, merchant, judge, real estate developer (founder of the City of Syracuse), legislator, and proponent of public improvement projects, notably the Erie Canal of which he was an early advocate. The Governor was impressed, and by the end of January 1829 he had submitted Forman's proposal to the legislature as "worthy of your deliberate attention."

The plan took its inspiration from the "regulation of the Hong merchants in Canton, where a number of men, each acting separately, have by the grant of the government the exclusive right of trading with foreigners, and are all made liable for the debts of each in case of failure." According to Forman, the Canton Guaranty System had "stood the test of experience for seventy years" and had given the hong merchants rock solid credit worldwide. The promise to pay of a "Hong merchant ha[d] acquired a credit over the whole world, not exceeded by that of any other security." The plan he proposed, which called both for deposit insurance and for public supervision of the insured banks, made rapid progress through the New York legislature. It was approved with amendments in March and was signed into law on 2 April 1829. Under the Safety Fund system, every bank chartered by the State of New York was required to remit one half percent of its paid-in capital to the Safety Fund annually until it had contributed a total of three percent of capital to the fund. If a bank failed, its assets would be liquidated and the Safety Fund would pay as much as was necessary to satisfy all claims against the failed bank.

4 The Crisis in the Chinese Port of Canton: 1829

The year 1829 found the experiment with unlimited collective liability for foreign debt at Canton approaching its fiftieth anniversary under great stress. Since the early 1700s, the conduct of China's maritime trade with the West had been vested in a small monopoly group known as the hong merchants. The Chinese government required the hong merchants to monitor foreign merchants and to collect taxes as a condition of their trading license. In addition to conducting an enormous import and export trade, these merchants also functioned as a bottom tier of the Chinese civil bureaucracy, serving as "quasi diplomats" (in the words of Weng Eang Cheong), mediating between restive Western traders and officials posted to Canton by the Qing government.

Success as a hong merchant thus required both: (1) strong skills as an export/import commodity trader; and (2) knowledge of and the ability to work within the regulatory constraints of the "Canton System," the rules which governed China's maritime trade with the West. The "Canton System" was thus similar to many regulated businesses of the present day. Knowledge of government regulations combined with the ability to work smoothly with sometimes demanding regulators could be every bit as important as skills in the stated line of business.

By 1829, the viability of the hong merchant monopoly was threatened. The volume of trade had soared since 1780, but so too had financial demands on the hong merchants individually and as a guild. Since 1780, the hong merchant body had been required to pay all the foreign debts of any member who became insolvent. The mechanism used for repayment was the Consoo Fund, maintained by the guild, which was to have been funded through a levy imposed on the trade (the *hangyong*), originally set in the amount of three percent (3%) but often collected in a higher amount. The original stated purpose of this tax was to fund the guaranty of foreign debts as well as other obligations due from the hong merchants to the Qing state. The burden of taxation on the hong merchants, both collective (*hangyong*) and direct (individual exactions) had since grown, driven both by mounting needs of the government in the difficult years of the early nineteenth century and by official venality. The high level of taxation had driven much legitimate trade—in tea and other commodities—outside the monopoly and into the hands of unlicensed "outside shopmen." The outside shopmen offered sharply lower prices for staple goods, and arranged either to smuggle them onto purchasers' ships or to deliver the discounted goods through weak "junior" hongs (while bribing hong proprietors and customs officers to look the other way). This unlicensed competition reduced effective tax collections and had the effect of increasing the tax burden on the residual legal trade.

At one time, membership in the thirteen hongs had been seen as a path to riches. By 1829, however, the prospect of becoming a hong merchant had long lost attraction on the streets of Canton. The official trading license was expensive, came with a high risk of financial loss (and dreadful penalties after failure), offered little prospect of a reasonable return on investment, and, even if one succeeded against these odds, it had been impossible since at least 1815 to retire from the guild or to withdraw one's capital.

As of 1829 the hong merchant body had dwindled to seven firms, of which only three were truly solvent. In that year, Governor-General Li Hongbin directed the hong merchants to recruit substantial people from among their friends. While the call produced some shaky recruits, it did not strengthen the hong merchant guild or arrest its decline. Individual hong merchant failures continued in the years that followed, and their debts continued to be shifted to the surviving hongs under the collective guaranty.

5 The 1829 Crises as Prologue

The crises at the Port of Canton and in New York State in 1829 capture financial worlds in transition. In China, the demise of the Canton System would soon be pronounced by the Treaty of Nanking of 1842. In the State of New York, a banking crisis led legislators to adopt a reform program—the Safety Fund—which was inspired by Chinese principles of financial collective responsibility. It is no small irony that both the Canton System, which inspired the New York reform, and the Safety Fund itself, were crippled by the same event—the depression that swept across the world in 1837.

History has only begun to draw lessons from the era of the Canton System, a remarkable commercial mingling of people, cultures and regulations under which the maritime trade of China was conducted for approximately a century and a half starting in 1684. It is a key fact that the "mature" form of this regulatory system (1780–1842), which included the collective guaranty by the hong merchants of the foreign debts of guild members, was bookended by threats by foreign creditors to use violence to collect such debts. At the outset, the threats were not executed. Nothing came of the threats made manifest by the repeated visits to Canton by Captain John Alexander Panton and his warship in the "Chinese Debts" crisis of 1779–80. At the end, in the Opium War of 1839–42, the threats made by the British in the "Chinese Debts" crisis of 1838–39 were executed with devastating force.

Civilization is defined by the rule of law. From its origins, law has sought to protect social order by reducing occasions for or by seeking to eliminate violence. In the English legal tradition, many common law rights have at their origin the goal of avoiding violence. In imperial China, "self help" (i.e., violent) debt collection was barred by statute. The fact that the origins of modern programs guaranteeing the payment of bank creditors arise from efforts by foreign creditors to use violence to collect from the state as implicit guarantor of a private guaranty fund is significant. The social or legal choice to pay or not pay debt involves the creation of winners and losers. Some creditors collect, and some do not, and the greater the amount that is caused to be collected from guarantors (whether individual or state), the greater the social cost. Within nations, and also between nations, the stresses caused by the "privatization of profit and the socialization of risk" are real and carry with them the threat of violence or social disorder. The social risks of the unlimited guarantee of private debt, under state auspices, are themselves unlimited.

The largely forgotten "Chinese Debts" crisis of 1838–39 began as a crisis of credit confidence brought on the withdrawal from trade of the British EIC—which had been a reliable purchaser from the hong merchants under stable long term share contracts. It deepened with massive hong failures coincident with the shock of the depression of 1837. It simply took a war to collect the defaulted guaranteed private debts in full. The total accrued liability for foreign debts of failed hong merchants as of 1842 was discharged with a lump sum payment of $3 million in cash that was delivered to the British consul at Canton on 23 July 1843.

In sharp contrast to this largely forgotten record, historians of American banking have paid considerable attention to the experiment with bank deposit insurance that was attempted by the State of New York between 1829 and 1866. The Safety Fund is recognized as having had many frailties. Thus it is that the Fund—like a poorly built ship, or indeed the Canton System itself—came undone under the force of the international depression of 1837. Yet unlike the Canton System, which had few mourners, the Safety Fund concept was long believed to represent a sound design. It inspired bank deposit insurance statutes in various states, national bank deposit insurance in the United States, and then such programs worldwide. It glowed as prologue: its possibilities stood . . . unlimited.

CHAPTER 2

Sources of the Canton Guaranty System

The early Manchu rulers of China had no interest in banking regulation. Their goals were to first complete the "great enterprise" of conquest and then to consolidate control over the entire nation. After years of careful preparation, the Manchus took Beijing in 1644 and achieved a surprisingly rapid conquest of Northern China.[1] Progress was much more difficult in the coastal south, far from Beijing, where the struggle raged on another forty years. After the devastated region had been brought under control, the Kangxi Emperor opened the south to maritime foreign trade. The regional economy responded quickly and positively to the stimulus. The Manchus sought the benefits of trade, but at the same time felt it important to maintain order among the traders and to assure the flow of customs tax revenues to Beijing. During the eighteenth century a body of rules, known as the Canton System, was evolved to advance these objectives. The regulatory structure that was developed for Canton drew on both Manchu and Chinese traditions. A collective guaranty of foreign debt—the Canton Guaranty System—was imposed in 1780 as a modification of those rules.

1 Conquest and Pacification

The Manchu began as a Jurchen Mongol tribe in the Liao valley in what is now Northeast China, a region of forest, steppe and agricultural lands.[2] Under a series of talented and aggressive rulers, notably the "great progenitor" Nurhaci (1559–1626), they rose rapidly from their original position, as one of a number of tribes contending for regional prominence, to a potent military force with ambitions to control China itself. Nurhaci organized a coalition of Jurchen Mongol tribes under his Aisin Gioro clan as leader, and bound them together culturally and militarily.[3] The coalition was defined as "Manchu," which

1 William T. Rowe, *China's Last Empire: The Great Qing* (Cambridge: Belknap Press of Harvard University Press, 2009), pp. 19 and 22.

2 Elliott, *The Manchu Way*, pp. 48–50; Rowe, *China's Last Empire*, p. 14; Gertrude Roth Li, "State Building Before 1644," pp. 9–72 in Willard J. Peterson, ed., *The Cambridge History of China, Vol. 9, The Ch'ing Dynasty to 1800, Part 1* (Cambridge: Cambridge Univ. Press, 2002), p. 9.

3 Elliott, *The Manchu Way*, p. 52.

 | DOI 10.1163/9789004276567_003

involved the creation of a written Manchu language (an adaptation of Mongol script). It was consolidated under a military system in which Manchu forces were organized in eight "banner" formations.[4] These banner forces carried out the "great enterprise" of conquest. The banner system was then adapted to control and to defend China itself.

Trading relations contributed to the rise of the Manchu and funded the cost of conquest. Their homeland was rich in natural resources, which the Jurchen Mongols exploited through hunting, fishing and agriculture, and active participation in regional trade in products such as furs and ginseng.[5] Several principal Manchu leaders, including Nurhaci, had early experience as traders.[6] The clan gradually developed an expertise in the ginseng trade and accumulated a monopoly of the import licenses issued by the Ming to sell their scarce and prized wild ginseng in China.[7] Rich profits realized from satisfying the enormous late Ming demand for high quality ginseng purchased weapons and contributed directly to the rise of Manchu military power.[8] The Japanese scholar Inaba Iwakichi therefore observed that the Qing dynasty "rose on ginseng and fell on opium."[9]

On 26 April 1644 the last Ming Emperor committed suicide by hanging himself atop Coal Hill in the Forbidden City in Beijing. In the context of Manchu military use of proceeds of the Ming ginseng trade, the suicide of the Chongzhen Emperor might be considered an example of the saying attributed to Lenin about selling the adversary the rope with which to hang himself, had Lenin only said so.[10] Beijing had fallen to rebels under Li Zicheng the day before. Manchu forces then streamed through the Shanhai Pass into China and

---

4 Elliott, *The Manchu Way*, pp. 39–42, 57–63 and 70; Rowe, *China's Last Empire*, p. 15; Frederic Wakeman, Jr., *The Great Enterprise: The Manchu Reconstruction of Imperial Order in Seventeenth-Century China* (Berkeley: Univ. of Calif. Press, 1985), Vol. 1, p. 55.

5 Rowe, *China's Last Empire*, p. 14; Van Jay Symons, *Ch'ing Ginseng Management: Ch'ing Monopolies in Microcosm* (Tempe, Arizona: Arizona State Univ. Press, 1981), pp. 9–10 and 73; Elliott, *The Manchu Way*, pp. 50–1; Li, "State Building Before 1644," p. 50.

6 Gang Zhao, *The Qing Opening to the Ocean: Chinese Maritime Policies, 1684–1757* (Honolulu: Univ. of Hawai'I Press, 2013) pp. 61–2.

7 Rowe, *China's Last Empire*, p. 14; Symons, *Ch'ing Ginseng Management*, pp. 3, 9 and 71–2; Zhao, *Qing Opening to the Ocean*, pp. 63–6.

8 Zhao, "Shaping the Asian Trade Network," pp. 110 and 120; Rowe, *China's Last Empire*, p. 14; Symons, *Ch'ing Ginseng Management*, pp. 9–10 and 72–4; Wakeman, *Great Enterprise, Vol. 1*, pp. 47–8.

9 Symons, *Ch'ing Ginseng Management*, pp. 24 and 72–73.

10 Paul F. Boller, Jr. and John George, *They Never Said It: A Book of Fake Quotes, Misquotes & Misleading Attributions* (Oxford: Oxford Univ. Press, 1989), p. 64 (debunking as "almost

defeated Li Zicheng's army in a great battle on 27 May 1644. The victorious Qing army entered a stunned Beijing without a fight. Mark Elliott offers a vivid description of the Manchu entry on 5 June 1644. Local residents "no doubt stared in curious amazement at the shaved foreheads and dangling queues of the Manchu soldiers riding by, daggers at their waists and short recurve bows of horn and wood by their sides."[11]

Stalwarts of the Ming Dynasty made their last stand against the Manchus in South China. Contending forces included Manchu military, Ming remnants, peasant rebels, turncoats, and commanders who were honored by the Qing for their services by being named hereditary feudal princes. The Manchu forces were soon caught up in bloody repression of local rebellions against the imposition of the queue, a traditional hairstyle of the northeast in which the forehead was shaved and remaining hair was wound up as a long braid.[12] In the south, the land was a constant challenge to the Manchu cavalry, which made difficult progress through often mountainous terrain with few roads and a countryside intersected with rivers and canals.[13] The city of Canton, in Qing hands as of January 1647, soon thereafter rose in rebellion.[14] It was besieged by Manchu forces under Shang Kexi for ten months in 1650. The defense was broken with an artillery barrage on 24 November 1650, after which the invaders plundered Canton with a horrific slaughter of the populace.[15] The city was devastated, but was gradually reconstructed by the Manchu rulers.

---

certainly a fake" the attribution to Lenin of the quotation that "The capitalists will sell us the rope with which to hang them.").

11 Elliott, *The Manchu Way*, pp. 1–2; Rowe, *China's Last Empire*, pp. 15–16; Wakeman, *Great Enterprise, Vol. 1*, pp. 1, 262–6 and 314–6.

12 Rowe, *China's Last Empire*, pp. 22–23; Wakeman, *Great Enterprise, Vol. 1*, pp. 646–55 and 659.

13 Elliott, *The Manchu Way*, pp. 187–191 (vivid description drawn from the surviving excerpts of a campaign memoir kept by a banner soldier named Dzengseo); Dzengseo, *The Diary of a Manchu Soldier in Seventeenth-Century China* (Nicola di Cosmo, tr.) (Abington: Routledge Books, 2006); E. C. Bowra, "The Manchu Conquest of Canton" (Part One), China Review, Vol. 1, pp. 86–96 (1872), p. 91; Zhao, "Shaping the Asian Trade Network," pp. 36–37.

14 Jerry Dennerline, "The Shun-chih Reign," pp. 73–119, in Willard J. Peterson, ed., *The Cambridge History of China, Vol. 9, The Ch'ing Dynasty to 1800, Part 1* (Cambridge: Cambridge Univ. Press, 2002), pp. 94–95; Wakeman, *Great Enterprise, Vol. 2*, p. 738.

15 Dennerline, "The Shun-chih Reign," p. 101; Robert B. Marks, *Tigers, Rice, Silk, and Silt: Environment and Economy in Late Imperial South China* (Cambridge: Cambridge Univ. Press, 1998), p. 149; Wakeman, *Great Enterprise, Vol. 2*, pp. 767–8 and 893.

> Local tradition affirms that the burial of the dead, neglected by the conquerors, was brought about by the exertions of a Buddhist priest, who attempted, single handed, to convey the corpses outside the city gates and give them decent burial. While engaged in his task—carrying a corpse on his shoulders—he was met by Shang Kexi, who asked him jeeringly whether he intended to bury all the slain? The priest replied that he did not look at the magnitude of the task or attempt to calculate its possibility; he merely did what was in his power and left the rest to Heaven. The spirit of the reply is said to have so pleased Shang Kexi, that he ordered the camp-followers to lend the priest their aid, and thus the bodies of the slaughtered were heaped in one huge pile and burned outside the east gate of the city, where the ashes were buried beneath an enormous mound which still exists and bears the significant name of the General Grave.[16]

Much of the forty year struggle for control of South China took place along the coast. Resistance on and near the Island of Taiwan was led by members of the family of Zheng Chenggong (Koxinga), who were and had long been heavily involved in international trade.[17] The Qing banned maritime trade in 1656, seeking to strangle the Taiwan resistance.[18] Zheng forces attempted a major assault on Nanjing from the sea in September 1659, which triggered a more forceful crackdown.[19] From 1661 through 1683, in order to prevent supplies from reaching the Zheng forces on Taiwan, the Qing directed and fiercely enforced a wholesale removal of the coastal population as much as ten miles or more inland from the adjacent mainland coast.[20] The only exception was Macao,

16 Quoted in Bowra, "Manchu Conquest of Canton," pp. 91–3 (the spelling of the name of Shang Kexi has been changed to Pinyin romanization)

17 Leonard Blussé, *Visible Cities: Canton, Nagasaki, and Batavia and the Coming of the Americans* (Cambridge: Harvard Univ. Press, 2008), pp. 25–6; Arthur Hummel, ed., *Eminent Chinese of the Ch'ing Period* (Washington, D.C.: U.S. Govt. Printing Office, 1943), pp. 108–10; Zhao, *Qing Opening to the Ocean*, pp. 71–2 and 86–91; Zhao, "Shaping the Asian Trade Network," pp. 54, 59, 86–7, 209 and 231; Jane Kate Leonard, *Wei Yuan and China's Rediscovery of the Maritime World* (Cambridge: Harvard Univ. Press, 1984), pp. 66–9; Marks, *Tigers, Rice, Silk, and Silt*, pp. 151 and 156; Ng Chin-keong, *Trade and Society: The Amoy Network on the China Coast 1683–1735* (Singapore: Singapore Univ. Press, 1983), pp. 48–55.

18 Ng, *Trade and Society*, p. 52.

19 Zhao, *Qing Opening to the Ocean*, pp. 71–2; Rowe, *China's Last Empire*, p. 27; Wakeman, *Great Enterprise, Vol. 2*, pp. 1046–9.

20 Ng, *Trade and Society*, pp. 52–53.

which was spared from this exercise of conquering will by a combination of good fortune and determined diplomacy.[21] The Qing ordered all oceangoing vessels burned; "not an inch of wood is allowed to be in the water."[22] The coast was devastated and the population suffered terribly. One source records that:

> People continued to drift around, unable to figure out how to survive. Fathers and sons, husbands and wives, abandoned each other; with anguished cries they parted ways. A son for a peck of grain, a daughter for a hundred cash for purchase by the powerful.[23]

As was observed by the Dutch Embassy of 1655–57, "you may ride in some Places [in Guangdong Province] for several miles together, and not see a Town or Village Standing, only great heaps of Stones, and the Ruines of many Places, which have been formerly very famous for Trade."[24] The Zheng forces finally surrendered on Taiwan in October 1683, after a crushing naval defeat by Qing forces under admiral Shi Lang.[25] Two years earlier, Manchu forces had suppressed the Revolt of the Three Feudatories, which marked the end of the era of the semi-independent princes appointed by the Qing in the early stages of conquest and their feudal privileges.[26]

---

21 Blussé, *Visible Cities*, p. 25; Cheong, *Hong Merchants*, pp. 21 n.14 and 66 n.2; Lawrence D. Kessler, *K'ang-hsi and the Consolidation of Ch'ing Rule 1661–1684* (Chicago: Univ. of Chicago Press, 1976), pp. 39–46; Donald F. Lach and Edwin J. Van Kley, *Asia in the Making of Europe, Vol. III (A Century of Advance), Book Four (East Asia)* (Chicago: Univ. of Chicago Press, 1993), pp. 1697–9; Leonard, *Wei Yuan*, p. 69; Marks, *Tigers, Rice, Silk, and Silt*, p. 151–3 and 167; Zhao, *Qing Opening to the Ocean*, pp. 73–4 and 89–90; John E. Wills, Jr., *Embassies and Illusions: Dutch and Portuguese Envoys to K'ang-hsi, 1666–1687* (Cambridge, Mass.: Harvard Univ. Press, 1984), pp. 16–17, 86–89 and 116–144; John E. Wills, Jr., *Pepper, Guns and Parleys: The Dutch East India Company and China 1622–1681* (Cambridge, Mass.: Harvard Univ. Press, 1974), pp. 86–89.

22 Marks, *Tigers, Rice, Silk, and Silt*, p. 167.

23 Quoted in Sucheta Mazumdar, *Sugar and Society in China: Peasants, Technology and the World Market* (Cambridge: Harvard Univ. Press, 1998), p. 205.

24 Quoted in Basu, "Asian Merchants and Western Trade," p. 47; White, "Hong Merchants," p. 31.

25 Jonathan D. Spence, "The K'ang-hsi Reign," pp. 120–229 in Willard J. Peterson, ed., *The Cambridge History of China, Vol. 9, The Ch'ing Dynasty to 1800, Part I* (Cambridge: Cambridge Univ. Press, 2002), at 146; Ng, *Trade and Society*, p. 52.

26 Hummel, *Eminent Chinese*, pp. 879–880; Leonard, *Wei Yuan*, p. 68; Marks, *Tigers, Rice, Silk, and Silt*, p. 156; Cheong, *Hong Merchants*, p. 30; Wakeman, *Great Enterprise, Vol. 2*, pp. 1099–1127.

The Qing rulers recognized that trade would help restore the badly damaged Guangdong economy and build the loyalty of the people.[27] In contrast to the Ming, which distrusted and indeed prohibited foreign trade for most of its history, the Qing had a positive view of trade founded in long beneficial experience in regional trade from the Manchu homeland.[28] The Kangxi Emperor strongly favored economic restoration of coastal regions in the interests of maintaining public order. In his directives, the Emperor encouraged officials to seek to achieve "prosperous people through trade" (*tongshang yumin*),[29] to "enrich the state by developing trade" (*tongshang yuguo*), and to "cherish merchants" (*xushang*).[30] These objectives have deep roots in Chinese

27 Blussé, *Visible Cities*, p. 28; Zhao, *Qing Opening to the Ocean*, pp. 53–6; Wills, *Embassies and Illusions*, p. 13; Thomas Metzger, "Ch'ing Commercial Policy," Ch'ing-shih Wen-t'i, Vol. 1, pp. 4–10 (1966), p. 10; William T. Rowe, "Domestic Interregional Trade in Eighteenth-Century China," pp. 173–192 in Leonard Blussé and Femme Gaastra, eds., *On the Eighteenth Century as a Category of Asian History: Van Leur in Retrospect* (Aldershot, England: Ashgate Publishing Ltd., 1998), p. 184 ("In the light of the current state of knowledge, the Qing seems perhaps the most pro-commercial regime in imperial Chinese history."); Lien-sheng Yang, "Government Control of Urban Merchants in Traditional China," Tsing Hua Journal of Chinese Studies, Vol. 8, new series, pp. 186–206 (1970), p. 188 ("Reviewing the overall picture of government control of urban merchants in the first two hundred years of the Ch'ing period, one is struck by the lack of obstacles preventing merchants from improving their status, the limited checks applied to their business activities, the relatively light (or not exceptionally heavy) taxation and extortion imposed on them, and whenever control was attempted, the reliance on two old key concepts of security and guaranty.").

28 Blussé, *Visible Cities*, p. 28; Li, "State Building Before 1644," p. 24 (substantial trade profits accumulated outside of the tribute system); Zhao, *Qing Opening to the Ocean*, pp. 77–8.

29 Blussé, *Visible Cities*, p. 28; Zhao, *Qing Opening to the Ocean*, p. 88; Zhao, "Shaping the Asian Trade Network," pp. 160, 164–6 and 168–9 ("tong shang yu min"); Leonard, *Wei Yuan*, pp. 71–2; Marks, *Tigers, Rice, Silk, and Silt*, pp. 166–7; Ng, *Trade and Society*, pp. 189 (objective "to facilitate commercial intercourse in order to benefit the populace" [tongshang bianmin], particularly with reference to trading in rice) and 191 ("The court always instructed officials 'to assist the merchants' [xu shang] not only 'to enrich the revenue' [yuke] but also 'to enrich the people' [yumin]."); Metzger, "Ch'ing Commercial Policy," p. 7; Pengsheng Chiu, "The Discourse on Insolvency and Negligence in Eighteenth-Century China," pp. 125–42 in Robert E. Hegel and Katherine Carlitz, eds., *Writing and Law in Late Imperial China: Crime, Conflict, and Judgment* (Seattle: Univ. of Washington Press, 2007), p. 129 (" 'provide equal benefit to merchants and their customers' (tongshang bianmin)").

30 Zhao, *Qing Opening to the Ocean*, pp. 72 and 87; Zhao, "Shaping the Asian Trade Network, pp. 165 ("xu shang") and 168; Angela Schottenhammer, "The East Asian Maritime World, 1400–1800: Its fabrics of power and dynamics of exchanges—China and her neighbors," pp. 1–83, in Angela Schottenhammer, ed., *The East Asian Maritime World, 1400–1800: Its Fabrics of Power and Dynamics of Exchanges* (Wiesbaden: Harrassowitz Verlag, 2007), p. 32.

PLATE 1 *The Kangxi Emperor, reigned 1661 to 1722, architect of the "open door" foreign trade policies implemented in 1683. Portrait in Court Dress, hanging scroll, ink and color on silk. Artist unknown. (The Palace Museum, Beijing, China. Photograph © The Palace Museum, by permission.)*

thought.[31] The Qianlong Emperor observed in 1748 that it was generally better to leave matters concerning the market to the people and allow free circulation of goods because government interference, however well intentioned, often failed to improve matters.[32] In 1683, however, the need for stimulus was urgent. Not only the south, but all of China suffered under an economic depression in the early Kangxi period, worsened by the heavy costs of suppression of the Revolt of the Three Feudatories.[33]

As of December 1683, two months after the victory on Taiwan, the Qing began to lift the ban on Chinese navigation overseas. At least fifty large and small coastal ports in four provinces were opened to foreign trade.[34] Initially, as later described by the Kangxi Emperor (who reigned from 1661 to 1722), "the following ports were opened for trade: Tianjin in Zhili, Dengzhou in Shandong, Yuntaishan in Jiangsu, Ningbo in Zhejiang, Zhangzhou in Fujian, and Macao in Guangdong. Later on, it was only maritime rebellions that necessitated closing these ports."[35] The Kangxi Emperor believed that opening these ports would benefit the national economy and also the livelihood of the general population (*guoji minsheng*).[36] Trade in military supplies and goods which were believed

31 "The phrase li-shang pien-min (make conditions materially advantageous for the merchants and the common people)...expressed a common official attitude with roots going back at least to Mencius and Hsun-tzu." Thomas A. Metzger, "The Organizational Capabilities of the Ch'ing State in the Field of Commerce: The Liang-huai Salt Monopoly, 1740–1840," pp. 9–45 in W. E. Willmott, ed., *Economic Organization in Chinese Society* (Stanford University Press, 1972), p. 44; Jennifer Cushman, *Fields from the Sea: Chinese Junk Trade with Siam during the Late Eighteenth and Early Nineteenth Centuries* (Ithaca: Cornell Southeast Asian Program, 1993), p. 121 ("Such expressions as [anmin tongshang] (pacify the people and encourage and facilitate the activities of merchants) and [yuguo xushang] (enrich the state while acting with sympathy for merchants) were common in the writings of Ch'ing officials.").

32 Yang, "Government Control of Urban Merchants," p. 199.

33 Zhao, *Qing Opening to the Ocean*, p. 86; Ramon H. Myers and Yeh-chien Wang, "Economic Developments, 1644–1800," pp. 563–645 in Willard J. Peterson, ed., *The Cambridge History of China, Vol. 9, The Ch'ing Dynasty to 1800, Part 1* (Cambridge: Cambridge Univ. Press, 2002), pp. 564–565. This period is sometimes referred to as the "Kangxi Depression." Mio Kishimoto-Nakayama, "The Kangxi Depression and Early Qing Local Markets," Modern China, Vol. 10, pp. 227–56 (1984).

34 Zhao, *Qing Opening to the Ocean*, pp. 6, 85, 92, 111, 128 and 170; Marks, *Tigers, Rice, Silk, and Silt*, p. 157; Cheong, *Hong Merchants*, pp. 10, 17, 21 n.14, 26, 50–53, 66 n.2 and 192.

35 Zhao, *Qing Opening to the Ocean*, pp. 6 and 85; Zhao, "Shaping the Asian Trade Network," p. 161.

36 Ng, *Trade and Society*, p. 188.

to be potentially useful to rebels, only, was still banned.[37] Of the newly opened ports, Xiamen [Amoy], Guangzhou [Canton], Macao and Ningbo attracted Western traders. At times, these ports competed among themselves for Western business.[38] Initially, "the ships were few and the customs duties meager,"[39] but the region enjoyed a rapid recovery under Kangxi's open trade policies.[40] Coastal residents returned, agriculture was restored, devastated junk fleets were rebuilt, and foreign and regional trade rapidly increased. Between 1685 and 1688 some 467 private Chinese vessels sailed to Japan; during the prior four years only twelve ships had made the voyage.[41]

As the Kangxi Emperor later explained, "Why have I opened trade along the coast? The development of maritime trade will benefit the people of Fujian and Guangdong. As the people of these two provinces get rich and commercial commodities circulate smoothly, this prosperity will benefit other provinces."[42] The powerful recovery that flowed from the trade liberalization policies of the late seventeenth century parallels China's late twentieth century economic revival in the wake of the "Cultural Revolution" of 1965–1971. Trade was encouraged by the modern Chinese political leadership—'to get rich is glorious'—as a means to spur recovery and maintain social order in those difficult years. In each case commerce was used to ignite the extraordinary energy of the Chinese people and to restore economic health after a period of crisis. The economies of these two eras were profoundly different, but the results of liberalization were the same.

In implementing an open trade policy, the Kangxi Emperor rejected Ming Dynasty policy that restricted foreign trade to limited business conducted in tandem with missions bearing tribute to the Chinese Emperor. The "tribute system" continued, but under Qing Dynasty policy it was separated from foreign trade.[43] The Kangxi Emperor acted to assure that tax revenue from foreign trade would flow smoothly to the Qing state. In 1684 the maritime

37 Zhao, "Shaping the Asian Trade Network," pp. 175–6.

38 Cheong, *Hong Merchants*, pp. 28–9 and 34 (the hong merchant Anqua told French traders at Canton, in 1699, that he had been sent to Batavia in 1694 by the Viceroy and other officials, to urge the Dutch to resume trade at Canton); Zhao, *Qing Opening to the Ocean*, p. 76; Van Dyke, *Canton Trade*, p. 10; White, "Hong Merchants," pp. 35–6.

39 White, "Hong Merchants," p. 32.

40 Wolfram Eberhard, *A History of China* (4th ed., Berkeley: Univ. of Calif. Press, 1977), pp. 282–3; Marks, *Tigers, Rice, Silk, and Silt*, p. 163.

41 Leonard, *Wei Yuan*, p. 69; Zhao, *Qing Opening to the Ocean*, p. 35.

42 Quoted in Zhao, *Qing Opening to the Ocean*, p. 88; Cushman, *Fields from the Sea*, p. 122.

43 Zhao, *Qing Opening to the Ocean*, pp. 99 and 109–115; Wills, *Embassies and Illusions*, pp. 166–7.

customs system (*haiguan*) was defined as having jurisdiction over the taxation of goods exported and imported by maritime ships, and trusted Manchu officials were appointed as the heads of the crucial Guangdong and Fujian maritime customs.[44] China's growing maritime foreign trade yielded substantial customs revenues thereafter. In the period from 1687 to 1755 the customs revenues of Guangdong Province grew from little more than 90,000 taels ($125,000) to over 500,000 taels ($694,444) annually. Scholarly estimates place the value of trade between China and nontribute countries in Europe and Southeast Asia in the late seventeenth and early eighteenth centuries at more than 5.4 million taels ($7.5 million) annually.[45]

The Qing recognized the dangers inherent in maritime trade. Successful as conquerors after a forty year struggle, they knew that anti-Manchu feeling existed among the majority ethnic Han population. The new rulers were wary that trade might facilitate contact with rebels who had escaped to the nearby Philippines and South China Sea (*nanyang*). They were equally watchful for anti-Qing or other unconventional ideas, coming from abroad, which might stir up the coastal population.[46] Further rebel activity in and near Taiwan led to reimposition of the ban on regional overseas trade in 1717. It was then gradually lifted in the years through 1727.[47] During this later ban, European ships continued to be allowed to call at Chinese ports, and general Chinese trade

44 Zhao, *Qing Opening to the Ocean*, pp. 118–22.

45 Zhao, *Qing Opening to the Ocean*, pp. 113 and 179. The Chinese tael was equivalent to one ounce (liang) of monetary silver. Frank H. H. King, *Money and Monetary Policy in China 1845–1895* (Cambridge: Harvard Univ. Press, 1965), pp. 27–8 ("The ideal nature of one tael being satisfied by one liang of monetary silver is based on the fact that 'liang' in Chinese was used both for the unit of account (tael) and for the weight of silver (Chinese ounce or liang) used to satisfy it.") and 47. On its accounts, the British EIC treated the Spanish dollar as equal to 0.72 tael. Morse, *Chronicles, Vol. 1*, p. xxii. That ratio has been used in preparing the tael (dollar) equivalents which appear throughout in this study. In practice, these calculations could become more complicated, given debasements, regional tael conventions, etc. King, pp. 47–50 ("The foreigner expected to find or thought he ought to find a unified national monetary system. Instead he found a system he might more usefully have compared with those of the Italian city states than with that of contemporary Britain."); Lien-sheng Yang, *Money and Credit in China: A Short History* (Cambridge: Harvard Univ. Press, 1952), p. 47. As a result, shroffs (money changers) were customarily used to test and validate the metal used in commercial transactions. King, pp. 32 and 87.

46 Leonard, *Wei Yuan*, pp. 34, 65, 69 and 73; Cheong, *Hong Merchants*, pp. 50–53; Wills, *Pepper, Guns and Parleys*, p. 188.

47 Cheong, *Hong Merchants*, pp. 50–53; Schottenhammer, "East Asian Maritime World," pp. 29 and 31–32; Ng, *Trade and Society*, pp. 186–7.

with Japan, the Ryukyu Islands (including Okinawa) and Annam (Vietnam) was also continued.[48]

As masters of a newly pacified land, the Qing rulers closely watched and were wary of the sometimes aggressive and seemingly uncivilized conduct of some of the Westerners who came to China to do business. Their burgeoning maritime commerce served Chinese interests, but the behavior of certain foreigners caused Qing officials to think constantly about public order and national defense. The first English expedition to China, which reached Canton in 1637 under Captain John Weddell, made itself memorable by using gunfire to force its way into the Pearl River.[49] In 1724 the hong merchant Youngqua was placed in chains by the Hoppo after his French tenant drew his sword on one of the Hoppo's officers.[50] In 1742, Commodore Anson of HMS Centurion threatened to force his way up the Pearl River to Whampoa. In response, an old law was revived prohibiting foreign warships beyond the Bogue forts. Regulations were announced banning the firing of ships' guns in port and requiring commercial vessels to surrender their cannons while in port, but these rules were largely ignored.[51] Commodore Anson then took his reprovisioned warship out to sea where he captured the annual Spanish galleon from Acapulco to Manila, *Nuestra Señora de Covadonga*, laden with £1,500,000 in silver. Anson brought his prize back to the Pearl River, where he disputed the customs duties assessed by the Chinese on the Centurion and the captured galleon.[52] After the 1754 death of a British sailor in fighting between French and British sailors, the Canton officials assigned what came to be called "French Island" to the French for recreation and "Danes Island" to the British and Danes for the same purpose.[53] On 17 August 1781 Captain John McClary of the English country ship *Dadoloy* captured the private Dutch ship *Goede Hoop* at the Whampoa anchorage. The Dutch protested to the Chinese, who scrambled some 2,000 troops and assembled a flotilla of private and government vessels which hemmed in the captured vessel while angrily demanding an end to this offense against Chinese sovereignty over inner waters. The Governor-General, Governor and Hoppo wrote the English supercargoes on 9 September 1781, stating: "This is to give notice to the supercargoes of the different nations in

48 Ng, *Trade and Society*, p. 57.

49 Frederic Wakeman, Jr., *The Fall of Imperial China* (New York: The Free Press, 1975), p. 129; Morse, *Chronicles, Vol. 1*, pp. 22–30.

50 Cheong, *Hong Merchants*, p. 221.

51 Cheong, *Hong Merchants*, p. 205.

52 Morse, *Chronicles, Vol. 1*, p. 284.

53 R. Randle Edwards, "Ch'ing Legal Jurisdiction Over Foreigners," p. 238.

order that they may inform their countrymen that the Emperor will not suffer them to bring war into his dominions, and that whoever does so in the future shall be treated as an enemy." Captain McClary then yielded his prize to the cheering Chinese flotilla and sailed off. He carried with him an iron chest containing pearls and gold consigned by Armenian merchants in India, with an invoice value of 89,128 rupees. Not long thereafter, Captain McClary further irritated the Chinese authorities by plundering a Canton junk he seized in the Bangka Straits, claiming that the goods he found on it were actually Dutch property.[54] On 19 March 1787, The hong merchant Howqua I (Lin Shimao) was taken hostage by a putative private creditor. He was held in the Imperial Factory by Mr. Dormer, purser of the *Nottingham* (a vessel Howqua I had not secured), who claimed that his hostage had somehow agreed to guaranty a failed transaction "with Small Merchants and Persons of that Description." He had no proof of guaranty, and the hong merchant refused to sign the new guaranty Dormer demanded. Howqua I was released, Dormer was reprimanded, and the EIC ordered the disgruntled supposed creditor to leave Canton on the next ship.[55] In 1808 thirteen British warships landed hundreds of soldiers and occupied a fort at Macao on the pretext of protecting Macao from the French navy. The Chinese authorities cut off British trade and marched an army in response, which caused the British forces to depart. Governor-General Wu Xiongguang was removed from office and ordered banished to Xinjiang for failure to respond sternly enough to the British occupation.[56] On 21 April 1833, private British country trader James Innes set fire to the Customs House, using rockets and blue lights, to express outrage at official inaction against a Chinese who he claimed had assaulted him.[57] The preceding is simply a collection of incidents, not a comprehensive catalog of aggressive activities. Fights—notably among foreign sailors or between sailors and the local population—occurred regularly, as did occasional murders of Chinese by foreigners, often enough in these

54 Michael Greenberg, *British Trade and the Opening of China 1800–42* (Cambridge: Cambridge Univ. Press, 1951), pp. 21–22; Liu Yong, "The Dutch India Company's Tea Trade with China, 1757–1781" (Ph.D. diss., Leiden University, 2006), pp. 111–7; Morse, *Chronicles, Vol. II*, pp. 63–5.

55 Morse, *Chronicles, Vol. II*, pp. 149–50.

56 Joanna Waley-Cohen, *Exile in Mid-Qing China: Banishment to Xinjiang, 1758–1820* (New Haven: Yale Univ. Press, 1991), p. 86; Austin M. Coates, *Macao and the British, 1637–1842: Prelude to Hong Kong* (Hong Kong: Hong Kong University Press, 2009), pp. 94–99.

57 Morse, *Chronicles, Vol. IV*, pp. 352–3; Greenberg, *British Trade*, p. 33 n.2; Downs, *The Golden Ghetto*, pp. 73–75.

brawls.[58] The Qing government had been given reason to consider Westerners a potential external risk to domestic order.

The Qing were also concerned about the potentially disruptive internal effects of unfair or deceptive business practices by Chinese who traded with Westerners. In the present, they saw shadows of the abusive trading practices that arose in the illicit maritime trade of the late Ming period. The *wokou* ("Japanese pirate") depredations of the mid to late 1500s were a particularly bitter memory. The *wokou* were Japanese and Chinese who had traded between China and Japan. As foreign trade was illegal, and subject to periodic crackdowns, the sea traders relied on prominent Chinese families which began to use the strained situation against them.[59]

> They received payment in advance from the Japanese traders but never delivered any cargoes or kept the cargoes without paying the cost. Waiting off coast in vain, the Japanese traders were desperately worried about the consequences if they went back to their lords with empty hands. With no other alternative, they resorted to violence. The prominent official families, acting for their own advantage, urged the local administration to expel them by force. But at the same time, they played the tricky game of deliberately informing their partners of the imminent military attacks just to make sure they could manage to escape in time for the gratefulness of the Japanese might bring them further benefit. After several similar occasions, the Japanese merchants became aware that they had been cheated.[60]

Vengeance by the Japanese traders escalated into large-scale raids, and even expeditions inland or up the Yangzi River, which caused terrible damage and took years of effort and great expense to suppress.[61] The Qianlong Emperor had the history of unpaid foreign merchants turning to piracy in mind during the years in which the Canton Guaranty System was developed. In a 1777

58 Edwards, "Ch'ing Legal Jurisdiction Over Foreigners," pp. 222–269; Liu, "Dutch India Company," p. 55.

59 John E. Wills, Jr., "Maritime Europe and the Ming," in John E. Wills, Jr., ed., *China and Maritime Europe, 1500–1800: Trade, Settlement, Diplomacy, and Missions* (Cambridge: Cambridge Univ. Press, 2011), p. 34.

60 Ng Chin-keong, "Gentry-Merchants and Peasant-Peddlers—The Response of the South Fukienese to the Offshore Trading Opportunities 1522–1566," Nanyang Univ. Journal, Vol. 7, pp. 161–174 (1973), pp. 168–9 (quoted text); Charles W. MacSherry, "Impairment of the Ming Tributary System as Exhibited in Trade Involving Fukien" (Ph.D. diss., University of California, Berkeley, 1952), p. 117; Sung, "A Study of the Thirteen Hongs," pp. 66–67 n.1.

61 Wills, "Maritime Europe and the Ming," p. 34.

edict which harshly criticized official handling of a relatively minor foreign debt case, the Emperor stressed the foreign relations importance of the matter.

> Moreover, our resolution of this point is not just for the particular case at issue. It comes after reflecting deeply on the fact that the dynasties of Han, Tang, Song and Ming, during their last years, came to ignore the proper way of showing benevolent disposition towards people from afar. When the foreign people were weak and incapable [to fight against China], [the rulers of the said dynasties] despised them and insulted or ill-treated them; while when they were strong and [China] got into trouble [with them], then [the Chinese rulers] showed their fear and sought for some kind of concession. [They] went with this type of appeasement, and acted without thinking. Consequently, serious ruptures occurred, and [the state of affairs] became unredeemable. The failure of the Song as well as the fall of the Ming was caused by mistakes of this kind. How can we not take warning [by these precedents]?[62]

2 The Organization of Merchants Engaged in Maritime Trade

Official management of Chinese merchants engaged in foreign trade from Canton dates from 1686, after the opening of foreign trade. In that year Governor Li Shizhen licensed a group of successful merchants as foreign goods firms (*yanghuo hang*).[63] The thriving business of these official merchants is described in a contemporary poem by Chu Dajun (1630–1696):

> Ocean-going ships compete to export the wares of official merchants
> As Shizimen opens on the two oceans
> The Guangdong silks and satins are highly prized
> And silver piles up in the thirteen hongs.[64]

62 Quoted in Ch'en, *Insolvency*, pp. 188–9; Cheong, *Hong Merchants*, p. 262; White, "Hong Merchants," pp. 68–9; On-cho Ng, "Ch'ing Management of the West: A Study of the Regulations, Homicide Cases and Debt Cases, 1644–1820" (M.A. Thesis, Univ. of Hong Kong, 1979), p. 146, see: "http://hub.hku.hk/bitstream/10722/32944/1/FullText.pdf" (accessed 10 May 2012).

63 Cheong, *Hong Merchants*, p. 31.

64 White, "Hong Merchants," pp. 15–16; Sung, "A Study of the Thirteen Hongs," pp. 24–5 and 73 (it is included in Chu's "poems on Canton," the Guangzhou Zhuzhici).

In these early years, the leading Chinese traders were spry and entrepreneurial. Their ships came and went from many places, notably the Philippines, Batavia and Annam (Vietnam). Some did business with Westerners in China, but that trade was insignificant. Early Chinese specialists in European trade were itinerant, associated primarily with home ports in neighboring Fujian Province such as Xiamen [Amoy] or Quanzhou.[65] They traveled to the ports European vessels visited according to a seasonal rhythm that long marked the trade. Their developing European business was fit into a timetable with other mercantile activities. The Western season began with the arrival of foreign ships with the southwest monsoon in about May or June and ended at the latest by mid-January when the ships left with the northeast monsoon.[66]

European trade was exempted from the renewed ban on overseas navigation which was imposed by the Kangxi Emperor from 1717 through 1727. The ban took the bloom off the regional junk trade and ended hong merchant involvement in it, at least for that period. While trade with Japan was also exempted, it too suffered, due to the austerity regime of the Japanese Shogun Yoshimune and falling Chinese demand for imported Japanese copper.[67]

From the early days of the trade, there was a divergence between the poetic image of hong merchant wealth and the less opulent reality of conducting trade between two worlds. While little detail survives about the finances of the early hong merchants, some became greatly indebted to foreign and domestic creditors. The unresolved burden of this debt—and mounting interest on it—placed an ongoing burden on their businesses. For example, many of the hong merchants are known to have been deeply in debt to official patrons and Armenian and other creditors in the early 1720s, in large part due to losses on tea shipments to Batavia.[68] The British EIC noted in its records in May 1723 that "almost all the merchants are broke, and there are not above two or three to be depended on for a contract."[69] In July 1723, the EIC noted that Suqua, Cowlo and several other merchants who had just arrived from Xiamen (Amoy) stated "that they have built large Hongs at Amoy, in order to live there, for that they can't bear the impositions of the Mandarines here, any longer, and wish the

65 Cheong, *Hong Merchants*, pp. 29, 32–4, 36–7, 41–2, 44–6 and 48; Zhao, "Shaping the Asian Trade Network," pp. 49–50, 55 and 86.

66 Cheong, *Hong Merchants*, p. 36.

67 Cheong, *Hong Merchants*, pp. 45, 49–50, 223 and 243 n.128; Zhao, *Qing Opening to the Ocean*, pp. 126–7 and 140–7.

68 Cheong, *Hong Merchants*, pp. 38, 45, 53 and 60; Li Tana and Paul A. Van Dyke, "Canton, Cancao, and Cochinchina: New Data and New Light on Eighteenth-Century Canton and the Nanyang," Chinese Southern Diaspora Studies, Vol. 1, pp. 1–28 (2007), p. 15.

69 Van Dyke, *Merchants of Canton and Macao*, p. 80.

English would go there."[70] The causes of hong merchant debt in the early 1700s were similar to those noted a century later: inadequate capitalization, heavy exactions by government officials, high operating and living expenses, and lack of business credit.

The lack of affordable domestic credit was a severe problem. The general trend of hong merchant history from the early 1700s forward is of a growing trade, and that trade is believed to have been generally profitable.[71] The demands of carrying on this increasing and highly competitive business strained hong firms from the start, and many turned to Western merchants for high interest rate credit.[72] Foreigners extended credit in the form of cash loans, which were used to finance large volume purchases, or in the form of import goods to be paid for in the future. Some domestic suppliers extended credit for large purchases by hong merchants, but a deposit was normally required.[73] Prior to the 1760 ban on foreign debt and mortgages, some foreign loans were secured by mortgages on real estate owned by hong firms.[74] The seemingly chronic indebtedness of the hong merchant firms had become a serious issue for the Western traders by at least the 1750s.[75]

The hong merchants had few other credit options. The principal lenders in China during this period were either family members or pawnshops. The latter grew in number and respectability during the eighteenth century, rising from 9,904 in 1723 to about 25,000 by the early 1800s.[76] Idle government funds were advanced to pawnshops to be lent out at interest, under a policy known as *fashang shengxi* (put the fund with merchants to produce interest).[77] There

---

70 Van Dyke, *Merchants of Canton and Macao*, p. 80.

71 Ch'en, *Insolvency*, pp. 43–88, 102–3 and 251.

72 Cheong, *Hong Merchants*, p. 102; Van Dyke, *Merchants of Canton and Macao*, p. 17.

73 Cheong, *Hong Merchants*, pp. 99, 114–6 and 283; Ch'en, *Insolvency*, pp. 170–1.

74 Ch'en, *Insolvency*, pp. 183, 307 and 432 n.199; Cheong, *Hong Merchants*, pp. 157–8, 171, 253 and 187 n.126; Morse, *Chronicles, Vol. v*, p. 74.

75 Cheong, *Hong Merchants*, pp. 254 and 278.

76 Yang, *Money and Credit in China*, pp. 73–74 (statistics drawn from Qing statutes); T. S. Whelan, *The Pawnshop in China* (Ann Arbor, Mich.: Center for Chinese Studies, Univ. of Michigan, 1979), p. 10; George Thomas Staunton, *Ta Tsing Leu Lee*; *Being the Fundamental Laws, and a Selection from the Supplementary Statutes of the Penal Code of China* (London: T. Cadell and W. Davies, 1810), p. 531.

77 Chung-li Chang, *The Income of the Chinese Gentry* (Seattle: Univ. of Wash. Press, 1962) p. 171; T. S. Whelan, *Pawnshop*, p. 10; Yang, *Money and Credit in China*, pp. 74 and 98–99. The Imperial Household Department (*neiwufu*) lent money to salt merchants in Changlu and Lianghuai, invested in pawnshops under its direct control, and loaned money at interest. Chang, "Economic Role of the Imperial Household," p. 268; Jonathan Spence, *Ts'ao Yin and the K'ang-hsi Emperor, Bondservant and Master* (New Haven, Conn.: Yale University Press, 1966), p. 103; Yang, "Government Control of Urban Merchants," p. 189; Yingcong Dai,

was no such thing as commercial finance.[78] George Staunton noted in 1810 that it was a "frequent practice in China, to lend upon pledges; and [that] accordingly, the shops of money-lenders, where deposits may be made of any kind of personal property, are extremely numerous in all parts of the empire, and, in general, upon a scale of greater respectability than establishments of a similar nature in Europe." He viewed the high interest rates and scarcity of credit in China as resulting from the "comparatively vague and undefined" state of property rights under Chinese law and difficulties enforcing such rights, adding:

> In a state of things so unfavorable to the accumulation and transfer of property, there cannot at any time be much floating capital; and the value of that capital, as far as it is denoted by the interest which it bears, it is natural to expect, will be high in proportion to its scarcity. In other words, where there are many borrowers and few lenders, and where it forms no part of the system of the government to grant to the former any peculiar degree of protection or encouragement, it seems a necessary consequence, that the latter will both demand and obtain a more than ordinary compensation in return for the use of his property. Trade, therefore, as far as it requires such aid, cannot be so extensively carried on, as it is in those countries, in which there being more available capital, that capital is procurable at a cheaper rate, and accordingly a smaller return of profit found adequate to the charges of commercial adventure.[79]

Undercapitalized hongs generally lacked the collateral required for pawnbroker loans, or did not have rich family members to call upon, or had previously drawn as much as family resources could bear. Credit was not to be had within the guild except on rare occasions. The wealthy hong merchants were reluctant to lend to the lesser merchants, because they could not offer good security, and were often patently unstable.[80] So it was that the hong merchant Goqua II (Xie Yuren of the Dongyu hong), who had long borrowed from the British EIC

"Yingyun Shengxi: Military Entrepreneurship in the High Qing Period 1700–1800," Late Imperial China, Vol. 26, No. 2 (2005), p. 11.

78 Elisabeth Kaske, "Fund Raising Wars: Office Selling and Interprovincial Finance in Nineteenth-Century China," Harvard Journal of Asiatic Studies, Vol. 71, pp. 69–141 (2011), p. 80 ("commercial borrowing was nonexistent").

79 Staunton, *Ta Tsing Leu Lee*, p. 531.

80 Ch'en, *Insolvency*, pp. 170–1.

as a lender of last resort, turned again to the EIC for credit in June 1828, saying that "no one [else] will help me with a loan."[81]

The difficult trading conditions of the 1720s led firms with a history of trading with Westerners to respond by building up that side of their businesses, exploiting existing connections in ports such as Manila and Batavia and good working relations with European traders. These were also years of outreach by Western national trading firms, which worked to develop more direct and therefore more efficient trade from the China coast to Europe.[82] As Canton became the lead port for China's developing trade with the West, the formerly itinerant Chinese traders began to settle there, along with returning overseas Chinese traders with close ties to the Philippines and Batavia. The seaport was in flux. Newcomers were rising to prominence in Canton's trade with the West, notably Puankhequa I (Pan Zhencheng of the Tongwen Hong) who had lived and worked for years in Manila.[83] The foreign trading community took root and grew up on the west side of Canton, in the area where the trading ships offices of the former Song and Ming dynasties had been located. These establishments became famous as the Thirteen Hongs and the Foreign Factories, the business premises of the Chinese and Western traders respectively.[84]

In the early 1700s, China's trade from Canton with Western merchants was managed through a series of chief merchants—notably Hunsunquin, Cawsanqua (Cudgin), and Suqua (Cumshaw). Each had close ties with officials

---

81 Basu, "Asian Merchants and Western Trade," pp. 351–2 ("I have hitherto been benefited by loans from your Company so that I was able to meet the payment of government duties… the Viceroy has ordered that all the Hongs no later than the twentieth of this month remit the [gongjia] (tribute to the Court) and the [sengjia] (ginseng duty). The total ginseng duty of this year is 68,712.2 taels and my share is 6,247.2 taels. As for [gongjia] the total is 61,400 taels and my share is 2,707.8192 taels. My total remittance thus amounts to 8,955 taels. I thought it over and over but could not find a way to raise the sum. My business is small in scale and being often deficient in capital, no one will help me with a loan… normally since your Company already helped me several times to pay off my duties, I should not have made this appeal again. Although I think hard, I can find no way out. In recent years, I have been relying on your Company for loans to pay off my share of duties, I therefore appeal to you gentlemen once more…"); Ch'en, *Insolvency*, pp. 19 and 41.

82 See Wills, *Embassies and Illusions*, pp. 196–7 ("And as the tea trade began to grow rapidly in the early eighteenth century [Dutch reliance on middlemen] proved disastrous: the English and even the Ostenders, trading directly to Canton, got consistently better quality in their tea and avoided the effects of a layover in a damp tropical warehouse.").

83 Cheong, *Hong Merchants*, pp. 29, 32–4, 36, 40–2, 48, 50, 52, 54, 56–8 and 63; Ng, *Trade and Society*, pp. 178 and 201; Basu, "Asian Merchants and Western Trade," p. 354.

84 Sung, "A Study of the Thirteen Hongs," pp. 88–91.

and used those ties to control or to obtain advantage in trade.[85] In the early years monopoly trading rights were sometimes purchased by an individual or group from the Canton officials.[86] The favored purchaser might in turn subcontract trading rights with particular ships to other merchants.[87] Individuals who traded under the name "Emperors Merchant" appeared at several foreign trade ports, seeking to enforce monopoly trading rights said to have been acquired from the Kangxi Emperor's fourth son, the future Yongzheng Emperor. The Emperor's Merchant who arrived at Canton in 1704 was an unsuccessful salt merchant who had acquired a monopoly of that season's trade for 42,000 taels ($58,333).[88] He sought to assert a general monopoly of Canton's foreign trade, but was rebuffed through the joint efforts of the European and Chinese merchants.[89]

To secure a collective monopoly of the Chinese side of the trade, a combination of the hong merchant body was attempted at Xiamen (Amoy) in 1704, at the behest of the local Emperor's Merchant. The organization did not last long.[90] In the course of the 1700s, the hong merchants tried on several other occasions to organize as one body that could negotiate on a more equal footing with the European trading corporations. In December 1720, a three-tiered guild of sixteen hong merchants known as the Cohong was organized at Canton with the support of the Hoppo and other officials. As described by Weng Eang Cheong:

> The members were graded into three groups of five, five and six merchants according to their wealth and ability. Admission to the third and lowest grade cost 1,000 taels; presumably the price for entry to the other grades was higher. Outsiders, known as shopkeepers, had to pay a levy of 40 per cent and 20 per cent respectively, to participate in the tea and porcelain trades monopolized by the Hong merchants; newly arrived merchants were required to observe the guild's practices and prices.[91]

---

85 Cheong, *Hong Merchants*, pp. 33–5, 37, 46 and 95–6.

86 Cheong, *Hong Merchants*, pp. 219–20; White, "Hong Merchants," pp. 40–41; Morse, *Chronicles, Vol. 1*, pp. 119–142.

87 See Morse, *Chronicles, Vol. 1*, p. 141.

88 Morse, *Chronicles, Vol. 1*, pp. 137–138; Cheong, *Hong Merchants*, p. 33.

89 Morse, *Chronicles, Vol. 1*, pp. 137–138; Cheong, *Hong Merchants*, p. 33.

90 Morse, *Chronicles, Vol. 1*, pp. 132 and 142.

91 Quoted from Cheong, *Hong Merchants*, p. 37 (footnotes omitted).

The Cohong monopolized the tea and porcelain trades at Canton and set practices and prices which had to be observed by all foreign trade merchants. Establishment of the guild seems to have been motivated by the desire of the incumbent traders to control their rising local competitors (the former itinerants), as well as to manage external trade with the increasingly powerful European chartered companies.[92] Although the organization was promptly dissolved in July 1721 under British East India Company pressure, its three tiered organization and the distinct functions of each tier governed the conduct of trade for many years thereafter.[93]

As Canton's maritime trade grew, official management of these outer seas merchants (the *waiyang hang* or *yang hang*) was separated from management of the junk trade merchants. Business with Western traders was monopolized in the hands of the outer seas hong merchants. The junk trade merchants were distinctly organized as the native ports hongs and as the Guangdong and Fujian hongs. The business of the merchants of the native ports hong (*bengang hang*) was international, specialized in trade with and tribute from Southeast Asia. The business of the merchants of the Guangdong and Fujian hong (*fuchao hang*) (Fu-jian, Chao-zhou hong) was regional, specialized in trade north up the coast. The history of these two sea trading hong organizations is obscure, but these hong merchants did business with the merchants of the outer seas hong, and appear to have been regulated in a similar manner.[94] Many other guild organizations existed at Canton during this period, and were subject to government regulation. Popularly known as the "seventy-two hong," the actual number of regulated guild organizations is said to have numbered ninety-seven guilds.[95]

92 Cheong, *Hong Merchants*, pp. 37, 41, 92 and 220; J. Y. Wong, *Yeh Ming-ch'en, Viceroy of Liang Kuang* (Cambridge: Cambridge Univ. Press, 1976), pp. 71–72.

93 Cheong, *Hong Merchants*, pp. 37, 42, 47, 61, 92 and 103.

94 Ch'en, *Insolvency*, pp. 6, 7 and 11; Cushman, *Fields from the Sea*, pp. 29 (the Fuchao hang had previously been known as the Hainan hang), 31 (the continuing inability of the bengang hang to meet its obligations led to its dissolution in 1795) and 107 ("The secondary literature is of equally little value in identifying these merchants more fully."); White, "Hong Merchants," p. 54. See Zhao, "Shaping the Asian Trade Network," p. 232 ("very few materials about the Qing regulation of Chinese private trade have survived").

95 Kato Shigeshi, "On the Hang or the Associations of Merchants in China," Memoirs of the Research Dept. of the Toyo Bunko, pp. 45–83 (1936), pp. 75 and 58 ("In China at present they use such an expression as 36 hang, 72 hang, or 360 hang, when they want to refer to the great varieties of trades.").

Virtually all of the Western firms doing business in China in this era were themselves state-chartered monopolies. Major European trading firms included the Dutch (*Vereenigde Oost-Indische Compagnie*) ("VOC"),[96] French (*Compagnie Française des Indes Orientales*),[97] and Swedish (*Svenska Ostindiska Companiet*)[98] East India Companies, as well as the aggressive and ultimately dominant British East India Company.[99] Each of these companies had monopoly rights in their home market, granted by the state. Lesser players included the Danish East India Company (*Asiatiske Kompagni*),[100] and private merchants operating under "flags of convenience," including the Imperial or Ostend Company (*Ostender Kompagnie*) (operated by private traders under a charter purchased in 1717 from the Austrian Emperor),[101] the Prussian or Emden company,[102] and companies chartered by Genoa and by Tuscany.[103]

96 Blussé, *Visible Cities*; Cheong, *Hong Merchants*, pp. 8–9, 50, 54, 56, 57, 109 and 332; Femme S. Gaastra, *The Dutch East India Company: Expansion and Decline* (Zutphen, The Netherlands: Walburg Pers, 2003); Els M. Jacobs, *Merchant in Asia: The Trade of the Dutch East India Company During the Eighteenth Century* (Leiden: CNWS Publications, 2006); C.J.A. Jörg, *Porcelain and the Dutch China Trade* (The Hague, Netherlands: Martinus Nijhoff, 1982), pp. 15–45; Earl H. Pritchard, "The Crucial Years of Early Anglo-Chinese Relations, 1750–1800," Research Studies of the State College of Washington, Vol. 4, Nos. 3–4 (Washington: Pullman, 1936), © Washington State University Press, pp. 186–9 and 194.

97 Cheong, *Hong Merchants*, pp. 9, 27, 29, 57 and 109; Pritchard, "Crucial Years," pp. 186–90 and 194.

98 Christian Koninckx, *The First and Second Charters of the Swedish East India Company* (1731–1766) (Kortrijk, Belgium: Van Ghemmert Pub. Co., 1980), p. 65 (the Swedish company went into receivership in 1809, being followed by company activities under a 5th and final charter which expired with its trading monopoly in 1813); Cheong, *Hong Merchants*, pp. 9, 50, 57, 111 and 145; Pritchard, "Crucial Years," pp. 186–90 and 194; Basu, "Asian Merchants," p. 355.

99 Cheong, *Hong Merchants*, pp. 9, 80, 108–9, 111–3 and 279; Michael Greenberg, *British Trade*, p. 18.

100 Cheong, *Hong Merchants*, pp. 9, 50, 57, 110, 111, 112, 145 and 283; Pritchard, "Crucial Years," pp. 186–7, 190 and 194.

101 Cheong, *Hong Merchants*, pp. 29, 57 and 145; Greenberg, *British Trade*, p. 25; Pritchard, "Crucial Years," pp. 186 and 190; Zhuang Guotu, "The Impact of the International Tea Trade on the Social Economy of Northwest Fujian in the Eighteenth Century," pp. 193–216 in Leonard Blussé and Femme Gaastra, eds., *On the Eighteenth Century as a Category of Asian History: Van Leur in Retrospect* (Aldershot, England: Ashgate Publishing Ltd., 1998), p. 196.

102 Pritchard, "Crucial Years," pp. 186–7 and 190–1 (of six ships which traded under the Prussian flag at Canton between 1783 and 1791, "two of which were certainly on Dutch account"); Liu, "Dutch India Company," pp. 25 and 156 n.22; Greenberg, *British Trade*, pp. 25 and 27.

103 Cheong, *Hong Merchants*, pp. 112; Pritchard, "Crucial Years," pp. 186–7 and 190–1 ("Expeditions were generally fitted out under these foreign flags [i.e., Imperial, Prussian,

These entities attempted to avoid monopoly rights existing in their promoters' respective European home countries. Private Spanish traders from Manila initially enjoyed privileged access to the important Chinese ports of Quanzhou and Xiamen [Amoy], granted early in the Qing period.[104] The various European East India companies competed among themselves, in Europe and in Asia,[105] and repeatedly sought to use their individual and collective power to seek economic advantage in trading with the licensed merchants of Canton. The scale of their operations grew strongly during the eighteenth century. While historical measurements of international trade are imprecise, various estimates have been offered. Trade between Canton and Europe is said to have grown "at the rate of 4 percent a year between 1719 and 1806, meaning that the volume of trade doubled every eighteen years."[106]

3 Official Roots of Collective Responsibility

The orderly conduct of maritime foreign trade at Canton was of direct personal importance to the Emperor at Beijing. Tax revenues from the trade were an important source of income for the Imperial Household Department (*neiwufu*), which funded court operations. The Emperor used Imperial Household Department personnel, posted to Canton, to monitor affairs at the port. While the procedures used to control and tax trade at Canton were distinctive, they were hardly unique. Elements of this system are similar to the structure of other monopolized businesses which were managed by the Imperial Household Department for the benefit of the Court, notably the important salt and ginseng monopolies. Each of these monopolies licensed merchants to trade in the monopolized matter, and held these merchants collectively responsible for unpaid taxes and other financial obligations to the state. The Chinese hong merchant scholar Liang Jiabin quotes his hong merchant grandfather as having said that "The licensed merchants of the hong system were much like the Salt Merchants."[107] Liang was right.

Genoese and Tuscan] by disgruntled English or French who hoped to profit by war-time conditions or by the smuggling trade into England. The ships under Genoese, Tuscan, and Prussian colors between 1787 and 1794 belonged without exception to [private British] Country traders who were attempting to avoid the regulations of the British Company."); Greenberg, *British Trade*, p. 28.

104 Cheong, *Hong Merchants*, pp. 6–7, 26 and 51; Pritchard, "Crucial Years," pp. 186–7, 191 and 194; Greenberg, *British Trade*, p. 47.

105 Pritchard, "Crucial Years," p. 186.

106 Myers and Wang, "Economic Developments, 1644–1800," p. 587.

107 Sung, "A Study of the Thirteen Hongs," pp. 78–9 and 31.

The Imperial Household Department (*neiwufu*) was at once the Emperor's personal treasury, the principal landlord, primary employer of workers and artisans, and the ultimate recipient of much national tax revenue collection.[108] Its key purpose was to maintain control of resources and enterprises to assure the financial stability of the imperial court.[109] Most of the Department's personnel were Manchu.[110] It was largely made up of bondservants (*baoyi*), a hereditary class organized in banners under the Manchu system. The significance of bondservant status varied by banner and ethnicity and changed over time. Many of the non-Manchu *baoyi* had come into the organization as captives and were originally held in slave-like conditions. At all times all bondservants owed a duty of service to the Court.[111] Jonathan Spence calls the Department the Emperor's "personal bureaucracy." Spence's invaluable study of the service of the bondservant Cao Yin to the Kangxi Emperor shows that communication within this bureaucracy could be direct and frank.[112] "The bondservants worked for the Emperor only; just because they were his servants, he protected them and appointed them to lucrative office, so that at some indeterminate point servility became prestige."[113] Spence posits that a significant purpose of the Emperor's use of this bureaucracy was to keep close watch on his household funds.[114] From the early 1700s, the major customs and salt administration offices were usually held by Imperial Household Department bondservants, who were regularly moved from one post to another.[115] The Hoppo often had prior experience elsewhere as a superintendent of customs or salt censor.[116]

The Imperial Household Department operated several schools which educated the sons of bondservants of the upper three banners for service in the

---

108 Chang, "Economic Role of the Imperial Household," pp. 251–4 (landlord operations), 254–6 (tribute revenue), 256–9 (customs revenue), 259–63 (ginseng and fur monopoly), 263–6 (incomes from fines against officials) and 266–8 (confiscations); Spence, Ts'ao Yin, p. 32.

109 Symons, *Ch'ing Ginseng Management*, pp. 79–80.

110 Chang, "Economic Role of the Imperial Household," p. 250; Spence, Ts'ao Yin, pp. 16–17 and 104.

111 Torbert, *Ch'ing Imperial Household Department*, pp. 53–80; Chang, "Economic Role of the Imperial Household," pp. 243–74, p. 245 (every banner had its combat units and bondservant units).

112 Spence, *Ts'ao Yin*, pp. xii, 17, 32, 184–9, 213, 227, 228, 234, 254 and 255.

113 Spence, *Ts'ao Yin*, pp. 17–18.

114 Spence, *Ts'ao Yin*, p. 191.

115 Ch'en, *Insolvency*, pp. 132–3; Chang, "Economic Role of the Imperial Household," pp. 249 and 256; Spence, *Ts'ao Yin*, p. 16.

116 Ch'en, *Insolvency*, pp. 132–3.

Department.[117] A small *baoyi* elite stood at the head of the Department, holding high office in Beijing or important financial positions in the provinces.[118] While the Department worked with other units of the government under a policy called "Government and Imperial Household working in unison" (*gongfu yiti*), little about it was known to contemporary Chinese. Its affairs were kept secret.[119]

Taxes were collected by the Qing government under a quotum system. At Canton, customs taxes were assessed and collected as regular quotum (*zheng'e*) or as surplus quotum (*yingyu*).[120] Regular quotum proceeds went to the Ministry of Revenue (*Hu Bu*). Surplus quotum went to the Imperial Household Department (*neiwufu*), bypassing the provincial government and the Board of Revenue.[121] While the assessment of regular quotum did not formally change from 1686 to 1843, the amounts collected as surplus quotum and related charges increased substantially over the years.[122] Surplus quotum revenue from the Canton customs averaged 855,500 taels ($1,188,194) annually during the period 1796–1821, representing 38% on average of national annual surplus quotum collection during that period (2,261,301 taels [$3,140,695]).[123] These revenues represented a significant part of the court's annual budget. Regular quotum revenue from the Canton customs exceeded 1,000,000 taels ($1,388,889) annually by 1796.[124]

The process by which the growing maritime trade of the port of Canton was taxed for the benefit of the Qing state was quite complicated, evolved over many years, and was a continual subject of vexation to Western traders who bemoaned the lack of a uniform customs table.[125] Such a table did exist, an official list of import and export goods and applicable duties charged per unit (not by value), but these charges had been fixed as of 1727 and represented a small part of the total duties payable by any given ship.[126] The Hoppo sought to maintain an equivalent balance between import and export duties charged.

117 Torbert, *Ch'ing Imperial Household Department*, pp. 37–39.

118 Torbert, *Ch'ing Imperial Household Department*, pp. 67, 77 and 81.

119 Chang, "Economic Role of the Imperial Household," pp. 243, 250 and 271.

120 Chang, "Economic Role of the Imperial Household," pp. 256–7; Cheong, *Hong Merchants*, pp. 197 and 213–4; Zhao, *Qing Opening to the Ocean*, pp. 124–5.

121 Chang, "Economic Role of the Imperial Household," p. 257.

122 Cheong, *Hong Merchants*, p. 215.

123 Chang, "Economic Role of the Imperial Household," p. 258; Cheong, *Hong Merchants*, p. 215.

124 Torbert, *Ch'ing Imperial Household Department*, pp. 98–99.

125 See, for example, John Phipps, *A Practical Treatise on the China and Eastern Trade* (London: William H. Allen, 1836), p. 149.

126 Cheong, *Hong Merchants*, pp. 197 and 214.

An excess of one over the other, such as heavy export duties contrasted with minimal import duties, might indicate smuggling.[127] The largest charges in terms of cash outlay were "anchorage" or "measurement" fees (assessed per vessel based on length and width measurements against which a uniform 20% discount was applied) and "cumshaw" or port charges (including the "emperor's present" which was 1,950 taels [$2,708] for English ships).[128] Surtaxes and supplements proliferated over time, ultimately exceeding the basic duty many times over.[129] The most prominent added charge was the tax imposed on the trade in 1780 to support the Consoo Fund (the *hangyong* levy), which ranged from as little as three percent to as much as seven percent depending on the exigencies of the moment.[130] Other significant charges, such as "native tribute" of 55,000 taels ($76,389) due to the Emperor, as much as 100,000 taels ($138,889) annually for singsong curiosities sent to Beijing, and the expense of forced purchases of ginseng which the Imperial Household Department had sent to the Hoppo for sale, all were deducted from the Consoo Fund.[131] To encourage the importation of rice, a significant import duty discount was given to vessels carrying large rice cargoes. Western traders made creative use of this rule in the open waters at Lintin Island, offloading inbound cargoes of opium onto storeships and taking on waiting rice cargoes for a short and tax-advantaged last leg of their voyage into Chinese waters.[132]

Customs duties were not collected on a current basis by the Qing government. They were required to be paid annually on the last day of the fiscal year of the Canton customs, a date that fell sometime between September and early November. In 1794, for example, the fiscal year ended on September 18th (the 25th day of the 8th moon), triggering the collapse of Gonqua's tax-delinquent Eryi hong.[133] Many financially troubled hong merchants took advantage of customs tax funds which were not due to be paid for up to twelve months, either by diverting them to other uses or by the expedient of "purchasing the privilege" of paying duties owed by others. When a hong merchant "purchased the privilege" of paying duties he received a discounted (smaller) sum from a third

127 Van Dyke, *Canton Trade*, p. 136.

128 Cheong, *Hong Merchants*, pp. 197, 214, 217 and 234 n. 15; Cushman, *Fields from the Sea*, p. 37; Van Dyke, Canton Trade, pp. 10 and 27–8 and Table 1, p. 27.

129 Cheong, *Hong Merchants*, pp. 214–5.

130 Ch'en, *Insolvency*, p. 91; Cheong, *Hong Merchants*, p. 232; Morse, *Chronicles, Vol. III*, p. 193; Greenberg, *British Trade*, p. 52 and n.3; Phipps, *Practical Treatise*, p. 151.

131 Ch'en, *Insolvency*, pp. 98–9; Cheong, *Hong Merchants*, pp. 97–8, 225 and 227; Phipps, *Practical Treatise*, p. 152.

132 Van Dyke, *Canton Trade*, pp. 135–7.

133 Ch'en, *Insolvency*, pp. 300–1; Van Dyke, *Canton Trade*, p. 131.

party and accepted in return the legal obligation to pay the customs duties due from the third party to the government in full on the due date. In reality this was a high interest rate short term loan, from a powerful and unforgiving involuntary lender (the Qing government).[134] The consequences of treating duties as an interest-free loan from the state were frequently disastrous for the weak hongs.

Tax collection performance was an important criterion for evaluating the work of Qing officials[135] The quotum system provided a motivation to understate or delay actual proceeds so as to avoid creating a new benchmark and a higher quotum for the following year which might prove impossible to pay.[136] Under the Qing statutes, if customs revenues came in at 10% (or more) below prior year revenues in any given year, the responsible officials could be held personally liable for the deficiency and also subjected to severe beating for the offense.[137] This discouraged custom collections by the Hoppo in peak years of the trade. During the 1780s, for example, trade surged. Gross stated collections from the customs (*shizheng*) increased from 450,000 taels ($625,000) in 1780 to 750,000 taels ($1,041,667) in 1786, and might have been greater than that.[138] The Hoppo regularly halted trade at Canton once the tax quotum was reached during these years, lest increased trade generate a higher quotum target for future years.[139] These revenues, and other fees and charges that were levied on foreign trade, contributed to the reputation of Canton postings among Qing officials as opportunities to grow rich. Officials who had built up personal debts to the Imperial Household Department for failure to meet required tax quota at other postings were often appointed to the Canton customs. The Canton position was viewed as an opportunity to pay down existing debt, the post rich enough on its own that existing debt was unlikely to get worse.[140]

---

134 Ch'en, *Insolvency*, p. 176. See Morse, *Chronicles, Vol. III*, p. 195.

135 Cheong, *Hong Merchants*, pp. 202 and 213–14.

136 Cheong, *Hong Merchants*, pp. 213–14.

137 William C. Jones, tr., *The Great Qing Code* (Oxford: Clarendon Press, 1994) (by permission of Oxford University Press), Art. 148, § 2, pp. 159–60; Staunton, *Ta Tsing Leu Lee*, § 148, p. 157; Susan Mann Jones and Philip A. Kuhn, "Dynastic Decline and the Roots of Rebellion," pp. 107–62 in John K. Fairbank, ed., *The Cambridge History of China, Vol. 10, Late Ch'ing, 1800–1911, Part 1* (Cambridge: Cambridge Univ. Press, 1978), p. 129.

138 Cheong, *Hong Merchants*, pp. 213–5 and 228.

139 Cheong, *Hong Merchants*, p. 228 n.152.

140 Ch'en, *Insolvency*, pp. 133, 135 and 99 (Xiangshao, who served as Hoppo from 1813 to 1818, had incurred tax collection arrearages in his prior service as salt censor of Changlu and Superintendent of the Huaian Customs, which he paid off during his service at Canton).

The ginseng monopoly, closely monitored by the Imperial Household Department, was an important traditional source of income for the Manchu rulers. To protect their homeland source of prized wild ginseng, the Qing closed Manchuria to immigration from China in 1668 and built "the famous willow palisade which stretched for several hundred miles in a great arc from the Wall at Shanhaiguan to the north of Kirin and southeastward to the Yalu river."[141] Wild ginseng production was organized for the benefit of the court, and bond-servant officials of the Imperial Household Department were required to act as monopoly product salesmen. Starting in 1757, a quantity of prime ginseng was sent annually to the officials in charge of the Lianghuai and Changlu salt monopolies, the Superintendents of the Imperial Silk Factories, and the Hoppo in charge of the maritime customs at Canton. Each was responsible to sell his allocation, and to return cash proceeds to Beijing.[142]

The ginseng monopoly was run by licensed merchants, who sent diggers into the Manchurian woods to find and return with the increasingly scarce fragile wild ginseng. Overharvesting caused ginseng yields to decrease sharply through the 1700s and into the early 1800s. As of 1739, the Court imposed collective responsibility on the ginseng merchant group. The body was made collectively liable for the actions of any one member of the merchant group, and was forced to guarantee that both the quality and quantity of ginseng collected would meet an overall quotum. As official quota were set high, it was hard to meet them.[143] Where a given quotum was not met, the guarantor had to pay an amount set by the Court as equivalent to the value of the shortfall. To the extent he was unable to do so, the other merchants had to pay the deficiency.[144] As of the early 1800s, diggers who failed to meet quotum were charged a penalty assessment of fifty ounces of silver for each ounce of ginseng by which they failed to meet quotum. Few diggers could pay. The Court directed the officials to collect, when necessary, from the merchants who had guaranteed the diggers.[145] Shortfalls became so severe that the officials were personally charged for failing to meet quotum, together with the ginseng merchants. The quality of the ginseng received by the Court in 1811 was so poor that the officials and merchants were made to purchase that entire crop, as the Imperial

141 John K. Fairbank, *Trade and Diplomacy on the China Coast: The Opening of the Treaty Ports 1842–1854* (Cambridge: Harvard Univ. Press, 1953), Vol. 1, pp. 40–1.

142 Symons, *Ch'ing Ginseng Management*, pp. 66–7 and 78.

143 Symons, *Ch'ing Ginseng Management*, pp. 14 and 21–22.

144 Symons, *Ch'ing Ginseng Management*, pp. 60–62.

145 Symons, *Ch'ing Ginseng Management*, p. 22.

Household Department could not sell it at a premium price.[146] These strictures applied up to and through the process of receipt and grading of harvested ginseng in Beijing. As Van Jay Symons relates:

> Government directives regarded all those involved in grading ginseng and transporting the root to the court to be guarantors of the quality of the harvest. Punishments established were so stringent that if cultivated ginseng was found in the tribute-grade ginseng sent to the court, even the Manchu Generals-in-Chief, Lieutenant-Generals…, Civil Governor of the Manchurian Province of [Fengtian]…, and the Vice President of one of the Six Boards…who was specially sent to assist in the grading process were subject to three step demotions in rank and transference to another post. They might also be required to make good any loss suffered by the court due to the poorness of the quality of the ginseng.[147]

The wholesale value of the annual ginseng harvest, which is estimated to have stood at between 128,000 taels ($177,778) and 208,000 taels ($288,889) in 1709, had plunged to 20,000 taels ($27,778) by the mid 1800s. More than half of the licensed ginseng merchants had been rendered insolvent by the first half of the nineteenth century. Of the 400 ginseng merchants in Shengjing in 1800, fewer than 150 remained in business as of 1847.[148]

The enormous wealth of the licensed salt merchants was well known in Qing China. In a directive to the Canton officials, the Qianlong Emperor stated that "there is no comparison between [the wealth of] these [Guangdong hong] merchants and that of the Liang-huai salt merchants."[149] Tax revenues generated from the salt administration were far greater than those from the Canton customs. Ping-ti Ho in his study of the salt merchants states that taxation of the Lianghuai merchants generated 36,370,968 taels ($50,515,223) for the imperial treasury during the period 1738–1804, nine times as much as the 3,950,000 taels ($5,486,111) paid by the hong merchants during the period 1773–1832.[150]

146 Symons, *Ch'ing Ginseng Management*, p. 23.

147 Symons, *Ch'ing Ginseng Management*, p. 37.

148 Symons, *Ch'ing Ginseng Management*, pp. 20 and 24.

149 Quoted in White, "Hong Merchants," p. 61.

150 Ho Ping-ti, "The Salt Merchants of Yang-Chou: A Study of Commercial Capitalism in Eighteenth-Century China," Harvard Journal of Asiatic Studies, Vol. 17, pp. 130–69 (1954), pp. 153–4 and 168 n. 109; Ch'en, *Insolvency*, pp. 92–5 and Table 2.6. The discrepancy may actually be greater. As Ping-ti Ho notes in footnote, the Guangdong statistics include revenues derived from the salt administration in that province, together with hong merchant

Lianghuai, in east central China, was the most important salt administration region, far exceeding all other regions in production, sale and revenue. Ho states that the salt merchants "owed their wealth and power to the monopoly which was granted to them by the government." The salt monopoly was abolished in 1831.[151]

Tax revenues from the salt administration were assessed on a quotum basis in accordance with general Qing policy.[152] The salt merchants were divided into two categories, factory merchants who produced salt, and transport merchants who distributed and sold salt. A group of about thirty leading merchants were chosen as head merchants of each, and these head merchants were held collectively responsible to pay taxes that were not paid by individual licensed salt merchants.[153] These individual merchants were guaranteed by the head merchants, and were required to register annually with the Lianghuai salt administration under the name of their head merchant guarantor.[154] The Lianghuai salt merchants contributed to a substantial "common box" fund which was used to pay various fees assessed by the salt administration officials.[155] This resembles the Consoo Fund of the Canton hong merchants, although it was not supported by a tax on trade and it is not known whether collective responsibility to the officials for unpaid salt taxes was paid from the Lianghuai "common box."

The common thread among these various Imperial Household Department enterprises was the bondservant administrators that shuttled between them. The Department was a small bureaucracy. Many of these administrators, particularly the leaders, would have been familiar with each others' work, reputation and ideas. This personal familiarity began with early training in Department schools and continued as bondservant administrators worked together with or succeeded each other in office. For example, many Hoppos were appointed to Canton for a one year term. Of necessity that service closely tracked the policies and procedures of preceding Hoppos.

As discussed above, collective responsibility to pay money to the state was imposed on the head merchants (*zongshang*) of the salt, ginseng and foreign

revenues. Kuo-tung Ch'en rightly observes that "light as it was, it was burdensome enough to the body of hong merchants." Ch'en, p. 92.

151 Ho, "Salt Merchants," pp. 130–1.

152 Spence, *Ts'ao Yin*, pp. 167, 181 and 208; Metzger, "Organizational Capabilities," p. 18.

153 Spence, *Ts'ao Yin*, pp. 180 and 199; Ho, "Salt Merchants," pp. 137 and 141; Metzger, "Organizational Capabilities," p. 25.

154 Metzger, "Organizational Capabilities," p. 25.

155 Spence, *Ts'ao Yin*, p. 189; Ho, "Salt Merchants," pp. 142–3 and 147–8.

trade monopolies run by the Imperial Household Department.[156] We may be sure that these merchants did not welcome this additional liability. The hong merchants certainly did not in 1780. The Department was more closely involved in ginseng administration than in salt affairs,[157] presumably because the salt business was thriving—in its "golden age" in Ping-ti Ho's words[158]—while the ginseng business was in decline. Whatever the reason, we know more about collective responsibility in the ginseng business. It was imposed on the head ginseng merchants in 1739, as a mutual responsibility to pay the state the value of any deficiency in quality or quantity of collected ginseng. This predates the practice at Canton by about fifteen years. The date of imposition of collective liability for unpaid taxes among the salt merchants is uncertain.

We do not know how Imperial Household Department managers judged the experience of collective liability in the ginseng monopoly in the years after 1739. It appears to have been seen as a successful risk control measure, for it was continued and tightened in practice over the next hundred years. It is therefore possible that the practice of collective liability in monopoly administration was first tested in the ginseng business (and possibly the salt business as well), and introduced at Canton only after it was judged to have been successful. The sudden appearance of collective liability in three aspects of administration of the Canton maritime customs in 1754–1755 suggests that these practices were specific innovations by Li Yongbiao, a bondservant who was first appointed to Canton as Hoppo in 1752.[159]

4 Collective Responsibility in Chinese Tradition

Collective responsibility dates from early Chinese history and has its roots in military organization. The practice of penalizing soldiers for the failures of comrades within defined groups can be traced back to the unifying first Emperor Qin Shi Huang Di. This practice developed into the registration of

156 Andrea McElderry, "Guarantors and Guarantees in Qing Government-Business Relations," pp. 119–37 in Jane Kate Leonard and John R. Watt, eds., *To Achieve Security and Wealth: The Qing Imperial State and the Economy* (Ithaca: Cornell Univ. Press, 1991), p. 122.

157 Symons, *Ch'ing Ginseng Management*, p. 79.

158 Ho, "Salt Merchants," p. 152 ("A study of official data reveals that it was due to the unusually good selling conditions that the eighteenth century is deservedly called the golden age of the Liang-huai salt merchants.").

159 Cheong, *Hong Merchants*, pp. 205–7 (Li Yongbiao served as Hoppo from 1752 to 1759); Torbert, *Ch'ing Imperial Household Department*, p. 60. The author has been unable to establish any prior direct connection between Li Yongbiao and either the salt or ginseng administrations.

household units which were held mutually responsible for conscription, policing and taxation duties owed to the state. As a large part of the tax revenues of the primitive state were used to support the military, there was an immediate early connection between personal military service and the collection of taxes needed to support the military forces that defended the state. Whether mustered in person or in the form of taxes paid, the early Chinese state based its defense on principles of collective responsibility laid equally on all of its subjects. Modern Chinese financial collective responsibility thus finds its origins in the taxation policies of the primitive state.[160]

The best known example of collective responsibility in Chinese tradition was the *baojia* system. This ancient program of social registration and responsibility was continued during the Qing Dynasty and is a near relative of the *hukou* system of household registration still in use in modern China.[161] Collective responsibility was observed in other ways as well. Among urban merchants, the concept of group liability to the state to pay something like taxes was recognized in the practice of *hangyi* payments. The government allowed a trade to be monopolized or controlled. The merchants in return accepted collective responsibility to pay *hangyi* to the state, dues in lieu of goods or services, plus other sums sought by the officials.[162]

The Western traders encountered collective responsibility in its raw form in Qing criminal cases, and spoke harshly about it.[163] When they encountered

---

160 Derk Bodde, "The State and Empire of Ch'in," pp. 20–102 in Denis Twitchett and Michael Loewe, eds., *The Cambridge History of China, Vol. 1, The Ch'in and Han Empires, 221 B.C.–A.D. 220* (Cambridge: Cambridge Univ. Press, 1986), pp. 36–37 and 58; Dewey, "Russia's Debt to the Mongols," pp. 255–258; Kung-chuan Hsiao, *Rural China: Imperial Control in the Nineteenth Century* (Seattle: Univ. of Washington Press, 1960), pp. 26–28; Joanna Waley-Cohen, "Collective Responsibility in Qing Criminal Law," pp. 112–131 in Karen G. Turner, James V. Feinerman and R. Kent Guy, eds., *The Limits of the Rule of Law in China* (Seattle: Univ. of Washington Press, 2000), pp. 112–114. Horace Dewey states that "Chinese administrators had devised a system of mutual guarantee for fiscal purposes as early as the fourth century B.C." Dewey, "Russia's Debt to the Mongols," p. 258.

161 Chin-chih Chen, "The Japanese Adaptation of the Pao-Chia System in Taiwan, 1895–1945," Journal of Asian Studies, Vol. 34, pp. 391–416 (1975), p. 393; Hsiao, *Rural China*, pp. 26–28; Fei-ling Wang, *Organizing Through Division and Exclusion: China's Hukou System* (Stanford: Stanford Univ. Press, 2005), pp. 32–35 and 40–42.

162 Sybille van der Sprenkel, *Legal Institutions in Manchu China: A Sociological Analysis* (London: The Athlone Press, Univ. of London, 1962), © Berg, by permission of Bloomsbury Publishing Plc, p. 90; Kato Shigeshi, "On the Hang," pp. 62–3, 67 and 69–70.

163 Edwards, "Ch'ing Legal Jurisdiction Over Foreigners," pp. 235 ("The fact that these statutes had never been applied to Westerners did not lessen the Westerners' distaste for the principle and their fear that it might be applied to them in the future.") and 245; Waley-Cohen,

the concept in its commercial aspect—the enforced collective responsibility of Chinese subjects for illegal hong debts due to foreigners—most embraced it warmly.

Kung-chuan Hsiao, a leading scholar, describes the *baojia* system of Qing China as a device the state used "to watch and check the number, movements, and activities of the people, through agents selected from the local inhabitants themselves." Like the Canton System, it was designed to address public order concerns. In a 1757 edict, the Qianlong Emperor stated that the system had been instituted to suppress sedition and maintain peace among the law-abiding.[164] Under the *baojia* system, Qing households were registered in succeeding decimal units (groups of ten) up to the level of a *bao*, of which a *baozhang* was appointed head.[165] All adult males were required to register and to report crimes and criminals. Failure to report brought punishment not just on the individual, but also on all of his neighbors in the ten person registered group.[166]

In its original concept, the *baojia* system involved social registration and monitoring, but not financial matters. A separate *lijia* system, intended to be distinct but in practice often overlapping, registered households in groups for tax purposes.[167] According to a popular Chinese story, the god of wealth had originally been a *lijia* tax gatherer.[168] The *baojia* and *lijia* systems were inconsistently administered, were sometimes confused in practice, and declined through the course of the Qing dynasty.[169] Efforts to reinvigorate the systems were occasionally made, notably the Qianlong Emperor's 1757 direction to the Governors-General and Governors to report on and improve local *baojia* compliance.[170] To improve reporting, as of the early 1800s, *baojia* heads had

---

"Collective Responsibility," pp. 116–117. See Waley-Cohen, *Exile in Mid-Qing China*, pp. 79, 85 and 221–2 (Appendix One, "The Application of [Criminal] Collective Responsibility under the Qing"). Waley-Cohen notes that the majority of the women who were ordered banished to Xinjiang "were convicted by virtue of collective responsibility, and as such were guilty of crimes too serious to be avoided by monetary redemption." Waley-Cohen, *Exile in Mid-Qing China*, p. 73.

164 Van der Sprenkel, *Legal Institutions in Manchu China*, p. 47.

165 Hsiao, *Rural China*, pp. 28 and 43–83; Van der Sprenkel, *Legal Institutions in Manchu China*, pp. 46–7.

166 Hsiao, *Rural China*, p. 45; Van der Sprenkel, *Legal Institutions in Manchu China*, pp. 46–7.

167 Hsiao, *Rural China*, pp. 31–6 and 84–143.

168 Hsiao, *Rural China*, p. 119.

169 Hsiao, *Rural China*, pp. 33–36, 46, 55 and 60–61.

170 Hsiao, *Rural China*, pp. 49 and 82; Van der Sprenkel, *Legal Institutions in Manchu China*, pp. 46–7.

to sign written pledges of mutual responsibility.[171] The precise meaning of such pledges is uncertain. A pledge of mutual responsibility was required from relatives of the defaulted *bengang* hong merchant Wayqua in 1777, which was a promise that the hong's foreign creditors would be repaid.[172] Pledges later became a key part of drug trade suppression efforts in the years leading into the Opium War. Household *baojia* groups were required to sign pledges in 1838 that members were not involved with opium, which became antecedents of the bonds Lin Zexu sought to obtain from British merchants soon thereafter.[173]

The Qing used a modified version of the *baojia* system to register seagoing vessels. This system followed Ming Dynasty practice by organizing vessels in decimal groups under appointed headmen. Under a 1707 regulation the groups pledged to guarantee each other and were mutually responsible for their conduct and activities while at sea. If any ship in the group was involved in piracy all were punished unless the errant vessel was denounced. Ship owners were also required to have their vessels guaranteed by a firm recognized by the officials at the port of departure.[174] Relatives, neighbors of crew members, and even members of the crew of the vessel itself could be required to be guarantors of a merchant ship, a situation Gang Zhao calls "a sort of financial hostage-taking."[175] As Andrea McElderry correctly notes, "[s]ecurity concerns, fears that supplies might go to potential rebels overseas, and worry over domestic grain shortages" lay behind this strong regulation.[176] These concerns carried over into the regulation of merchants who traded overseas. Head merchants were appointed among groups of merchants involved in trade with Japan and the Southern Seas (*nanyang*) from various Chinese ports in the years after 1728, and these leaders were held mutually responsible for enforcing various government regulations and guarding against piracy.[177]

---

171 Hsiao, *Rural China*, pp. 53–4.

172 White, "Hong Merchants," p. 67.

173 Fairbank, *Trade and Diplomacy*, Vol. I, p. 78; Hsiao, *Rural China*, pp. 58–9; Frederic Wakeman, Jr., *Strangers at the Gate: Social Disorder in South China, 1839–1861* (Berkeley: Univ. of California Press, 1966), p. 32.

174 Richard James Aston, "The Merchant Shipping Activity of South China 1644–1860" (M.A. Thesis, Univ. of Hawaii, 1967), pp. 119–120; Basu, "Asian Merchants and Western Trade," p. 32; Cushman, *Fields from the Sea*, p. 50; Dian H. Murray, *Pirates of the South China Coast 1790–1810* (Stanford: Stanford Univ. Press, 1987), pp. 106–7; Ng, *Trade and Society*, pp. 153–4; Andrea McElderry, "Guarantors and Guarantees," pp. 123–6; MacSherry, "Impairment of the Ming Tributary System," pp. 202–3.

175 Zhao, *Qing Opening to the Ocean*, p. 127.

176 McElderry, "Guarantors and Guarantees," p. 125.

177 McElderry, "Guarantors and Guarantees," p. 123.

Licensed brokers (*yahang*) played a vital role in local markets in the Qing period, and were required to guarantee due completion of transactions in which they were involved including financial responsibility in case of default. To be licensed, brokers were required to have guarantors of their solvency and personal conduct. These guarantors could be held liable along with the brokers if a problem arose. Guarantors who reported misdeeds by brokers whom they had guaranteed might escape punishment.[178]

Collective responsibility was also enforced among Qing officials. Among some officials, like the three commissioners who managed the imperial textile factories in Nanjing, Suzhou and Hangzhou, it was imposed on the basis of status. Without fixed rank and having been specially appointed by the Emperor, the textile commissioners were considered to be bound in a special relationship of mutual responsibility and surveillance.[179] Otherwise officials were subject to "joint liability" (*lianzuo*) under Qing administrative law, which implies a mutual obligation. Officials could be held liable for the actions or omissions of their subordinates—whether or not they were involved and whether or not they had knowledge—for failure of their overall duty of supervision.[180] In this light, we may surmise that Qing officials considered application of collective responsibility among the monopoly merchants to be entirely fair. The officials themselves were subject to collective responsibility with their colleagues. They were also subject to the tax penalty rule that made them personally liable to pay any deficiency in the tax quotum established for their term in office. To fund these respective exposures, Qing officials had only their salary and the various fees and exactions they were able to collect while in office. By contrast, the head merchants could draw on the presumably bountiful profits of the trade from which the liability arose, and could cushion collective liability by spreading it out among the entire responsible group. The Qing officials likely reminded the merchants that many of them had sought out and purchased official rank, and that some burdens came with the honor of an official title.

The topic of collective responsibility leads directly into that of guaranty; i.e., exactly what the group members were held responsible for. Here the records become somewhat obscure. This uncertainty may result from vagaries in records of actual practice, is perhaps also one of translation, and may just as well reflect defenses or justifications asserted after the guaranteed affairs went awry. Assurances freely offered on a sunny day are often found to be riddled with conditions—not plainly expressed until after the skies have darkened.

178 McElderry, "Guarantors and Guarantees," pp. 120–2.

179 Spence, *Ts'ao Yin*, pp. 82–3.

180 Waley-Cohen, "Collective Responsibility," pp. 114–5.

As Sybille van der Sprenkel notes, a gradation of meaning existed in China between a guarantee that was in the nature of a promise to exercise suasion and a guarantee which meant that cash would be paid following default by the primary obligor.

> The two forms of guarantee existed side by side—no doubt varying also with locality—and care had to be exercised (as European merchants found when they came up against the system in the nineteenth century) to know what was intended. Sometimes the responsibility of the guarantor was limited to bringing pressure on the debtor to pay up, as is indicated by a saying current in Hupei, 'A go-between cannot undertake to produce children, a guarantor cannot undertake to repay money.'[181]

The word "guaranty" also has multiple and nuanced meaning in the English language and legal tradition. It can mean a firm commitment to pay money, the subject matter of this study. It can also mean something less definite, an offer to vouch or confirm. For this and other good reasons, a "guaranty" must usually be in writing and signed before it has legal effect in Anglo-American law. "Guaranty" (*bao*) has a similar gradation of meaning in Chinese, but what may seem to be one word—*bao*—in Pinyin romanization may yet be one of three different words distinguished by separate characters and tones. As analyzed by Lien-sheng Yang, three characters must be distinguished:[182]

> (1) Bao (保) (third tone), meaning 'security, guarantee of no failure.' This character is used in the Chinese term baojia, and also in the Canton trade terms which are translated in English as 'security merchant' (baoshang) (保商) and 'security merchant system' (baoshang zhidu) (保商制度).
> (2) Bao (包) (first tone), meaning 'to contract, to guarantee certain achievement.'
> (3) Bao (報) (fourth tone), meaning 'reciprocity, retribution, etc.'

Lien-sheng Yang states that the first character *bao* (保), defined as meaning "guarantee of no failure," was used throughout Qing political, social and economic life. "Taking civil service examinations, entering officialdom, securing a loan, applying for a passport, to name only a few examples, all required guaranty from persons of certain standing or from shops or firms ... up to a

181 Van der Sprenkel, *Legal Institutions in Manchu China*, pp. 108–9.

182 Yang, "Government Control of Urban Merchants," pp. 188–9.

certain grade."[183] In most of these cases, however, default did not trigger an unconditional obligation of financial performance by the 'guarantor,' either individually or on a collective basis. Over two centuries have passed since the high years of the Canton Guaranty System, and we know little of the original content of Chinese promises of guaranty to foreigners. It does seem clear, as Van der Sprenkel states, that confusion existed as to the content of guarantees, and that there were more than a few ways such confusion might have arisen.

Elements drawn from both Manchu and Chinese traditions were used by the Qing government in framing the regulatory structure of the Canton System and of the system of collective liability for foreign debt (the Canton Guaranty System) during the period 1684 through 1780. When the Kangxi Emperor decided to open Southern China to maritime trade in the years after 1683 he drew on Manchu experience that regional trade, properly regulated, could both promote general prosperity and advance state objectives. Public order concerns, much on the mind of the new rulers in the wake of the forty year struggle to conquer Southern China, dictated that overseas trade would need to be closely regulated. The trade regulations which were promulgated in the century after China was opened to foreign trade in 1683 drew on Chinese and Manchu traditions, and were administered by a Qing bureaucracy which was comprised of Han Chinese and ethnic Manchu officials.

183 Yang, "Government Control of Urban Merchants," p. 189.

CHAPTER 3

Evolution of the Canton Guaranty System

The rules used to manage China's maritime foreign trade with the West began to be assembled shortly after completion of the Manchu conquest. They were formulated in a time of trade liberalization, after a forty year period of conquest, during which the maintenance of internal order was a major concern of the new rulers. This process, which took place principally between 1684 and 1780, produced a set of governing regulations with layers of official supervision which came to be known as the Canton System. The system evolved through experiments and a series of crises between and among national officials, local officials, Chinese merchants, and Western trading firms operating on the China coast. At its core, the Canton System was founded upon reliance by the Qing state on a group of official merchants (*guan shang*) who had specific duties to and ties with the government.

1 Official Management of Maritime Foreign Trade

Close relations between powerful local officials and the leading foreign trade merchants dates from the earliest days of the Qing. During the conquest period, local officials were interested in maintaining internal order and in securing trade revenues, either through direct participation in trade or by licensing and taxing official merchants.[1] Merchants wanted protection, and to increase their own profits by controlling parts of the trade.[2] Various types of favored relations between officials and merchants accordingly developed during these years. Certain merchants associated with the transitional princes of the coastal provinces of Guangdong and Fujian came to be known as "King's Merchants" by foreign traders.[3] The Dutch term used to describe these official merchants was "factoor," which can mean either an agent or an active partner in partnership (with a governmental sponsor).[4] In Guangdong Province, long before the 1683 adoption of "open door" policies by the Kangxi Emperor,

1 Wills, *Pepper, Guns and Parleys*, p. 42.

2 Cheong, *Hong Merchants*, p. 219; White, "Hong Merchants," pp. 38–41; Wills, *Embassies and Illusions*, p. 108.

3 Cheong, *Hong Merchants*, p. 30.

4 Wills, *Embassies and Illusions*, p. 109.

 | DOI 10.1163/9789004276567_004

PLATE 2 *Shang Kexi, 1604–1676, Prince Pacifier of the South.* (*Engraving, from Johann Nieuhof, Die Gesantschaft der Ost-Indischen Geselschaft in der Vereinigten Niederländern an der tartarischen Cham und nunmehr auch sinischen Keiser, Amsterdam, 1666.*)

Shang Kexi, the "Prince Pacifier of the South" (*ping nan wang*), recognized official merchants (*guan shang*), who paid for the privilege of trading with foreigners. Shang Kexi's official merchants collected customs taxes, which were forwarded to Beijing.[5] During the period of his control, Shang Kexi had considerable indirect and direct involvement in trade from Canton and Macao and accumulated an enormous personal fortune, then estimated at one million taels ($1,388,889).[6] When the princes were abolished in 1681, patronage shifted. The leading foreign trade merchants now became associated with new official patrons, i.e., the "Tartar-General's Merchant," the "Viceroy's Merchant," and so forth. In the early 1700's, several "Emperor's Merchants," associated with Beijing patrons including the future Yongzheng Emperor, attempted to involve

5 White, "Hong Merchants," pp. 29–30; Marks, *Tigers, Rice, Silk, and Silt*, p. 156 n.78; Hummel, *Eminent Chinese*, pp. 635–6; Spence, "K'ang-hsi Reign," p. 137.

6 Zhao, *Qing Opening to the Ocean*, pp. 73–5; Wills, *Embassies and Illusions*, pp. 42–4 and 88; Wills, *Pepper, Guns and Parleys*, pp. 108–9; Bowra, "Manchu Conquest," pp. 231 and 234.

themselves in and to assert seasonal or product monopolies of foreign trade with the West in several coastal cities, including Canton.[7]

This close relationship, at first evidenced by the use of trading names which emphasized the merchant's tie with a leading official, was always at the heart of the Canton System. Over the years, it changed in several ways. For the merchants, their choice of a trading name was both an important expression of brand identity and a key marketing device in dealing with Westerners who did not speak Chinese. In the early 1700s, that brand identity shifted from the former connection with a specific individual patron (i.e., a prince) to status group membership (i.e., one of the official merchants). In their trading names, the hong merchants came to generally adopt the suffix "qua" (*guan*, as in *guan shang*), indicating official merchant status.[8] Examples include the trading names Beau Khequa (Li Guanghua of the Ziyuan hong) (d. 1758), Puankhequa I (Pan Zhencheng of the Tongwen hong) (1714–1788) and Howqua II (Wu Bingjian of the Yihe hong) (1769–1843). Invocation of a specific champion quickly became obsolete.[9] Thus "qua," denoting official status, became a core statement of brand identity among the hong merchants of Canton. Hong merchants also established official status connections through the purchase of civil rank. In the early days of the trade, when such ties had more business significance, local Europeans often added the prefix "Mandarin" to the trading names of hong merchants who held official titles.[10] In hong merchant portraits, badges of purchased official titles, such as embroidered square surcoat decoration, hat, or button are commonplace.

All of the leading hong merchants held official titles.[11] According to scholar Ann Bolbach White, more than half of all of the individual heads of hong

---

7 Cheong, *Hong Merchants*, pp. 31–5, 59, 133, 219 and 300; Earl H. Pritchard, "Anglo-Chinese Relations During the Seventeenth and Eighteenth Centuries," Univ. of Ill. Studies in the Social Sciences, Vol. 17, Nos. 1–2 (March–June 1929), pp. 77–8. See Zhao, *Qing Opening to the Ocean*, p. 75 (overseas venture activities of Manchu princes).

8 Sung, "A Study of the Thirteen Hongs," p. 13.

9 Cheong, *Hong Merchants*, pp. 32, 37–8 and 107; Fairbank, *Trade and Diplomacy*, Vol. 1, pp. 50–1; Sung, "Study of the Thirteen Hongs," pp. 13, 30 and 104–5.

10 Van Dyke, *Merchants of Canton and Macao*, p. 87.

11 Sung, "A Study of the Thirteen Hongs," p. 13. Sale of public titles and degrees which did not directly qualify the holder for public office, through the Contribution Office (juannafang) of the Board of Revenue, was formalized on a permanent basis during the Qianlong era (1736–96). See Elisabeth Kaske, "Fund Raising Wars," pp. 90–93; Elisabeth Kaske, "The Great 1830 Forgery Case: Metropolitan Clerks and Venality in Qing China" (unpublished paper presented at The Fairbank Center for Chinese Studies, October 24, 2008), pp. 3–4.

firms purchased official title and rank.[12] Puankhequa I purchased a title, and was awarded the Blue Sapphire Button of a third rank official in about 1780 for military campaign contributions.[13] Eequa (Wu Zhaoping of the Fengtai hong), Wayqua (Ni Hongwen of the Fengjin hong) (purchased *Jiansheng* title), Yngshaw (Yan Shiying of the Taihe hong), and Kewshaw (Zhang Tianqiu of the Yuyuan hong), each purchased titles and degrees.[14] The senior hong merchants Howqua II, Mowqua II and Puankhequa III all proudly held *hualing*—peacock feathers—conferred as a special reward for their 1832 public service contributions for the suppression of a Yao rebellion in Guangdong Province.[15]

Each such transaction tied the official merchant more closely to the supervising Qing officials. The merchant thus became explicitly linked in and beholden to a chain of command that ran from the Emperor in Beijing down to the individual hongs in Canton. The purchase contributed to the coffers of the state. As the purchase was almost always of an expectant or honorary title, no duties devolved on the purchaser. Yet the acquisition of title raised the status of the titled merchant in local Canton society, and its loss carried great social stigma.[16]

The administration of China's foreign trade with the West was supervised by civil officials, who were appointed by and reported to Beijing. Key officials were the Governor-General (also known as the Viceroy), the Governor and the Hoppo. Their offices were all located at Canton. These officials were assisted by the *weiyuan* (a military official attached to the Hoppo), by their respective staffs, by military officers posted to Canton, and by district (*xian*) magistrates in matters of local administration.[17] Jurisdiction was divided by district among the magistrates of Nanhai district (Canton), Panyu district (including

12 White, "Hong Merchants," pp. 150, 154–6 and 173–4.

13 Cheong, *Hong Merchants*, p. 162; Hummel, *Eminent Chinese*, p. 605.

14 Cheong, *Hong Merchants*, pp. 107 and n.101, 211 and 264; Ch'en, *Insolvency*, pp. 187–8 and 191. Singyquan (Wang Shengyi), an Anhui merchant who traded with the EIC in the mid-1700s, had a purchased title as a candidate at the Imperial College. Cheong, pp. 100 and 107 n.101. The elder brother of the Tongshun hong merchant Samqua (Wu Tianyuan), Wu Tianxian, purchased the rank of expectant daodai, and Wu Jianzhang, a near relative, purchased the academic title of Imperial College student. Chang, *Chinese Gentry*, pp. 155–6; Fairbank, Trade and Diplomacy, Vol. I, p. 395; Sung, "A study of the Thirteen Hongs," p. 28.

15 White, "Hong Merchants," p. 149.

16 Cheong, *Hong Merchants*, pp. 107, 108 and 268.

17 Ch'en, *Insolvency*, pp. 24–9; Downs, *The Golden Ghetto*, p. 76.

Whampoa) and Xiangshan district (including Macao), with the respective magistrates sometimes acting jointly in judicial matters involving foreign trade.[18]

Most important in the daily management of trade was the Commissioner of the Guangdong Province Maritime Customs, the official Western traders called the Hoppo. The Western term is a corruption of part of the Hoppo's Chinese language title: *Duli Guangdongsheng Yanhaidengqu Maoyishuiwu Hubufensi* (Commissioner of the Board of Revenue [*Hu Bu*], in Charge of the Customs Duties on the Trade of the Maritime Area of the Province of Guangdong).[19] First appointed at Canton in 1684, the Hoppo played a key role in the management of maritime foreign trade under the Qing Dynasty. The post of Hoppo was typically held by an ethnic Manchu, on a one year assignment from Beijing. In the years after 1750, this increasingly regularized post was exclusively held by members (*baoyi*) of the Imperial Household Department (*neiwufu*), appointed from and reporting directly to the Imperial Court in Beijing. The Canton customs administration, known as the *yuehaiguan*, eventually consisted of five sub-stations and some sixty collection points.[20] The Hoppo stood at the top of a large bureaucracy which was in constant contact with the Chinese and foreign traders. As described by Dilip Basu, the Canton Customs administration:

> was led by a head clerk (*jincheng*) who presided over upwards of two hundred writers (*danshu*). On the seventh moon of every year, they drew lots as to who should be deputed to the seventy-odd customs houses in the province. The losers remained to act as tide-waiters, examining goods daily brought up to or sent down from Canton. The Hoppo usually did all

---

18 Cheong, *Hong Merchants*, p. 194; Van Dyke, *Canton Trade*, p. 22; Edwards, "Ch'ing Legal Jurisdiction Over Foreigners," p. 227.

19 It is said that the term "Hoppo" was derived from "Hu Bu" (the Qing Board of Revenue). Ch'en, *Insolvency*, p. 24; Frederic Wakeman, Jr., "The Canton Trade and the Opium War," pp. 163–212 in John K. Fairbank, ed., *The Cambridge History of China, Vol. 10, Late Ch'ing, 1800–1911, Part 1* (Cambridge: Cambridge Univ. Press, 1978), p. 163. In his 1887 Leiden treatise, Abram Lind offers an intriguing alternative attribution. Lind proposes that the term "Hoppo" might have derived from a Chinese term for surety, on account of the Hoppo's financial responsibility to the state for customs duties. This explanation seems unlikely, as there is little evidence of foreign trader awareness of the term Lind cites, as opposed to Hu Bu, an important national office of which there was considerable knowledge. Abram Lind Jr., *A Chapter of the Chinese Penal Code* (Leiden: E.J. Brill, 1887), p. 30. The author is grateful to Koos Kuiper for bringing Abram Lind to his attention and for sharing Mr. Kuiper's considerable insights about this important early Leiden scholar of Chinese law.

20 Ch'en, *Insolvency*, p. 24; Cheong, *Hong Merchants*, p. 194; Zhao, *Qing Opening to the Ocean*, pp. 122–4.

> his business through the head clerk who often bought the office for a five year tenure. He acted as the Hoppo's alter ego, charging a Hongist $1,000 to get an appointment with the Hoppo. Next to the head clerk, were three accountants with five in the office of records, 'each of whom has to pay a fee of two or three hundred dollars.' The Hoppo's Customs House posse consisted of seven head runners who required 'seven or eight hundred dollars to get this appointment.' Each head runner had thirty assistants under him. Every year the two hundred-plus among them drew lots 'to ascertain who shall be sent to the outer customs-houses, who shall go to watch alongside the ships, and be, what is at Whampoa called, Hoppo-men, and who shall attend daily at the shipping off or receiving goods at the Hongs.' Then there were numerous personal servants and attendants at the Hoppo's establishment. Their number varied 'according to the number of persons recommended by the various official men in Canton, who have dependents to be provided for.' There were four 'superior ones' (*dangshang*) who received duties and four 'personal confidants' (*qinxin*) who went around inspecting customs-houses for the Hoppo. No doubt each and every one of these jobs yielded a handsome amount in perquisites and profits.[21]

The Hoppo's close Beijing connections, notably the personal privilege of being able to present memorials directly to the Emperor, gave him considerable independent power. These Court links are said to have given the Hoppo functionally equal status with the Governor-General (*zongdu*) (of the provinces of Guangdong and Guangxi) and the Governor (*fuyuan*) (of the province of Guangdong).[22] The original function of the Governor-General was military. Like the Hoppo, the Governor-General was typically an ethnic Manchu. He served as supreme commander of the forces maintaining order in his viceroyalty. While civil affairs were supposed to be handled by provincial Governors, Governors-General often became involved in such matters.[23] Between 1750 and 1792, the Governor-General of Guangdong and Guangxi was co-supervisor of the Guangdong Maritime Customs, but he rarely interfered with customs

---

21 Basu, "Asian Merchants and Western Trade," pp. 268–9 (quoting from "Concerning European Ships and Trade to Canton," by a Native Chinese, translated from the original manuscript (undated), British Museum, pp. 30–38) (Pinyin Romanization has been supplied in the place of the Wade-Giles Romanization in the original); Zhao, *Qing Opening to the Ocean*, pp. 118–22.

22 Ch'en, *Insolvency*, p. 27; Wong, *Yeh Ming-ch'en*, p. 4.

23 Wong, *Yeh Ming-ch'en*, pp. 38 and 48.

matters.[24] When problems with foreigners arose, initial decision was reserved to ethnic Manchu officials. Thus, when the armed frigate *Sea Horse* (Captain Panton) arrived at Canton from Madras in September 1779 seeking to collect debts from hong merchants, the matter came before Governor Li Zhiying, a Manchu bannerman and Imperial Household Department member. Governor-General Yang Jingsu (Han Chinese) was excluded.[25]

2 The Security Merchant System and Origins of Collective Responsibility

The activities of security merchants or *fiadors* are recorded in the 1720s, but are believed to be of earlier origin, possibly derived from trade at Macao.[26] The practice was initiated at Canton in the 1730s, a period during which officials sought to improve their control of foreign trade. In order to strengthen official control, Weng Eang Cheong observes, "the Hoppo, perhaps unintentionally, had to strengthen the merchants' control of the foreigners and the trade."[27] As of the 1730s, hong merchants made their commitment to stand security by a written contract delivered to the Hoppo after the measurement (for tax purposes) of each arriving foreign ship.[28] By about 1735, foreign traders at Canton were required to engage a hong merchant to stand as security for each ship.[29] These security merchants (*bao shang*) were given a monopoly of the ship's business, were bound to assure orderly trade and the good conduct of its crew, and were held liable as guarantor for full payment of all import and export duties on the ship's cargo.[30] This monopoly was porous within the guild. Foreign merchants often traded with other hong merchants (who would sometimes make payment to the original security merchant), as is evident from the pattern of purchases among various hong merchants seen during the controversy over liability for the purchase cost of "singsongs" in 1754.

---

24 Ch'en, *Insolvency*, pp. 27 and 408 n.58.

25 Ch'en, *Insolvency*, pp. 198 and 408 n. 58.

26 Cheong, *Hong Merchants*, pp. 65, 104 and 92 n.51; Van Dyke, *Canton Trade*, pp. 11–2 and n.21 and 165.

27 Cheong, *Hong Merchants*, p. 202.

28 Van Dyke, *Canton Trade*, p. 25.

29 Ch'en, *Insolvency*, pp. 8–9 n.19.

30 Cheong, *Hong Merchants*, pp. 92 and 95; Robert Bennet Forbes, *Remarks on China and the China Trade* (Boston: Samuel M. Dickinson, 1844), pp. 11–2.

The security merchants were licensed by the government. Little is known about the definition and form of this license right. No license records have survived. The license seems to have been a non-transferable personal right, granted to one man,[31] to operate a non-limited liability enterprise as a hong or security merchant. Its issuance appears to have involved written undertakings by the licensee, specific commitments made to the state. This is evidenced by amendments, as when the hong merchants were compelled over strong protest to assume collective responsibility for debts in 1780, and in entrance terms, as when the five new hong merchants of 1782 agreed to guarantee each other (because the incumbents refused to do so) and in the 1760 registration rules for five merchant groups of outside shopmen.

License issuance was tightly controlled by the Canton officials. One reason was that the licensee merchants were expected to perform security duties for the state (risk management). A second reason was the revenue the state received upon the issuance, transfer, assignment or withdrawal of license rights. The amount of these fees varied with the strength of the applicant and the circumstances of the moment, but the amounts involved were significant. Admission fees ranged from $30,000 to $80,000, and are said to have reached as high as $200,000 in some cases.[32] Transfer or assignment fees ranged from $30,000 to $100,000 to the high of $500,000 charged to Howqua II (Wu Bingjian) for license transfer to his son in 1826.[33] Withdrawal or retirement was almost impossible. Yanqua was allowed to retire in 1804, fee unknown. Puankhequa II is said to have paid $500,000 in 1807 for permission to retire, but the authorization granted him was later revoked.[34] Licensing fee revenues were shared among the Governor-General, the Governor, the Hoppo, and their assistants. The Hoppo and Governor-General are said to have received the largest share.[35] It has been argued that the issuance of hong licenses was motivated primarily by fee revenues, as evidenced by a concentration of license issuance among just a few Hoppos, many of whom had reached Canton indebted to the Imperial Household Department. Of the thirty-six hong merchants licensed between 1760 and 1843, twenty-nine were licensed during the terms of office of only six

31 Ch'en, *Insolvency*, pp. 123, 126, 329 and 349.

32 Ch'en, *Insolvency*, pp. 123 and 317; Cheong, *Hong Merchants*, p. 221.

33 The 1826 fee was occasioned by transfer of the license of the Yihe hong to Howqua's son Wu Yuanhua. The son died in 1833, triggering re-transfer of the license, additional fee unknown. Ch'en, *Insolvency*, pp. 123 and 126.

34 Ch'en, *Insolvency*, pp. 126, 316 and 394 n.58; White, "Hong Merchants," pp. 93–4.

35 Ch'en, *Insolvency*, p. 123; Cheong, *Hong Merchants*, p. 221 (dating the practice to the 1780s).

Hoppos (of the thirty who held office in this period).[36] For various reasons, including but not limited to these fees, there was a sharp decline in the quality of the licensees accepted during these years. Scholar Kuo-tung Ch'en accordingly observes that "over time those who were appointed came from lower and lower strata of society: a number of Hong merchants made in the course of the nineteenth century, or their partners, had been opium-dealers, linguists, compradores, and even a domestic; similar backgrounds cannot be found for the Hong merchants of the eighteenth century."[37]

The security merchant system (*baoshang zhidu*) received its original imperial approval in 1745, on a memorial submitted by Governor-General and Hoppo Ce Leng (a Manchu). In approving the system, the Qianlong Emperor directed that the security merchant group should be limited to wealthy and respectable men, to safeguard the payment of state revenues they were required to guarantee.[38] The timing of approval suggests that national security concerns were directly involved. Reports of a Dutch massacre in 1740 of some 10,000 ethnic Chinese at Batavia had horrified China. Proposals to impose economic sanctions against the Dutch by closing or restricting foreign trade had been made and seriously considered in Beijing. The Qianlong Emperor rejected sanctions in 1742 after careful consideration. During this volatile period, the Hoppo cautioned two Dutch ships that it would be wise to trade at Macau to avoid trouble at Canton.[39]

The foreign trade monopoly of the licensed hong merchants was defined a decade later in three edicts issued jointly at Canton in May 1755 by Governor-General Yang Yingzhu, Governor Honian and Hoppo Li Yongbiao.[40] A parallel edict, issued in January 1758, enforced the monopoly by requiring European

---

36 Ch'en, *Insolvency*, pp. 133–137 and 253.

37 Ch'en, *Insolvency*, p. 257.

38 Ch'en, *Insolvency*, pp. 10–1; Cheong, *Hong Merchants*, pp. 92–3, 105, 205 and 237 n.49.

39 Leonard Blussé, *Strange Company: Chinese Settlers, Mestizo Women and the Dutch in VOC Batavia* (Dordrecht, Foris Publications, 1986), pp. 94–6; Ch'en, *Insolvency*, pp. 10–11; Cheong, *Hong Merchants*, pp. 92–3, 105, 205 and 237 n.49; Jennifer W. Cushman, "Duke Ch'ing-fu Deliberates: A Mid-Eighteenth Century Reassessment of Sino-Nanyang Commercial Relations," Papers on Far Eastern History, Vol. 17, pp. 137–56 (1978), pp. 145–56; Cushman, *Fields from the Sea*, pp. 129–130; Edwards, "Ch'ing Legal Jurisdiction Over Foreigners," p. 227; Fairbank, *Trade and Diplomacy*, Vol. 1, pp. 51–2; Rowe, *China's Last Empire*, p. 142; Van Dyke, *Merchants of Canton and Macao*, p. 74; White, "Hong Merchants," p. 48; Zhao, *Qing Opening to the Ocean*, pp. 76–7 and 180.

40 Cheong, *Hong Merchants*, p. 205; Pritchard, "Crucial Years," pp. 126–7; Morse, *Chronicles, Vol. V*, pp. 29–30 and 37–44 (Appendix AI) (text of edicts).

ships to trade exclusively at Canton.[41] The occasional practice of issuing joint edicts by the three senior Canton officials manifested their combined resolve and the importance of the subject matter. The two exceptions to the new monopoly rules were at Macao and Xiamen (Amoy), where foreign trade was permitted to be conducted, but only by the Portuguese and Spanish respectively.[42] These edicts, and other measures defining hong merchant responsibilities which were put in place during the period roughly from 1735 through 1758, are properly viewed in the context of controls that were imposed on the Hoppo during the same period.[43] The Canton System was being regularized on direction from above. As Weng Eang Cheong observes, "[a]fter 1760, the emphasis of the [Hoppos's] function shifted to the interpretation and enforcement of laws and guidelines to the system."[44] In the first half of the eighteenth century, foreigners were able to obtain personal audiences with the Hoppo at his residence in Canton. From the 1750s forward, access to the Hoppo was channeled through the hong merchants or linguists who received and transmitted foreign petitions.[45]

As of 1755 the hong merchant monopoly of maritime foreign trade, which had begun as seasonal rights purchased by leading merchants and had since evolved into an informal combination of the merchant elite, was formally recognized without time limit.[46] The 1755 edicts maintained the existing three-tiered structure of the outer seas merchant (*waiyang hang*) guild. The thirteen merchants of the first and second tiers had the exclusive right to trade with foreigners under the state enforced monopoly, becoming known collectively as the *yang hang* (foreign [trade] firms).[47] The six senior merchants of the first tier also had the right to serve as security merchants for foreign ships, evidently in order of seniority. These senior merchants—Beau Khequa, Chai Suequa, Chetqua, Chai Hunqua, Sweetia and Puankhequa—now came to be called capital merchants by foreign traders. The seven junior merchants of the

41 Cheong, *Hong Merchants*, pp. 101–2 (edicts closed Ningbo to European trade in December 1757 and expelled the English from that port in January 1758).

42 Greenberg, *British Trade*, pp. 46–8.

43 Cheong, *Hong Merchants*, p. 208.

44 Cheong, *Hong Merchants*, p. 231.

45 Liu Yong, "The VOC Business Culture in China: How the VOC Did Business in Canton in the Eighteenth Century," pp. 235–248 in Evert Groenendijk, Cynthia Vialle and Leonard Blussé, eds., *Canton and Nagasaki Compared 1730–1830: Dutch, Chinese, Japanese Relations* (Leiden: Institute for the History of European Expansion, 2009), p. 241.

46 Cheong, *Hong Merchants*, p. 156.

47 Cheong, *Hong Merchants*, pp. 31 and 95.

second tier were allowed to trade and ship abroad, but not to secure foreign ships.[48]

Each arriving vessel was assigned by the Hoppo to a hong merchant, who was to serve as its security merchant. As new business tended to be welcome, the assignments were generally accepted, but refusal was possible as in the 1754 general refusal to secure incoming EIC ships carrying singsongs in their cargo. Assignments were usually made according to a seniority list, with the turn to secure going first to the senior merchants.[49] Assignments of EIC ships, which had once been negotiated, evolved over time into an agreement under which security merchants were assigned to EIC vessels in rotation.[50] The cargo of a foreign ship could be sold to any of the hong merchants, although it became customary to pay the vessel's security merchant the fixed sum of $700 for his expenses and risk.[51] It was the duty of the hong merchants to cause foreigners whose vessels they secured to comply with the rules of the Canton System. The hong merchants could be and were punished for infractions by Western traders whose vessels they secured, variously fined or imprisoned or both, depending on the gravity of the offense. Their role was thus "quasi-diplomatic," in Weng Eang Cheong's apt phrasing.[52] When the system worked, the hong merchants themselves and all the various Chinese engaged in dealings with foreigners were supposed to report any untoward activity they observed. As described by Jacques M. Downs,

> Thus the comprador collected information from his coolies, cooks, guards, and the shroff and reported to the linguist, who, in his turn, informed the mandarinate. In this way local officials had a reporting service that delivered data independently of the Cohong.[53]

Collective responsibility for debt among the Canton hong merchants makes its first appearance in 1754–1755. The burden varied among the three tiers of the guild. The senior merchants of the first and second tiers were made subject to limited collective responsibility. The capital merchants of the first tier were collectively liable, among their own group only, for customs duties due to the

48 Cheong, *Hong Merchants*, pp. 93 and 105.

49 Cheong, *Hong Merchants*, p. 95.

50 Ch'en, *Insolvency*, p. 11.

51 Greenberg, *British Trade*, p. 59.

52 Cheong, *Hong Merchants*, pp. 102–8 and 299.

53 Downs, *The Golden Ghetto*, p. 78.

state but not paid by any member of the group.[54] The exact date when the first tier was made collectively liable for unpaid customs duties is uncertain.[55]

The second imposition of collective financial responsibility concerned the heavy cost of subsidizing opulent imported gifts sent by the Canton officials to Beijing. When an uproar arose among the security merchants, who were outraged by the excessive burden they were forced to bear individually for the purchase of "singsong" curiosities, Hoppo Li Yongbiao directed in 1754 that this expense would henceforth be shared collectively.[56] The word "singsong" is a pidgin English term used to describe European luxury objects such as musical boxes, mechanical toys, clocks and watches which were sent as official gifts to the Court in Beijing.[57] Many of these elaborate presents, notably mechanical clocks produced in London, have survived. They are popular exhibits at the Forbidden City today, much as they were delighted upon two centuries ago. These objects were a matter of immediate interest to the Hoppo upon the arrival of any Western trading ship, and the selection of singsongs and direction to the security merchant to acquire desired objects was an official priority.[58] Their acquisition was originally funded with a general levy on foreign trade. Over time, the Hoppos shifted to a system of coerced purchase

---

54 Ch'en, *Insolvency*, pp. 184–5.

55 Collective liability for unpaid customs duties was enforced after 1755 in the cases of Beau Khequa (1758), Yngshaw and Kewshaw (1780) and Geowqua (1798). Ch'en, *Insolvency*, pp. 182–3 (Beau Khequa), 206 (Yngshaw and Kewshaw) and 217 (Geowqua); Cheong, *Hong Merchants*, p. 158 (Beau Khequa). The date of imposition of such liability is uncertain. No provision making the hong merchants collectively liable for customs duties is found in the EIC's English language translations of the foreign trade regulations of 1755 or 1760. Morse, *Chronicles, Vol. V*, pp. 29–30 and 37–44 (Appendix AI) (text of 1755 edicts) and 94–98 (Appendix AK) (text of the 1760 regulations) (text attached to this study as Appendix 2).

56 Morse, *Chronicles, Vol. V*, pp. 13–4; Cheong, *Hong Merchants*, pp. 156, 225 and 274; Pritchard, "Anglo-Chinese Relations," p. 116.

57 Cheong, *Hong Merchants*, pp. 166, 281 and 349; Van Dyke, *Canton Trade*, pp. 25 and 97; Morse, *Chronicles, Vol. V*, p. 154. The term "sing-song" was also used to describe Chinese musical stage presentations. Downs, *The Golden Ghetto*, p. 80; Robert Burts, *Around the World: A Narrative of a Voyage in the East India Squadron* (New York: Charles S. Francis, 1840), Vol. II, p. 253; Greenberg, *British Trade*, pp. 22–3.

58 Van Dyke, *Canton Trade*, p. 25; Van Dyke, *Merchants of Canton and Macao*, p. 98; Morse, *Chronicles, Vol. V*, p. 14 (in August of 1754 the Hoppo "asked as a favour that he might have a first view of the curiosities brought in the ships, and that the prices might be reasonable. He was informed in reply that the supercargoes would use their influence in the matter, but that they had no control over these curiosities, which were the private property of the officers of the ships.").

PLATE 3 *A singsong. Financial collective responsibility was first imposed at Canton in 1754 in response to hong merchant protests over the high acquisition cost of "singsongs," elaborate contraptions the Canton officials forced the merchants to buy so that they could then send them as gifts to the Court in Beijing. Pictured: Mechanical clock with a writing figure, gilded copper, made in England by Timothy Williamson, about 1770. The most complex and dramatic part of this clock is the mechanical man on the lowest floor who is able to write eight Chinese characters on paper. The robot is dressed as a European gentleman. Half-kneeling, he is poised in writing position and rests his left hand on the desk. When the mechanical device is activated, the robot writes characters meaning that other countries all worship China and send emissaries to pay homage to the Chinese Emperor. (The Palace Museum, Beijing, China. Photograph © The Palace Museum, by permission.)*

PLATE 4 *A singsong. Elaborate and expensive "singsong" devices, imported at Canton and sent as gifts to the Emperor and other high officials in Beijing by the Canton officials, remain popular exhibits at the Palace Museum, Beijing. Pictured: Mechanical clock supported by four goats, gilded copper, agate and glass, made in England by William Hughes, about 1770. Crystal-like glass pillars surround a sumptuously decorated cosmetics box on the upper level which contains a glass perfume bottle, a pair of scissors, a pair of tweezers and other items. In the center panel of the box is a painting of a Greek goddess standing in a chariot made from a seashell and pulled by imaginary sea creatures. Perched on the box's lid are two angels holding a two-hand dial in the shape of a flower vase. When the clock is activated music plays and the people in the box's lower section dance merrily.* (The Palace Museum, Beijing, China. Photograph © The Palace Museum, by permission.)

PLATE 5 *A singsong. The practice of financial collective responsibility at Canton, the source of the idea for bank deposit insurance in New York, began in the year 1754 when the Hoppo made all hong merchants equally responsible to pay the amounts required for the purchase of elaborate imported "singsong" devices the officials sent as gifts to Beijing. Pictured: Mechanical clock with a peacock and a timekeeping figure, gilded copper and enamel, made in England by Timothy Williamson, eighteenth century. The gilded copper stand of this clock is a musical box on the face of which is inlaid three enamel panels. The center panel is made of silver and depicts a European style hall, while the flanking panels feature scenes of three female artists. Between two enamel columns resting on the box is a sculpted scene of a peacock perched on a tree stump watched by a shepherdess and her three sheep. In the pavilion above the clock a figure holds a copper hammer to strike the time. When he strikes the bell music plays, the peacock spreads its tail, and the shepherdess and her sheep move. (The Palace Museum, Beijing, China. Photograph © The Palace Museum, by permission.)*

PLATE 6 *A singsong. The idea that inspired bank deposit insurance in the State of New York had its origin, at Canton, in the practice of making all hong merchants jointly liable to pay the enormous cost of "singsong" devices imported at Canton and sent to Beijing as gifts by the Hoppo and other Canton officials. Pictured: Automaton in the form of a chariot pushed by a Chinese attendant and set with a clock, gold, with diamonds and paste jewels set in silver, and pearls, white enamel, brass and steel, made in London, England by James Cox, 1766. (The Metropolitan Museum of Art, New York, New York. Photograph © The Metropolitan Museum of Art, by permission.)*

directly from the hong merchant who secured the ship that had the desired object on board, sometimes paying as little as 25% of cost.[59] This penalized the security merchant responsible for a vessel with "singsongs" in its cargo, for that merchant alone paid the great part of the purchase cost of these gifts.[60] The high cost of these prized objects, which in the case of the British EIC came to China exclusively as the private venture cargo of its officers, became a management problem for the EIC which grew concerned that the expense of buying private cargo from its own ships might ruin the hong merchants.[61] The hong merchant body was openly restive about this unequal and unpredictable burden by the early 1750s.[62] In 1754, four merchants refused to serve as securities for six British EIC ships, due to potential losses on the inbound "singsong" cargo they carried. Tsai Suequa alone said that he might be willing to secure these vessels, but only temporarily and jointly with other merchants who did significant trade with the secured ships.[63] The Hoppo responded in August 1754 by directing that the burden would be shared, presumably among the first and second tier hong merchants only.[64]

Collective liability for foreign debts—unlimited in amount—was imposed on the third tier shopkeepers under the 1755 edicts. In order to be allowed to trade with foreigners, shopkeepers had to register in groups of five with the Nanhai *xian* magistrate. Registration required the written commitment, from all members of each five person group, that each would be jointly liable for any unpaid foreign debts of other members of the five person registered group.[65]

---

59 Cheong, *Hong Merchants*, pp. 166, 205, 225, 227, 255 and 281; Morse, *Chronicles, Vol. V*, p. 71; Lo-shu Fu, *A Documentary Chronicle of Sino-Western Relations* (1644–1820) (Tucson: Univ. of Arizona Press, 1966), p. 220, quoted with permission of the Association for Asian Studies, Inc., see: *www.asian-studies.org*.

60 Morse, *Chronicles, Vol. V*, p. 10 ("A still further disadvantage is that the Security is looked upon by the Hoppo and other Mandarines, as the only Person to procure for them any Curiosities or Merchandize brought on that Ship, and this at the moderate Rule perhaps of One fourth of what the Security pays for them.").

61 Cheong, *Hong Merchants*, pp. 226 and 281; Pritchard, "Crucial Years," p. 200; Morse, *Chronicles, Vol. II*, p. 15, Vol. V, p. 154.

62 Cheong, *Hong Merchants*, p. 156 n.118.

63 Morse, *Chronicles, Vol. V*, p. 11.

64 Morse, *Chronicles, Vol. V*, pp. 13–4; Cheong, *Hong Merchants*, pp. 156, 225 and 274; Pritchard, "Anglo-Chinese Relations," p. 116.

65 Morse, *Chronicles, Vol. V*, pp. 29, 39 ("that every five of them enter into written Contract to be answerable for all their transactions in trade and fair dealing jointly and Seperately.") and 41–4 ("joint bonds"); Cheong, *Hong Merchants*, pp. 94 and 205 n.64; White, "Hong Merchants," p. 56; Pritchard, "Crucial Years," p. 127.

The officials declared that their concern was that the shopkeepers were not always truthful in their dealings with foreigners, but they were also concerned that Western trade was increasingly being conducted outside the guild. It was believed, correctly, that much of this traffic was not being reported and that customs duties were being evaded.[66] Repeated crackdowns on shopkeepers sought to protect the hong merchant trade monopoly, to suppress or inconvenience smuggling, and to defend the collection of maritime customs revenues.

It is unclear whether the 1755 regulation imposing collective responsibility on registered third tier shopkeepers was enforced. It is not known if any shopkeeper was ever held collectively liable for debt, whether for customs duties or for amounts due to foreign traders. Nor is it known how long and how carefully, if at all, the 1755 shopkeeper registration regulations were observed. By definition, the debts for which the shopkeepers might be held collectively responsible were small. This was inherently a minor business. The Canton officials would soon be required to devote much more attention to the substantial debts incurred by merchants of the first and second tiers of the outer seas merchant (*waiyang hang*) guild.

3 The Formal Regulation of Maritime Foreign Trade

The European trading corporations chafed under the restrictions of the Canton System. The monopoly regulations of the 1755 edicts were found particularly irksome. Foreigners saw the new rules as tending to increase their costs, including official exactions levied on the trade.[67] The British EIC repeatedly protested to the Canton authorities, and certain of its officers came to believe that its petitions might be more successful if they could only reach the Emperor's attention.

The British East India Company tried in 1757 and again in 1758 to reopen trade up the coast at Ningbo, where it had done business as recently as 1736. It hoped to take advantage of lower customs duties and reduced inland goods transportation costs available at that port.[68] This initiative was favored by

---

66 White, "Hong Merchants," p. 59 (official concern about "clandestine thieves [who] connive at the loss of the nation's taxes").

67 Pritchard, "Crucial Years," p. 127.

68 Cheong, *Hong Merchants*, pp. 100–1 and 255; Edward L. Farmer, "James Flint Versus the Canton Interest," Papers on China, Vol. 17, pp. 38–66 (East Asian Research Center, Harvard University) (1963), p. 44; Pritchard, "Crucial Years," p. 128.

domestic Ningbo interests, but they lost out in Beijing to a range of economic,[69] internal order,[70] and partisan concerns which favored concentrating and managing China's Western trade at Canton in the south.[71] Efforts were thereafter made to discourage foreign trade at Ningbo, starting with sharp increases of customs fees.[72] The Qianlong Emperor issued edicts in December 1757 and January 1758 first closing Ningbo to European trade, and then expelling the British.[73] British representatives at Canton were given a written "obligation" in which they were asked to agree not go to Ningbo in the next season, which they refused to sign.[74]

The British EIC decided in 1758 after further unsuccessful local protests to directly petition the Emperor in Beijing.[75] A petition was prepared, in formal Chinese, seeking the right to trade at ports other than Canton, and detailing a string of grievances with trading conditions at Canton including the unsettled debts of the first tier hong merchant Beau Khequa (Li Guanghua of the Ziyuan hong) who had died insolvent in 1758.[76] The petition was placed in the hands of James Flint, a Chinese speaking EIC employee, who sailed north on a small 70 ton snow ironically named *Success* (which was lost at sea with all hands on its return to Canton).[77] Turned away at Ningbo, Flint continued north to the port of Tianjin, about seventy miles from Beijing, where he presented the petition to local officials on 21 July 1759.[78] The first memorial reporting his appearance, sent to Beijing on 23 July by Zhili Province Governor-General

69 White, "Hong Merchants," p. 52.

70 Officials were troubled by reports of the presence of non-European foreigners on British vessels calling at Ningbo. Furthermore, the Europeans were disruptive and seemed to require close supervision. In September 1754, not long before Flint sailed north, an English seaman had been killed by a French seaman in a brawl at Canton. The episode required official intervention, with French trade at Canton finally having to be halted on British demand until the guilty man was delivered up for imprisonment (being ultimately freed by a royal act of grace). Cheong, *Hong Merchants*, p. 101; Pritchard, "Crucial Years," pp. 124–5 and 129.

71 Pritchard, "Crucial Years," p. 129.

72 Cheong, *Hong Merchants*, pp. 101–2; Pritchard, "Crucial Years," pp. 128–9; Farmer, "James Flint," pp. 45–7 (the 1756 Ningbo customs fee increase was rumored to have been secured with a 20,000 tael [$27,778] bribe paid by Canton merchants to Beijing officials).

73 Cheong, *Hong Merchants*, pp. 101–2.

74 Farmer, "James Flint," pp. 47–8.

75 Pritchard, "Crucial Years," pp. 129–30.

76 Pritchard, "Crucial Years," p. 130; Cheong, *Hong Merchants*, pp. 254–5.

77 Pritchard, "Crucial Years," p. 130; Farmer, "James Flint," pp. 50 and 55; Morse, *Chronicles, Vol. 1*, pp. 301–5.

78 Farmer, "James Flint," pp. 38–66, pp. 50 and 52.

Fang Guangcheng, commented that Flint "is an insignificant barbarian from a small country; if there does not really exist an injustice, how would he dare to bother us with his petition?"[79] An edict to the Grand Council, issued the same day by the Qianlong Emperor, reported that the incumbent Hoppo Li Yongbiao had been ordered removed from office and that senior officials had been dispatched to go quickly to Canton and conduct a careful joint investigation. "This affair concerns the foreign barbarians, and the prestige of the empire is involved. You must investigate thoroughly in order to manifest imperial justice."[80] Flint himself traveled back to Canton by courier horse with one of the investigating officials.[81]

The official investigation, conducted from September through November 1759, focused on public corruption and on identifying the Chinese who had prepared the petition presented by James Flint. Liu Yabian, a minor Sichuan trader who was indebted to the British EIC, was identified as translator. Liu was publicly executed on 6 December 1759 pursuant to Imperial edict. James Flint was ordered imprisoned at Macao for three years, and then forever banished from China.[82] These punishments reflected the severe violation of Chinese law involved in an attempt to communicate directly with the Emperor in Beijing.[83] Incumbent Hoppo Li Yongbiao and his *weiyuan* were impeached for corruption and removed from office. Property found in the Hoppo's official mansion was confiscated.[84] This discipline is said to have had the effect of finally stamping out any further direct participation by officials in the trade.[85] The politically well-connected Governor-General Li Shiyao, who had advised the Court early in August 1759 that there would be no further troubles with foreigners and that their "speech and manner were respectful and obedient," remained at his post

79 Quoted in Fu, *Documentary Chronicle*, pp. 215–6; Farmer, "James Flint," p. 53.

80 Quoted in Farmer, "James Flint," pp. 53–5.

81 Fu, *Documentary Chronicle*, p. 216; Pritchard, "Crucial Years," p. 130.

82 Fu, *Documentary Chronicle*, pp. 222–4; Pritchard, "Crucial Years," pp. 130–1; Farmer, "James Flint," pp. 54–7; Morse, *Chronicles, Vol. V*, pp. 81–3; White, "Hong Merchants," pp. 63–4.

83 R. Randle Edwards, "The Old Canton System of Foreign Trade," pp. 360–378 in Victor H. Li, ed., *Law and Politics in China's Foreign Trade* (Seattle: Univ. of Washington Press, 1977), p. 363 ("This action violated a fundamental rule of traditional Chinese foreign relations which prohibited direct foreign contact with Peking, with the exception of envoys from tributary states, who came very infrequently in accordance with a schedule prescribed by the Chinese court."); Zhao, *Qing Opening to the Ocean*, pp. 114–5.

84 Cheong, *Hong Merchants*, pp. 107, 158–9, 205, 206 and 225; Fu, *Documentary Chronicle*, pp. 217–9; Farmer, "James Flint," pp. 42 and 54–6.

85 Cheong, *Hong Merchants*, pp. 107 and 158–9.

and was appointed acting Hoppo.[86] The investigating officials proposed some administrative reforms to be made to Chinese procedures and changes in port charges at Canton, but little came of them.[87]

The lasting consequence of James Flint's 1759 petition was a tightening and formalization of the rules of the Canton System. On 28 March 1760, "Regulations for the Control of Trade at Canton" (the *fangyi zhangcheng*) were announced at Canton.[88] These regulations, which were at once a restructuring and a codification of existing practice, had been solicited and approved by the Qianlong Emperor.[89] Translations of the 1760 Regulations are attached to this study as Appendix 1 (a modern translation by Lo-shu Fu) and Appendix 2 (a contemporary translation prepared for the British EIC).[90] Together with orders issued jointly by the Hoppo and the Governor-General, the 1760 Regulations formalized security merchant control duties and improved the competitive position of the outer seas merchant guild (the *waiyang hang*). Collective responsibility for customs duties not paid by an individual merchant was now applied to the full guild (no longer just among the upper tier members).[91]

The 1760 Regulations dealt with the thorny issue of hong merchant debt by declaring foreign loans to be illegal. "If the people of this Country do hereafter on any pretence whatsoever take up money of Foreigners, he [the Emperor] requires that they should be severely punished. and that all the Goods also of those who borrow money be Confiscated."[92] All accounts between foreign

---

86 Quoted in Farmer, "James Flint," pp. 52, 55 and 40–2; Hummel, *Eminent Chinese*, pp. 480–2 ("At any rate, owing to the European trade, official posts at Canton were regarded for more than a century as among the most lucrative in the empire, and Li Shih-yao, being the highest official there for more than fourteen years (longer than any other Governor-General in that port in the Ch'ing period), probably amassed a fortune."); Cheong, *Hong Merchants*, p. 205; Fu, *Documentary Chronicle*, p. 216.

87 Farmer, "James Flint," p. 58.

88 Farmer, "James Flint," p. 59 (received on 24 March and publicly announced on 28 March 1760); Ch'en, *Insolvency*, p. 185 (a copy of the text of the regulations was obtained by the EIC and translated and recorded by them on 12 April 1760); Morse, *Chronicles, Vol. V*, pp. 89–90 (same).

89 Ch'en, *Insolvency*, pp. 9–11 and 184–5; Cheong, *Hong Merchants*, p. 106 n.99; White, "Hong Merchants," pp. 53 and 63; Pritchard, "Crucial Years," pp. 131 and 133–4 (table showing various Canton regulations as of 1760 and their dates of origin); Farmer, "James Flint," p. 58.

90 Fu, *Documentary Chronicle*, pp. 224–6 (modern translation of the 1760 Regulations) (text attached to this study as Appendix 1); Morse, *Chronicles, Vol. V*, pp. 94–8 (Appendix AK) (contemporary translation of the 1760 regulations) (text attached to this study as Appendix 2).

91 Ch'en, *Insolvency*, pp. 9–10.

92 1760 Regulations, Rule No. 3, Appendix 2 to this study (contemporary translation) (Morse, *Chronicles, Vol. V*, pp. 96) (quoted). Also, 1760 Regulations, Rule No. 3, Appendix 1 to this

traders and hong merchants were required to be settled before a foreign ship left Canton.[93] The regulation directed prosecution of violations of the loan ban under "the law by which we punish criminals who communicate with a foreign country, borrow money or hold their goods or money without payment"[94]—the Qing Code substatute under which many hong merchants were ordered banished to Ili in distant Xinjiang.[95] The confiscation penalty, which the regulation provided for separately and in addition to punishment under the substatute, created confusion. Debtors usually had little left to "confiscate." Did the confiscation provision give the government the right to seize *the debtor's* last remaining assets, in derogation of the rights of other creditors? Or did it mean that *the interest of the foreign lender* in a loan made in violation of the law was subject to forfeiture[96]—either by being voided (held unenforceable) or by being taken by the Qing government ("confiscation")? Chinese officials stated in 1779[97] and again in 1780[98] that European loans were subject to

---

study (modern translation) ("We should forbid Chinese merchants from borrowing capital from the foreign barbarians... The money which they borrow should be confiscated by the government.") (Fu, *Documentary Chronicle*, p. 225).

93 1760 Regulations, Rule No. 3, Appendix 1 to this study (modern translation) (Fu, *Documentary Chronicle*, p. 225) and Appendix 2 to this study (Morse, *Chronicles, Vol. v*, pp. 95–6).

94 1760 Regulations, Rule No. 3, Appendix 1 to this study (modern translation) (Fu, *Documentary Chronicle*, p. 225).

95 Cheong, *Hong Merchants*, pp. 159 and 255; Waley-Cohen, *Exile in Mid-Qing China*, p. 5. Although Cheong states that foreigners were subject to banishment from Canton under the 1760 Regulations, this possible penalty is not found in texts of the regulations the author has seen, nor is it mentioned by other scholars. The substatute under which the hong merchants were banished, "collaborating with foreigners and cheating them out of their money," applied to Chinese subjects by its terms.

96 Cheong, *Hong Merchants*, p. 159.

97 Josiah Quincy, *The Journal of Major Samuel Shaw, The First American Consul at Canton* (Boston: William Crosby & H. P. Nichols, 1847), p. 312 (Governor Li Zhiying told Captain Panton on 22 October 1779 "that the emperor, in 1760, having been informed of the distresses occasioned to the merchants, in consequence of borrowing money from the Europeans at a high premium, had issued an edict, forbidding such loans upon any conditions, under penalty to the European of a forfeiture of his money, and of banishment to the Chinese,—a circumstance well known to all the Europeans and Chinese in Canton, the edict having been published in the usual manner, and translated into several European languages.").

98 Morse, *Chronicles, Vol. II*, pp. 53–4 (On 29 February 1780 a joint communication was received from the Governor and Hoppo in which the foreigners "were 'reminded' of the Imperial Decree of the 25th year of Kienlung [Qianlong] (1760), by which the taking of loans at interest by Chinese from Europeans, or by Europeans from Chinese, was strictly prohibited under penalty of banishment (transportation) to Ili for the Chinese, and

forfeiture under the 1760 Regulations as approved by the Emperor, but the threatened penalty was never enforced.[99]

Also in question is whether the 1760 loan ban was violated by the mere act of borrowing money from a foreigner, even though the loan was being repaid. The answer to this question seems to be no. First, the applicable substatute punished nonpayment. Second, the ban itself was modified—changed to a cap of 100,000 taels ($138,889)—by an imperial edict issued in 1794 in the case of Gonqua (Shi Zhonghe, also known as Shy Kinqua II, successor head of the Eryi hong). As of 1794, only debts in excess of 100,000 taels required immediate payment.[100] Although hong debts after 1794 often exceeded 100,000 taels, no hong merchant was ever punished simply for being so indebted (although many were). As of 1815, the disclosure of debts and a plausible payment plan seem to have been all that was required for a Chinese debtor to be in technical compliance with the loan ban.[101] Payment default, not the loan itself, triggered the severe penalties provided for under the "cheating foreigners" substatute.

As a practical matter, there would have been little upside for the Canton official who acted to enforce the loan prohibition against foreign lenders during the period of the Canton Guaranty System, 1780–1842. As discussed in Chapter Two, customs taxes were collected and remitted to Beijing on a quotum basis, and if there was a material deficiency, officials had to pay it out of their own pocket. This was perhaps the principal risk involved in holding public office in imperial China. In this context enforcement of the loan ban, while theoretically possible, became problematic. The consequences of enforcement were potentially ruinous, to the system and to the official personally. First, the mere refusal to enforce foreign loans would have brought an uproar from the foreign

forfeiture of the loan for the Europeans; they were also 'reminded' of the provision of Chinese law that accumulated interest should not be allowed to exceed the original principal of a loan, i.e., that no loan should be more than doubled by interest.").

99 A memorial on proposed punishments, prepared during the "Chinese Debts" crisis of 1780, suggested that foreigners who lent money to hong merchants in future should have their money confiscated and that foreign offenders should be banished ("driven out back to his own country"). Ng, "Ch'ing Management of the West," p. 156.

100 Ng, "Ch'ing Management of the West," p. 164 ("hereafter, when the hong merchants owe the barbarians money for their goods, the annual amount shall not exceed 100,000 liang [i.e., taels]. If the debt exceeds that amount, the debt will be ordered to be cleared immediately. This law is in effect starting from this year.").

101 Ng, "Ch'ing Management of the West," pp. 174 ("the handling of the present case [of the junior hong merchants] was done in accordance with this law, as the amount of debts had been investigated and arrangement had been made for their repayment. If after the time limit of six years was up, and still the debts were not cleared, then the hong merchants would be punished according to the law.") and 176.

community at Canton. The foreigners had come to view the collective guaranty of hong merchant debt as a cornerstone of the Canton System. For their part, Qing officials long used relief under the collective guaranty as a means of placating the restive Western traders. While loans to hong merchants were unlawful, the officials enforced them nevertheless, if sometimes with a lecture about the need to respect Chinese laws. Foreign traders would have taken any change as an abrogation and might have been expected to respond sharply. A stoppage of foreign trade might be expected, as happened in 1829–1830. Second, any stoppage of trade would reduce the amount of collected taxes flowing to Beijing, with the enforcing official liable for the deficiency. Personal financial ruin was thus a possible consequence that had to be considered in deciding whether to actively enforce the loan ban. Third, many years' experience had shown that when the foreign trade of Canton was interrupted, unemployment soared and social disorder followed. The domestic order consequences of trade interruption may have been the most frightening prospect that officials weighed in considering enforcement of the loan ban. Collectively, this range of dismal prospects may have suppressed any inclination to enforce the loan prohibition the officials continued to proclaim to all concerned. It was safer, indeed almost the only viable choice for Qing officials at Canton, to ignore the foreign loan problem and leave it for a later day. There was plenty of money on the Canton waterfront. Officials who chose not to stir up trouble could draw their share and move along quietly to another posting. The risk of substantial personal liability if there was a disruption of trade, and the ability to do well for the moment while hoping that problems might solve themselves with time, discouraged enforcement of the loan ban against foreign lenders.

Under the 1760 Regulations, foreign merchants were barred from sending messages into the interior of China, or adopting any means of determining inland commodity prices.[102] Administrative enforcement of this rule is said to have barred the hong merchants, as well, from further direct contact and negotiation with inland suppliers.[103] Foreigners were prohibited from hiring Chinese servants, except "the Established Linguists and Compradores."[104] This enforced a prior rule that foreigners were not allowed to study or translate

102 1760 Regulations, Rule No. 4, Appendix 1 to this study (modern translation) (Fu, *Documentary Chronicle*, pp. 225–6) and Appendix 2 to this study (contemporary translation) (Morse, *Chronicles, Vol. V*, pp. 96–7); White, "Hong Merchants," pp. 52–3; Pritchard, "Crucial Years," p. 134.

103 Cheong, *Hong Merchants*, p. 102.

104 1760 Regulations, Rule No. 3, Appendix 1 to this study (modern translation) (Fu, *Documentary Chronicle*, p. 225) and Appendix 2 to this study (contemporary translation) (Morse, *Chronicles, Vol. V*, pp. 95–6); Pritchard, "Crucial Years," p. 134.

Chinese, except in the imprecise pidgin language form used by the merchants and licensed linguists.[105] These Chinese restrictions on communication by foreigners can be compared to an existing rule, imposed by the Hoppo in 1731 on foreign request, which prohibited the hong merchants from communicating directly with Western firms in Europe. The earlier rule had its origins in foreign complaints about the repeated efforts of Tan Hunqua (Chen Fangguan) to complain directly to the EIC and VOC about alleged overpricing and kickbacks in contracts made between other hong merchants and local representatives of the European firms. Paul Van Dyke sees the 1731 communication rule as "one of the first policies to clearly lay down the foundation of the system that disadvantaged Chinese merchants in international trade compared to their foreign counterparts."[106]

When resident at Canton, under the terms of the 1760 Regulations, foreign traders had to reside at properties owned and maintained by hong merchants.[107] In the off-season, foreign traders were still required to leave, but they were now officially permitted to stay at Macao as an alternative to traveling all the way home.[108] Provincial coastal defenses were ordered strengthened, to

105 Morse, *Chronicles, Vol. V*, pp. 27–8; Pritchard, "Crucial Years," p. 134; Cheong, *Hong Merchants*, p. 107.

106 Van Dyke, *Merchants of Canton and Macao*, pp. 105–110 (quotation at p. 110). Although the 1731 ban on communication with European firms is said to have been on pain of death, there is no record of enforcement of the rule with this penalty. "Tan Hunqua" was also known as "Ton Hunqua." Van Dyke, *Merchants of Canton and Macao*, p. 104. The rule prohibiting foreigners from studying or translating Chinese had an independent basis in the Chinese concern that foreigners might coopt or control Chinese citizens with whom they had open and uncontrolled contact. See Ng, "Ch'ing Management of the West," pp. 140–1 and 170–1.

107 1760 Regulations, Rule No. 2, Appendix 1 to this study (modern translation) (Fu, *Documentary Chronicle*, pp. 224–5) and Appendix 2 to this study (contemporary translation) (Morse, *Chronicles, Vol. V*, p. 95) ("At present there are Vagabonds [i.e., persons who have not been licensed as hong merchants] who build Handsome houses to allure Strangers for which they receive great Rents, who let them do many bad things, who come and go, occasion trouble, carry on illicit trade, defraud the Customs, and commit such like disorders."); Cheong, *Hong Merchants*, pp. 159 and 255–6; White, "Hong Merchants," pp. 52–3. Foreigners paid rent for the 'foreign factory' properties they occupied, and sometimes acted as landlord in turn, contracting with other foreigners as subtenants. Downs, *The Golden Ghetto*, pp. 90–1 (boardinghouse operations); William C. Hunter, *Bits of Old China* (Shanghai: Kelly and Walsh Ltd., 1911), pp. 33–5 (anecdote of the termination of an unauthorized attempted subtenancy of the Canton premises of the then absent Senn Van Basel).

108 1760 Regulations, Rule No. 1, Appendix 1 to this study (modern translation) (Fu, *Documentary Chronicle*, p. 224) and Appendix 2 to this study (contemporary translation)

prevent further disorders. Contingents of troops near the foreign anchorage at Whampoa were ordered to be increased, and were directed to stand constantly on duty from the arrival through the departure of the foreign ships. The Panyu district (Whampoa) magistrate, charged with keeping the foreigners in order, ultimately assessed and collected a weekly fee from the trade for these ongoing control efforts.[109]

The provisions barring foreigners from lending money to hong merchants, and requiring the foreigners to reside at Canton in properties owned by hong merchants, ended the occasional former practice of hong merchants mortgaging real property as security for foreign loans. While such loans continued to be made, the ban on the transfer or mortgage of hong properties was respected, presumably because the Nanhai magistrate would no longer accept the necessary mortgage documents for filing. This meant that the loans foreigners extended to hong merchants after 1760 were entirely unsecured (without lien protection).[110]

Five in number, the 1760 Regulations are the earliest promulgated form of the "Eight Regulations," the set of rules which governed the maritime foreign

---

(Morse, *Chronicles, Vol. V*, pp. 94–5; Pritchard, "Crucial Years," p. 133. See Liu, "Dutch India Company," pp. 91 and p. 169 n.2 (the off-season varied among the various European companies in the 18th century. "[G]enerally speaking, the off-season of roughly four months would start from the end of February, March, or April, and last to the end of June, July, or August.").

109 1760 Regulations, Rule No. 5, Appendix 1 to this study (modern translation) (Fu, *Documentary Chronicle*, p. 226) and Appendix 2 to this study (contemporary translation) (Morse, *Chronicles, Vol. V*, pp. 97–8) ("The Foreign Ships have a great number of People, many of them are of a wild brutish Nature, and may easily occasion trouble, The Villainous Boat Men connect themselves with them, which occasions continual disturbances."); White, "Hong Merchants, pp. 52–3; Pritchard, "Crucial Years," p. 134; Van Dyke, *Canton Trade*, p. 66.

110 In traditional China, land was the preferred form of security to be pledged for a loan. Van der Sprenkel, *Legal Institutions in Manchu China*, pp. 11, 105–7 and Appendix 2 at 133–4 (examples of deed of sale, mortgage and loan documents). Tehanqua (Teunqua I) mortgaged his Yihe hong to the EIC early in 1756. After his father's death on 3 November 1759, Teunqua II visited the EIC offices with Tinqua and paid off the mortgage by tendering 3,000 taels. Ch'en, *Insolvency*, pp. 307 and 432 n.199; Cheong, *Hong Merchants*, pp. 171, 253 and 187 n.126 (suggesting that the payoff was spurred by the imminent mortgage ban of the 1760 Regulations); Morse, *Chronicles, Vol. V*, p. 74. The following documents were executed and delivered in 1756 to perfect the EIC mortgage on Teunqua I's Yihe hong: (a) an assignment by Teunqua; (b) a certificate from the Nanhai Xian of the assignment; (c) the "Writing or Deeds of Yee-ho Hong"; and (d) an attested assignment of these papers by the EIC. Morse, *Chronicles, Vol. V*, p. 74 (listing documents delivered to the hong merchant mortgagor by the EIC when the mortgage was paid off).

PLATE 7 *Chinese people reading notices posted on a wall. Sketch by George Chinnery, October 1841. (Private collection. Photograph by courtesy of the Martyn Gregory Gallery, London.)*

PLATE 8 *View of Mingqua's hong and Old China Street, showing a large number of notices posted on the wall, Canton, 28 November 1838. Pen, ink and watercolor sketch by Warner Varnham. (Private collection. Photograph by permission.)*

trade of Canton through 1842.[111] These rules are the public face, presented openly to the Western traders by being posted on walls and by other means, of the far larger body of laws, edicts, rules and procedures which guided the Canton officials and the hong merchants in the management of foreign trade. The Eight Regulations are only seen in histories in summary form, such as the abridged version of the 1835 regulations that William C. Hunter included in his 1882 book *The 'Fan Kwae' at Canton*, which is attached to this study as Appendix 5.[112] (Complete versions of the 1831 Regulations and the 1835 Regulations are attached to this study as Appendix 3 and Appendix 4 respectively.) The shortened versions of the Eight Regulations have tended to focus on rules of personal conduct, rather than the trade regulations themselves (which were not always restated in later enactments). This abridgement process has had the effect of trivializing and sometimes producing comic effects entirely absent from the original Chinese regulations. For example, per Hunter, Rule No. 2 of the Eight Regulations (1835) provided that "Neither women, guns, spears, nor arms of any kind can be brought to the Factories."[113] This seeming equation of women with weaponry is the product of summarization, the *reductio ad absurdum* combination of two distinct parts of the original three paragraph Rule No. 2.

William C. Hunter, who had long experience at Canton as a clerk and then partner with the American firm of Russell & Co., states that the foreigners assumed that the Eight Regulations were "in force always," although some of the rules "came to be disregarded by the foreign community." He recounts that the Eight Regulations "were now and then brought to the Factories by a Linguist, as an intimation that they were not to be considered a 'dead letter.'[114] The Chinese authorities admitted that some of these rules were being ignored by all concerned. The 1831 version of the "Eight Regulations" opens with the statement that "through length of days they [the 1760 Regulations] have gradually

111 Fu, *Documentary Chronicle*, p. 224 n. 180 ("The original regulations had five articles—but article II was divisible into two articles. These regulations were repeatedly revised until there were eight of them by which China regulated foreign trade prior to the Opium War.")

112 William C. Hunter, *The 'Fan Kwae' at Canton Before Treaty Days 1825–1844* (London: Kegan Paul, Trench & Co., 1882), pp. 28–30. While Hunter does not date his abridged version, its substance is identical to the content of the translation of the 1835 Regulations in the Chinese Repository, Vol. 3, pp. 579–584 (April 1835). The full text of the 1835 Regulations as published in the Chinese Repository and of the Hunter abridgement are attached to this study as Appendices 4 and 5, respectively.

113 1835 Regulations, Rule No. 2, Appendix 5 to this study (Hunter, Fan Kwae, p. 28).

114 Hunter, *Fan Kwae*, p. 28.

been neglected and the execution of them relaxed.[115] The 1835 enactment, produced four years later, refers to the rules of 1760, 1810 and 1831, adding that "during the length of days they have been in operation, either they have in the end become a dead letter, or there have gradually sprung up unrestrained offenses."[116] Some of the rules, such as the bans on collecting inland price information and on learning Chinese, would have been fairly easily evaded and also difficult to enforce.[117]

R. Randle Edwards, a historian of Chinese law, states that the "Eight Regulations" "were not simply posted on the wall in the Chinese language but were delivered, translated, and fairly well understood by the European community.... Comparison of some of these translations with the original Chinese documents reveals that most of the translations are faithful renderings of the original; some are superbly done."[118] While this is true, the regulations were neither modern in style nor models of clear presentation. The trade regulations reached the foreigners in the elaborate form in which they had been presented to the Emperor for approval, framed as a Memorial to the throne, with a preamble, with explanations and reports of official investigation, and often with what might otherwise be considered strictly internal directives to Chinese civil and military officers (for example, coastal defense directives in Rule No. 5 of the 1760 Regulations). The regulations are thus typical of legal enactments in imperial China, having been framed from the perspective of the state, either from within looking out ("barbarian merchants") or from the top looking down ("for them to obey and act accordingly").[119] Penalties to foreigners that might result from the violation of particular rules may be suggested, but they are rarely provided for in detail, and often no penalty for violations appears at all. No fixed order is observed in the various iterations of the regulations. Given rules appear and disappear in different versions, with rules which were not repeated still remaining effective. The rule prohibiting foreign debt

---

115 1831 Regulations, Appendix 3 to this study (Morse, *Chronicles, Vol.* IV, pp. 293–301 (Appendix AB) (contemporary translation of the 1831 regulations)), p. 294.

116 1835 Regulations, Appendix 4 to this study (Chinese Repository, Vol. 3, pp. 579–584 (April 1835) (contemporary translation of the 1835 regulations), p. 584.

117 Basu, "Asian Merchants and Western Trade," p. 276 ("it was always possible for the foreign community to enlist the aid of a Chinese language instructor or the drafter of their petitions. In fact, the East India Company developed an elaborate intelligence-gathering apparatus which gave them access to secret documents and communications.").

118 Edwards, "Ch'ing Legal Jurisdiction Over Foreigners," p. 244.

119 1835 Regulations, Appendix 4 to this study (Chinese Repository, Vol. 3, p. 579) ("also to command the hong merchants and linguists to enjoin orders on the barbarian merchants of every nation, for them to obey and act accordingly.").

is unusual as it appears in most versions, albeit continually renumbered (Rule No. 3 in 1760, No. 2 in 1831, and No. 7 in 1835). Yet even in the 1835 Regulations it appears only as an allusion in a separate rule ("or incur debts to the barbarians"), not as a full restatement. Nor was there a consistent number of rules. The number eight (of trade regulations), as with the number thirteen (of licensed hong merchants), appears to represent little more than the use of a number considered auspicious in Chinese tradition. The "thirteen hongs" only rarely attained the number of thirteen.[120] The "Eight Regulations," as revised from time to time, also rarely—if ever—stood at that number.

The personal conduct and residence components of the "Eight Regulations," which increased with the passage of time, loom large in the popular memory of the Canton System. The foreign traders found them particularly irksome.[121] Today they might be thought of as akin to school dormitory (parietals) or "nanny state" rules. The Qing state acted like an overprotective parent, and the foreign trader children showed no gratitude whatsoever. The foreigners were not allowed to enter the city of Canton. During the trading season of about four to five months they were confined to a foreign enclave on the waterfront at the Western edge of the city, with the exception of escorted visits to parks, not more than three times monthly, and sometimes to hong merchant residences by permission.[122] Their river travel was closely monitored, although foreign officers in properly flagged service boats were usually permitted to pass

120 There were thirteen hongs in the years 1808, 1809, 1830, 1836 and 1837, and fourteen hongs in the year 1835. Ch'en, *Insolvency*, pp. 14–18. Weng Eang Cheong suggests that the term "thirteen hongs" may have "accidental and mundane" origins, such as the fact that there were thirteen first and second tier hong merchants in 1755 when the key organizational edicts were proclaimed. However, the term is of significantly older origin. It was used, for example, by Chu Dajun (d. 1696) in his "poems on Canton," the Guangzhou Zhuzhici. Cheong, *Hong Merchants*, p. 95 ("erudite speculation" on origins of the number thirteen); White, "Hong Merchants," p. 15–16; Sung, "A study of the Thirteen Hongs," pp. 10 (Liang Jiabin has "abundant evidence to prove that the so-called Thirteen Hongs had already existed before K'ang-hsi 59 (1720) and that this year was merely the year when the merchants of the Thirteen Hongs were organized collectively (Kung-hang [Co-hong]). (See Chapter 1, Section 2.)."), 24–5 and 73. See Kato Shigeshi, "On the Hang," p. 58 ("In China at present [1936] they use such an expression as 36 hang, 72 hang, or 360 hang, when they want to refer to the great varieties of trades.").

121 Greenberg, *British Trade*, p. 58.

122 1835 Regulations, Rule No. 5, Appendix 4 to this study (Chinese Repository, Vol. 3, pp. 582–3) and Appendix 5 to this study (Hunter, *Fan Kwae*, p. 29); Edwards, "Old Canton System," p. 364.

through the customs checkpoints without inspection.[123] Foreigners were originally prohibited from hiring any Chinese employees, except "the Established Linguists and Compradores,"[124] but were later allowed to hire up to eight registered servants per factory property to perform specified duties.[125] With the passage of time, more personal conduct rules were added, prohibiting women from visiting the foreign factories,[126] restricting boating on the river,[127] barring use of sedan chairs,[128] and so forth. The foreign traders muttered about and ignored or evaded these rules as best they could. They were inconveniences which burdened a trade that was profitable for the foreign merchants, and generally well managed.

The American China trader Robert Bennet Forbes, writing at the end of 1831, praised the Canton System by comparison with the London alternative. "[W]ho would barter the present free trade in all descriptions of goods for a regular commercial system of duties, entries, permits, etc., myriad of forms, like those in London? The facilities of trade have always been remarkable here and those who have had most experience are perfectly willing to put up with a continuation of the same."[129] Business went on.

Under the regime of the 1760 Regulations, the competitive position of the hong guild was strengthened against the Western merchants. It was now

---

123 1831 Regulations, Rule No. 7, Appendix 3 to this study (Morse, *Chronicles, Vol. IV*, pp. 299–300; 1835 Regulations, Rule No. 5, Appendix 4 to this study (Chinese Repository, Vol. 3, pp. 582–3); Van Dyke, *Canton Trade*, pp. 23, 117–8 and 166.

124 1760 Regulations, Rule No. 3, Appendix 1 to this study (modern translation) (Fu, *Documentary Chronicle*, p. 225) and Appendix 2 to this study (contemporary translation) (Morse, *Chronicles, Vol. V*, pp. 95–6).

125 1831 Regulations, Rule No. 3, Appendix 3 to this study (Morse, *Chronicles, Vol. IV*, p. 297; 1835 Regulations, Rule No. 4, Appendix 4 to this study (Chinese Repository, Vol. 3, p. 582) and Appendix 5 to this study (Hunter, *Fan Kwae*, p. 29).

126 1831 Regulations, Rule No. 5, Appendix 3 to this study (Morse, *Chronicles, Vol. IV*, pp. 298–9; 1835 Regulations, Rule No. 2, Appendix 4 to this study (Chinese Repository, Vol. 3, p. 581) and Appendix 5 to this study (Hunter, *Fan Kwae*, p. 28); Edwards, "Old Canton System," p. 360; Morse, *Chronicles, Vol. IV*, pp. 234–5 and 238.

127 1831 Regulations, Rule No. 7, Appendix 3 to this study (Morse, *Chronicles, Vol. IV*, pp. 299–300; 1835 Regulations, Rule No. 5, Appendix 4 to this study (Chinese Repository, Vol. 3, pp. 582–3) and Appendix 5 to this study (Hunter, *Fan Kwae*, p. 29); Morse, *Chronicles, Vol. IV*, p. 174.

128 1831 Regulations, Rule No. 5, Appendix 3 to this study (Morse, *Chronicles, Vol. IV*, p. 299); Morse, *Chronicles, Vol. IV*, pp. 235 ("that hereafter Foreigners … must all, as of old, walk on foot—they must not overstep their station, or rank, and go about in chairs."), 238 and 244.

129 Quoted in Edwards, "Old Canton System," p. 369 n. 29.

officially recognized as an independent body, the *gonghang* (or Cohong).[130] Little is known of the details of its internal organization. Some contemporary Westerners spoke of the hong merchants acting through the Cohong of 1760 in a 'corporate capacity.' This did not signify a legally independent corporate body in the modern sense, but simply that the Cohong acted as a unified body which set prices and maintained collective discipline in dealings between its members and the Western firms.[131] The hong merchant scholar Weng Eang Cheong describes the Cohong of 1760 as having been

> more like an exclusive club, with members paying different fees for different classes of membership entitling them to different privileges in the trade. Privileges could be inherited by succeeding heads of the firms as in corporate membership, but the shares were not negotiable in the open market.[132]

A French correspondent, writing in December 1760, stated that ownership of the Cohong was held in 75 shares priced at 1,000 taels ($1,389) each, for an initial capitalization of 75,000 taels ($104,167). Puankhequa I, who became Chief Merchant, held twelve shares.[133] The new body of about ten became known

130 It remains uncertain whether the Cohong of 1760 had Imperial level authorization. Ann Bolbach White could not find any evidence that Governor-General Li Shiyao had sent a Memorial to the Emperor on the subject of this merchant group. White, "Hong Merchants," pp. 53–54; Cheong, *Hong Merchants*, p. 126 n.99 (merchants and Europeans were uncertain); Liu, "Dutch India Company," p. 96 (when the Dutch pressed this question at a 15 August 1760 meeting with the hong merchants, "the Hong merchants fell silent.").

131 At a 21 August 1760 meeting at the Dutch factory the ten hong merchants had "solemnly declared... that they united in a corporation to conduct all sorts of trade at the instigation of the high-ranking mandarins, but that the Dutch were still free to negotiate with those members with whom they wanted to deal. It mattered not one jot to them whether the Dutch traded with the corporation or one particular member since all the eggs were in the one basket." Liu, "Dutch India Company," p. 98.

132 Cheong, *Hong Merchants*, p. 269.

133 Dermigny, *La Chine et L'Occident*, Vol. 2, p. 834 (lettre de Michel à Rothe, 31 Déc. 1760) ("Nos marchands hannistes forment à présent une société à laquelle on a donné le nom de Compagnie chinoise; et, quoique tout le monde soit liqué contre elle, elle subsiste toujours et n'on fait pas moins la loi. Les intéressés dans cette Compagnie, qui s'avisent de prendre le titre de Directeurs, sont Pankekoa [Puankhequa], le grand Souikoa [Sy Hunqua], Souitsia [Sweetia], Chet-koa fils du vieux Sioukoa [Chetqua], Tamkoa [Tinqua], Tsankoa, Hykoa Conscience, Foutcha [Fotia] et Fatoukoa. Les voilà selon le rang qu'ils tiennent: Pankekoa comme chef a douze parts, le grand Souykoa 10, etc. Tioukoa qui étoit aussi de la Compagnie est mort depuis peu de temps, et Fatoukoa est à l'agonie; ce n'est

as the *waiyang hang* merchants, all of whom were eligible to serve as security merchants. Those merchants who would not accept the terms of the Cohong were forced into the non-Western trading *bengang hang* or *fuchao hang* or made to retire entirely.[134] Ton Anqua, who strongly opposed the Cohong, was arrested by the Governor-General, and finally ordered to move with his family back to Quanzhou in Fujian Province.[135] The only criterion for nomination to the guild was that a prospective merchant must be "rich and financially sound" (*yinshi*), as previously.[136] As under the 1755 regulations, shopkeepers were still excluded from the hong merchant monopoly of the principal articles of trade. Shopkeepers could trade only in less important articles such as porcelain and silk fabric.[137]

Puankhequa I, who became Chief Merchant, was a driving force behind the creation of the Cohong of 1760. The EIC believed that he was motivated by his own debts, which had grown large by the late 1750s.[138] Puankhequa I had close influence with Governor-General Li Shiyao and a deep distrust of foreigners dating to having seen Chinese abused by the Spanish when he traded in the Philippines.[139] Governor-General Li Shiyao is said to have received a cut from the increased revenues enjoyed by the new Cohong, and presumably the new Hoppo Yu Bashi did as well.[140] A footnote to the British EIC translation of the 1831 Regulations, inserted by Morse, mentions a "tradition" that Governor-General Li Shiyao "had a share in Puankhequa's house."[141]

---

pas une grand perte. Nous regrettons davantage le vieux Sioukoa et le tisserand Foukien, quoiqu'ils soient remplacés, l'un par son fils et l'autre par son frère. Tantinkoa qui étoit aussi un des Directeurs a été disgrâcié et renvoyé dans son pays de Chinchiou. Ankoa s'est retiré volontairement du commerce. Le fonds de la Compagnie est de 75 actions de 1,000 taels chacune."); Cheong, *Hong Merchants*, p. 220; Van Dyke, *Merchants of Canton and Macao*, p. 116 ("Tan [or Ton] Hunqua was included as a member of the Co-hong in August 1760, but his family was now among the smallest of the licensed Hong merchants. He and Foutia were the only two members who were asked to contribute a minimum of 2,000 taels. . . . The largest houses paid 10 to 12,000 taels.").

134 Ch'en, *Insolvency*, p. 11.

135 Ch'en, *Insolvency*, p. 11 n.27.

136 Ch'en, *Insolvency*, p. 10 n.22.

137 White, "Hong Merchants," p. 56.

138 Cheong, *Hong Merchants*, pp. 254 and 257.

139 White, "Hong Merchants," pp. 53–5.

140 Cheong, *Hong Merchants*, p. 165. Yu Bashi was posted to Canton as Hoppo in 1760. Cheong, p. 209.

141 1831 Regulations, Appendix 3 to this study (Morse, *Chronicles, Vol. IV*, pp. 293–301 (Appendix AB), p. 294 n.1.

The foreign community vigorously protested against the introduction of the Cohong of 1760. Western company representatives variously complained, negotiated and stalled, delaying the landing of their inbound cargoes. The Chinese stood firm, maintaining a united front and insisting upon uniform prices.[142] By the middle of August 1760 Hoppo Yu Bashi demanded to know why the foreign ships had not yet begun to unload. He stated "that the new procedure had been approved by the Emperor, and that conformity was imperative." The Hoppo added, perhaps fatefully, that "the Association was designed to make the Merchants jointly answerable for every trouble, great or small, that the Europeans might occasion."[143] The foreign community finally landed their cargoes and traded, thus accepting the new terms upon which the Canton trade would be conducted thereafter.[144]

During the same time period in which the Chinese government promulgated the 1760 Regulations and recognized the Cohong of 1760, the unpaid debts of the deceased Ziyuan hong merchant Beau Khequa were finally resolved. It is unclear from surviving records precisely when and how this occurred.[145] Beau Khequa's British EIC debt had stood at 50,000 taels ($69,444) on his death in 1758.[146] In proceedings before the Nanhai and Panyu magistrates, the Taihe hong merchant Sweetia—who had traded on joint account with Beau Khequa—was held liable for half of the debts of his deceased sometime joint venture partner. This liability arose either from Sweetia's relationship with the deceased hong merchant as joint venture partner, or from the deceased's occasional practice of acting as joint guarantor with other merchants in connection with specific business that they transacted. The hong merchant Chowqua paid

---

142 Liu, "Dutch India Company," pp. 92–100.

143 Morse, *Chronicles, Vol. v*, p. 92; Pritchard, "Crucial Years," p. 131; Cheong, *Hong Merchants*, p. 209.

144 Morse, *Chronicles, Vol. v*, p. 93.

145 Simon Yang-chien Tsai, "Trading for Tea: A Study of the English East India Company's Tea Trade with China and the Related Financial Issues, 1760–1833" (Ph.D. diss., University of Leicester, 2003), p. 295.

146 The 50,000 tael figure may represent (more risky) unsecured debt only; it is unclear whether this total includes the balance due on a 10,600 tael mortgage loan the EIC had made to Beau Khequa in 1754. Ch'en, *Insolvency*, p. 183; Cheong, *Hong Merchants*, pp. 157–8 and 253–54; Farmer, "James Flint," pp. 52–53 (in the 23 July 1759 Memorial of Zhili Province Governor-General Fang Guangcheng, Flint is quoted as having said that "The merchant Li Kuang-hua [Beau Khequa] borrowed more than 50,000 taels capital from me and did not return it."); White, "Hong Merchants," p. 64 (although White states that Beau Khequa died owing 50,000 taels to James Flint, the actual creditor was Flint's employer the EIC).

off Beau Khequa's 10,600 tael ($14,722) mortgage loan to the EIC in January 1759 and various foreign creditors accepted private settlements. Sweetia agreed to assume additional debt in exchange for new business with foreign firms, and to maintain good customer relations.[147] The entire hong merchant body was ordered by the government to pay tea duties owed by the Ziyuan hong, funds for which had been advanced by the EIC but diverted by the failing firm and not paid to the state. The hong merchants raised these funds through an *ad hoc* surcharge on the trade. This levy is considered to have been a prototype for the later surcharge in support of the Consoo Fund that was established in 1780.[148] The Ziyuan hong settlements piled more debt onto Sweetia's already weak Taihe hong, which owed creditors 118,800 taels ($165,000) as of 1759. Sweetia then died in 1761. The burden of this debt and its accumulating interest contributed directly to the 1780 failure of the Taihe hong under successor proprietor Yngshaw (Yan Shiying).[149]

A pattern in hong merchant debt cases, which recurs in cases after 1780, is evident in the 1759–1760 resolution of debts of Beau Khequa's Ziyuan hong. First, most of the hong's debt was not "paid" at all but rather was assumed (with the burden of paying interest) by another hong merchant. Second, that debt assumption was tied to the transfer of existing contracts between the debtor and foreign firms to the assuming hong merchant (aiding the rescuer).[150] Third, the dead weight of this assumed and still interest bearing debt then became a material factor in the later failure of the rescuer.

The merchants of the 1760 Cohong stood their ground and maintained price unity for several years. While the guild enjoyed some trading prosperity, most of its members remained in difficult financial condition, burdened with old debt. An employee of the British EIC noted in 1761 that "[m]ost of the

147 Cheong, *Hong Merchants*, pp. 81, 149, 158 n.23 and 254; Ch'en, *Insolvency*, pp. 183, 225 and 273; Morse, *Chronicles, Vol. V*, p. 73; Van Dyke, *Merchants of Canton and Macao*, p. 91. Van Dyke states that as of 1753—five years before Beau Khequa died—Beau Khequa, Sweetia, Suqua and son, and Tan Anqua were operating as a consortium and had advertised that they would be standing security for each other. The 1758 determination by the Nanhai and Panyu magistrates that only the Taihe hong merchant Sweetia would be liable for the deceased's debts, and for only half of that sum, indicates either that the consortium had ceased general operation by this date or that the mutual assumption of liability by its members was less sweeping when contracts were made than in the original advertisements or solicitations to contract.

148 Ch'en, *Insolvency*, p. 185.

149 Cheong, *Hong Merchants*, pp. 141, 149 and 254; Ch'en, *Insolvency*, p. 273.

150 Van Dyke, *Merchants of Canton and Macao*, p. 191.

merchants are considerably in our debt."[151] Some borrowed still more from foreigners, and at high interest, despite the stern prohibitions of the 1760 Regulations.[152] These debt problems received little official attention, except in 1762 and 1764 when the Hoppo suspended trade until guild debts were cleared, which of course did not really happen. Records that the Canton officials allowed inland tea merchants to contract directly with foreigners in 1764 for as much as 30% of that year's business, in breach of the Cohong monopoly, are a strong indication of instability (i.e., the licensed merchants lacked the capital to complete that year's tea contracts on their own).[153] Hong merchant debt to private Western creditors continued to grow and be ignored through the late 1770s, although many of the creditors were closely affiliated with European trading companies at Canton and should have understood the consequences.[154]

Just ten years after the organization of the Cohong of 1760, it was dissolved at the behest of Puankhequa I, its original proponent and leader. Puankhequa told the British EIC in 1768 that he would buy all of its cotton that season at a higher price than that set by the Cohong, as he had been unable to persuade his colleagues to raise the price to be paid by the guild.[155] In 1771, Puankhequa procured the formal dissolution of the body. The EIC advanced 100,000 taels ($138,889) to Puankhequa which he used to motivate Governor-General Li Shiyao to this purpose.[156] After dissolution, the right to serve as security merchant was now extended to all viable hong merchants, who would be assigned to vessels by seniority by the Hoppo.[157] While this ended the former priority rights of the capital (senior security) merchants, that priority meant little in

151 Cheong, *Hong Merchants*, pp. 228, 245 n.154, 256 (quotation) and 261–2.

152 Pritchard, "Crucial Years," p. 200; Pritchard, "Anglo-Chinese Relations," p. 143; Cheong, *Hong Merchants*, p. 257 (troubled condition of the various hongs during the 1760s); Van Dykc, *Canton Trade*, p. 20.

153 Van Dyke, *Canton Trade*, p. 20.

154 Cheong, *Hong Merchants*, pp. 228, 245 n.154, 256 and 261–2.

155 Morse, *Chronicles, Vol. v*, p. 142.

156 Ch'en, *Insolvency*, pp. 9–11 and 184–5; White, "Hong Merchants," pp. 53 and 58; Pritchard, "Crucial Years," p. 200; Cheong, *Hong Merchants*, pp. 110 and 165; Farmer, "James Flint," pp. 38–66, p. 41 and 42 ("Surely, Li Shih-yao and his father must have found some way to profit from the father's position on the Board of Revenue while the son was governor-general at Canton, and Li's fondness for that position was surely the result of its money-making potential. Often the English sources contain more information on such matters, as the bribe mentioned above or the rumor recounted below that the Canton people had spent 20,000 taels at Ningpo to influence trade policy. Chinese sources offer more numerous, but usually less lurid hints of what went on beneath the surface.").

157 Cheong, *Hong Merchants*, p. 95.

practice. Of the original six, most had died, failed or withdrawn from trading by 1771.[158] Although dissolution of the Cohong was hailed as a success by the British EIC, its historian Earl Pritchard instead records the 100,000 tael bribe as having accomplished a "disaster" for EIC interests. The dissolution of the Cohong of 1760 "broke the bargaining power of the Hongists, prices decreased, and the demands of the officials fell upon the merchants individually instead of collectively."[159] These destabilized market conditions led directly to the "Chinese debts" crisis of 1779–80, and spectacular hong merchant failures in its wake.[160]

The difficult post-Cohong decade of the 1770s was marked by several hong failures, which were brought before the local magistrates and resolved according to Chinese law. The hong merchant body had no liability for the debts of Sy Anqua (Seunqua II) whose Zhufeng hong was determined to be insolvent early in 1775, or for the debts of Coqua whose Guangshun hong failed in 1778. In both cases, assets were liquidated and applied first to the payment of arrears of customs duties due to the government, and then to the claims of foreign creditors. The business of the Zhufeng hong was determined to be viable. Governor-General Li Shiyao directed Sy Anqua (Seunqua II) to continue trading for the benefit of creditors and to pay 192,018 taels ($266,692) in allowed foreign claims over ten years without interest. The foreign loans were not confiscated, nor were the foreign lenders otherwise punished by the Chinese officials. Only one 10% installment was subsequently paid. When foreign creditors later complained of nonpayment the Canton authorities noted their procedural failure to either acknowledge or accept the payment plan, but expressed hope that

158 Of the six capital merchants of 1755 (Beau Khequa, Chai Suequa, Chetqua, Chai Hunqua, Sweetia and Puankhequa), Puankhequa I (Pan Zhencheng of the Tongwen Hong) stood unchallenged as chief merchant as of 1771. Cheong, *Hong Merchants*, pp. 86, 93 and 95. Beau Khequa (Li Guanghua of the Ziyuan hong) had died insolvent in 1758. Cheong, p. 254. The Taihe hong merchant Sweetia had died indebted in 1761. Cheong, pp. 141 and 254. The Yifeng hong merchant Chai Suequa had died in 1761 (Yokqua took over the firm but did not succeed to the right to secure ships). Cheong, pp. 84, 94, 141 and 254. The Guangshun hong merchant Chetqua died indebted on 13 March 1771 (the hong was liquidated in 1778 after the failure of his successor Coqua). Cheong, pp. 141–3, 254 and 261; Ch'en, *Insolvency*, p. 271; Pritchard, "Crucial Years," p. 202; Van Dyke, *Merchants of Canton and Macao*, pp. 97–8 and 128. The Chufeng hong merchant Chai Hunqua had withdrawn from trade in 1768, leaving his heavily indebted firm to fail in the hands of his successor Sy Anqua (Seunqua II) in 1775, the year Chai Hunqua died. Cheong, pp. 84–5, 94–5 and 260–2.

159 Pritchard, "Crucial Years," pp. 200 and 234.

160 Pritchard, "Crucial Years," p. 234; Cheong, *Hong Merchants*, p. 107.

when the young Cai Zhaofu (later Seunqua III) "grows up and gains money by his business, he shall pay his father's debts."[161] Net assets of the hong merchant Coqua after liquidation and payment of his customs duty debt stood at under 14,400 taels ($20,000), as against 1,028,239 taels ($1,428,110) in creditor claims. The EIC's 11,530.630 tael ($16,015) claim was a small part of this total. The hong merchants resisted EIC efforts to persuade them to assume Coqua's debts in proportion to their business with the Company, but agreed that the merchant who took up Coqua's EIC business might become liable for those debts. The hong merchant Munqua (Cai Shiwen of the Fengyuan hong) took on and satisfied Coqua's EIC debts over two years, contributing to the imminent failure of his own Fengyuan hong. As in the 1775 Sy Anqua case, the EIC and other foreign creditors failed to participate or assert claims in the 1778 proceedings on debts of Coqua's Guangshun hong. This was later found to constitute a waiver of their rights as creditors.[162]

A pivotal moment came in 1776–77, when the EIC pressed to collect another relatively small debt—11,725.75 taels ($16,286) owed by Wayqua (Ni Hongwen of the Fengjin hong). The Fengjin Hong was originally a *bengang* hong, but was licensed as an outer seas hong after the 1771 dissolution of the unified Cohong. The EIC's repeated attempts to collect this debt, starting in the spring of 1772, resulted in a late 1776 report from Governor Li Zhiying to the Board of Punishments in Beijing. The Governor advised that Wayqua had been deprived of his purchased *Jiansheng* title, and punished by beating.[163] The Governor saw the offense as simply involving bad debt,[164] but the Board disagreed. As the case involved foreigners, the charge it considered applicable was the more serious crime of "collaborating with foreigners and cheating them out of their money."[165] The Board recommended, and the Emperor agreed, that Wayqua should be beaten, and imprisoned, and given a year to pay his debt, failing

161 Ch'en, *Insolvency*, pp. 264–5 (quotation), 409 n.68 and 422 n.30; Cheong, *Hong Merchants*, pp. 85, 88, 257 and 260; Morse, *Chronicles, Vol. II*, p. 55.

162 Cheong, *Hong Merchants*, pp. 143, 172 and 259; Ch'en, *Insolvency*, pp. 226–7, 271–2 and 409 n.69; Van Dyke, *Merchants of Canton and Macao*, Plate 10.07 (between pp. 78–9) (communication to the VOC dated 18 April 1778, in Dutch, from Ingsia (Inksja), Chowqua (Tan Tsjoqua), Monqua (Munqua) and Tsjonqua, stating that although they had delivered a sealed letter to the Governor-General and Governor in Canton three days earlier on 15 April 1778, that letter had been returned to them unopened with the explanation that a report had already been sent to the Emperor, a month previously, concerning the matter).

163 Ch'en, *Insolvency*, pp. 186–8; Cheong, *Hong Merchants*, p. 257; Pritchard, "Crucial Years," p. 201.

164 Ch'en, *Insolvency*, p. 181.

165 Ch'en, *Insolvency*, pp. 188 and 182 n.6.

which he would be banished. In his 3 January 1777 approval edict, the Emperor dismissed Wayqua's commercial defenses to nonpayment. "Excessive borrowing is no way to cherish foreigners."[166] The Qianlong Emperor stressed the foreign relations importance of the matter, invoking precedents from the Han, Tang, Song and Ming Dynasties.[167] As foreigners were barred from presenting their grievances in Beijing, the Emperor told the Governor and the Governor-General that the duty therefore fell upon them to 'show benevolence.' The officials were ordered to be fairminded in cases involving foreigners, and not to show partiality to Chinese parties.[168] "If governing officers are petty, permitting local ruffians to insult people and never giving redress for complaints that are brought to them, can [foreigners] help but despise and laugh at such a governor or governor-general?"[169] The Emperor criticized Governor-General Li Shiyao for his negligence in the matter. Governor Li Zhiying was reprimanded by the Board of Punishments for his handling of the case.[170]

Wayqua was jailed and beaten in response to the Imperial edict. He died in prison at Canton on 30 June 1777, likely due to judicial beatings, before the banishment order was carried out. Relatives came forward with 6,000 taels ($8,333), leaving a 5,725.75 tael ($7,952) balance due to the British. Canton officials, from the provincial level down to the *xian* level, were ordered to pay the remainder out of their salaries. The officials recouped this sum from the hong merchant body.[171] This forceful resolution, albeit in a small matter, served to encourage private British "country traders" with large claims arising from high interest loans to hong merchants to come forward.[172]

---

166 Ch'en, *Insolvency*, p. 188; White, "Hong Merchants," p. 68.

167 This part of the text of the 3 January 1777 edict is quoted in Chapter Two. Ch'en, *Insolvency*, pp. 188–9; Cheong, *Hong Merchants*, p. 262; White, "Hong Merchants," pp. 68–9; Ng, "Ch'ing Management of the West," p. 146.

168 Ch'en, *Insolvency*, pp. 188–9; Cheong, *Hong Merchants*, p. 262; White, "Hong Merchants," pp. 68–9.

169 White, "Hong Merchants," p. 69.

170 White, "Hong Merchants," pp. 67–8.

171 Ch'en, *Insolvency*, p. 190; Cheong, *Hong Merchants*, p. 262; White, "Hong Merchants," p. 67; Pritchard, "Crucial Years," p. 201; Ng, "Ch'ing Management of the West," p. 144 ("If after one year, the sum could still not be cleared, then all the officials responsible for his case, namely, the viceroy, governor, the circuit intendant (ssu-tao), the prefect of the prefecture (chih-fu), magistrate of the county (chih-chou) and the magistrate of the district (chih-hsien) had to make up for the sum by deducting proportional amount from their salaries. These officials were further ordered to announce the emperor's edict to the foreigners so that they knew their money would be repaid and could go back home.").

172 Ch'en, *Insolvency*, pp. 195 and 200.

4 Debt Collection Under the Canton System

In the years after the 1759 failure of the Flint mission, the British EIC redirected its attention from improving trading conditions toward strengthening its bargaining position at Canton.[173] One of the tactics it employed was to use Chinese legal process to collect unpaid hong merchant debts, thereby seeking redress for its "trouble[s], great or small." At least in this respect, the EIC and other foreign traders accepted Hoppo Yu's invitation and the text of the 1760 Regulations, which invited bringing infractions of the new rules to the "Knowledge of the Mandarines."[174]

The procedures for debt collection that were made available to Western creditors differed from the normal debt collection process available to Chinese citizens. In many ways it was a special form of justice, significantly better than most Chinese could obtain from their own officials. To the extent that they were preferred, foreign creditors either did not realize they were getting a better deal, or tended to view their preferential treatment as justified given other inconveniences of the Canton System. The foreigners certainly disliked the Chinese law that was enforced through this process. While harsh penalties for unpaid foreign debt tended to operate in their favor, Chinese rules reduced the collectability of foreign debt by requiring creditor participation in the debt process (or claims were considered to have been waived) and barring the collection of interest in excess of the principal amount of a claim (*yi ben yi li*). Twenty years after promulgation of the 1760 Regulations, as a result of the "Chinese debts" crisis of 1780, foreigners were given the further benefit of a collective guaranty of the payment of hong debt, enforced by the state against the entire hong merchant body.

---

173 Pritchard, "Crucial Years," p. 132.

174 Morse, *Chronicles, Vol. V*, pp. 95 ("If there be any who abuse the Credit given them, and are Guilty of Rogueries, and it should come to the Knowledge of the Mandarines, they shall be severely Judged according to the laws of the Country, and punished without any Grace.") and 92 (assertion by the Hoppo that the Cohong of 1760 had been "designed to make the Merchants jointly answerable for every trouble, great or small, that the Europeans might occasion."); Pritchard, "Crucial Years," p. 211 (EIC "policy of appealing to the officials when the merchants could not meet their debts"); Liu, "Dutch India Company," p. 99 (in a 22 August 1760 communication to the Dutch from the Governor-General, Governor and Hoppo, the officials said "you should realize without entertaining a single shred of doubt that everything had been done for your own benefit; if the merchants do not behave magnanimously under the present conditions, we shall punish them severely and our unfailing scrutiny will certainly make their deeds known to us in due time [for steps to be taken].").

In imperial China, debt might be collected either through public process, entered through the doors of the magistrate's *yamen*, or through private process, which took the form of mediation or other procedures administered by guilds or local village or family groups.[175] Contracts were in frequent use,[176] business disputes were common, and large amounts of private litigation occupied the time of Qing magistrates.[177]

The sources of law varied. A considerable body of customary law or guild or kinship rules existed which was applied in private process.[178] The law that was applied in public cases included the Qing statutes, substatutes, reports of decided cases, and also imperial edicts.[179] The Qing statutes, notably the Qing Code (*da qing lu li*), were organized according to the departments of government and, as such, reflected the perspective of the Emperor.[180] Statutes (the *lu*) might be applied if they addressed the situation. Substatutes (the *li*), which

175 Jerome Alan Cohen, "Chinese Mediation on the Eve of Modernization," California Law Review, Vol. 54, pp. 1201–26 (1966), pp. 1216–22 and 1210–1 (private mediation sometimes occurred as part of or in tandem with public judicial process); William C. Kirby, "China Unincorporated: Company Law and Business Enterprise in Twentieth-Century China," Journal of Asian Studies, Vol. 54, pp. 43–63 (1995), p. 45.

176 Madeleine Zelin, "A Critique of Rights of Property in Prewar China," pp. 17–36 in Madeleine Zelin, Jonathan K. Ocko and Robert Gardella, eds., *Contract and Property in Early Modern China* (Stanford: Stanford Univ. Press, 2004), pp. 17–8 ("county magistrates everywhere were innundated with litigation of an economic nature.") and 23–4 ("Contracts were commonly used in an enormous variety of transactions, including household division (fenjia), betrothal, adoption and uxorilocal marriage, purchase of real and personal property, conditional sale, purchase of people, loan agreements, promissory notes and bills of exchange, partnership agreements, employment agreements, rotating credit agreements, contracts to transport goods (especially interesting because they deal with indemnification and insurance), pooling of resources for irrigation, social welfare, group investment, and the creation of lineage trusts, pawn, and contracts to agree to accept the decision of a mediator."); Edwards, "Old Canton System," pp. 369–71.

177 Jones, *Great Qing Code*, p. 6; Zelin, "Critique of Rights of Property," p. 27 (a growing body of scholarship "indicates that people in late imperial and early modern China were highly litigious.").

178 Van der Sprenkel, *Legal Institutions in Manchu China*, pp. 80–96.

179 Jones, *Great Qing Code*, p. 2; Cushman, *Fields from the Sea*, pp. 118–9 ("Imperial edicts, which became law until countermanded, provided the emperor and bureaucracy with a flexible medium for approaching contemporary problems. An edict was authoritative only as long as it was not rescinded by succeeding edicts, unless it was incorporated into the Ch'ing Code itself. Because edicts reflected imperial policy at one particular time, they should not be cited to document policy from another period until the sources have been thoroughly searched for any later edicts that may have nullified the earlier.").

180 Jones, *Great Qing Code*, p. 6.

were detailed rules based on prior interpretations or decisions, were instead to be applied if they more precisely addressed the problem.[181] In all sections of the Qing Code "the arrangement is consistent: a *lu* or general law is stated and then followed by *li*, specific conditions for its application or for exemption from its provisions, and then by commentary to explain both."[182] Enforcement of the Qing Code was by specified punishments. This has caused it to be called a penal code, which is an inadequate explanation of its function, for many civil elements are included.[183] As explained by Qing Code scholar William C. Jones,

> The aim [of the drafters of the Qing Code] seems to have been to create a sort of giant grid on which any legally relevant act, such as eating another's melons, including all the ways of varying the basic fact pattern, such as the relationship between trespasser and owner, could be located. When this was done properly, the precise punishment required would be discovered. If no punishment could be found, the act was not legally significant. This is similar to a finding in Western law that no action lay.[184]

The location of some statutes within the Qing Code can seem a little strange. The relatively few Articles devoted to commerce and industry are in the section of the Qing Code devoted to the Board of Revenue (*Hu Bu*). Sybille van der Sprenkel speaks of this arrangement as being "rather as if our commercial law were an appendix to the Inland Revenue Department regulations."[185] The Code stood nonetheless as an integrated whole, reflecting the attitude of the Emperor in his administration of the officials who governed China. It thus was, per William C. Jones,

> in part a collection of rules that deal with particular fact situations, sometimes in great detail. Nevertheless, it is not just a compendium of rules. The rules themselves have been refined and harmonized to a considerable degree. General principles have been factored out. It is, in other

181 Jones, *Great Qing Code*, p. 3 (Jones suggests the term "codified precedent" as a better translation of *li*, which has traditionally been translated as "substatute").

182 Van der Sprenkel, *Legal Institutions in Manchu China*, pp. 59 and 131 (Appendix 1) (layout of a specimen page of the Qing Code with an explanation of its arrangement and content).

183 Jones, *Great Qing Code*, p. 7.

184 Jones, *Great Qing Code*, p. 12. See Jones, *Great Qing Code*, Art. 99, p. 121 (provision penalizing eating melons or other fruit without authorization).

185 Kirby, "China Unincorporated," p. 44; Van der Sprenkel, *Legal Institutions in Manchu China*, p. 89.

> words, a true code, and as such can be taken to represent the considered view of some of China's leading jurists as to ways to think about law, to think about what law is. It was to show the way to analyze legal problems and to provide methods for applying legal rules to them.[186]

Local magistrates were vested by the Code with authority in debt disputes. The Code specified certain debt rules and penalties, and it regulated markets in a limited way.[187] At least officially, public judicial process under the Qing Code preempted local and informal dispute resolution.[188] In particular, it provided for severe punishment of those creditors who did not use the public process but instead attempted "self help" debt collection by using (unauthorized) violence to take property from debtors.[189]

---

186 Jones, *Great Qing Code*, p. 3. See Jones, *Great Qing Code*, Art. 44, p. 74 (direction to decide cases by analogy from the closest provision if no statute or rule precisely addressed the matter).

187 Zelin, "Critique of Rights of Property," pp. 21–2 ("Debt is one of the few areas of civil law in which the Code specifically assigns responsibility for adjudication to the state.").

188 Cohen, "Chinese Mediation," p. 1209 ("It is true that there was tucked away in the Official Commentary to the Ch'ing Code (ta ch'ing lu li) a provision inherited from the Ming dynasty (1368–1644) that authorized certain rural leaders and elders (li-lao) to reconcile the parties to disputes over 'petty matters' such as those relating to domestic relations and real property. But all other disputes were beyond the legal competence of the local leaders and elders and were required to be brought to the county (hsien or chou) magistrate, who served as both trial judge of general jurisdiction and the national government's principal administrative officer in the area.... And, regardless of the nature of the dispute, once it had been brought to the attention of the magistrate, the Code precluded the local leaders from disposing of it and prohibited private settlement of any kind.").

189 "If a powerful or influential person (in regard to those who are obligated to him because of a breach of contract) does not prosecute [a matter] before the official having jurisdiction, but, enforcing his private obligation, takes the domestic animals and property of another away by force, he will receive 80 strokes of the heavy bamboo. (If he does not take excess interest, permit [the obligor] to redeem [the items taken] but [the obligee] is not to be levied on [for them].) If when the price of the (domestic animals and property that have been taken away by force) is calculated, it exceeds principal and interest, calculate the excess, (and if the punishment [for that amount as illegally obtained property] is greater than 80 strokes of the heavy bamboo), sentence for illegally obtained property [Art. 345] (The punishment is limited to 100 strokes of the heavy bamboo and penal servitude of three years.) As (for the excessive) quantity, levy and return to (the obligor)." Qing Code, Art. 149, § 3. Jones, *Great Qing Code*, p. 162 (italics in the original). See also Staunton, *Ta Tsing Leu Lee*, § 149, p. 160. As translator Jones explains, "the interlinear commentary [included in the Qing Code] is indicated by italics within parentheses. Square brackets

Public judicial process was initiated by accusation, which was made in the form of a written petition presented at the magistrate's *yamen* (office compound). The magistrate was required to investigate the facts, question the witnesses, and render a preliminary decision in the dispute.[190] He had to ascertain

> (a) whether the defendant was in fact guilty of the action of which he stood accused (and, if so, a confession of guilt had to be extracted from him); (b) which section of the [*Da Qing Lü Li*] covered this misdeed; and (c) circumstances which were relevant to determining his degree of criminality. He then had to decide according to (b) and (c) what punishment was appropriate.[191]

Much of this work was performed by unpaid or underpaid *yamen* clerks, who were notorious throughout China for exacting heavy fees from those involved at every stage of the proceedings.[192] Beating to obtain a confession was permitted, but only during trial.[193] "At the trial the parties and witnesses were flanked by guards wielding bamboo staves and other implements and were required to remain in a kneeling position on the ground before the magistrate's high bench."[194]

> The proceeding could be quite dreadful for everyone, including the complainant. All persons concerned, including witnesses, were usually imprisoned under appalling conditions pending final conclusion of the matter. The term which when translated is the innocent word 'interrogate' often involved torture. Even the lightest punishment—beating—could be crippling or even fatal.[195]

Even conscientious and even-tempered magistrates administered a law that was largely unknown to the populace governed by it. This was expressed in the saying, "Of ten reasons by which a magistrate may decide a case, nine are

([ ]) are used to enclose explanatory material by the translators that is not contained in the Chinese text of the Code and the interlinear commentary." Jones, p. 29.

190 Jones, *Great Qing Code*, pp. 9–11.

191 Van der Sprenkel, *Legal Institutions in Manchu China*, pp. 66–9.

192 Van der Sprenkel, *Legal Institutions in Manchu China*, pp. 75 and 138; Cohen, "Chinese Mediation," p. 1213.

193 Van der Sprenkel, *Legal Institutions in Manchu China*, pp. 66–9.

194 Cohen, "Chinese Mediation," p. 1214.

195 Jones, *Great Qing Code*, p. 11.

unknown to the public."[196] The preliminary decision of the magistrate, once rendered, required higher review and approval before it could become final.[197] If the outcome was a finding that the original accusation was false, then the punishment for the crime that was charged was to be imposed on the accuser under the principle of *fan zuo*. George Staunton, writing in 1810, viewed this sanction as similar to Western penalties for willful perjury. Sybille van der Sprenkel agrees that it at least appeared to act in the interests of justice, but submits that *fan zuo* "probably in fact worked against it, i.e., as a deterrent to denouncing the influential but no protection to those who needed it."[198] As she explains,

> The unavoidable consequence of a legal case once started was punishment for at least one person. It could end in punishment for the accused, if judged guilty; if he were not, punishment would be assigned to the unjustified accuser; it was also likely that witnesses would, during the course of the proceedings, incur punishment, while the magistrate was exposed throughout the case to the risk of reprimand or degradation for making a mistake in procedure or in application of the code.[199]

From a Confucian standpoint, simply being involved in a lawsuit, even with a legitimate grievance, was somewhat disreputable, as a disruption of natural harmony was involved.[200] The harsh treatment of participants in legal process was thus somewhat intentional, an attempt by the system itself to cause the maintenance of the condition of (at least apparent) harmony in society that was the Confucian ideal. Confucius himself is said to have stated: "In hearing cases I am as good as any one else, but what is really needed is to bring about that there are no cases."[201] The Kangxi Emperor (reigned 1661–1722) once challenged the very ideal of justice in litigation. He had expressed concern that:

> law-suits would increase to a frightful amount, if people were not afraid of the tribunals, and if they felt confident of always finding in them ready

196 Cohen, "Chinese Mediation," p. 1212; Van der Sprenkel, *Legal Institutions in Manchu China*, p. 135.

197 Jones, *Great Qing Code*, p. 11.

198 Van der Sprenkel, *Legal Institutions in Manchu China*, p. 67 n. 1; Jones, *Great Qing Code*, Art. 336, pp. 317–21; Staunton, *Ta Tsing Leu Lee*, § 336, pp. 364–71.

199 Van der Sprenkel, *Legal Institutions in Manchu China*, p. 69; Jones, *Great Qing Code*, p. 10.

200 Cohen, "Chinese Mediation," pp. 1206–7.

201 Jones, *Great Qing Code*, p. 28.

> and perfect justice. As a man is apt to delude himself concerning his own interests, contests would then be interminable, and the half of the Empire would not suffice to settle the lawsuits of the other half. I desire therefore that those who have recourse to the tribunals should be treated without any pity, and in such a manner that they shall be disgusted with law, and tremble to appear before a magistrate. In this manner the evil will be cut up by the roots; the good citizens, who may have difficulties among themselves, will settle them like brothers, by referring to the arbitration of some old man, or the mayor of the commune. As for those who are troublesome, obstinate, and quarrelsome, let them be ruined by the law-courts—that is the justice that is due to them.[202]

Such was justice for the average subject of the Emperor of China.[203] The lack of any reliable or convenient system for collecting debt certainly discouraged risk taking in the form of the general extension of credit, as discussed above. When a hong merchant was owed money by a foreign debtor, he had little recourse under Chinese law, and the foreigner was usually overseas. The hong merchant Conseequa thus ended up mired in disastrous litigation trying to collect from debtors in the United States, as discussed below. In an 1814 petition in which he sought assistance from the American President, Conseequa told James Madison that "[w]hen such Debtors come to, or reside in, China, he cannot claim the aid of the Laws of the Imperial Dynasty in his behalf. They

202 Van der Sprenkel, *Legal Institutions in Manchu China*, pp. 76–7; Evariste Régis Huc, *A Journey Through the Chinese Empire*, Vol. 1 (New York: Harper & Brothers, 1856), pp. 124–5.

203 The elites fared better. The Qing Code specifies eight classes of persons whose cases are to receive special consideration, with interrogation (i.e., beating) prohibited except after disclosure to and approval from the Emperor. Jones, *Great Qing Code*, Art. 3 and 4, pp. 36–38. Sybille van der Sprenkel cites a passage from the famous early Qing novel, The Dream of the Red Chamber, as evidence of the favored treatment of local elite families. In the novel, "a magistrate newly arrived at his post (and particularly conscientious since he has just been reinstated after losing a previous appointment on account of his unsatisfactory conduct) is full of zeal to arrest a murderer, until he discovers that the suspect is related to one of the families which, his staff inform him, should on no account be implicated. Every yamen, it is explained, has its 'hu kuan fu,' magistrate's protective charm, that is, a list of families who have important connections with government circles (or at least who have relatives who hold important posts elsewhere) against whom the magistrate would proceed at his peril." Van der Sprenkel, *Legal Institutions in Manchu China*, p. 73.

prohibit such confidences, as he has placed in Subjects of the United States."[204] Collection even by hong merchants from hong debtors was difficult. So it was that in 1767, when Puankhequa I was asked by the British EIC and agreed to pay off a debt due to the EIC from his guild colleague Conqua (Chen Shiji of the Yuanlai Hong), Puankhequa requested (and was granted) the accommodation of having the bond (promissory note) from Conqua for the amount due plus interest made payable to Mr. Robert Gordon, surgeon to the EIC.[205] While the EIC's 1780 discussion of the Conqua note says that it arose in a "peculiar circumstance," notes payable to Europeans as designees for Chinese were drafted occasionally, and by this stratagem the sophisticated Puankhequa created an obligation that could be enforced—by its European holder—against Puankhequa's Chinese debtor.

Normal Chinese procedures were modified when Western creditors sought to collect debts from hong merchants. They were not "treated without any pity," but rather had their complaints heard and acted upon. Westerners who used the Chinese public debt collection process were not penalized for presenting their petitions to the wrong official in the local hierarchy,[206] were not beaten by *yamen* staff, were not forced to kneel when present at hearings, and were not penalized if their accusations were later determined to be untrue. They were required to present an accusation, a written petition that was usually submitted to the Hoppo. In most cases, the Hoppo referred the dispute to the local magistrate with appropriate jurisdiction for investigation and initial decision. This was usually the magistrate of the *Nanhai xian* (Canton). The initial questions considered by the magistrate—whether the foreign petitioner had extended credit and whether the hong merchant debtor had failed to pay the debt—were usually not a point of contention, though the true amount of unpaid debt was often disputed. After investigation, creditors and the hong debtor presented their cases at a trial before the magistrate. Process in the investigatory and trial stages of proceedings on foreign debt complaints seems to have been somewhat *ad hoc*, simpler in smaller cases and more elaborate in

---

204 Petition of Conseequa, a Hong Merchant of the City of Canton in China, 10 February 1814 (contemporary English language translation). Despatches of United States Consuls at Canton, Volume I, National Archives, Washington, D.C.; published in File Microcopies of Records in the National Archives, No. 101, Roll 1; Tyler Dennett, *Americans in Eastern Asia* (New York: The MacMillan Co., 1922), p. 86; Fu, *Documentary Chronicle*, pp. 391–3 (modern translation).

205 Van Dyke, *Merchants of Canton and Macao*, p. 118.

206 Jones, *Great Qing Code*, Art. 332, p. 314.

larger or more complicated cases.[207] The debt complaints of Western creditors were received and adjudicated according to an established process which in many ways is comparable to the debt collection process that then existed in their home nations.[208]

Chinese creditors typically came in as participants in foreign debt cases and joined foreign creditors in demanding payment. The domestic creditors tended to have better information about the activities of the indebted firm than did the foreign petitioner. The local creditors were also in a better position to press the *yamen* clerks to forcefully investigate debtors, their relatives, or employees or other witnesses who might assist in the recovery of assets or funds. Surviving records show that it was the domestic creditors who generally pressed the *yamen* staff for the physical beating of debtors to force them to pay debts. The records do not indicate that this tactic produced appreciable added value for creditors except as a means of sometimes reaching into the pockets of horrified relatives and friends of the beaten debtors.

A critical initial determination by the magistrate concerned the solvency of the debtor, i.e., whether there was any reasonable prospect that the hong would be able to pay its debts within a reasonable time. Where the business of the indebted hong was determined to be viable, it was invariably ordered to continue trading to generate a dividend for creditors. Business goodwill or reorganization value was thus realized for creditors. Where the hong was not viable, its assets were liquidated and used to pay creditors in order of priority: customs debt first, paid to the government, and unsecured debt second, paid to foreign and domestic creditors.[209] The magistrate also directed punishment of the debtor, meted out according to the type of offense that was found to have occurred, and the terms of repayment to creditors. Under the regime of collective responsibility, starting in 1780, the magistrate first tried to get foreign creditors and the surviving hong guarantors to reach an agreement on repayment terms. If agreement could not be reached, the magistrate imposed a repayment schedule, a series of equal annual payments by the hong merchant body,

207 As a detail, it is unclear whether the foreign creditors' initial petition stood as their "claim" against the debtor, or whether an opportunity for amendment was provided when other creditors were allowed to submit claims after a debtor was determined to be insolvent.

208 See, for example, Bruce Mann, *Republic of Debtors: Bankruptcy in the Age of American Independence* (Cambridge: Harvard Univ. Press, 2002); Edward J. Balleisen, *Navigating Failure: Bankruptcy and Commercial Society in Antebellum America* (Chapel Hill: Univ. of North Carolina Press, 2001).

209 See generally Van Dyke, *Merchants of Canton and Macao*, p. 17. There does not seem to have been a firm rule as to the priority of distribution of the proceeds of liquidation of the assets of debtors as between foreign and Chinese creditors.

without interest. These various orders were assembled as a preliminary decision by the magistrate, which was submitted to his superiors for review and approval (or modification). Records of the hong merchant debt cases invariably reflect long periods of time during which the debtor and creditors alike waited for final judgment from Beijing.

In contemporary records, the Chinese debt process decribed above is sometimes spoken of as involving the "bankruptcy" of the hong debtor. Historians have picked up this usage. The failed hongs were certainly "bankrupt" in the sense that they could not pay their debts. The term "bankruptcy," however, implies an established public legal process for the permanent resolution of debts that brings in and binds the debtor and all affected creditors.[210] While the Chinese process involved domestic creditors in debt cases filed by foreign creditors, it served no such public end. It was not a bankruptcy system.[211] This study accordingly avoids the use of the term "bankruptcy," and uses the terms "insolvency" or "debt" by preference.

To foreign creditors, the most important part of the magistrate's decision was the allowance or disallowance of claims. In these often controversial rulings, the magistrate applied settled Chinese laws concerning debt. The most important of these was the rule that recoverable interest could not exceed the principal amount of the loan (*yi ben yi li*).[212] A joint communication from the Governor and Hoppo, dated 29 February 1780, "reminded" foreigners of this provision of Chinese law.[213] (On at least two other occasions, in 1801 and in 1821, Canton officials provided instruction in Chinese law by having parts of the Qing Code translated into English and delivered to the local head of the British EIC.)[214] Many foreign claims were slashed under the rule of *yi ben yi li*.

210 See, for example, United States Constitution, Art. 1, § 8, cl. 4, which authorizes Congress to enact "uniform Laws on the subject of Bankruptcies throughout the United States."

211 Lind, *Chapter of the Chinese Penal Code*, p. 19 ("A doctrine of contracts, laws on bankruptcy etc. are totally unknown.").

212 Jones, *Great Qing Code*, Art. 149, § 1, p. 161; Staunton, *Ta Tsing Leu Lee*, § 149, p. 158; Cheong, *Hong Merchants*, p. 256; Jing Junjian, "Legislation Related to the Civil Economy in the Qing Dynasty," pp. 42–84 in Kathryn Bernhardt and Philip C. C. Huang, eds., *Civil Law in Qing and Republican China* (Stanford: Stanford University Press, 1994), pp. 72 (Qing Code Art. 149) and 77 (origins of the statutory rule of *yi ben yi li*).

213 Morse, *Chronicles, Vol. II*, pp. 53–54; Pritchard, "Crucial Years," p. 209 (the creditors claimed ignorance of this rule of law).

214 Edwards, "Ch'ing Legal Jurisdiction Over Foreigners," p. 244 (in 1821, translations of the statutes on jurisdiction over aliens (*hua wairen*), homicide in a fight (*dou'ou sharen*) and policemen killing in self defense an offender resisting arrest (*gesha*) were delivered "for the instruction of the barbarian.").

Full analysis of the practical consequences of the rule is beyond the scope of this study, but a few may be noted. First, the rational creditor who believed that the debtor (or guarantor) had the ability to pay a given debt had good reason under this rule to cooperate with the debtor during the period that interest was accruing but did not yet equal the amount of principal. This creditor would expect the loan to be profitable, i.e., to receive full return at the agreed interest rate, during this time period. Second, at some point as the interest total neared the Qing statutory cap this expectation of profit ceased. The prospect of loss now beckoned, if the debtor defaulted and debt collection by Chinese public process was required. This would be a real loss to the extent the creditor had other profitable uses for its funds. Third, when the amount of interest exceeded the amount of principal (the statutory cap), any hope of legal profit in return for cooperation with the debtor ceased. An economic incentive for aggressive collection efforts thus existed during the time period when the amount of accrued interest approached the principal amount cap above which there could be no recovery by legal process—in order to liquidate and collect the loan in full. If assets were believed to exist in an amount sufficient to pay the debt in full, whether held by the debtor or by the hong merchant body as his collective guarantors, there was no incentive for further cooperation. Finally, the rule tended to promote extralegal or secret collection activity from that point forward. The creditor's only remaining hope to collect further interest would be to collect it from the debtor through private action kept away from the magistrate and out of the knowledge of other potentially affected creditors.

In criminal matters involving foreigners, by contrast, the Qing did not assert criminal jurisdiction, except in cases in which a Chinese citizen was killed. Otherwise, as R. Randle Edwards succinctly explains, "the foreign community was held responsible for maintaining order in its ranks and the Chinese government was not particular about how it was accomplished."[215] Where a foreigner was the victim of a crime committed by a Chinese citizen, the Qing authorities typically responded quickly and severely.[216]

When a Qing official was presented with a foreign petition complaining of unpaid debt owed by a Chinese citizen, the crucial question he had to address was identification of the offense to be charged under the Qing Code. When Beijing identified errors in the decisions made in hong debt cases, it was apt to be that the wrong offense had been charged, resulting in the wrong punishment. Such mistakes, and the officials who made them, were subject to

215 Edwards, "Ch'ing Legal Jurisdiction Over Foreigners," pp. 230, 243 and 259.

216 Edwards, "Ch'ing Legal Jurisdiction Over Foreigners," pp. 255–9

PLATE 9 *The trial of the Neptune sailors. Painting by an unknown Chinese artist, ca. 1807. (Collection of Anthony and Susan Hardy. Photograph by courtesy of the Martyn Gregory Gallery, London.)*

correction and harsh criticism. These were crucial matters, for, as William C. Jones notes, "determination of the proper punishment was the fundamental task of the law" under the Qing Code.[217] Precisely such an imperial rebuke was issued in 1777—three years before imposition of collective liability among the hong merchants for the foreign debts of failed guild members—in the relatively minor 11,725.75 tael ($16,286) debt case of Wayqua (the Fengjin hong). Wayqua had been ordered punished for his default by beating, by being ordered to repay the debt, and by being stripped of his purchased *Jiansheng* title. Revocation of purchased official title was required when its holder was sued for debt, and Qing practice required that the disgrace be reported to the Board of Punishments in Beijing. Governor Li Zhiying accordingly reported the matter and its disposition, in which he had applied the normal bad debt penalties.[218] The Board, and the Emperor, strongly disagreed with his handling of the matter. In their view, the appropriate punishments were beating, imprisonment for one year, and banishment to Ili (in Xinjiang) if the debt had not been paid within that year. As the case involved foreigners, the applicable charge

217 Jones, *Great Qing Code*, p. 12.

218 Ch'en, *Insolvency*, pp. 181, 188 and 191.

was the crime of "collaborating with foreigners and cheating them out of their money"[219]—the same substatute the 1760 Regulations specified for punishment of violations of the foreign loan ban. In his 3 January 1777 edict, quoted above (and at length in Chapter 2), the Qianlong Emperor sharply rebuked the officials involved for their failure to apply the correct offense and penalties. The Emperor singled out the negligence of Governor-General Li Shiyao, "a remarkable performance... for one who had always been so diligent in the handling of barbarian affairs."[220] The Emperor emphasized the foreign relations and defense implications of the mistreatment of maritime traders to whom Chinese were indebted. The *Wokou* raids of the late Ming Dynasty, and their perceived relation to dynastic decline, stood as a living instruction to the Qing rulers of China.

The charging tension seen in the Wayqua matter haunted hong merchant debt cases through the years of the Canton System. The applicable punishments were quite different, depending on whether the matter was seen as one of common bad debt, or as involving cheating foreigners. The nature of the latter offense, as Joanna Waley-Cohen has observed, "bordered, at least, on political territory."[221] The choice was stark:

> Common bad debt. Such cases were prosecuted under the authority of Articles 24 and 345 of the Qing Code (concerning illegally obtained property) (*zang*), which were applied in debt cases by analogy.[222] Punishment in common bad debt cases included: a restitution order, beating, imprisonment for a half year (and/or being forced to wear the neck yoke, also called the cangue), with the possibility of release after the half year period if the debtor satisfied the magistrate that he truly lacked the

219 Ch'en, *Insolvency*, pp. 188 and 182 n.6.

220 White, "Hong Merchants," p. 68.

221 Waley-Cohen, *Exile in Mid-Qing China*, p. 87 ("The law under which they [the hong merchants] were sentenced penalized commercial relations with foreigners that risked inspiring unruliness and thus potentially endangering the state; after 1760 this law was extended to apply specifically to Hong merchants indebted to foreigners.").

222 Ch'en, *Insolvency*, pp. 181 (*zang*) (loot or illicitly acquired property) and 188; Jones, *Great Qing Code*, Arts. 24 and 345, pp. 54–56 and 330–32; Pengsheng Chiu, "Refining Legal Reasoning from Precedents: Economic Crimes and Rhetoric in Ming-Qing Casebooks" (paper prepared for Annual Meeting of the Association for Asian Studies, New York City, 2003), p. 23, see: "http://idv.sinica.edu.tw/pengshan/OnEcoLegalReasoningdraft.pdf" (accessed 3 June 2012).

ability to pay the debt.[223] As noted below, debtors in common debt cases (such as Wayqua) were also stripped of their purchased official titles, but that disgrace occurred as a matter of administrative practice, not as a punishment for violation of the Qing Code.

Cheating foreigners. The term "collaborating with foreigners and cheating them out of their money" (*jiaojie waiguo kuangbian caiwu*) is the short title of the *li* (substatute) that was applied in most of the hong merchant debt cases. It is found in the part of the Qing Code devoted to the Board of War, organized as the first substatute under *lu* (statute), Art. 224, entitled "Interrogating Spies" (*panjie jianxi*).[224] There is no standard translation of the title of this substatute, which has been rendered in variant ways,[225] such as the "law by which we punish criminals who communicate with a foreign country, borrow money or hold their goods or money without payment,"[226] or the law "which punishes criminals who plot with a foreign country, borrow money or hold their goods or money without payment."[227] The punishment directed for violation of this substatute included: a restitution order, beating, imprisonment for a year,

223 Ch'en, *Insolvency*, p. 181 (in 1837, Governor-General Deng Tingzhen described the law governing *zang* (loot or illegally obtained property) as follows: "According to the established substatute of the Celestial Empire, for the loot that should be restored to its original owner, [the offender in question] should be put in jail for the period of half a year and pressed for the restoration. If [at the expiration of that said period] it is vindicated that [the offender is] really in want of means to complete the whole, the press for recovery should cease. In the meantime, orders should be given [to the offender] to procure an affidavit [to that effect] and to file a petition for the exemption [of the remainder].").

224 Ch'en, *Insolvency*, pp. 188 and 182 n.6; Edwards, "Old Canton System," p. 374 n.61; Jones, *Great Qing Code*, Art. 224, pp. 215–6 (substatute not reproduced); Staunton, *Ta Tsing Leu Lee*, § 224, pp. 237–8 (substatute not reproduced).

225 Such as, "the law governing intercourse with foreign nations and borrowing with intent to swindle, . . ." White, "Hong Merchants," p. 63 (quoting the 1760 Regulations as directing the punishment of violations per the substatute).

226 1760 Regulations, Rule No. 3, Appendix 1 to this study (modern translation) ("Hereafter, if anyone violates the prohibition and borrows money from the foreigners and engages in intrigue with them, he should be punished according to the law by which we punish criminals who communicate with a foreign country, borrow money or hold their goods or money without payment.") (Fu, *Documentary Chronicle*, p. 225) (quoting the 1760 Regulations as directing the punishment of violations per the substatute).

227 Ng, "Ch'ing Management of the West," p. 141 ("Hereafter, people who violate the prohibition and borrow money from the foreigners and conspire with them would be punished according to the law which punishes criminals who plot with a foreign country, borrow

> and banishment to Ili if the debt had not been paid within that year.[228] Banishment to Xinjiang, itself, was an extraordinary penalty under Qing law—ranking second only to execution.[229]

Some of the Canton officials believed that the penalties that were applied in common bad debt cases were proper in hong merchant debt cases as well. This was true in the Wayqua case in 1776, in the Hingtae case in 1837,[230] and probably on other occasions. Leniency tended to favor domestic economic interests. Yet the 1760 Regulations and the edict in the Wayqua case, both directly issued by the Emperor, mandated the harsh punishments of a substatute that at least nominally sought to protect foreigners as a special class (penalizing "collaborating with foreigners and cheating them out of their money"). The true objective of this "protection," however, was to prevent Chinese subjects from becoming so beholden to foreigners that they would work to advance foreign interests. In a memorial sent to the Emperor at the time of adoption of the 1760 Regulations, Li Shiyao expressed concern that indebted hong merchants tended "to be very toadying and obsequious [to foreigners] so as to invite their favour."[231] An 1815 joint memorial to the throne from the Governor-General, Governor and Hoppo expressed concern about the economic consequences of the control foreign lenders achieved over "treacherous" Chinese subjects:

> As the people of Kwangtung rush towards profits like ducks, the first thing to do is to scrutinise the treacherous people of China.... However, now, there are ten hong merchants but only three or four are really affluent. The rest, though they are guaranteed by their colleagues, are not rich but simply hold the position as hong merchants. After they have assumed their positions, as they are incompetent in doing business, they fall into debts to the barbarians inevitably. As they owe the barbarians money, they have to buy goods on credit from merchants in other provinces in order to clear the debts owed to the barbarians. Debts accumulate and become too large an amount to be returned. Consequently, they are

---

money or hold their goods or money without payment.") (quoting the 1760 Regulations as directing the punishment of violations per the substatute).

228 Ch'en, *Insolvency*, p. 188; White, "Hong Merchants," p. 63 ("the law governing intercourse with foreign nations and borrowing with intent to swindle, the punishment for which was exile.").

229 Waley-Cohen, *Exile in Mid-Qing China*, pp. 17 and 56.

230 Ch'en, *Insolvency*, pp. 181–2.

231 Ng, "Ch'ing Management of the West," p. 140.

> controlled by the barbarian merchants. The fixing of the price of goods will as a result be unfair and the merchants from the other provinces will suffer in the process. The current rule is that when foreign ships are leaving, they will receive the chop from the customs superintendent's office which will receive a note on which is written "no debt between each other". But this has become a formality and cannot be trusted any more.[232]

Maintaining domestic public order was the true objective of the protection of foreigners provided in the "cheating foreigners" substatute.[233]

Many Chinese hong merchant debtors were punished in accordance with the "cheating foreigners" substatute during the period 1777 through 1842. Although the substatute specified only one (1) set of punishments, the indebted hong merchants had actually committed two (2) distinct offenses:

> being indebted to foreigners in violation of the substatute (the rule of the Wayqua case); and
> violating the loan ban imposed by the 1760 Regulations.

Each of these offenses specified that violations would be punished as provided in the "cheating foreigners" substatute. In cases in which offenders were Chinese, this was easily accomplished. So it is that Wayqua in 1777,[234] Yngshaw and Kewshaw in 1780,[235] Eequa in 1791,[236] Wyequa in 1796,[237] Fonqua in 1809,[238] Gnewqua II, Ponqua and Ashing in 1811,[239] Pacqua in 1828,[240] and Manhop II in 1828,[241] were all severely punished and ordered banished to Ili. Little is known of the fate of the hong merchants in Xinjiang except for a report that was prepared for the Qianlong Emperor in 1795. The Emperor had asked about the condition of these exiles. The local officials in Ili reported that the former hong

232 Ng, "Ch'ing Management of the West," pp. 170–1.

233 Ng, "Ch'ing Management of the West," pp. 140–1.

234 Ch'en, *Insolvency*, pp. 189–90.

235 Morse, *Chronicles, Vol. II*, pp. 57–8.

236 Morse, *Chronicles, Vol. II*, p. 190.

237 Ch'en, *Insolvency*, p. 306; Morse, *Chronicles, Vol. II*, p. 271.

238 Ch'en, *Insolvency*, p. 322.

239 Ponqua died in prison on 15 February 1811, before the banishment order could be carried out. Ch'en, *Insolvency*, pp. 239–241; Cheong, *Hong Merchants*, p. 92 n.49; Morse, *Chronicles, Vol. IV*, p. 83, and Vol. III, pp. 153 and 192.

240 Morse, *Chronicles, Vol. IV*, p. 173.

241 Chen, *Insolvency*, pp. 350–1; Morse, *Chronicles, Vol. IV*, pp. 150 and 173.

merchants, because they were literate, had been put to work as bookkeepers in the government boatyards and were thus able to support themselves.[242]

The correct prosecution of foreign offenders under these rules was problematic. Violation of the 1760 loan ban, by definition, involved two parties (a foreign lender and a Chinese debtor). Yet the members of the class that stood ***protected*** by the criminal substatute (which penalized cheating foreigners) were equally ***offenders*** when the 1760 loan ban was violated. There was never any doubt that the substatute provided for severe punishment of Chinese subjects who violated the loan ban, but it was unclear whether the same applied to foreigners.[243] Senior Canton officials stated that loans made by foreign lenders were subject to forfeiture (confiscation) as a punishment for violating the ban on loans to hong merchants. While this was said repeatedly, that stern sanction was never imposed.[244] No foreign lender was ever penalized. The opposite took place: loans made in violation of the 1760 ban (as regularly restated in the Eight Regulations) were enforced. Not only were the loans enforced against the original debtors (who stood *in pari delicto* as equal violators of the ban) but they were enforced against other innocent members of the hong guild after 1780 as a matter of collective responsibility. The threatened penalties for foreign violations of the loan ban proved illusory, and the warnings proved meaningless as well.

Perhaps it is that the Qing Dynasty officials were caught in an enforcement dilemma not unlike that which confronted their Ming predecessors. The debts that were owed by Chinese to Japanese traders in the Ming period, which some Chinese refused to pay (provoking the *Wokou* depredations), were incurred in a foreign trade that was illegal under Ming law. Creditor and debtor alike equally violated Chinese law by engaging in this trade. In the Qing period, the debts

242 Ch'en, *Insolvency*, pp. 208–9 and 411 n.92; Waley-Cohen, *Exile in Mid-Qing China*, p. 143. See Waley-Cohen, p. 55 (although banishment "theoretically involved close surveillance and labor in public works at the place of banishment, the reality was often markedly less restrictive. The individual exile tended to be left alone as long as he did not commit further crimes or attempt to escape, with the result that the boundaries between these convicts and other local residents were somewhat blurred.").

243 1760 Regulations, Rule No. 3, Appendix 1 to this study (modern translation) (Fu, *Documentary Chronicle*, p. 225); 1760 Regulations, Rule No. 3, Appendix 2 to this study (contemporary translation) (Morse, *Chronicles, Vol. v*, p. 96); Ch'en, *Insolvency*, p. 184; Cheong, *Hong Merchants*, pp. 159 and 255; Morse, *Chronicles, Vol. II*, pp. 53–54; Pritchard, "Crucial Years," p. 200; Quincy, *Journal of Samuel Shaw*, p. 312; White, "Hong Merchants," p. 63; Ng, "Ch'ing Management of the West," pp. 59–60, 141 and 155.

244 Morse, *Chronicles, Vol. II*, pp. 53–54; Quincy, *Journal of Samuel Shaw*, p. 312; Ng, "Ch'ing Management of the West," p. 156.

that hong merchants owed to Europeans were incurred through extensions of credit in violation of the 1760 ban (as restated in the Eight Regulations). Once again, creditor and debtor alike were in equal violation of Chinese law. Yet the Qing—unlike the Ming—permitted foreigners to collect these debts using the Chinese public debt process. The foreigners seem to have enjoyed some type of legal shelter when they came before Qing courts. We can only speculate as to the reason.[245] Perhaps it is that the magistrates believed the foreigners were protected under the "cheating foreigners" substatute which seemed to favor them as a class in debt cases. Perhaps the increasingly common practice of delivering goods on credit (to be paid for in the future) was seen as outside the loan ban, although the delivery of goods represented an extension of credit that required the same payment in the future as a cash loan. Perhaps Qing officials recognized the heavy dependence of both the Chinese state and the Chinese economy on maritime foreign trade, and were loathe to take any action that might result in either the suspension or interruption of this internally important commerce.

Whatever its reason, the policy choice that resulted in Qing officials not only failing to enforce the loan ban they repeatedly proclaimed against foreign lenders, but actively assisting foreigners in collecting the large loans they made in violation of the ban, provided a dangerous lesson. The inference that all Chinese prohibitions were as likely to be meaningless as meaningful could be drawn from this experience. This conclusion was indeed drawn by some Western traders. This erroneous instruction in local law played at least some role in the brazen development of the opium trade in and near Canton. In 1806, a private British country trader stated that "there are few things in China that cannot be had by paying for them." Speaking of the opium trade, an employee of the British EIC said in 1835 that "It could safely be stated that there was no officer of the Canton Government whose hands were clean." The importation

245 The active enforcement of the loan ban against hong merchant debtors who defaulted in payment, and then suffered the full severe punishment specified in the "cheating foreigners" substatute, shows that the loan ban was not mere "political rhetoric." To the extent the loan ban, as proclaimed to foreigners, was revealed through inaction to be just talk, this message was taken by opium traders as a green light because they believed that prohibitions in Chinese law were meaningless. As discussed in text above, the consequences were pernicious. See Van Dyke, *Merchants of Canton and Macao*, p. 437 n.20 ("Officials issued many edicts forbidding Chinese from borrowing from foreigners, but when those illegal loans were revealed, they were honoured. Thus, even though there were no specific laws to protect foreign investment capital, local practice filled in the gap and ensured repayment.... As late as the 1830s, Chinese officials were still warning Hong merchants not to borrow from foreigners, but all this talk was simply political rhetoric.").

of opium was illegal under Chinese law. That prohibition, as with the empty prohibition of foreign loans to hong merchants, was repeatedly proclaimed to the Westerners at Canton. Opium had first been banned by an edict issued in 1729, and again by an edict issued in 1799, but the prohibition was spottily enforced, only notably in the crackdown of 1821 which drove the trade out to Linton Island. In daily practice, the opium ban was easily evaded by smuggling and functionally 'waivable' with well placed bribes. The illegal trade in opium, as with the illegal loans to hong merchants, grew large. It thrived in an atmosphere in which some foreigners believed that no prohibition imposed under Chinese law had any real meaning, except perhaps as the excuse given by officials for requests for higher fees to allow the practice to continue. This belief held sway at least until the year 1839, when Commissioner Li Zexu arrived at Canton from Beijing angry at pretty much all of the local officials and merchants and authorized to act finally and utterly to enforce the opium prohibition.[246] The crackdown he instituted led into the First Anglo-Chinese (Opium) War of 1839–1842, which brought on the trade disruptions and the social, internal order and economic consequences the Canton officials had long sought to avoid.[247]

5 The 1780 Crisis and Imposition of the Collective Guaranty

Starting in the 1760s, many of the hong merchants borrowed significant amounts from private Western creditors. These loans were at high interest, many from 16 to 20 percent per annum, and some at rates as high as 40 percent. More loans were made in 1773–74, when the British EIC was unable to offer bills on London to private parties. The high return on money attracted capital

---

246 Greenberg, *British Trade*, pp. 73 and 110; Charles C. Stelle, "American Trade in Opium to China, Prior to 1820," Pacific Historical Review, Vol. 9, pp. 425–444 (1940), p. 426 n.9 (prohibitory edicts); Charles C. Stelle, "American Trade in Opium to China, 1821–39," Pacific Historical Review, Vol. 10, pp. 57–74 (1941). See Morse, *Chronicles, Vol. III*, pp. 233–4 (when the Governor-General became upset upon being informed in 1815 that 100,000 taels ($138,889) in bribes were being paid to squelch an imperial solvency inquiry, the British EIC recorded the following: "Altho' there is scarcely any affair that can be arranged in China without the good wishes of the Officer under whose authority the affair may be being previously purchased, still a certain form and shew of justice must be exhibited; and the bribe is neither received openly or avowedly, but is generally arranged thro' the medium of some third person. The Viceroy is stated to be extremely tenacious of these external marks of Purity, altho' it is currently said that he obtains considerable sums.").

247 Wakeman, *Strangers at the Gate*.

to Canton from as far away as France. Substantial loans were made by British and French traders and investors. The principal British creditors said that their loans were the proceeds of fortunes made in India, sent to China in order to be transferred home as EIC bills, but which had been lent to Chinese debtors as the EIC was temporarily unable to remit private funds to London by company bills.[248] The 1775 default of Sy Anqua (Seunqua II) frightened the creditors, who refused to lend or to extend the maturity of existing loans, and tried to collect amounts then due. The debtor hong merchants found themselves in a vice. They could not pay old debts, could not make new or refinancing loans, and found it increasingly difficult to pay even basic operating expenses. This deadlock was patently dangerous for the Canton trade and all parties involved. Writing in 1936, Earl Pritchard presciently described the situation in 1779–80 as "reminiscent of that produced by the cessation of American loans to Germany after 1929."[249] According to an EIC investigation at Canton in 1779, the total debt claimed by British country traders and supercargoes representing private interests then stood at $4,347,300.[250] These claims were evidenced by 248 bonds (promissory notes). Having reviewed the best information it could gather, the British EIC concluded that of the total claimed "the Chinese never received in money or goods more than $1,078,976."[251] With French creditor claims, which are estimated to have exceeded $600,000,[252] the total face amount of foreign claims against hong merchants stood at about $5 million as the crisis broke.

Four of the principal Madras traders sent a representation to London on 17 December 1777, complaining of unpaid "Chinese Debts" and seeking active

248 Pritchard, "Crucial Years," pp. 200–1 and 204; Dermigny, *La Chine et L'Occident, Vol. 2*, pp. 822–6. Jessica Hanser identifies some of these funds as the proceeds of "post-Plassey plunder, … the process by which many Company servants (the most notorious being Robert Clive) personally enriched themselves through plunder, 'gifts' and private contracts with local Indian leaders." Jessica Hanser, "Mr. Smith Goes to China: British Private Traders and the Interlinking of the British Empire with China, 1757–1793" (Ph.D. diss., Yale University, 2012), p. 14.

249 Pritchard, "Crucial Years," pp. 201–2; Hanser, "British Private Traders," pp. 59–60.

250 Pritchard, "Crucial Years," p. 206 ("Of this amount $539,224 was apparently owed to non-English in partnership with or represented by Englishmen, and $3,808,076 was owed to English, not more than $1,078,976 of which represented money and goods advanced. The difference represented accumulated interest compounded annually at 18 to 20 per cent. The debts were owing from one to eleven years, but most of them had been incurred within seven years."); Morse, *Chronicles, Vol. II*, pp. 44–5.

251 Hanser, "British Private Traders," p. 77.

252 Cheong, *Hong Merchants*, p. 258 (French claims totaled $617,460); Dermigny, *La Chine et L'Occident, Vol. 2*, pp. 826, 898–9 and 908.

assistance from the British EIC. The traders warned of a danger of general bankruptcy among the hong merchants, and reported that the French were also seeking governmental assistance in collecting Chinese debts. On 23 December 1778, the Court of Directors in London sent instructions to the supercargoes at Canton to do all in their power, consistent with the interests of the EIC, to help collect these private debts.[253]

In July of 1779, the Madras creditors pressed for help from Rear Admiral Sir Edward Vernon, commander-in-chief of the British fleet in India, promising him ten percent of the amount of debt collected through his efforts.[254] The Madras creditors took heart from the forceful resolution of the Wayqua case by the Qianlong Emperor and from a 1779 letter from Jean-Baptiste-Joseph de Grammont, a Jesuit missionary in Beijing, to a missionary in Macao which stated that if the Emperor knew of the debts to Europeans he would see that they were paid at once.[255] Also, at this early date, there was a belief among some creditors that all of the hong merchants would answer for each others' debts, and that the Chinese government might stand behind this implied guarantee in turn.[256] Admiral Vernon dispatched the frigate *Sea Horse* under Captain John Alexander Panton, which reached Canton on 23 September 1779. His arrival dismayed the local EIC servants. The Supercargoes warned Captain

253 Pritchard, "Crucial Years," pp. 203–4 and 205.

254 Ch'en, *Insolvency*, p. 196; Pritchard, "Crucial Years," pp. 205–6; Quincy, *Journal of Samuel Shaw*, p. 307 ("For these good offices, the agents engaged to give Sir Edward a tenth part of the amount recovered.").

255 Pritchard, "Crucial Years," p. 208. De Grammont (1736?–1812) was a French Jesuit who was posted as a musician and mathematician to the Imperial Court. He arrived in Beijing in September 1768, learned Manchu, and was thereafter useful in diplomatic negotiations. In 1785 he was allowed to go to Canton by the Emperor, for health reasons, but was recalled to Beijing in 1790. Lord Macartney described de Grammont as "certainly a very clever fellow [who] seems to know this country well, but as he is said to be of a restless, intriguing turn it is necessary to be a good deal on one's guard with him." J. L. Cranmer-Byng, *An Embassy to China: Lord Macartney's Journal, 1793–1794 (1962); rpt.*, Patrick J. N. Tuck, *Britain and the China Trade 1635–1842* (London: Routledge, 2000), p. 357 n.6; Pritchard, "Crucial Years," pp. 336 (same) and 343; http://ricci.rt.usfca.edu/biography/view.aspx?biographyID=626 (database of the Ricci 21st Century Roundtable on the History of Christianity in China) (accessed 26 March 2014). During the period of his residence in the suburbs of Canton (1785–1790), according to Major Samuel Shaw, de Grammont was regarded with suspicion by both Chinese and Europeans, who "consider[ed] him as a spy from the court." Quincy, *Journal of Samuel Shaw*, p. 315 n.*.

256 In the view of George Smith [of Canton], in 1779 European creditors held "undoubted" security because each guild member was "responsible for the other, and the guardian of the whole." Hanser, "British Private Traders," p. 39.

Panton that his representation to the Canton officials would result in the bankruptcy and banishment of several hong merchants, as well as the restoration of the Cohong, but Panton intended to persist.[257] Concerned that he was about to damage the EIC's ongoing trade, the Supercargoes presented Panton with a formal protest on 19 October 1779 warning him that he would be held responsible in damages "for all losses of Goods, Monies, demorrage [demurrage] for detention of Ships, and every ill consequence that may (and we think will) attend the present premature representation to the Viceroy of Canton for Debts owing to private Persons from the Chinese Merchants."[258] The hong merchants sought private negotiations. They offered Panton $40,000, unsuccessfully, to withhold his letter and remonstrance.[259]

On 24 October 1779, Captain Panton appeared before Governor Li Zhiying and Hoppo Tu-ming-a, with representatives of the major foreign trading companies. Governor Li was somewhat bewildered by the vague petition that had been presented to him by Captain Panton, which failed to identify the debtors, their creditors, or even the amounts sought to be recovered. Evidently John Crichton, who was to have prepared a detailed statement of the hong debts, had "suddenly became so desponding that he could not give any assistance towards forwarding a plan which he had projected," and Captain Panton ended up sailing for Canton without a specific statement of the claims he sought to have paid.[260] At this first session, or at a meeting soon thereafter with representatives of the British EIC, the Chinese insisted that an accounting of the foreign debts must be provided, distinguishing loans made before and after the 1760 edict. The British offered to send a boat to Madras, to "investigate the names of the people involved and the amounts of silver owed." They were told to do so quickly.[261]

In response to Captain Panton's claims, the local trading company chiefs presented a petition asking that their business not be harmed by Panton's conduct. In his record of the initial audience in October 1779, the American Samuel Shaw states that "all the chiefs of the trading companies" had been

257 Pritchard, "Crucial Years," p. 207; Morse, *Chronicles, Vol. II*, p. 47; Quincy, *Journal of Samuel Shaw*, pp. 310–1.

258 Pritchard, "Crucial Years," p. 207; Morse, *Chronicles, Vol. II*, pp. 47–8.

259 Ch'en, *Insolvency*, pp. 197–8 and 408 n.56; Pritchard, "Crucial Years," pp. 203–7; Quincy, *Journal of Samuel Shaw*, pp. 307, 310, 312–4.

260 Ch'en, *Insolvency*, p. 198; Hanser, "British Private Traders," p. 74; Pritchard, "Crucial Years," p. 207; Quincy, *Journal of Samuel Shaw*, pp. 312–3; Morse, *Chronicles*, Vol. 2, pp. 48–9.

261 Hanser, "British Private Traders," p. 74.

summoned to attend in person. All attended, except the representatives of the French East India Company. Addressing the Europeans, Governor Li Zhiying

> demanded if they had any claims, in behalf of their respective companies, against the estates of the bankrupt merchants; to which they replied in the negative. To the further question, whether, individually, any of them had a claim for himself or friend, the answer was also in the negative. It was necessary that they should give such an answer, for an acknowledgment that they were creditors of the Chinese would have been a virtual admission that they had acted contrary to their engagements with their own companies. But in this instance, the English had the advantage of all the others, as that nation alone allows its subjects in India to carry on a trade with China, independently of the company. Accordingly, the English gentlemen observed, that, though, for the company, or for themselves individually, they had no claims, yet, as agents for British subjects who had, they begged justice from the viceroy in their behalf, and hoped that he would be pleased to take some measures for the relief of such persons, who, with their families, had suffered greatly by the said bankruptcies.

British EIC records corroborate Shaw's account. They state that the company chiefs "all declared [that] no private debts were owing from the Chinese merchants to individuals of their respective nations," and that these representations were untrue, as "the servants of the Dutch, Danish and Swedish Companies are greatly involved [in hong lending]." Only the British EIC admitted that British citizens had claims against the insolvent hong merchants.[262] Addressing the naval officer from Madras,

> [H]is Excellency [Governor Li Zhiying] assured Captain Panton that proper inquiries would be made; and likewise told him, that the emperor, in 1760, having been informed of the distresses occasioned to the merchants, in consequence of borrowing money from the Europeans at a high premium, had issued an edict, forbidding such loans upon any conditions, under penalty to the European of a forfeiture of his money, and of banishment to the Chinese,—a circumstance well known to all the Europeans and Chinese in Canton, the edict having been published in the

262 Dermigny, *La Chine et L'Occident*, Vol. 2, p. 912; Hanser, "British Private Traders," pp. 74–5; Morse, *Chronicles, Vol. II*, pp. 48–9; Pritchard, "Crucial Years," p. 207; Quincy, *Journal of Samuel Shaw*, pp. 312–3.

> usual manner, and translated into several European languages. He added, that, notwithstanding this flagrant violation of the emperor's edict, his Majesty should be made acquainted with the present application, and Captain Panton might come back for his answer the succeeding year.[263]

On 6 November 1779, Captain Panton received the reply of the Governor and Hoppo, stating that "Justice [will] be done agreeable to Imperial Laws." He departed for Madras on 8 November 1779, emptyhanded.[264] Before departure, the Captain issued a proclamation, forbidding the lending of money to the Chinese by British subjects.[265]

Captain John Alexander Panton was not the only foreigner who vexed the Canton authorities in 1779–80. There was also the remarkable Abraham Leslie, a junior surgeon employed by the British EIC, who had lent much of his savings to Coqua at high interest, and stood to lose $11,000 in his insolvency. On 4 October 1779, with loaded pistols in hand, and the support of several Lascars and large dogs, he seized Coqua's hong and all its contents. Leslie posted his name above the door and raised a blue flag reading "Leslie, an English merchant, has taken possession of this hong until he is paid," in English and in Chinese. He then remained in possession for two (2) years, refusing orders by Chinese officials to vacate the premises, and orders by the EIC to return to quarters. After debt proceedings were commenced against Yngshaw, Leslie broke the official seals that secured the door to Yngshaw's shuttered hong and seized it on 22 September 1780, now as agent for a third party creditor. Again, he posted signs, stating that possession had been taken until the creditor was paid. He took down the lanterns marked with the name of Yngshaw's hong (Taihe) and replaced them with lanterns marked with his name in Chinese. The Chinese carpenter who helped Leslie prepare the signs was put in irons for the translation offense. Leslie put up a sign in English advertising rooms for rent, the income to be applied to reduce debt, and rented a room in the Taihe hong to an English captain from a private ship. He defied Chinese and EIC demands to vacate both hong premises, and posted Lascar guards to prevent approach. The Chinese authorities grew increasingly frustrated that the British either would not or could not control their own employee. "[S]carcely a month passed in which the Chinese authorities did not demand angrily why the supercargoes did not coerce him into being obedient to the laws and doing

263 Quincy, *Journal of Samuel Shaw*, p. 312.

264 Ch'en, *Insolvency*, p. 198; Morse, *Chronicles*, Vol. 2, pp. 48–9; Pritchard, "Crucial Years," p. 207; Quincy, *Journal of Samuel Shaw*, p. 312.

265 Quincy, *Journal of Samuel Shaw*, p. 312; Morse, *Chronicles, Vol. II*, pp. 48–9.

PLATE 10 *View of the foreign factories at Canton, 1780. Gouache on silk panel, by an unknown Chinese artist. The author is grateful to Paul A. Van Dyke and Maria Mok for their assistance in dating this view of the foreign factories. (Peabody Essex Museum, Accession No. E82734.1. Photograph by courtesy of the Peabody Essex Museum, Salem, Mass.).*

right and justice." At the end of 1780, the incumbent Governor, Li Hu, offered $17,500 as a lump sum in satisfaction of the Coqua, Yngshaw and Kewshaw debts, to induce Leslie to yield up the premises. Leslie accepted, and the money was paid through Puankhequa on 17 January 1781, but he then refused to leave. Abraham Leslie was finally arrested, delivered to Macao, imprisoned there for a period of time, and deported.[266]

On 29 February 1780, three months after Captain Panton returned to Madras, the Governor and Hoppo issued a joint communication:

> The Select Committee were 'reminded' of the Imperial Decree of the 25th year of Kienlung [Qianlong] (1760), by which the taking of loans at interest by Chinese from Europeans, or by Europeans from Chinese, was strictly prohibited under penalty of banishment (transportation) to Ili for the Chinese, and forfeiture of the loan for the Europeans; they were also 'reminded' of the provision of Chinese law that accumulated interest should not be allowed to exceed the original principal of a loan, i.e.

266 Morse, *Chronicles, Vol. II*, p. 66 (text quoted); Ch'en, *Insolvency*, pp. 207–8; Cheong, *Hong Merchants*, p. 259; Van Dyke, *Canton Trade*, p. 98.

> that no loan should be more than doubled by interest. A statement was to be drawn up, distinguishing between money lent before and money lent after the twenty-fifth year; and efforts were to be made to effect a settlement.[267]

All of the supercargoes and creditors claimed ignorance of the decree prohibiting foreign loans.[268] An accounting of foreign debt, distinguishing between loans made before and after the date of the 1760 edict, was requested, and provided. At a 22 March 1780 meeting of the Hoppo and EIC representatives, the Hoppo "appeared surprised at the largeness of the Sum; which he observed greatly exceeded" the debtors' estimates. Negotiations ensued, but the private British creditors, emboldened by armed naval support from Madras, rejected the Chinese proposals.[269] The creditors' account of a final May 1780 meeting with the Nanhai magistrate states that the official "behaved rudely, and in an overbearing manner. He was certainly not well pleased for he went away without taking any notice of anybody and to show his authority, called out in the middle of the factory, to the linguists, to see that those people meaning the Bondholders, went to Macao immediately."[270]

The sums involved in the "Chinese Debts" crisis of 1779–80 were large indeed. British creditors asserted $4,296,650 [3,093,588 taels] in claims, including substantial accrued interest. The amount of the claims of other nationals is unknown, but the claims of French citizens alone have been estimated at over $600,000. It appears that claims of foreigners other than the British were not paid in the wake of the crisis. In the 22 October 1779 audience before Governor Li Zhiying and Hoppo Tu-ming-a, the other trading company chiefs had stated that they had no such claims. The Dutch, Danish, French and Swedish communities were dismayed that the dividend to pay claims was funded by a tax put on their trading; "for, though there were creditors of the bankrupt Chinese among their respective companies' servants, yet they did not dare avow their claims, and of course were entirely excluded."[271]

All the hong merchants were involved. The primary debtors were Yngshaw (Yan Shiying of the Taihe hong), Coqua, Seunqua III (Cai Zhaofu of the Yifeng hong), and Kewshaw (Zhang Tianqiu of the Yuyuan hong), who owed, respec-

267 Morse, *Chronicles, Vol. II*, pp. 53–54; Pritchard, "Crucial Years," pp. 208–9.
268 Pritchard, "Crucial Years," p. 209.
269 Morse, *Chronicles, Vol. II*, p. 55; Pritchard, "Crucial Years," p. 209.
270 Hanser, "British Private Traders," p. 87.
271 Quincy, *Journal of Samuel Shaw*, pp. 314–5.

tively: $1,354,713, $1,151,299, $634,784 and $438,735 to British creditors.[272] The Seunqua III debt was largely the original principal amount plus accruing interest brought forward from the 1775 failure of his father Seunqua II's Zhufeng hong. Yngshaw's hong had long struggled under the burden of debts assumed by former proprietor Sweetia in the Beau Khequa settlements of 1759–60. In addition to debt to British creditors, Yngshaw owed customs duties and $1,300,000 to Chinese creditors.[273] Puankhequa I paid off his $75,672 debt on 28 February 1780.[274]

Yngshaw, Kewshaw and Munqua (Cai Shiwen of the Fengyuan hong) had their debts brought before the magistrates in 1780, in proceedings evidently instigated by Puankhequa when debt settlement negotiations stalled.[275] Puankhequa is said to have paid officials 30,000 taels ($41,667) to speed the Yngshaw and Kewshaw matters, seeking to acquire their properties cheaply in a distress sale.[276] Munqua avoided bankruptcy by entering into and performing a plan under which his British creditors agreed to accept payment of their $141,112 in claims over three years with 5% interest. Munqua then assaulted Puankhequa, unsuccessfully trying to kill him "with a dagger to the chest."[277]

The spectacular failures of 1780 left six surviving hong merchant firms, only four of which had appreciable business—Puankhequa, Chowqua, Shy Kinqua and Munqua. The Canton officials put intense pressure on these merchants to agree to resolve the massive debts of their failed guild colleagues. Hoppo Tu-ming-a ordered them to come to his office, daily, waiting from morning to night, but never received by him. This was a ruinous diversion from active business. The Hoppo's deputy, the *weiyuan*, questioned the merchants over and over about paying the debts of the bankrupts. The merchants adamantly refused to do so. Their collective responsibility as security merchants was limited. They might be required to pay unpaid customs duties only, but not all debts incurred by other hong merchants. The *weiyuan*, increasingly exasperated, said he would disgrace the merchants by putting chains upon their necks unless they signed an agreement to assume these liabilities. The four merchants replied by offering to surrender their licenses and withdraw from

272 Ch'en, *Insolvency*, pp. 199, 200 and 203; Morse, *Chronicles, Vol. II*, p. 45.

273 Ch'en, *Insolvency*, p. 202.

274 Ch'en, *Insolvency*, p. 199.

275 Cheong, *Hong Merchants*, pp. 165, 167, 172 and 223.

276 Cheong, *Hong Merchants*, pp. 167, 223 and 242 n.116.

277 Cheong, *Hong Merchants*, pp. 165, 167, 172, 223 and 242 n.116; Ch'en, *Insolvency*, pp. 201 and 308. Cheong suggests that the change of the name of Munqua's hong, from Fengyuan to Wanhe, occurred at this time. Cheong, p. 172.

foreign trade. The surviving records offer no further detail as to the persuasive force that was put to bear on the hong merchants in these "negotiations," but they were pressed very hard by the officials. If they did not agree, their lives would be made miserable. The four hong merchants ultimately gave in and signed an agreement assuming collective liability for foreign debts. The final terms did not represent total surrender, but they rather reflect negotiation with the Canton officials. The hong merchants agreed to accept liability for the foreign debts of failed colleagues, as demanded. For their part, the officials agreed to impose a new tax on the trade that would be used to support a newly created guaranty fund, to be maintained by the hong merchant body under state supervision. The fund was supposed to cover debt repayment on a current basis and in the future. The hope was that the burden on the guild would be minimized, with the repayment expense being passed on to foreign customers in the form of the new tax.[278]

In theory, the collective guarantee of foreign debt accomplished a Confucian ideal. Should a debt problem arise, a guaranty payment would solve it. Any occasion for dispute and legal process would be obviated, and harmony would be maintained between the Chinese and foreign trading communities. Unfortunately, the results of the actual practice of collective liability for debt did not conform with Confucian theory.

In addition to collective liability for foreign debts, which was enforced against them by the state, the hong merchants were also burdened with two other types of guaranty liability to foreign traders. The first type of guaranty was based on kinship. There was an expectation that, to the extent possible, sons, near relations, business co-venturers, and even other merchants who were close friends would step forward and pay the debts of a failed hong merchant. This was generally conceived as a social duty. However, where property was held in common, whether in a joint venture or by a family group, collec-

278 Ch'en, *Insolvency*, p. 204; Cheong, *Hong Merchants*, p. 260. According to the records of the British EIC, the Canton officials confronted the hong merchants with "a paper setting forth, that the underwriting persons, were willing to enter into an agreement, to contribute every thing in their power towards the payment of the debt; This paper being offered to Khequa, Chowqua, and Shykinqua and Munqua; they refused to sign it; on which the wooyuen ordered chains to be brought in, which being done the merchants were threatened with having them put about their necks. Whether this threat would have been carried into execution is not certain, but the merchants not choosing to run the risk of so much disgrace, signed the paper and were then dismissed.... The four merchants are certainly frightened, they threaten to give up their Hong Chops being very apprehensive lest they should be made to contribute to the discharge of debts they do not owe." Hanser, "British Private Traders," pp. 80–1.

tive liability might exist under Chinese law. In that situation, "the [common] debts of the father became the debts of the sons, who themselves could be held accountable for the others' bad business dealings."[279] The second type of guaranty existed in the tea trade, which was the heart of the export business of Canton. Here a liberal return credit had long been customary in cases of defective or substandard teas, an effective guaranty which could be held applicable even to teas shipped years earlier. Numerous examples of this practice appear in the records of the British EIC, and also in the records of collection suits by hong merchants against American debtors.[280] "By the mid-eighteenth century, it was generally assumed by all companies that any tea that could not sell in Europe for the normal going market prices must have been in some way contaminated when it was packed, and so the Chinese merchants must bear the loss. What this meant, of course, was that in practice, Chinese merchants guaranteed the profitable sale of every chest they sold to the companies."[281]

279 Zelin, "Critique of Rights of Property," p. 32.

280 Edwards, "Old Canton System," p. 371 (describing British EIC practice). The deposition testimony of Mr. Blight in Conseequa's United States litigation with Willings & Francis established that, with respect to the British EIC, "where the sales in England show the inferior quality of the teas, documents are sent to Canton stating their quality; and if they were inferior to the quality contracted for, they are charged back according to their quality; that is, if they appear to have been third instead of first quality, the Hong merchant is charged the difference between first and third quality, in reference to the prime cost." Mr. Kuhn testified that upon his return to Canton following the auction sale of the cargo of the Ganges at Amsterdam, he presented Conseequa with a statement of the claim of Willings & Francis for inferior quality tea provided to them by Conseequa. "Consequa required a day or two for consideration, and for the purpose of consulting a friend, and he afterwards agreed to allow 19,000 dollars on account of this claim and another for cassia, sent in the same vessel." *Willings v. Consequa*, 30 F. Cas. 55, 60–61 (C.C.D. Pa. 1816) (No. 17,767). In 1807, upon the return of William Jones's supercargo to Canton with a complaint of the "bad quality of the defendant's teas," the hong merchant Chunqua was alleged to have made an agreement "reciting this representation by Mr. Gray [the supercargo], of the bad quality of the teas; and promising to settle with the defendant [Mr. Jones], upon the same terms that other respectable houses at Canton had done; and, in case of a difference of opinion between the parties, to submit the same to arbitration." *Cheongwo v. Jones*, 5 F. Cas. 544, 545 (C.C.E.D. Pa. 1818) (No. 2,638) (Chunqua is plaintiff) ("This [settlement agreement] was denied by the plaintiff's counsel; and no settlement was effected by Mr. Gray, relative to the defendant's teas.").

281 Van Dyke, *Merchants of Canton and Macao*, p. 41 and Plate 08.10 (between pp. 78–9) (list dated 17 January 1801, in Dutch, of mispacked teas for which the VOC received reimbursement during the period 1780 to 1800).

In the wake of the "Chinese Debts" crisis, the claims of foreign creditors against the stricken hong merchants were decided under Chinese law. Aggressively pressed by foreign creditors, the terms of claim resolution by the Chinese authorities were firmly expressed as well. European claims against Coqua were entirely disallowed, on the basis that they had been waived by not being asserted when Coqua was petitioned against in 1779. Claims for accumulated interest were slashed, under the traditional rule capping allowable interest at no more than the original principal amount of the loan. The amount of "Chinese Debts" thus ordered repaid was about twenty percent of the face amount of stated claims.[282] The result was reported in a 15 May 1780 joint memorial to the Emperor by Governor Li Zhiying and the Hoppo. After referral to and upon the joint recommendation of the *Li Bu* (Civil Office) and *Xing Bu* (Justice Office) in Beijing, the memorial was approved by the Qianlong Emperor on 7 July 1780.[283] The hong merchants thus assumed approximately 600,000 taels ($833,333) in British creditor debts of Yngshaw and Kewshaw, which they thereafter paid without interest in ten annual installments, completed in 1790.[284]

The Imperial Edict of 7 July 1780 required that in future the hong merchants should fix uniform prices and be under direct official supervision. To accomplish this, the merchants of the outer seas guild (*waiyang hang*) would henceforth meet at a stated place under the direction of the *Weiyuan*. The Hoppo's representative would have a say in prices, levies and perquisites voted at meetings, as well as access to the books of member merchants. This knowledge facilitated subsequent exactions by the Canton officials, timed "as they found the trade able to bear."[285] Meetings of the merchants of the outer seas guild took place at their guild hall (*gongsuo*), which the foreign traders called the Consoo House, a grand building of stone and polished teak with several interior courtyards filled with flower gardens.[286]

The hong merchants were required to establish a fund for payment of the Yngshaw and Kewshaw debt, and other common obligations. The foreign

282 Ch'en, *Insolvency*, pp. 203 and 272.

283 Ch'en, *Insolvency*, pp. 205–7; Pritchard, "Crucial Years," p. 210.

284 Ch'en, *Insolvency*, pp. 96 (Table 2.7) and 206–7.

285 A representative of the Hoppo had been attending guild meetings at least since 1762. Cheong, *Hong Merchants*, pp. 211 and 228; Pritchard, "Crucial Years," p. 210; Morse, *Chronicles, Vol. II*, pp. 58–9 (suggesting that the real powers of decision were in Puankhequa, the dominant merchant, and the weiyuan).

286 Downs, *The Golden Ghetto*, p. 76; Van der Sprenkel, *Legal Institutions in Manchu China*, p. 91 n.1 (term *gongsuo*).

traders called it the Consoo Fund, after the name of the guild hall where it was initially kept in specie in a chest or chests.[287] The merchants of the native ports hong (*bengang hang*) were likewise ordered to establish a Consoo Fund in 1780, and it too was funded by a levy on trade. Some of these merchants incurred considerable foreign debt, which exhausted their distinct Consoo Fund, and with that the native ports hong was ordered abolished in 1795. Individual outer seas hong merchants were subsequently ordered to pay the remaining debts of the native ports hong merchants on a rotating basis, which was done until about the year 1803.[288]

The purpose of the Consoo Fund of the outer seas guild (*waiyang hang*) was to pay charges sought by the government from the hong merchants. These included:

> Payments on account of unpaid customs duties or foreign debts incurred by insolvent hong merchants;
>
> Governmental demands for funds for public service projects, such as military defense or flood relief;
>
> The collective obligation of all members to share in the cost of purchasing singsong curiosities as official presents for the Emperor; and
>
> Fees, donations and gratuities paid each year to various officials.

Each hong merchant was required in 1780 to make an initial 6,000 tael ($8,333) contribution to establish the fund. The Consoo Fund was also to receive the income stream from a set of surcharges on traded goods, which became known as the *hangyong*, or "disbursement for [hong merchant] trade." Puankhequa, as head merchant, reported the surcharges to the EIC's Council of Supercargoes on 16 March 1781.[289] A few years later, Hoppo Li Zhiying authorized an increase in the number of goods subject to Consoo Fund charges to sixty-nine.[290] The only goods not subject to Consoo Fund charges were woolens, calicos and iron, articles in which Puankhequa had a near monopoly of trade and which he

287 Cheong, *Hong Merchants*, pp. 206–7 and 262.

288 Cushman, *Fields from the Sea*, pp. 31 and 107. The levy in support of the Consoo Fund of the native ports hong ranged from 3% to 6% charged on selected imports and exports. Cushman, p. 31. White, "Hong Merchants," p. 90 n.12.

289 Cheong, *Hong Merchants*, pp. 206–7 and 262; Ch'en, *Insolvency*, pp. 88 and 92–102; Pritchard, "Crucial Years," pp. 140 and 210; Morse, *Chronicles, Vol. II*, p. 69; White, "Hong Merchants," p. 75.

290 Ch'en, *Insolvency*, p. 89.

caused to be exempted from the levy on the trade.[291] This list of import and export items monopolized by the hong merchants and surcharged for the benefit of the Consoo Fund was continued to the end of the hong system.[292]

In August 1780, before the Emperor's edict had arrived, Captain Panton and the *Sea Horse* once again appeared at Canton. This time Panton had been sent by Admiral Sir Edward Hughes, successor to Admiral Vernon, to press the Governor-General for "a statement of his intentions regarding the debts 'justly due His Majesty's subjects.' " The voyage was made in spite of the objection of the Governor and Council of Fort St. George (Madras). Captain Panton was seen in audience by the Chinese Governor-General, and he presented Admiral Hughes' letter to him, but no explicit assurances were provided by the Chinese authorities.[293] The "Chinese Debts" matter was soon resolved with the arrival of the Imperial Edict of 7 July 1780, discussed above. The EIC thereafter declined further requests for cooperation in the matter of the collection of these debts.[294] Earl Pritchard summarizes the results of the unfortunate episode:

> Thanks to the Private creditors' usurious demands backed up by gun-boat diplomacy, of the $4,400,222 claimed by them not over $1,198,189, slightly more than the total principal, was ever required to be paid them. Had they not called in the aid of the Navy and had they accepted the supercargoes' advice in 1779, over twice this amount might have been realized, Yngshaw and Kewshaw saved from bankruptcy, and the establishment of the Co-hong and the Consoo fund prevented.[295]

At Canton, order finally prevailed. The two year tempest with foreign creditors concerning hong debts stood resolved. While payment was required to be made by the entire guild, it was in an amount substantially less than the total claimed to be due by foreign creditors, and was stretched over ten years without interest. A tax had been imposed on the trade to fund debt repayment and also other guild obligations to the state. The Consoo Fund, immediate recipient of the tax, existed in the form of cash in chests, secure in the guild hall. Although the fund did not have independent management, employees, or supervision, it was closely watched by the hong merchants and by the

291 Greenberg, *British Trade*, p. 52 n.3; Phipps, *Practical Treatise*, p. 151.

292 Ch'en, *Insolvency*, p. 89; White, "Hong Merchants," pp. 192–195.

293 Morse, *Chronicles, Vol. II*, p. 56; Pritchard, "Crucial Years," pp. 209–10.

294 Pritchard, "Crucial Years," pp. 210–1 and 240–1.

295 Pritchard, "Crucial Years," p. 211. Some of the Madras creditors also suffered terribly. Pritchard, "Crucial Years," pp. 177–8.

supervising Canton officials. While this new arrangement—the Canton Guaranty System—had been imposed on the hong merchants under duress, there was reason to hope that the *hangyong* tax would cover all expenses and that little would really change. A long period of difficulties had been resolved and the future looked bright.

CHAPTER 4

The Fund is Drained, 1780–1799

The hong merchant body had reason to be optimistic as of 1780. In July, the guild was recognized by imperial decree and was authorized to fix uniform prices. Revenues improved thereafter. A French observer estimated that higher prices were yielding the guild an additional 768,900 taels ($1,067,917) annually by 1786.[1] The hong merchants had to pay 600,000 taels ($833,333) in debts of Yngshaw and Kewshaw, but no interest was due and payments were spread out over ten years.[2] The Consoo Fund had been created and funded, had a cash balance, and the *hangyong* tax on foreign trade assured that money would come into the fund for years to come. The British EIC estimated *hangyong* tax collection at 300,000 taels ($416,667) in the year 1781.[3]

Unfortunately, several hong merchant firms failed during the twenty year period 1780 to 1799. These resulted in substantial foreign creditor claims under the collective guaranty. Seunqua III failed at last in 1784, leaving a 166,000 tael ($230,555) liability. The failures of Eequa (1790) and Gonqua (1794) generated foreign claims of 255,000 ($354,167) and 600,000 taels ($833,333) respectively. Despite the prohibition of foreign debt under the trade regulations, the foreign claims were allowed by the Canton officials. The hong merchants were ordered to pay these substantial debts over six years.[4] It is recorded that the cash balance of the Consoo Fund had been consumed by about 1790.[5] When one includes the 1780 failures of Yngshaw and Kewshaw (debts ordered to be paid over ten years), the hong merchant body was held liable for the massive sum of 1,621,000 taels ($2,251,388) in debts of defaulted colleagues in the period 1780 to 1799. The problem then got worse. Over the years 1800 to 1842, an additional 6,225,000 taels ($8,645,833) in debts were charged to the hong merchants.[6]

1 Cheong, *Hong Merchants*, p. 228.

2 Ch'en, *Insolvency*, pp. 14 (Table 1.1), 96 (Table 2.7) and 206–7.

3 Ch'en, *Insolvency*, p. 91.

4 Ch'en, *Insolvency*, p. 96 (Table 2.7).

5 Ch'en, *Insolvency*, pp. 89 and 91.

6 Ch'en, *Insolvency*, pp. 95–6 and Table 2.7.

 | DOI 10.1163/9789004276567_005

1 The Hong Merchants, 1780–1799

Whether its members had reason to be optimistic or not, the outer seas guild had shrunk from its normal complement of about twelve members. After the spectacular failures of the "Chinese Debts" crisis, only six firms remained in business in 1780. Of the six survivors, only four had appreciable business—Puankhequa I, Chowqua, Shy Kinqua and Munqua. While Puankhequa I seemed wealthy, he owed significant debt.[7] Chowqua alone had little debt but that was because his firm did little business. He died in 1789 and was succeeded by his son in whose hands the family hong failed in 1792.[8] Credit for the hong merchants was exceptionally tight after the Yngshaw and Kewshaw settlements of 1780.[9]

The Canton officials sought to replenish guild membership. The Hoppo licensed twenty hong merchants between 1780 and 1799. Yet no more than eleven were ever guild members at the same time. Five were appointed in 1782: Sinqua, Geowqua, Pinqua, Seequa and Lunshaw. As the incumbents refused to extend their collective debt guaranty to these five, the Hoppo made them guarantee each other. This contractual firewall did not last long. These five soon failed and the incumbents ended up having to contribute to Consoo Fund payment of their debts in the 1780s and 1790s. As Weng Eang Cheong dryly notes, "the Hoppo had his way after all on this point."[10]

While all of the merchants who were licensed between 1780 and 1799 had some background in the trade, they were all undercapitalized, "men of straw" per Cheong.[11] Each had failed by 1799, along with three of the four firms that had survived the debt crisis of 1780. Weng Eang Cheong calls this "a wholesale extinction of merchants recruited before 1790." He rightly sees in this turnover the end of an era of "merchant bureaucrats" who mediated between the Canton authorities and the various European trading companies, and the advent of merchants adapted to the very different trading world of the

7 Cheong, *Hong Merchants*, pp. 88 (Puankhequa I "was apparently wealthy although this is debatable") and 257 (Puankhequa I "had large but manageable current debts"). When the "Chinese Debts" crisis broke in 1780, British creditors complained that Puankhequa I owed them $75,672. He promptly paid this debt, on 28 February 1780. Ch'en, *Insolvency*, p. 199.

8 Cheong, *Hong Merchants*, pp. 88 and 264.

9 Cheong, *Hong Merchants*, pp. 115 and 116.

10 Morse, *Chronicles, Vol. II*, p. 82; Cheong, *Hong Merchants*, p. 273 (quotation); Pritchard, "Crucial Years," pp. 210–1.

11 Cheong, *Hong Merchants*, pp. 88–9 (Table 9) and 263.

nineteenth century.[12] The January 1798 failure of Geowqua (Wu Guozhao of the Yuanshun hong), himself "a trader of little importance," had transitional significance. As a trader, he "was the last of a type and a generation of Hong merchants."[13] Geowqua's nephew Puiqua, who later rebranded himself with a different trading name as the proprietor of the Yihe hong, went on to become a giant of the new era, the senior hong merchant Howqua II (Wu Bingjian).[14]

12 Cheong, *Hong Merchants*, p. 79.

13 Ch'en, *Insolvency*, pp. 216–7, 311–2 and 414 n.129; Cheong, *Hong Merchants*, pp. 18 and 115 n.122; Morse, *Chronicles, Vol. II*, p. 299.

14 More than a little confusion exists concerning the personal trading name Howqua (Houqua) and its association with members of the Wu (伍) family who made the name famous. The name Howqua (in variant forms) had been used by a number of different persons before the Wu family gave it renown. "The identity of [the] Houqua [who worked for the hong merchant Chetqua as a writer in the 1760s] is not known, and there were several other men with similar names. One of Tsia Hunqua's sons was called Hauqua, the chief writer in Tiauqua's house was Hoyqua/Huiqua, both Poankeequa and Monqua had writers in the 1770s with names of Hanqua and Houqua (respectively), and a man who later became a Hong merchant was called Howqua (Lin Shimao 林時懋)." Paul A. Van Dyke, "Tan Suqua and Family: Merchants of Canton 1716–1778," ARI [Asia Research Institute, National University of Singapore] Working Paper, No. 50, Sept. 2005, see: "http://www.ari.nus.edu.sg/docs/wps/wps05_050.pdf" (accessed 17 November 2008) (italics added). See Van Dyke, *Merchants of Canton and Macao*, p. 457 n. 66. The first "Howqua" to be admitted as a member of the outer seas guild, a disreputable type who bore the surname Lin (林), became a hong merchant in 1784 but failed and fled Canton in 1788. Ch'en, *Insolvency*, pp. 14, 20 and 279–83. Not being a member of the family (Wu) that made the trading name famous this prior hong merchant has no proper place in the numerical sequence by which Wu family members trading as Howqua are known. That order begins with the first Wu, father and progenitor Wu Guoying (1731–1810) ("Howqua I"), who founded the Yihe hong in 1783. His second son, Wu Bingjun (1777–1799), was admitted as a hong merchant in 1792 and did business under the name "Puiqua" until his death. The third son, Wu Bingjian (Wu Dunyuan) (1769–1843) ("Howqua II") succeeded his brother as proprietor of the Yihe hong in 1801, trading initially as "Puiqua." He gradually rebranded himself as "Howqua"—the famous Howqua II. Two sons of Wu Bingjian (Howqua II) then used the personal trading name Howqua in turn, sometimes at the same time as their renowned father. The sons were Wu Yuanhua (Wu Shouchang) ("Howqua III") and Wu Chongyue (Wu Shaoyong) ("Howqua IV"). Basu, "Asian Merchants and Western Trade," pp. 356–8; Ch'en, *Insolvency*, pp. 15–18 and 20; Wolfram Eberhard, *Social Mobility in Traditional China* (Leiden: E.J. Brill, 1962), pp. 83–4; David Faure, *Emperor and Ancestor: State and Lineage in South China* (Stanford: Stanford Univ. Press, 2007), p. 235; Hummel, *Eminent Chinese*; Sung, "Study of the Thirteen Hongs," p. 4; White, "Hong Merchants," pp. viii, 95–6 and 187–91.

2 The Demands of Government, 1780–1799

Defaulted foreign debt was not the only government directed expense that came out of the Consoo Fund, or out of the tills of individual hongs. Guild members were continually forced to pay other official fees and exactions. The government quickly recognized the Consoo Fund as a convenient source to tap for state needs. These soared in the difficult years of the 1790s and early 1800s. Public needs charged to the Consoo Fund included *hegong zhuan* (Yellow River works), *jigu zhuan* (drought and famine relief), *tanggong zhuan* (coastal defense maintenance), military supplementary taxes, flood relief, and other occasional needs.[15] In addition, the Canton officials required heavy payments from the hong merchants to support local public operations and for their personal use. The draw from the Consoo Fund and the hong merchants in these two directions was enormous, and grew as the years passed.

It was an objective of the Canton Guaranty System, as with most if not all modern bank guaranty programs, that the tax imposed on participants would be sufficient to cover all of the expenses of the guaranty fund. The intention as of 1780 had been that the three percent (or more) *hangyong* tax would cover all collective expenses, including the guaranty of defaulted foreign debt. Under the Canton scheme, in contrast to modern bank guaranty programs, there was never any systematic effort to predict future losses or other amounts that would need to be paid from the Consoo Fund or to adjust the tax according to anticipated draw on the fund. The enormous cash demands of the first twenty years emptied the fund and appear to have exceeded the ability of the tax to cover draw from the Consoo Fund on a current basis. To the extent the *hangyong* tax did not cover these expenses, they had to be taken from the resources of individual merchants. As individual hong merchants—many of whom lived on the edge—failed to make good by paying their respective obligations to the Consoo Fund on time and in full, the burden fell the more heavily on those who could pay.[16] This added cost of doing business necessarily meant higher

15 Cheong, *Hong Merchants*, pp. 224–25.

16 It is difficult to give great weight to the fact that a 70,000 tael ($97,222) credit balance with the Consoo Fund appears on the statement of Eryi hong assets that Gonqua presented to the Hoppo in September 1794. Ch'en, *Insolvency*, p. 302; Cheong, *Hong Merchants*, p. 229 (citing the credit balance as evidence that the fund showed a profit). This entry may be evidence that the book entries in the Consoo Fund ledgers balanced on their face as of that date. It might be evidence of a substantial payment made into the Consoo Fund by Gonqua, on time or possibly even in advance of its due date. Yet it tells us nothing of the reality behind the entries on the Consoo Fund's ledgers, a crucial matter as its cash is said to have been exhausted by about 1790. Were all the individual hong debtors able to fully

prices, in order for the hongs to survive. Contemporaries learned during the 1790s that debt payment under the collective guaranty had an immediate and possibly destabilizing effect on the marketplace. This recognition is explicit in the reluctance EIC officers expressed about commencing debt proceedings against hong merchants in the first decade of the 1800s.[17]

There is no surviving comprehensive list of government exactions from the hong merchants, or of total annual draw from the Consoo Fund, but some highlights are known. Total draw from the Consoo Fund is recorded at 272,500 taels ($378,472) in 1793 and 279,788 taels ($388,594) in 1796. In each of these years, 100,000 taels ($138,889) was for singsong gifts to the Court in Beijing, 55,000 taels ($76,389) was "native tribute" to the Emperor, and 25,000 taels ($34,722) was for military use in Sichuan. In 1793, 50,000 taels ($69,444) went for military expenses in Fujian. Debt repayments were 42,500 taels ($59,028) in 1793 (Eequa) and 99,788 taels ($138,594) in 1796 (Gonqua).[18] As the domestic situation grew troubled in the 1790s, the hong merchants were hit with charges for military mobilization. The campaign in Taiwan (1787) cost 300,000 taels ($416,667) (or possibly 400,000 taels—$555,555—sources disagree), the campaign against the Gurkhas (1792) cost 300,000 taels ($416,667), the campaign in Huguang (1799) 120,000 taels ($166,667), and the campaign in Sichuan and Shenxi (1800) another 120,000 taels ($166,667).[19]

Weng Eang Cheong sees the increased trade and hong merchant profits of the decade of the 1780s as having given rise to official expectations which led in turn to a "steep increase in official exactions." As Cheong recognizes, the reasons for this increase were somewhat complicated. Among Qing officialdom, postings were sometimes spoken of in terms such as *feique* or *meique* (rich post), *zhongque* (medium post) or *jique* (lean post). Many officials took a rich posting as an opportunity to require fees or exactions to meet legitimate expenses of office, many of which were not officially provided for, and also to build up some private wealth. This was understood and expected within

---

and timely pay their respective obligations to the Consoo Fund? Is the 70,000 tael Gonqua credit a correct statement of sums actually paid in, or an optimistic guess by a struggling debtor who has given himself the benefit of unstated offsets and credits in a desperate effort to avoid this liability? As the obligation of a hong merchant to pay into the Consoo Fund itself had no priority over other debts, and is not known to have been enforced by criminal or other magistrate process, it is difficult to conceive of why Gonqua's cash poor Eryi hong would choose to prepay this obligation. It is reasonable to assume that the obligation to pay into the Consoo Fund was often deferred by weak hong merchants.

17 Morse, *Chronicles, Vol. III*, p. 111.

18 Morse, *Chronicles, Vol. III*, p. 62.

19 Ch'en, *Insolvency*, p. 93 (Table 2.6); Van Dyke, *Merchants of Canton and Macao*, p. 194.

a certain tolerance,[20] but customary limits were pressed and exceeded by a national climate of venality that existed in the late 1700s and thereafter. During his six month term as Hoppo in 1795, Shuer is said to have exacted $240,000 from the hong merchants for his own use.[21] Sun Shiyi and Fu Kangan arrived at Canton from Beijing in 1784 charged with investigating abuses in the trade and taxation; both left richer, one said to have received seventeen piculs of gold for clean reports on the local officials and merchants.[22] Sanyizhu, whom the hong merchants considered to have been a relatively mild Hoppo, managed in two years to exact more than $600,000 from the hong merchant body for himself (as of 29 November 1803). Exact amounts of official exactions in subsequent years are unknown, but are estimated by Kuo-tung Ch'en to have been in the range of from 200,000 to 300,000 taels ($277,778–$416,667) annually.[23]

Officials used rich postings as opportunities to pay down their own debts to the state. The Imperial Household Department (*neiwufu*) repeatedly posted officials to Canton who owed large debts to it, anticipating beneficial results. As but one example, Li Zhiying was posted to Canton as Hoppo in 1781 after he had incurred a 256,000 tael ($355,555) personal debt to the *neiwufu*. The appointment of five new hong merchants in the year 1782, and other exactions of the period, are believed to have been motivated by his desire—need—to generate funds with which to pay this substantial debt.[24] The British EIC was doubly pleased with the quality of the 1782 appointees. Some were men of substance, and the EIC hoped that collectively the new merchants "will at least

---

20 Cheong, *Hong Merchants*, pp. 228-9; Zhao, "Shaping the Asian Trade Network," pp. 249–50 ("Criticisms have tended to gloss over the basic problem faced by Chinese officials: they received only a miniscule salary and were expected to supplement this pittance with squeeze. In other words, without collecting a certain amount of additional fees, the maritime customs office of the four coastal provinces would have ceased to operate.").

21 Cheong, *Hong Merchants*, pp. 223–4; Morse, *Chronicles, Vol. II*, p. 264; Pritchard, "Crucial Years," p. 369.

22 Cheong, *Hong Merchants*, pp. 223–4 (citing several other examples in this period). A picul has the weight of 133.33 pounds, and a tael the average weight of 1.333 pounds. In other words, a picul was equivalent to 100 taels. Morse, *Chronicles, Vol. I*, p. xxii; Cuthbert Collingwood, *Rambles of a Naturalist on the Shores and Waters of the China Sea* (London: John Murray, 1868), p. 225. By weight, seventeen piculs (gold) equaled 1,700 taels (gold). The conversion rate between gold and silver varied through the period of this study; in 1782, one pound of gold was equivalent in value to twenty pounds of silver. Yang, *Money and Credit in China*, pp. 47–48. Seventeen piculs of gold would therefore be equivalent in value to 34,000 silver taels ($47,222).

23 Ch'en, *Insolvency*, pp. 131 and 136.

24 Ch'en, *Insolvency*, pp. 133–7 (and Table 3.3); Cheong, *Hong Merchants*, p. 211.

alleviate the [burden on] the other merchants & perhaps preserve some of them from ruin by contributing to the exorbitant demands of the Mandareens which are now become almost intolerable."[25] The *neiwufu* practice of posting indebted officials to Canton continued for decades. All of the Hoppos posted to Canton between 1813 and 1828 arrived with customs deficiency debt in baggage, in amounts ranging from 136,000 taels ($188,889) to 324,000 taels ($450,000). Xiangshao, who served as Hoppo from 1813 to 1818, had incurred tax collection arrearages in his prior service as salt censor of Changlu and Superintendent of the Huaian Customs, which he paid off during his service at Canton.[26]

Had these exactions been publicly exposed and criticized, one can imagine the officials noting in defense the opulent lifestyles and excesses of the hong merchants themselves. The foreign merchants certainly noted hong merchant high living with disapproval, especially when they were creditors holding unpaid bills. Perhaps these outward signs of prosperity inspired the Canton officials to ask the merchants to help the state and its servants just a bit more than they might otherwise.

3 Trading Conditions, 1780–1799

The trading world of Canton changed markedly during the twenty year period 1780 through 1799. The English share of trade soared, in part the result of enactment of the Commutation Act in 1784 and in part the result of a cycle of wars which began with the February 1793 declaration of war by France on Britain and the Netherlands.[27] This marked the end of the period of competition by continental European trading firms at Canton, and the substantial importations of silver into China with which they paid for much of their export cargoes.[28] The advent of United States trade with China, which began in 1784, proved well-timed as the American traders brought considerable bullion (specie) to buy their export cargoes. This period also saw the beginning of the rise of private country traders, who carried India goods to China with the blessing of the EIC. Toward the end of this period, pirate activity and social insta-

25 Ch'en, *Insolvency*, p. 135.

26 Ch'en, *Insolvency*, pp. 99 (Xiangshao), 133, 135, 136 (quotation) and 137 (Table 3.3) (debts incurred variously in the Huaian, Jiujiang and Hushu Customs and the Changlu Salt Administration).

27 James R. Fichter, *So Great a Proffit: How the East Indies Trade Transformed Anglo-American Capitalism* (Cambridge: Harvard Univ. Press, 2010), pp. 56–72.

28 Cheong, *Hong Merchants*, pp. 283–4.

PLATE 11 *View of the foreign factories at Canton, ca. 1782–1784. Oil on glass painting by a Chinese artist. The author is grateful to Paul A. Van Dyke and Maria Mok for their assistance in dating this view of the foreign factories.* (*Private collection. Photograph by courtesy of the Martyn Gregory Gallery, London.*)

bility began to increase in South China. Demands by the Canton officials for payments from the hong merchants, both for military defense and for venal purposes, increased in turn. So it is that much at the same time as the British successfully stimulated both trade and the domestic demand for tea by slashing customs duties (the Commutation Act), the Qing marched off in the opposite direction, gradually increasing both the direct and indirect tax burdens on the hong merchants and the trade conducted within the Canton monopoly.

The most important changes in the maritime trade of Canton in this period concerned Great Britain. It had responded to the high debts and poor performance of the EIC by attempting the then radical remedy of cutting taxes on goods being brought into England in order to increase trade. Under the Commutation Act of 1784, import duties on goods coming into England and export duties on such goods leaving England were reduced from over 100 percent to 12.5 percent. Prices fell, consumer demand soared, and the formerly troubled EIC was able to undersell all competitors in its home market. British imports from China quadrupled in the following decade, with tea comprising ninety percent of the total. EIC scholar Earl Pritchard believes that it was this increase in demand that caused the great increase in tea prices noted in the mid-1780s, not the re-establishment of the Cohong in 1780 which the EIC blamed.[29] The sharp increase in EIC domestic tea sales meant commensurate losses for the continental firms which had long supplied British smugglers.[30]

The EIC was now directed by statute to sell British woolen goods in China, and those exports soared. Unlike cotton, for which substantial Chinese demand existed, woolens were not attractive to Chinese buyers. The EIC accordingly adopted a practice of directly tying the sale of its woolen imports to its export purchases of tea from the hong merchants (a practice called "truck"). The hong merchants adopted various strategies in turn for dealing with truck goods. Sometimes their own tea acquisitions might be tied to the sales of British woolens to inland tea merchant suppliers, after the EIC method, truck thus following truck. In general, the truck business was unfavorable for the hong merchants.[31]

In the decade after 1784, the EIC exported more than two thirds of the tea that came out of China. The hong merchants thus became more dependent than ever on this single dominant firm.[32] The rising force of the EIC is reflected in the respective debts between it and the hong merchants. Debtor in the 1780s, the EIC then became a massive creditor in the 1790s (itself a portent). In the 1780s, the EIC was indebted to the hong merchants in amounts ranging from 266,560 taels ($370,222) in 1782 to 1,352,292 taels ($1,878,183) in 1787. The EIC then swung into surplus, with guild members now owing money to it. Hong merchant debt to the EIC soared in the 1790s to a high of 1,606,669 taels ($2,231,485) in 1793.[33]

The private country traders, who exported opium, cotton and other India goods to China with the approval of the British EIC, grew in importance during this period.[34] The massive exportations of Indian opium and cotton to China

---

29 Pritchard, "Crucial Years," pp. 165–6 and 212; Greenberg, *British Trade*, p. 64.

30 Ch'en, *Insolvency*, pp. 44 and 46; Cheong, *Hong Merchants*, pp. 112 and 216–7 ("but by 1819 [British duties] had risen back up to 100 per cent of the landing price"); Fichter, *So Great a Proffit*, p. 29; Greenberg, *British Trade*, p. 3; Pritchard, "Crucial Years," pp. 165–6 and 212.

31 Ch'en, *Insolvency*, pp. 53–61; Cheong, *Hong Merchants*, pp. 112, 114 and 278; Greenberg, *British Trade*, pp. 7–8 and 59; Van Dyke, *Merchants of Canton and Macao*, pp. 22–3. See David Graeber, *Debt: The First 5,000 Years* (Brooklyn, N.Y.: Melville House Publishing, 2011), pp. 34 and 291 (noting that in the century or two before the time of Adam Smith (1723-1790) "the English words 'truck and barter,' like their equivalents in French, Spanish, German, Dutch, and Portuguese, literally meant 'to trick, bamboozle or rip off.'").

32 Ch'en, *Insolvency*, pp. 29–30 and 45 (Table 2.2); Cheong, *Hong Merchants*, pp. 112 and 283.

33 Cheong, *Hong Merchants*, pp. 114–115.

34 Ch'en, *Insolvency*, pp. 32–3 and 69–82; Cheong, *Hong Merchants*, pp. 112–3; Greenberg, *British Trade*, pp. 9–13 and 20.

relieved the EIC of the need to bring in silver to fund its tea exports. In the words of trade historian Michael Greenberg, "the resources of India were utilized to finance the purchase of China tea for England."[35] The country traders bought opium from the EIC in Calcutta, and carried it to China under a license granted by the Company. As Greenberg notes,

> From 1816 there was a clause in that license declaring it to be void if any opium other than the Company's were carried. But in the sailing orders of every Company's Indiaman bound for China was embodied a strict prohibition against carrying opium, 'lest the Company be implicated' with the Chinese! By 1800, the East India Company had perfected the technique of growing opium in India and disowning it in China.[36]

Measured by value, raw cotton imported into China more than tripled during the years 1780–1785 and then tripled again during the years 1795–1815.[37] Trading in cotton and opium could be difficult and was subject to sharp price variation.[38] Bulky light cotton became known as the "white tiger" and dense compact opium as the "black tiger." Much money could be made or lost in these commodities and the country traders developed a reputation for sharp trading practices. There were big winners and big losers in this trade, such as the hong merchant Eequa, who was brought down in 1790 by unsuccessful cotton speculations.

The early United States voyages to China provided competition for Chinese export goods as well as liquid funds, both welcome in the Canton marketplace.[39] As the Americans lacked products for which there was much Chinese demand, they instead brought great amounts of specie (silver coins) with which to buy export goods. Where a European needed time to sell his woolens, cotton, spices, or other imports before he could buy Chinese export goods, the American, cash in hand, was by contrast often ready to buy immediately on arrival. The Americans experimented with ginseng and fur imports for the Chinese markets as alternatives to shipping silver coins. United States ginseng was considered low grade, and the New England forest supply was quickly

35 Greenberg, *British Trade*, p. 11.

36 Greenberg, *British Trade*, pp. 109–10.

37 Marks, *Tigers, Rice, Silk, and Silt*, p. 178 and Figure 5.3.

38 White, "Hong Merchants," p. 85.

39 Jacques M. Downs, "American Merchants and the China Opium Trade, 1800–1840," Business History Review, Vol. 42, pp. 418–442 (1968), pp. 419 and 421; Greenberg, *British Trade*, p. 68; White, "Hong Merchants," p. 96.

PLATE 12 *The Spanish dollar, the primary currency of China's maritime foreign trade during the period 1780–1842, as hard currency and as a work of porcelain art. Photograph contrasting the obverse and reverse of a Spanish dollar produced by the Mexico mint in 1795 (top) with the front and back of a porcelain pillbox in the form of a Spanish dollar, made by a Chinese artist, ca. 1830–1840 (bottom). The pillbox was originally owned by Warren Delano II. (Private collection. Photograph by permission.)*

depleted.[40] The rush to supply furs for the Chinese market wreaked ecological havoc on the Pacific Northwest coast where vast numbers of sea otters were slaughtered. The resulting oversupply at Canton, where top quality pelts were no longer a rarity, caused prices to plummet.[41] Until the development of opium as a profitable import cargo in the early 19th century, Americans brought silver coins to China as a matter of commercial necessity. This association of United States traders with hard cash seems to have made the Americans especially

40 James R. Gibson, *Otter Skins, Boston Ships, and China Goods: The Maritime Fur Trade of the Northwest Coast, 1785–1841* (Seattle: Univ. of Washington Press, 1992), pp. 100–1.

41 Gibson, *Otter Skins*, pp. 28, 30–9, 54–61, 101 and 200-3; Greenberg, *British Trade*, p. 88.

inviting candidates for credit when they wanted more goods than they had coins to pay for at the time of sale.

The Chinese economy experienced difficulties toward the end of the twenty year period 1780–1799. Devastating flooding along the Yellow River sharply suppressed Chinese consumer demand for woolens in the period 1794–95.[42] Pirate activity became a serious problem along the coast of Guangdong Province in the 1790s.[43] The Canton officials accordingly pressed the hong merchants to fund government works ranging from flood control and relief, to military preparedness, to pirate control. The state saw the Consoo fund as a convenient liquid source for the immediate payment of pressing needs. Such demands on the fund and individual merchants only increased, as, for example, the problem of coastal piracy grew worse in the years that followed.

Starting with the *hangyong* levy of 1780, and then through frequent exactions or supplements, the Qing gradually increased the tax burden on trade conducted through the hong merchant monopoly. The natural result of tax increases was that legitimate goods—those sold by the licensed monopoly traders—became more expensive. The Americans and a small but growing number of English private traders were increasingly attracted to Chinese merchants who were not guild members. These "outside shopmen" undercut the foreign trade monopoly, selling tea and other export goods at prices perhaps 10 to 15 percent less than hong merchants.

Outside shopmen often traded under the cover of an inadequately capitalized hong merchant through the use of the hong's seal or chop. Sometimes they engaged in smuggling, occasionally paying money to low level customs officers to make sure they looked the other way.[44] Outside goods were quality goods, as the American trader Samuel Russell pointed out in a March 1821 letter to Edward Carrington:

> outside men . . . take particular pains to select the best and choicest teas, and they are all of them so situated that they can ship off their teas at Hong duties and will actually sell lower than the Hong merchants, as they buy for cash and sell for the same. They are all of them very tenacious of their reputation, and will not put their names on teas that are not good.

42 Ch'en, *Insolvency*, pp. 83–4.

43 Ch'en, *Insolvency*, p. 86; Leonard, *Wei Yuan*, pp. 80-3; Murray, *Pirates of the South China Coast*.

44 Cheong, *Hong Merchants*, p. 284; Greenberg, *British Trade*, pp. 53 and 60; White, "Hong Merchants," p. 112.

> We should like to do more business with these people than we have it in our power to do.[45]

Despite periodic official attempts to defend the foreign trade monopoly, such as an 1817 crackdown in which over 200 outside shops were shut down and their goods confiscated, the hong merchants continued to lose significant amounts of business to outside shopmen competitors.[46]

4 The Collective Guaranty of Debt, 1780–1799

There were numerous hong firm failures during the period 1780–1799, only a few of which resulted in calls on the collective guaranty. The 1784 failure of Cai Zhaofu (Seunqua III), successor head of the Yifeng hong, was simply the terminus of a slow motion train wreck that began ten years earlier. In 1775 Sy Anqua (Seunqua II) had been directed to continue trading for the benefit of creditors and to pay $266,692 in foreign claims over ten years. Only one installment was paid. When foreign creditors complained, the officials noted that they had failed to either acknowledge or accept the payment plan, and expressed hope that when the young Cai Zhaofu (Seunqua III) "grows up and gains money by his business, he shall pay his father's debts."[47] The young man was not successful. He had lost the right to secure foreign vessels by 1781, then sold the Dutch Hong (his last property) to Pinqua to raise money to pay duties, and was finally stripped of his hong license in 1783. The hong merchant body was ordered to pay the foreign debts of the Yifeng hong, 166,000 taels ($230,555) in total, over ten years. As he had not personally incurred the debts ordered to be paid by the hong merchant guild, Seunqua III was not punished as a debtor.[48]

The 1790 failure of Eequa (Wu Zhaoping) was the result of speculative cotton trading. Eequa was successor head of the Fengtai hong his father Sinqua

---

45 White, "Hong Merchants," pp. 109–110.

46 Greenberg, *British Trade*, pp. 55 and 69; White, "Hong Merchants," p. 111.

47 Ch'en, *Insolvency*, pp. 21, 264–5, 409 n.68 and 422 n.30; Cheong, *Hong Merchants*, pp. 85, 88, 257 and 260; Morse, *Chronicles, Vol. II*, p. 55; Van Dyke, *Merchants of Canton and Macao*, pp. 131–5 and Plate 10.12 (between pp. 78–9) (communication to the VOC dated 22 August 1776, in Dutch, from Chowqua (Tan Tsjoqua), Monqua (Munqua), Geowqua (Kiouqua) and Pinqua, stating that these men would stand security for each other and that all of the goods they supplied to the VOC in the current season would be applied as credits against the debt they owed, remaining from the insolvency of the Yifeng hong).

48 Ch'en, *Insolvency*, pp. 96 (Table 2.7), 267–8 and 411 n.93; Cheong, *Hong Merchants*, p. 264; Van Dyke, *Merchants of Canton and Macao*, p. 134 and Plate 07.07 (between pp. 78–9).

had founded in 1782. He had played the system hard and was unpopular within the guild. As of early 1790 he owed over $400,000 to country traders (largely Bombay Parsis) and could not raise the funds. The Parsis petitioned the Hoppo in person, with the result that Eequa was jailed, stripped of his purchased degree, and his case reported to the Emperor. The auction of Eequa's properties yielded enough to pay customs duties of 38,520 taels ($53,000) but left the bulk of his 289,100 tael ($401,600) foreign debt unsatisfied. In January 1791 the Hoppo directed repayment of 255,000 taels ($354,167) in six annual installments, and reported the case to the Emperor. The decree of the Qianlong Emperor, issued on 31 May 1791, instead ordered that the foreign debt should be immediately paid from customs funds, to be repaid by the hong merchants over six years. Immediate payment from the provincial treasury was ordered because the Emperor thought that installment payments were not sufficiently favorable to foreign creditors. The Emperor harshly criticized lax supervision by the officials and directed reporting improvements in order to more effectively monitor the work of the Canton customs. Effective as of 1790, double blind submission of confidential financial reports was required from the officials who supervised the Canton customs.[49]

The position of senior or head merchant of the outer seas guild fell open in 1788 upon the death of Puankhequa I. His son Puankhequa II refused to succeed his father. The Hoppo ordered Munqua (Cai Shiwen of the Wanhe hong) to take the position—with its burdens—as he was second in seniority among the hong merchants.[50] Munqua's hong was not strong. It had narrowly escaped foreign creditor insolvency proceedings in 1780 through agreement to pay creditors over time. Shortly after Munqua was made head merchant, the marginal hong of the early Howqua (Lin Shimao)[51] failed in December 1788 during a bungled transaction with Americans.[52] Munqua was required to lead the guild in paying substantial customs duty arrears and in arranging settlements

49 Ch'en, *Insolvency*, pp. 96 (Table 2.7), 209, 283–91 and 411 n.94; Cheong, *Hong Merchants*, pp. 91, 115 n.120, 197, 211 and 264; Fairbank, *Trade and Diplomacy, Vol. I*, p. 49; Morse, *Chronicles, Vol. II*, p. 181; Fu, *Documentary Chronicle*, pp. 317–8.

50 Ch'en, *Insolvency*, pp. 22 and 308.

51 This Howqua (surname "Lin") had no family or other connections with the better-known, and reputable, members of the "Wu" family who traded as Howqua. Ch'en, *Insolvency*, pp. 279–80; Van Dyke, "Tan Suqua and Family," p. 21 n.49.

52 The episode was described by Samuel Shaw in his journal. "He delayed performing his contract,—absented himself almost continually from his hoang,—smoked opium,—absconded on the 24th of December,—was declared bankrupt, and his effects were seized." Quincy, *Journal of Samuel Shaw*, p. 301.

of foreign creditor claims against that failed hong in 1789.[53] These and other expenses pressed on Munqua as head merchant were worsened by business difficulties his firm experienced in the 1790s. Munqua then became ill. In 1795 he let his brother Seequa come in to manage his firm's affairs, which deteriorated further. Munqua tried to commit suicide and failed. Pressed for payment by tea suppliers, he committed suicide by swallowing opium and died on 10 April 1796. "Everything in his hong was left in confusion."[54] Seequa was authorized to carry on the hong, with a license "free of every expense," but the firm failed when more customs debt, previously unknown, came to light in the summer of 1797. The Hoppo directed Mowqua I (Lu Guanheng of the Guangli hong) to take responsibility for settlement of the hong's affairs. The justification was that Mowqua I had traded on his own account, but under Munqua's hong license, before becoming a hong merchant in 1792. Mowqua I carried out the Hoppo's order, but negotiation and compromise were required to make debt assumption work. The hong merchants agreed that the *hangyong* levy would not be charged against new contracts made by Mowqua I in order for him to generate profits to recoup his Munqua expenses.[55]

The 1795 collapse of Gonqua's hong was triggered by a request for extension of the 18 September 1794 deadline for paying customs taxes to the government. Gonqua (Shi Zhonghe) (also known as Shy Kinqua II), successor head of the Eryi hong founded in 1788 by his father Shy Kinqua I (Shi Mengjing), had enjoyed exceptionally trusting relations with the British EIC. In October 1794, he admitted having dipped into 94 sealed chests of EIC funds (containing $470,000) that had been entrusted to his care. He was also in arrears to his tea suppliers. The EIC nevertheless decided to work with Gonqua and to complete his tea contracts, to mitigate the loss. About three weeks earlier, Gonqua had petitioned Hoppo Shuxi for an extension of the customs tax payment deadline. The Hoppo asked for and received a statement of financial condition from Gonqua, which listed the following Eryi hong assets and their values.

Few hong merchant statements of financial condition have come to light. Gonqua's is known because its contents were leaked from the Hoppo's *yamen* (office compound), sending Chinese creditors into a panic and accelerating the collapse of the Eryi hong.[56]

53 Ch'en, *Insolvency*, pp. 214 and 283; Cheong, *Hong Merchants*, p. 115.

54 Ch'en, *Insolvency*, pp. 215 and 308–9; Cheong, *Hong Merchants*, pp. 170 and 172.

55 Ch'en, *Insolvency*, pp. 20, 51–2, 215–6, 309 and 311; Cheong, *Hong Merchants*, pp. 170 and 172–3; Morse, *Chronicles, Vol. II*, pp. 300–1.

56 Ch'en, *Insolvency*, pp. 275–6 and 297–302; Morse, *Chronicles, Vol. II*, pp. 255 and 261–2.

TABLE 1 *List of the Assets of the Eryi hong, and their values*

Asset	Value
House and paddy grounds	608,856 taels
New and old unsold teas	229,428 taels
Unsold goods in warehouse	130,075 taels
Collection of watches and clocks (singsongs)	222,650 taels
Debts owed by Europeans	118,160 taels
Debts owed by shopkeepers	50,000 taels
Debts owed by Chinese	9,388 taels
Credit from the Consoo Fund	70,000 taels
Share of Loqua's property	40,000 taels

The Hoppo responded to these disclosures and the alarm of the hong's Chinese creditors by directing the five principal hong merchants (Munqua, Puankhequa II, Geowqua, Mowqua and Puiqua) to manage and liquidate its affairs "without having recourse to the Emperor" if possible. According to the English supercargoes, the Hoppo was "very anxious that the business should not reach the Emperor's ears."[57] In entrusting Gonqua's hong to liquidating agents or trustees, the Hoppo replicated the process that had been initiated two years earlier in response to the 1792 failure of the Yuanchuan hong of Loqua (Chowqua II). The four trustees appointed in the prior case had operated that hong, sold assets including Loqua's famous Honan gardens, and fully completed creditor settlements by 1797.[58] Gonqua's debts however were far larger. He owed almost 200,000 taels ($277,778) in customs duties alone. The EIC estimated total foreign debt at 1,735,465 taels ($2,410,368): 1,000,000 taels ($1,388,889) to it; 310,465 taels ($431,201) to American and country ships; and 425,000 taels ($590,278) in promissory notes (time obligations). There is no surviving estimate of Gonqua's tea merchant and other domestic debts, but they were certainly large as well. Some recoveries were made for the benefit of creditors, notably teas and nankeen cloth valued at more than 600,000 taels ($833,333) which were delivered to the EIC by Wyequa (Shi Huailian),

57 Ch'en, *Insolvency*, p. 303.

58 Ch'en, *Insolvency*, p. 295.

Gonqua's brother and advisor.[59] The five trustees for the Eryi hong (three of whom were also trustees for the Yuanchuan hong) did what they could, but could not harmoniously resolve the affairs of the Eryi hong.

Gonqua demolished the prospects for any further foreign business on 10 April 1795 when, to the outrage of his foreign creditors, he gave his tea merchant creditors the title deeds to his houses and estates, in near proportion to the debts owed to each of them. The title deeds were later redeemed from the tea merchants upon the payment of over 100,000 taels ($138,889), chiefly in gold, delivered on behalf of Gonqua by Wyequa in May 1795.[60] The EIC and other private creditors responded by petitioning the Hoppo, complaining of the unpaid debts of Gonqua's Eryi hong.

Gonqua's failure, the second largest in the history of the trade, was reported to the Emperor late in July 1795. After payment of customs debt from the liquidated assets of the hong, 600,000 taels ($833,333) remained due to foreign creditors. The hong merchants were ordered to pay this sum in six annual 100,000 tael ($138,889) payments.[61] The amount due to the EIC each year (28,532 taels) ($39,628) was actually paid by book entry, not in cash; "it was agreed that in each season the supercargoes should debit each merchant's account with the sum payable by each to the Company. This was acceptable to both sides."[62]

Gonqua and Wyequa were arrested by the Nanhai magistrate soon after the debt petition was filed. They were allowed to stay in a rented house, under guard, for a fee.[63] On 23 June 1795, at his request, Gonqua was brought to Macao by the Magistrate, where he begged to speak with President Henry Browne of the EIC's Select Committee. Browne at first refused, but relented, and went to the Magistrate's office. He spoke for a few minutes with the Nanhai Magistrate, and then Gonqua was brought in. As noted by the EIC in its records, Gonqua

> immediately prostrated himself and repeatedly hit the Ground with his forehead, with all the appearance of that abject Humiliation which

59 Ch'en, *Insolvency*, pp. 301-3; Cheong, *Hong Merchants*, pp. 127 n.120, n.122 and n.123 (Cheong states that Gonqua owed 934,000 taels to the EIC and 586,922 taels to country traders); Morse, *Chronicles, Vol. II*, p. 262.

60 Ch'en, *Insolvency*, pp. 299–301 and 304–5; Morse, *Chronicles, Vol. II*, pp. 261–3.

61 Ch'en, *Insolvency*, pp. 305 and 96 (Table 2.7); Cheong, *Hong Merchants*, p. 212; Morse, *Chronicles, Vol. II*, pp. 271, 284 and 298.

62 Morse, *Chronicles, Vol. II*, p. 272. The second Gonqua dividend, which was paid on 12 May 1797, was 28,532 taels ($39,628) to the EIC, and 69,300 ($96,250) to private Europeans—97,832 taels ($135,878) total. Morse, *Chronicles, Vol. II*, p. 284. The third Gonqua dividend, in 1798, was in the same amounts. Morse, *Chronicles, Vol. II*, p. 298.

63 Ch'en, *Insolvency*, p. 304.

> Criminals in this Country are obliged to submit to, till ordered by the Mandarin to rise, who with all his Attendants and the other two Merchants [Munqua and Puankhequa] immediately left the room. He then again attempted to prostrate himself, to entreat the Compassion of [Browne], who prevented him.... This Prisoner was habited in a coarse Jacket & drawers, with white [mourning] Shoes, but no Stockings, his Hair was grown to a considerable length [instead of being shaven clean] a Chain round his Neck and on both his wrists, and his whole appearance squalid, and suited to the part he was intended to act, though it is impossible not to feel for a Man under such a Reversal of Fortune, and such Sensations would be more particularly excited in those who have lived with him in Habits of Friendship, and confidential intercourse, [Browne] could not help remarking an appearance of Art & Studied distress, which greatly diminished their force.[64]

Creditors believed that Gonqua and Wyequa had hidden funds, and that the Hoppo and Governor-General could recover the money. These were fatal beliefs. Gonqua was held in prison at Canton, where he died on 27 February 1796, as the result of repeated beating by the Hoppo's agents, forcefully "pressing" him as demanded by angry tea merchant creditors. Gonqua "had suffered the Bastinado three times, the last of which was on the Face, & so severe as to cause a violent inflammation in consequence of which all his teeth dropped out: this was succeeded by the fever which after a duration of two days put an end to [his] existence..." His brother Wyequa was banished to Ili on 22 January 1796, and appears to have survived in exile.[65]

The Gonqua case has been reviewed in detail because records of this case are unusually complete. The cause of his failure remains unclear. Unlike Eequa (who failed in 1790), Gonqua seems to have been well liked and highly trusted. His failure may be no more than the result of business losses built up over time. Gonqua could mask losses easily as he was thought to be solid, and doubtless he yearned for better days ahead. When the crisis broke, the foreigners were relatively relaxed. They had always liked the man, and had the benefit of the collective guaranty to pay his debts. Gonqua's uninsured domestic creditors were furious, and all the more so for the breach of the high confidence that had long existed. Historians have picked up some of this antidebtor fury, as well as the absolute belief as of 1795 that Gonqua and Wyequa had hidden a

64 Morse, *Chronicles, Vol. II*, pp. 270–1.

65 Ch'en, *Insolvency*, pp. 305–6; Morse, *Chronicles, Vol. II*, pp. 271–2.

"considerable fortune." The evidence however equally supports an opposite view of the circumstances.[66]

Gonqua died in prison, under the horrific circumstances related above. Wyequa was banished to Ili in distant Xinjiang, itself a miserable venue. It is true that payments for the benefit of creditors came in from these debtors or their relatives, but the amounts of the payments decreased sharply over time. First, 600,000 taels ($833,333) was paid—in teas and nankeen cloth. This would seem to have been trade merchandise. Next, 100,000 taels ($138,889) was paid—largely in gold. Might this have been family savings? Finally, 1,680 taels ($2,333) was paid almost a decade later by Wyequa's mother Madame Cai—trying to end her son's banishment. Might these funds have been her own? It is quite possible that each of these payments were outside funds, paid by family members or others who cared for Gonqua or Wyequa and hoped to halt or forestall the judicial beatings to which they were subjected. If the debtors actually had funds in "secret storage," those funds appear either to have been tapped out quite early or to have been so effectively secured that the debtors themselves could not get at them in their hour of need. One would expect the debtors to have done everything they could to save themselves by bringing in cash from every possible source. Indeed, the purpose of the judicial beatings was to motivate them to do just that. It is hard to conceive of Gonqua choosing death over emptying his private savings account. It may therefore be more constructive to think of these three payments as a mirror of the process of equity contribution into the Eryi hong business—but thrown into reverse operation. First back in were current trading assets (goods). Next back in were accumulated profits from prior trading, held as savings (largely in gold). Last back in was the original family money that started the hong, a small amount assuredly, but representing the seed from which the large tree had grown that fell in 1795.

As hong merchant firms continued to fail, the Consoo Fund came under pressure in the 1780s and 1790s. This reflects business pressures on the guild,

---

66 Ch'en, *Insolvency*, pp. 303 ("out of their hidden property"), 305 ("took out from their secret storage") and 307 ("it is manifest that he was still in possession of a considerable fortune"). The surviving records of hong merchant debt cases were most often kept by creditors, and as such these accounts, as in the foregoing examples, present only the victorious creditor's view of the subject events. Historical accounts have picked up, probably inadvertently, an antidebtor bias that runs through this primary source material. See, for example, Ch'en, *Insolvency*, pp. 306 (Wyequa's "deserved punishment" in 1796) and 350–1 (quoting an EIC reference to the 1828 departure of Manhop II for banishment "in a style better suited to the station of a wealthy mandarin than that of a degraded bankrupt merchant about to undergo his punishment."). The hong merchants deserve more neutral reporting.

including the end of the era of competing European state trading corporations at Canton, also increased piracy, and the old problem of inadequate capitalization. More fundamentally, the reduced state of the Consoo Fund reflects the frailty of the guaranty system that was adopted in 1780. Neither the Consoo Fund nor the *hangyong* tax that supported it had any independent existence or protection. While the fund and the tax were closely monitored by the hong merchants and by the state, each supervisor had a severe conflict of interest. The interests of foreign creditor beneficiaries of the fund, whether existing or potential, was a first concern of neither. Government officials often dipped into the Consoo Fund for their own needs, and the monitoring function helped them to know when best to draw. Payments to the state were among the original list of purposes of the fund. State needs soared during these years, reflecting civil disorder and a climate of venality that existed in the late years of the Qianlong reign. For their part, the hong merchants had no motivation to keep the fund at a maximum level. As with certain modern private pension schemes, they paid in the minimum that was required. The hong merchants were under stress, and doubtless felt it wise to hold onto their funds and invest the money for return rather than to simply deposit cash that would then sit idle in Consoo Fund chests. The *hangyong* tax was duly collected from the trade and paid into the fund but it was consumed by current expenses. There was no surplus, and the chests of the Consoo Fund were empty by the end of the 1700s.

As reviewed immediately above, foreign creditors made substantial claims against the fund during the period 1780–1799. These claims were largely allowed by the Canton officials and were directed to be paid by the hong merchants despite their origin in loans that were illegal under Chinese law. Even with these benefits, foreign creditors began to understand, during the 1790s, that nothing came free under the guaranty scheme of 1780. Foreign traders, and their customers, paid the costs of the Canton Guaranty System. They paid the general tax on the trade, the *hangyong*, and were also subject to indirect price increases which tended to follow foreign demands for collective guaranty payments from the empty Consoo Fund chest. This understanding drove the foreign response to the hong merchant insolvencies of the early years of the 1800s, when trading conditions grew even more difficult.

CHAPTER 5

Three Plagues: War, Piracy and Litigation, 1800–1814

In the first twenty years of the regime of hong merchant collective liability for debt the process was direct. There were many hong firm failures. In the lesser cases, liabilities rolled on to successors or were settled. In major cases, the claims of creditors were determined through Chinese public debt process and the other hong merchants were ordered to pay allowed claims against failed guild members over time without interest. Under the public process, the hong merchant body was held collectively liable for 1,621,000 taels ($2,251,388) in defaulted foreign debt during the period 1780–1799.

During the next fifteen years, the period 1800–1814, wars in Europe and in Asia, piracy along the South China coast, and bad debts and collection litigation in the United States afflicted both Chinese and Western participants in the Canton trade. As but one example of the problems of these years, two American ships were seized by Danish privateers in 1810 with $128,000 in goods owned by Chinese merchants. One carried $58,000 in tea that was owned by Puiqua (also known as Howqua II) and $32,000 in tea owned by Conseequa. The other carried $38,000 in tea that was owned by various Canton merchants.[1] The hong merchant Puiqua was financially sound as of this date, the exception who could tolerate the loss. As of 1810, Conseequa was embroiled in severe debt problems compared to which his $32,000 Danish loss may have seemed almost negligible. In this difficult period, foreign creditors generally avoided the use of Chinese public process to collect hong debts, for fear that heavy calls on the collective guaranty might bankrupt the entire hong merchant guild.

The basic trade system, described above, stood unchanged. When a foreign vessel arrived at Canton it was assigned to a hong merchant who became responsible (as security merchant) for customs duties owed by the ship, and also for the conduct of its crew and officers. Customs duties were levied under a complex set of rules, applied beginning with the measurement of the arriving vessel, which the foreign traders found difficult to understand. The sale of the ship's import cargo and the purchase of its export goods did not have to be with the hong merchant who secured the vessel, but that merchant usually received some payment from the hong merchant with whom the ship's business was done. The Canton trade was of national significance to China, and a large number of types of commodities were exported and imported. Tea

1 Mazumdar, *Sugar and Society in China*, pp. 115–6.

 | DOI 10.1163/9789004276567_006

was the leading Chinese export of the period, but many other products were shipped, for example, rattan mats, bulk and fine porcelain, and fireworks.[2] The principal import products included specie, rice, and cotton, as well as illegal and untaxed opium brought in from India and Turkey. Transactions with Chinese merchants were carefully negotiated. Initially this was the work of the supercargo (the commercial officer of the Western vessel), but with time firms with local contacts and trade expertise arose at Canton which contracted directly with the hong merchants as agents for distant foreign principals.

Under the Canton System, the hong merchants were required to report to the local officials as a condition of the foreign trade monopoly. The Chinese official most immediately concerned was the Hoppo, the Superintendent of Maritime Customs. The Hoppo reported directly to the Imperial Household Department in Beijing. The two other senior officials at Canton, the Governor-General (also known as Viceroy) and Governor, occasionally become involved in more serious issues or disputes involving foreign trade. When a claim was made by a foreign creditor under the collective guaranty, and it was directed to be paid by the hong merchant body, that order was not final until it had gone up through the Canton officials and received ultimate approval from Beijing.

While the process of the Canton System thus remained much the same as in prior years, the trade itself took on a new character in the years 1800–1814. The era of competition among chartered European state trading corporations had come to an end, and the British East India Company was now the dominant foreign trading company at Canton. Independent traders, from the United States, Great Britain, and other nations, were rising in importance. Although their ships tended to be smaller, they arrived in increasing number and their activities altered the trade. The hong merchants were forced to adjust to the demands of the powerful British EIC and also to changes brought on by the private foreign traders. The illegal trade in opium was on the rise, and the trade monopoly of the hong merchants was increasingly evaded through transactions with outside merchants. Specie carried to Canton by vessels from the United States helped replace the bullion that had formerly been brought in by European trading corporations, and made the supercargoes of American ships desirable trading partners. Howqua II built strong alliances with Americans in these transitional years. Conseequa also traded heavily with independents, but extended large loans to Americans, ending up a casualty of these difficult years.

2 See Nancy Ellen Davis, "The American China Trade, 1784–1844: Products for the Middle Class" (Ph.D. diss., The George Washington University, 1987).

1 The Hong Merchants, 1800–1814

The outer seas guild was in a frail condition in 1800, reduced by the failures of the last years of the eighteenth century. It had eight members. Puankhequa II (Pan Zhixiang of the Tongwen hong) and Mowqua I (Lu Guanheng of the Guangli hong), both in sound condition, were the senior merchants.[3] The other six members were:

> Yanqua (Ye Shanglin of the Yicheng hong) (est. 1792);
> Puiqua (Howqua II) (Wu Bingjian of the Yihe hong) (est. 1792);
> Gnewqua II (Zheng Chongqian, successor proprietor of the Huilong hong);
> Ponqua (Ni Bingfa of the Dacheng hong) (est. 1792);
> Chunqua I (Liu Dezhang of the Dongsheng hong) (est. 1794); and
> Conseequa (Pan Changyao of the Liquan hong) (est. 1796).[4]

Yanqua, who had prospered in his decade as a hong merchant, sought and obtained the Hoppo's permission to retire in 1804. This was the first successful withdrawal by a hong merchant with his capital since 1760. The EIC saw this as a positive sign, which might encourage "respectable" people to join the guild without the fear of becoming trapped by it.[5] The portent however had no significance. Mowqua I attempted to retire in 1804, but was thwarted and obliged to continue in business until his death in 1812. Three years later Puankhequa II is said to have paid $500,000 to obtain permission to retire, but the authorization granted him in 1807 was revoked in 1815. Howqua II asked for but was denied permission to retire in 1807, and ended up as head hong merchant in 1812 upon the death of Mowqua I.[6] Even in "retirement," Yanqua and his family continued to be pressed by the Canton officials to pay money for state needs.[7]

The Hoppo reported the weakened financial condition of the hong merchant body to the Court in the Spring of 1813. The Memorial alarmed senior officials and it was soon proposed that two or more senior hong merchants should be appointed as managers of the guild, with general powers over contracts

---

3 Ch'en, *Insolvency*, pp. 15 and 20–21; Hummel, *Eminent Chinese*, p. 605.

4 Ch'en, *Insolvency*, pp. 15 and 19–21.

5 Ch'en, *Insolvency*, pp. 312–7; White, "Hong Merchants," p. 93; Van Dyke, *Merchants of Canton and Macao*, pp. 195–7.

6 Ch'en, *Insolvency*, pp. 126, 316 and 394 n.58; White, "Hong Merchants," pp. 94–5.

7 Ch'en, *Insolvency*, p. 316; Van Dyke, *Merchants of Canton and Macao*, p. 196.

PLATE 13 *A hong merchant. Oil portrait by Spoilum, ca. 1800.* (*Private collection. Photograph by courtesy of the Martyn Gregory Gallery, London.*)

and pricing. The British EIC adamantly resisted, refusing to unload its ships in response, until the proposal was withdrawn as of February 1814.[8]

Of the eight members of the guild of 1800, only four survived through 1814: Puankhequa II (recalled to business in 1815); Puiqua (Howqua II); Chunqua I;

8 Greenberg, *British Trade*, p. 52; Morse, *Chronicles, Vol. III*, pp. 194–7 and 202–3.

and Conseequa.[9] As of 1813 Conseequa was on life support as one of the five junior hong merchants who were placed in receivership by the EIC and other foreign creditors that year. Conseequa's experiences as a debtor at Canton and as a creditor in numerous courts in the United States, a remarkable and instructive story, is discussed below. Of the seven hong merchants who were admitted to the guild between 1800 and 1814, four ended up subject to the junior merchant receivership of 1813 (along with Conseequa): Goqua I (Xie Jiawu of the Dongyu hong);[10] Loqua (Exchin II);[11] Manhop (I and II); and Poonequa.[12] Inqua, admitted in 1802, failed in 1810. Fonqua (Mu Shifang of the Wancheng hong), who was admitted in 1807, failed in 1809 in part because the $70,000 he paid for a hong license left him with little operating capital.[13] Fatqua I (Li Xiefa of the Wanyuan hong) had exactly the same problem but struggled on

9 Ch'en, *Insolvency*, p. 16.

10 In 1806 the Hoppo allowed Goqua I, a head linguist who wanted to become a trader, to join the hong the struggling Lyqua (Zhou Xinzhao) had founded at the end of 1804. Within two years Lyqua was out, ordered to retire by the Hoppo, and Goqua became the full licensed representative of the hong. Ch'en, *Insolvency*, pp. 19 and 317.

11 Loqua (also known as Exchin II) (Li Yanyu) joined the outer seas hong in 1802 as the proprietor of the Xicheng hong. The firm, established by his father Exchin I (d. 1796), had long engaged in a modest but profitable trade supplying chinaware to the EIC. The father had managed to dodge admission to the guild; the circumstances under which Loqua became a member are unclear. Despite its modest origins and its presumably modest capital, the firm expanded quickly, growing its portion of the EIC's tea business to two shares as of 1809. Loqua extended much credit to Americans, sometimes unsuccessfully, and became involved in speculative trading with India agency houses and Parsis. As the decade 1800–1810 neared an end, the Xicheng hong was deeply in debt and often unable to pay customs duties to the government when due. Ch'en, *Insolvency*, pp. 339–41; *Exsching Looqua v. Dexter*, June term 1815, Records of the Circuit Court of the United States for the District of Rhode Island, Record Group 22, Federal Archives and Records Center, Waltham, Mass. (collection lawsuit: whether it resulted in the payment of money to Loqua is unknown).

12 The Tongtai hong, established by Poonequa (Mai Jinting) in 1811, follows a pattern similar to that of Loqua's Xicheng hong. Poonequa had a good reputation, and Youqua, who was either an employee or partner in the firm, was thought to have excellent judgment in choosing teas. Its business flourished. As of the season 1811–12, the firm had two shares of the EIC's tea business. Unfortunately, the firm's business judgment seems to have been worse than its judgment of teas. It was in severe financial trouble in 1811. As of 1812, the EIC believed that the Tongtai hong owed about $600,000 to country traders and about $400,000 to domestic Chinese creditors. Ch'en, *Insolvency*, pp. 345–6.

13 Fonqua was treated warily by the EIC, did business with country traders whom the other hong merchants believed took advantage of him, and failed within two years. Ch'en, *Insolvency*, pp. 19, 317–8 and 320.

with financial assistance from Mowqua I, to whom he was related, and others.[14] The perhaps happy exception, Kinqua I (Kingqua I) (Liang Jingguo of the Tianbao hong), although financially stressed and said to have been involved in the dangerous practice of "purchasing the privilege" of paying customs duties in the period 1813–1815, survived and remained in business for years thereafter.[15]

Two of the eight members of the guild of 1800 were immediately troubled. Gnewqua II was considered on the edge of failure in the seasons ending 1800 and 1801, but was rescued by a $20,000 loan from other hong merchants to pay customs duties in 1801.[16] Ponqua's Dacheng hong had resorted to desperate practices including "purchasing the privilege" of paying customs duties owed by outside shopkeepers or the agents of country traders. It was near collapse by the end of the 1802–03 season, burdened with over $2.1 million in debt.[17] Ponqua reached an agreement with creditors under which the claims of his Chinese creditors would be deeply discounted and all debts would be paid over a period of years, and brought in help to operate the hong.[18] The Gnewqua II and Ponqua businesses struggled along. The EIC decided that it would prefer to continue to work with Gnewqua II and Ponqua, rather than see them collapse with negative consequences for the entire trade.[19]

2 The Demands of Government, 1800–1814

Demands made by the Canton officials on the Consoo Fund and on the hong merchants individually increased significantly in the troubled years of the early nineteenth century. As noted by British EIC historian Hosea B. Morse, the Consoo Fund "was drawn on so heavily to supplement ordinary taxation that it was not available for the very purpose for which it had been established"—paying the debts of failed hong merchants.[20] Of the climate of official "squeeze" that developed at Canton and across China in this era, John

14 Ch'en, *Insolvency*, pp. 19 and 363.
15 Hummel, *Eminent Chinese*, p. 501; Morse, *Chronicles, Vol. III*, p. 195; White, "Hong Merchants," pp. 99 and 155.
16 Ch'en, *Insolvency*, pp. 229–30 and 327.
17 Ch'en, *Insolvency*, pp. 175–6, 231, 323; Morse, *Chronicles, Vol. III*, p. 195.
18 Ch'en, *Insolvency*, pp. 231–2 and 323; Morse, *Chronicles, Vol. II*, pp. 403–4.
19 Ch'en, *Insolvency*, pp. 231–3.
20 Morse, *Chronicles, Vol. III*, p. 112.

King Fairbank states, "[s]een more sympathetically, the dynasty after 1800 was, no doubt, clutching at every straw to maintain itself."[21]

The records of the British EIC show that payments out of the Consoo Fund increased dramatically in the early years of the nineteenth century. There were no disbursements to pay foreign debts from 1801 to 1808, as the debts ordered to be paid over time in the late 1700s had been satisfied. (See Table 2 and Chart 1.) The three failures of 1809–1810 generated 1,706,000 taels ($2,369,444) in foreign claims, ordered to be paid over a period of years. Despite the magnitude of these claims, there is no record of any attempt ever having been made to adjust the *hangyong* tax on the trade to these losses, or to assess future risk or to adjust the amount of tax in accordance with any estimation of risk. Foreign creditors were deeply concerned that despite the passage of eight years since the satisfaction of the last of the claims ordered to be paid in the 1790s, and the collection of a tax for the benefit of the Consoo Fund, that the fund was unable to satisfy the claims that arose in 1809–1810. The British EIC made a determined effort at this time to understand the fund's income and the expenses, and the limited information that survives concerning Consoo Fund finances for the period are products of that effort. The EIC determined as of 1813, "though with some difficulty," that total annual payments from the Consoo Fund in recent years had been as follows:[22]

21 Fairbank, *Trade and Diplomacy, Vol. I*, p. 52 ("At all events, the result at Canton seems clear—a tradition of 'squeeze' was developed such as had seldom been equaled in Chinese history, even allowing (as Sansom puts it) for the customary 'difference between principle and practice.'").

22 Morse, *Chronicles, Vol. III*, p. 193 ("The above sums include as far as we can learn the whole of the charges made on the Merchants on account of Quan Suie contributions levied by order of Government to meet the exigencies of the State generally for the payment of Troops and Armaments employed in quelling Disturbances—The Repairs of the Embankments of the Wh'ang ho River and other principal Rivers and Canals—The Dividends on Bankrupt Merchants Debts—The payments on account of Clocks Watches and other pieces of Mechanism and the annual payments in the shape of fees donations and gratuity to the several Officers of Government and which are all annually levied on the Hong Merchants in their corporate capacity. The mode of connection appears to be that when the sum required by Government is ascertained a percentage on the Imports and Exports of foreign Trade is levied formerly 3 per cent was deemed sufficient this however from the increase of the charges and the decrease of Foreign Trade is by no means adequate to the Demand and the charge in fact may be considered as exceeding 7 per cent.").

TABLE 2 *Payments from the Consoo Fund, 1806–1813*

1806–1807	691,000 taels ($951,722)
1807–1808	592,000 taels ($822,222)
1808–1809	740,000 taels ($1,027,778)
1809–1810	885,000 taels ($1,229,167)
1810–1811	619,000 taels ($859,722)
1811–1812	763,000 taels ($1,059,722)
1812–1813	698,000 taels ($969,444)

In the years 1802 and 1803 "native tribute" remitted from the Consoo Fund to the Emperor soared to the amount of 150,000 taels ($208,333) annually, rather than the usual 55,000 taels ($76,389). This is said to have followed a series of confrontations between the strained hong merchants and Hoppo Jieshan, who sought retribution against the guild by reporting their "voluntary" agreement to a sharp payment increase to the throne.[23] In the years 1805 and 1806, for which there is more detail, 55,000 taels in "native tribute" went to the Emperor annually, plus singsong gifts to the Court in Beijing (expenses of 150,000 taels in 1805 and 200,000 taels in 1806), and 5,400 taels ($7,500) annually for presents to high officials. Boat construction for anti-pirate operations cost 30,000 taels ($41,667) in 1805 and 70,000 taels ($97,222) in 1806, and Yellow River flood control and relief cost 37,500 taels ($52,083) in both 1805 and 1806. Other military expenses, local and national, were 80,000 taels ($111,111) in 1805 and 81,666 taels ($113,425) in 1806.[24] Total draw from the Consoo Fund for these purposes is recorded at 357,900 taels ($497,083) in 1805 and 449,566 taels ($624,397) in 1806.

In 1817 six of the junior merchants, who sought financial support from the British EIC, were required by the EIC to disclose the payments that had been made out of the Consoo Fund during the prior ten years. The detailed list they provided of payments from 1807 through 1816 shows that a total of 3,438,057 taels ($4,775,079) had been paid out of the Consoo Fund during this period.[25] The annual total ranged from a high of 568,000 taels ($788,889) in 1811 to a low of 194,166 taels ($269,675) in 1807. The average annual draw was 343,805.7 taels ($477,508). Foreign debt payments totaled 1,338,000 taels ($1,858,333), or 39%

23 Ch'en, *Insolvency*, pp. 97–98.

24 Morse, *Chronicles, Vol. III*, p. 62.

25 Morse, *Chronicles, Vol. III*, pp. 309–11; Cheong, *Hong Merchants*, pp. 224–25.

of total payments out of the fund during the ten year period.[26] The only consistent annual expenditure was 55,000 taels ($76,389) in "native tribute" sent to the Emperor, amounting to 16% of total payments from the fund over the ten year period (550,000 taels) ($763,889). Other significant recurring expenses were: Yellow River flood control and relief, 553,500 taels ($768,750) (16% of the total);[27] piracy suppression efforts, 339,800 taels ($471,944) (1807–1812) (10% of the total);[28] military expenses, local and national, 329,757 taels ($457,996) (10% of the total);[29] and Shandong Province famine relief, 90,000 taels ($125,000) (1814–1816) (3% of the total). Nonrecurring expenses included: 120,000 taels ($166,667) for presents for the Emperor's birthday in 1809; and 73,700 taels ($102,361) in non-foreign debt expenses resulting from Gnewqua's failure, including arrears of customs duties and his own arrears due to the Consoo Fund itself (all amounting to 193,700 taels [$269,028] or 6% of the total). While their disclosure might be questioned both on the basis of whether these junior merchants had access to complete and accurate Consoo Fund data, and of the bias inherent in disclosure to the EIC in support of pleas for loan support, the numbers provided generally square with other information available about the amounts of and trends in government exactions.

3 Trading Conditions, 1800–1814

The first quarter of the nineteenth century was a period of high risk and potentially high reward for merchants engaged in foreign trade. The Napoleonic Wars, fought in Europe and Asia, had a substantial effect both on foreign

---

26 Morse, *Chronicles, Vol. III*, pp. 309–11 (1809, 84,200 taels (Gnewqua II); 1810, 128,800 taels (foreign debts); 1811, 398,100 taels (foreign debts); 1812, 146,400 taels (foreign debts); 1813, 145,500 taels (foreign debts); 1814, 145,000 taels (foreign debts); 1815, 145,000 taels (foreign debts); and 1816, 145,000 taels (foreign debts)).

27 Morse, *Chronicles, Vol. III*, pp. 309–11 (Yellow River flood control and relief: 1807, 37,500 taels; 1808, 150,000 taels; 1809, 52,500 taels; 1812, 60,000 taels; 1813, 73,500 taels; 1814, 60,000 taels; 1815, 60,000 taels; and 1816, 60,000 taels).

28 Morse, *Chronicles, Vol. III*, pp. 309–11 (suppression of piracy: 1807, 60,000 taels; 1808, 20,000 taels; 1809, 149,800 taels; 1810, 50,000 taels; 1811, 30,000 taels; and 1812, 30,000 taels).

29 Morse, *Chronicles, Vol. III*, pp. 309–11 (Military expenses: 1807, 41,666 taels (Sichuan and Shanxi); 1808, 41,666 taels (Sichuan and Shanxi) and 10,000 taels (Macao); 1809, 20,000 taels (river barriers and forts) and 10,000 taels (Macao); 1810, 41,600 taels (Sichuan and Shanxi); 1811, 41,600 taels (Sichuan and Shanxi) and 43,300 taels (Macao); 1812, 41,600 taels (Sichuan and Shanxi) and 33,300 taels (Macao); and 1816, 5,325 taels (Bogue forts, first installment)).

trade with China and on the domestic Chinese economy. The flow of silver to China, the lifeblood of the trade, was repeatedly interrupted. The Embargo of United States trade imposed on 22 December 1807 halted the shipment of American silver until it was lifted in March 1809, in the course ruining many American merchants who traded with China. The flow of American silver was also impaired by the War of 1812, fought between Britain and the United States until 1815. Revolts in Spanish America sharply cut the historic flow of South American silver via Manila, and the opening of trade between India and London raised prospects of quick return in that trade which drew funds away from China. The maritime trade of Canton was accordingly affected by a serious cash squeeze in the years 1800 to 1814. Foreign traders responded by developing the use of private notes and bills to finance a trade which to this point had largely been conducted in cash.[30] The hong merchants had no such easy alternative. Their debts to foreign creditors soared through this period.

Already a problem in the 1790s, coastal piracy grew worse yet, at once a symptom and a cause of problems with the regional economy. The pirates (ladrones) had large numbers of ships and operated with impunity. Seaborne trade was disrupted and at points in 1802 and 1805 pirate fleets threatened Canton and the foreign factories. U.S. Consul Edward Carrington reported in 1807 to Secretary of State James Madison that "The Coast of China and particularly the entrance to this Port, have for a long time been infested by China Ladrones or Pirates, in very alarming and considerable forces." Government forces proved largely useless against the pirates, until coordinated action finally bore fruit with a mass pirate surrender in April 1810.[31]

The hong merchants were severely affected by these trading conditions. As the American merchant Peter Snow related in an August 1811 letter to Edward

30 Weng Eang Cheong, "Trade and Finance in China: 1784–1834, A Reappraisal," Business History (Liverpool), Vol. 7, pp. 34–56 (1965), pp. 40–1; Weng Eang Cheong, "The Beginnings of Credit Finance on the China Coast: The Canton Financial Crisis of 1812–1815," Business History (Liverpool), Vol. 13, pp. 70–92 (1971), p. 87; Fichter, *So Great a Proffit:*, pp. 56–72; John D. Forbes, "European Wars and Boston Trade, 1783–1815," New England Quarterly, Vol. 11, pp. 709–730 (1938); Gibson, *Otter Skins*, p. 103; Kenneth S. Latourette, "The History of Early Relations Between the United States and China," Transactions of the Connecticut Academy of Arts and Sciences, Vol. 22, pp. 1–209 (1917), p. 27 n.3; Stelle, "American Trade in Opium to China, Prior to 1820," pp. 425 and 443; Herbert J. Wood, "England, China, and the Napoleonic Wars," Pacific Historical Review, Vol. 9, pp. 139–56 (1940).

31 Ch'en, *Insolvency*, pp. 85–6; Gibson, *Otter Skins*, p. 189; Leonard, *Wei Yuan*, pp. 80–3; Murray, *Pirates of the South China Coast*, pp. 85, 87–8, 105, 111, 119, 131 and 137–50; Morse, *Chronicles, Vol. III*, pp. 7–8; Anonymous, "Chinese Pirates," Chinese Repository, Vol. 3, pp. 62–83 (June 1834).

Carrington, "The Hong Merchants with a few exceptions as you may have anticipated before your departure are in a bad state—all but Mouqua Houqua and Chunqua are unable to pay their duties, and some of them I am told are in want even of the common necessaries of life." He spoke of an outside shopman. "Old Tuckee pays me a visit about once a week—he says that China Man this time to muche hot for money—and chin chins hard for your ship to come—I tell him no fear. He heaves a heavy sigh and departs."[32]

Many American traders were troubled as well. Large numbers had been ruined by the Embargo, which held their vessels idle in port running up bills while depriving them of the revenues to pay those and other expenses. They lacked funds to pay loans taken before the Embargo, and perhaps more distant creditors could be more easily ignored. As Helen of Troy is remembered as the face that launched a thousand ships, the Embargo of 1807–09 should be remembered as the force that launched innumerable lawsuits. With many Americans debtors having defaulted on loans made to them by Chinese merchants before the Embargo, credit now available to Americans at Canton was constricted,[33] and many lawsuits were brought in the United States by Chinese merchants to collect these debts.[34] Chinese who filed collection actions in American federal and state courts in the early nineteenth century include the hong merchants Chunqua I, Conseequa, Loqua (Exchin II), Howqua II and Pacqua (Exchin III), along with the outside merchants Cowqua, Eshing, Keetshing, Kingling, Namshing, Thonching and Youqua.[35]

---

32 Letter from Peter W. Snow (Canton) to Edward Carrington, 11 August 1811, Edward Carrington Papers, MSS 333, SG I, Series 1, Box 13, Rhode Island Historical Society, Providence, Rhode Island.

33 Dennett, *Americans in Eastern Asia*, p. 85.

34 Frederic D. Grant, Jr., "Hong Merchant Litigation in the American Courts," Proceedings of the Massachusetts Historical Society, Vol. 99, pp. 44–62 (1987); Stelle, "American Trade in Opium to China, Prior to 1820," pp. 436–7.

35 Grant, "Hong Merchant Litigation," pp. 44–62. It is almost certain that other lawsuits were filed by Chinese merchants for which records have not been found, as for example in the Court of Common Pleas of Philadelphia County, the records of which court for this period have been lost. Carelessness and inconsistency in the transcription of the trading names of Chinese merchant litigants by American merchants, lawyers, court clerks and court reporters make it difficult to match Chinese litigants with known hong merchants and outside shopmen. An original promissory note found in the files of the case styled as *Chomqua v. Mason*, 5 F. Cas. 649 (C.C.D.R.I. 1812) (No. 2,693) establishes that the plaintiff "Chomqua" is the hong merchant Chunqua. Chunqua's name was also rendered as Cheongwo and Cheonqua. *Cheongwo v. Jones*, 5 F. Cas. 544 (C.C.E.D. Pa. 1818) (No. 2,638); *Cheonqua v. Tagert*, Apr. term 1816, No. 45, Records of the Circuit Court for the District of Pennsylvania. The hong merchant Loqua (Exchin II) is the plaintiff in *Exsching Looqua*

4 The Collective Guaranty of Debt, 1800–1814

Heavy demands were placed on the collective guaranty during this troubled period, all in its later years. Proceedings after the 1809 failure of Fonqua resulted in 259,000 taels ($359,722) in allowed foreign claims, which were ordered to be paid by the hong merchant body in three annual installments without interest. The 1810 proceedings on the insolvencies of Gnewqua II and Ponqua produced an additional 1,447,000 taels ($2,012,609) in allowed foreign claims, which the hong merchants were ordered to pay in ten annual installments without interest. In all of these cases, the Canton officials recognized and directed the payment of claims that arose from extensions of credit that were illegal under Chinese law.

The total collective guaranty liability that was assessed in the fifteen year period 1800–1814 is 1,706,000 taels ($2,369,444), which averages at 113,733 taels ($157,963) annually. While this sum might not seem that bad for hard times, the collective guaranty liability, as an annual average, was up sharply from the prior twenty year period. Total collective guaranty liability assessed to the hong merchant body in the period 1780–1799 was 1,621,000 taels ($2,251,388), an average of 81,050 taels ($112,569) annually. The average annual assessment under the collective guaranty for the period 1800–1814 was 32,684 taels ($45,394) more than in the earlier period, a forty percent (40%) increase.[36]

The first imposition of collective liability after 1800 was in a case in which the hong merchant body complained about the sharp practices of country traders with weaker members of the guild. Fonqua (Mu Shifang) had become deeply indebted to country traders within two years of opening his Wancheng hong. In 1809 the hong merchants were pressed by two Parsi creditors, Hormajee Dorabjee and Dosabhae Monackjee, to pay these debts, or else they would petition the authorities. The guild saw the debts as excessive, and replied that the creditors had taken advantage of Fonqua's weakness by overpricing Indian

v. Dexter, June term 1815, Records of the Circuit Court of the United States for the District of Rhode Island, Record Group 22, Federal Archives and Records Center, Waltham, Mass., and the hong merchant Pacqua (sometimes Pakqua) is the plaintiff in *Pacqua v. Pleasants*, Apr. term 1822, No. 4, Records of the Circuit Court for the District of Pennsylvania. Morse, *Chronicles, Vol. III*, pp. 208, 234, and Vol. IV, p. 57. Actions commenced by outside merchants include: *Keetshing v. Wells*, Apr. term 1822, No. 36, Records of the Circuit Court for the District of Pennsylvania; *Kingling v. Read*, Apr. term 1805, No. 68, Records of the Circuit Court for the District of Pennsylvania; *Namshing v. Coe*, Apr. term 1826, No. 25, Records of the Circuit Court for the District of Pennsylvania; and *Thonching v. Coe*, Apr. term 1826, No. 28, Records of the Circuit Court for the District of Pennsylvania.

36 Ch'en, *Insolvency*, p. 96 (Table 2.7).

goods they sold him on credit. Members would agree to pay this debt, but a levy of one tael per picul would need to be imposed on imports of Indian cotton to cover the cost. With negotiations thus at an impasse, word of the proposed cotton levy reached the EIC which told the guild it would be an unacceptable burden on the country trade. The creditors then petitioned Hoppo Changxian and Governor-General Bailing about the Wancheng hong debts, as they had threatened. The Governor-General directed the hong merchants to reach an agreement with the creditors. This brought on a second round of negotiations, opening with a proposal by the hong merchants to pay the debt in three equal annual installments without interest. Several proposals were in turn rejected by the creditors, who finally accepted the last proposal. Just then, the Governor-General issued an order in which he directed payment of Fonqua's debts in three equal annual installments without interest (the hong merchants' opening offer). In a joint memorial to the throne, the Governor-General, Governor and Hoppo reported that the matter had been resolved under the precedents in which hong merchants who violated the 1760 debt prohibition and borrowed money from the foreigners and engaged in intrigue with them were punished under the law concerning criminals who plotted with a foreign country and cheated foreigners of their goods and money. Fonqua's assets were liquidated, he was stripped of his purchased official title, and he was banished to Ili. The hong merchants were ordered to assume 259,000 taels ($359,722) of Fonqua's debts. These debts were paid in three annual installments, the second having been significantly delayed due to the 1810 failures of Ponqua and Gnewqua. Fonqua's EIC debt was satisfied by delivery by Mowqua to the EIC of teas of equivalent value.[37]

The difficult period 1800–1814 saw two notable attempts to evade the Canton Guaranty System. In form and in substance, each is quite different from the types of behavior which are seen as attempts to escape the restrictions of modern bank guaranty schemes. The first was the 1810 receivership of the hongs of Gnewqua II and Ponqua. That evasion was terminated almost immediately with the arrest of the Chinese subject who acted as receiver for the British EIC, discussed in the following pages. The second was the 1813 receivership of five junior hong merchants, discussed further below. As the latter attempt did not directly interfere with hong operations under official monopoly license, it was allowed to run its course. The element that these evasions have in common with certain modern examples is that each failed, with the result that large—

37 Ch'en, *Insolvency*, pp. 96 (Table 2.7) and 319–323; Ng, "Ch'ing Management of the West," pp. 166–7.

and probably increased—claims ended up being filed, allowed and paid by the hong merchants under the Canton guaranty process.

5 The Abortive 1810 Receivership of Gnewqua II and Ponqua

The EIC became aware in 1809 that two massively indebted hongs were about to fail. Resort to the collective guaranty threatened to shift a debt burden exceeding $2 million onto the other hongs, many of which were themselves troubled. That summer, Ponqua (Ni Bingfa of the Dacheng hong)[38] had been petitioned against for $240,000 due to the Parsi merchant Hormajee Dorabjee. The Governor-General ordered the hong merchants to pay this debt in three annual installments.[39] In November 1809 the EIC learned that Ponqua had not used the proceeds of woolens it had delivered to him to pay advances to tea merchants, as he was supposed to, and concluded that upon the deadline for duties to be paid to the government, Ponqua would fail.[40] In December 1809 it received word from Ahoy, a recently admitted business partner of Gnewqua II (Zheng Chongqian of the Huilong hong),[41] who had fled Canton. Ahoy reported that he had just learned that this hong owed massive secret debt to Chinese creditors, and that Gnewqua II had been borrowing money on desperate terms, further jeopardizing its affairs. By contrast, Ponqua's recently admitted partner See Samyee (Shi Sanyo) did not flee Canton until February 1810.[42]

The EIC decided that it would not petition about the unpaid debts of Gnewqua II or Ponqua. Its concerns, as noted in its records, were realistic.

> Should these merchants be allowed to break, and the amount of their debts to Europeans and for duties fall upon the other Merchants, it is more than some of them would be able to support, the Hong generally consisting of young Merchants who cannot be expected to do more than discharge their own immediate claims; from the accumulated pressure

38 Ponqua, who was licensed to operate the Dacheng hong in 1792, was pushed to the edge by imposition of his share of collective responsibility for debts of Gonqua in 1795 and had been in financial distress for many years. Ch'en, *Insolvency*, pp. 214–5, 229 and 294–5.

39 Morse, *Chronicles, Vol. III*, pp. 110–1.

40 Ch'en, *Insolvency*, pp. 232–4.

41 Gnewqua II assumed control of the Huilong hong, established by his father Gnewqua I (Zheng Shangqian) in 1793, upon the father's death in 1795. Ch'en, *Insolvency*, pp. 212, 229 and 327.

42 Ch'en, *Insolvency*, pp. 233 and 235–6; Morse, *Chronicles, Vol. III*, p. 111.

> therefore that would ensue, it is difficult to say where the evil would end, but it appears certain that a total loss of confidence and the most serious difficulties to the trade must be the result.[43]

If a debt petition were to be presented, officials would "no doubt either on their own authority or by reference to Peking direct the payment of debts to Europeans in a certain number of years—from the magnitude of the debts, six, is perhaps the least that can be expected, but more probably eight or even ten."[44] These concerns are echoed in observations on the collective guarantee written in November 1807 by John Gibson, a trader from Philadelphia. Gibson's comments are notable both for his early view that the Consoo Fund enjoyed the further guarantee of the Chinese government ("the Emperor ultimately guarantees them"), and for his cold realism about the system's practical frailities. "This gives a degree of security greater than you find in any other country. But nothing would be more Erroneous than to trust this security for should you ultimately gain redress by an application to the laws of the Land, the delays would perhaps be equally destructive to your prospects as the loss of the original debt."[45]

The EIC determined that it would assume management of the two failing hongs and try to pay foreign debts from their operating (liquidating) profits. It opted to act through a receiver, under its direction—"confidential persons working in the interest of the bankrupts, but under the supervision of the Committee." The EIC further decided to save money by consolidating operations, bringing the business of Ponqua's Dacheng hong under the umbrella of the Huilong hong licensed to Gnewqua II. The hong merchants did not assent to the EIC plan for consolidation and liquidation but EIC records state that they "did not resist it strenuously," either. Private foreign creditors agreed to give the plan a chance, but reserved final decision.[46]

Ashing (Wu Shining), who had been head clerk of Ponqua's hong, was hired by the EIC to act as receiver. He took charge in February 1810, continuing the business of the Ponqua and Gnewqua II hongs under the name of the Huilong

43 Morse, *Chronicles, Vol. III*, p. 111.

44 Ch'en, *Insolvency*, p. 224.

45 John Gibson, "Observations on the manner of trading at Canton," 13 November 1807, Philadelphia, Pennsylvania (Collection of Cornell University, Kroch Library Rare and Manuscript Department) (32 pages), pp. 8–9 ("The Co-hong consists of eleven members appointed by the Emperor to Trade with Foreigners. They mutually agree to Guarantee the Debts of each other contracted with those Foreigners, & the Emperor ultimately Guarantees them.").

46 Ch'en, *Insolvency*, pp. 224 and 236–7; Morse, *Chronicles, Vol. III*, pp. 112–3.

hong. He made contracts with tea merchants for the new season under his own seal, *shengji*, rather than under the seal of the Huilong hong. The purpose of the variant seal was to prevent creditors of Gnewqua II from seizing these teas if Gnewqua II became involved in debt proceedings.[47]

The authorities promptly arrested Ashing. In May 1810 he was brought before Governor-General Bailing for multiple violations of Chinese law. The most serious charge was that he had violated the trade monopoly by making tea contracts for foreign trade without a government license. Ashing was also charged with having violated the law barring Chinese from working for foreigners. He had previously worked for the EIC as a menial servant, and the receivership was viewed as a continuation of that service. Prosecution was triggered by petitions to the authorities from the remarkable number of sixty-four Chinese creditors, complaining of the receivership. For its part, the EIC believed Chunqua I had tipped off the authorities, in order to secure the debtors' shares of EIC business. The Governor-General told the EIC that Ashing stood accused of conspiring "and in the dark making use of the foreigners wealth [he] carried on Gnewqua's hong to the detriment of the inland tea dealers." Ashing duly confessed, providing a detailed description of his activities as receiver to the Canton authorities.[48]

With Ashing imprisoned, and the receivership terminated, Gnewqua II and Ponqua were arrested and their property was seized. On 6 October 1810, the Hoppo entered an order determining the amounts of duties they respectively owed, directing the sale of their assets, and ordering the hong merchant body to pay the rest of the arrearage of customs duties. The Hoppo also directed foreign creditors of Gnewqua II and Ponqua to file statements of the amount of their claims. Foreign claims, through termination of the EIC receivership, totaled 1,447,000 taels ($2,012,609). On 24 November 1810 the Nanhai Magistrate, acting for the Governor-General, announced that these claims would be paid by the hong merchants in ten equal annual installments without interest. "Protests from the Committee were met by indignant surprise that any one should venture to resist or criticize the Viceroy's decree." On 18 April 1811, foreign creditors were told that this ruling had been approved by the Emperor.[49] Gnewqua II,

47 Ch'en, *Insolvency*, pp. 62–3, 237–9 and 354; Morse, *Chronicles, Vol. III*, pp. 151–2.

48 Ch'en, *Insolvency*, pp. 62–3, 237–9 and 354; Morse, *Chronicles, Vol. III*, pp. 148 and 151–2.

49 Ch'en, *Insolvency*, pp. 62–3, 96 (Table 2.7), 237–9, 241 and 354; Morse, *Chronicles, Vol. III*, pp. 105 and 148–52. The debtors also owed large amounts to the government. At failure, Gnewqua II and Ponqua respectively owed 89,000 taels and 88,000 taels in unpaid customs duties. Jointly they owed another 30,000 taels in piracy control assessments. Morse, *Chronicles, Vol. III*, pp. 150–1 and 192 and Vol. IV, p. 83; Cheong, *Hong Merchants*, p. 92 n.49.

Ponqua and Ashing were ordered banished to Ili, in accordance with the law that penalized Chinese citizens who plotted with or cheated foreigners, and were stripped of their purchased official titles Given the gravity of his offense, Ashing was subjected to the further punishment of being forced to wear the cangue (a form of yoke) for a period of three months. Ponqua died in prison at Canton on 15 February 1811, at the age of fifty, before he could be exiled, and Gnewqua II died shortly after arrival in Ili.[50] Ashing survived and returned to Canton twelve years later in 1823.[51]

The EIC made at least one attempt to secure relief for Ashing. A remarkable exchange occurred in April 1811, upon the arrival in Canton of Governor-General Songyun. George Staunton of the EIC knew Songyun, having met him twenty years earlier when as a young man he had traveled to Beijing with the British Macartney embassy of 1793. Songyun agreed to see Staunton. Their private meeting was convivial through the moment Staunton presented a written note in Chinese about Ashing. The Governor-General read it quickly. He looked at Staunton and told him that the case "was serious and was already and finally settled" and refused to accept the letter.[52]

Six months later, it was Songyun who raised the subject of Ashing. The hong merchants had responded to an October 1811 demand for funds to meet national exigencies by complaining that this expense was simply too great on top of the burden of the recently failed hongs. In response, the Governor-General proposed to extend the repayment period of the Gnewqua II and Ponqua debt from ten to sixteen years. He sweetened his offer by saying that Ashing and Gnewqua II would be freed from prison if the EIC consented. The EIC refused to modify. It also took the position that it had no right to change the settlement on behalf of other foreign creditors.[53] While the EIC was concerned about Ashing's plight, its concern had only modest cash value.

In the middle of 1810, while in the midst of dealing with the abortive Ashing receivership which itself had been triggered by the flight of the newly admitted junior partners of the Dacheng (Ponqua) and Huilong (Gnewqua II) hongs, the

50 Ch'en, *Insolvency*, pp. 239–40 and 327; Cheong, *Hong Merchants*, p. 92 n.49; Morse, *Chronicles, Vol. III*, p. 153; Ng, "Ch'ing Management of the West," p. 169.

51 Ch'en, *Insolvency*, p. 241 ("The Select Committee, feeling responsible to provide a living for the rest of Ashing's life, granted him two 'chops' (lots) of tea through one of the Hong merchants, for three consecutive years [after his 1823 return]. By such an arrangement, the Committee gave Ashing a total sum of about 12,000 taels in the form of profit."); Morse, *Chronicles, Vol. IV*, p. 83.

52 Morse, *Chronicles, Vol. III*, pp. 169–70.

53 Ch'en, *Insolvency*, pp. 240–1; Morse, *Chronicles, Vol. III*, p. 153.

British EIC learned that yet another hong partner had taken flight. Now it was Inqua (Deng Zhaoxiang) who had fled—he never was found—abandoning his Fulong hong and his partner Manhop I (Guan Xiang) burdened with roughly 700,000 taels ($972,222) in debt to foreign creditors, plus unpaid customs duties and debt to Chinese creditors. Manhop I was pressed to stay in place and to assume together with his son Manhop II (Guan Chengfa) the liabilities Inqua had incurred. The Manhops did so. The Hoppo cooperated to the extent of reissuing the Fulong hong license in the name of the son as of the end of the 1810–11 season without payment of any fee. The Fulong hong was thus restarted as of 1811, under new management, but still mired in debt.[54]

6 The 1813 Receivership of the Junior Hong Merchants

In the wake of the failure of the Ashing receivership, there was grave concern about the viability of seven "junior merchant" firms: Conseequa, Goqua I, Loqua (also known as Exchin II), Manhop (I and II), Poonequa, Kinqua I and Fatqua I. Their debts were significant. As of March 1809, Conseequa owed 670,769 taels ($931,027) to the British EIC alone.[55] In 1812, the EIC decided to intervene in the cases of the five principal debtors, paying current hong expenses, and deducting them from the given merchant's account at the end of the season. Under EIC leadership, private creditors of these five debtors—Conseequa, Goqua I, Loqua (Exchin II), Manhop (I and II) and Poonequa—agreed to work together, appointing three trustees as of January 1813 to superintend affairs and pay existing debts. Private creditors agreed "to stop charging any interest on the debts contracted by the five merchants in question prior to 1813, and to wait for the gradual liquidation of their claims from the commercial profits of these merchants expected in the years to come." The EIC had effective control over the trusteeship; two of the three trustees were its employees (James Molony, junior supercargo, and Alexander Pearson, surgeon), and the third trustee,

54 Ch'en, *Insolvency*, pp. 213, 328–30, 349 and 375 n.36; Morse, *Chronicles, Vol. III*, p. 135. Although Manhop II (Guan Chengfa) was also known as "Fatqua," he is not referred to by that name herein, in order to avoid confusion with Li Xiefa and Li Yinggui (the son of Li Xiefa) who traded during the same period under the names Fatqua I and Fatqua II respectively (of the Wanyuan hong). Ch'en, *Insolvency*, pp. 19–20, 349 and 363–4.

55 Frederic D. Grant, Jr., "The Failure of the Li-ch'uan Hong: Litigation as a Hazard of Nineteenth Century Foreign Trade," American Neptune, Vol. 48, pp. 243–60 (1988), pp. 259–60.

Hollingsworth Magniac, was a British private trader.[56] In contrast to the receivership of Gnewqua II and Ponqua, the trustees of the junior hong merchants did not attempt to operate the subject hongs or to control the official hong seal under which these hongs did business. The EIC increased cash flow to the debtors by allocating extra shares of its business to the insolvent merchants. Claims against the trust (all pre-1813) totaled $3,964,297: Conseequa, $822,906; Goqua, $341,953; Loqua (Exchin II), $820,610; Manhop (I and II), $1,237,681 (891,130 taels); and Poonequa, $741,147.[57]

Yet already by the summer of 1813, the junior merchants were again in trouble. In June Conseequa appealed again to the EIC for help paying his customs duties and other sums owed to the government. The situation worsened with the 17 August 1813 arrival of a new Hoppo, who refused to take over from the old Hoppo until the hong merchants brought their customs duties completely current. In desperation, four of the junior hong merchants (Conseequa, Goqua, the Manhops and Poonequa) sought funds at forty percent interest for this need, but even at that premium they could not borrow enough money. The EIC finally stepped in as lender of last resort to advance the 166,000 taels ($230,556) required to pay off the customs duties, but it had to borrow this sum from Howqua II and Mowqua as the EIC did not have sufficient cash in its own treasury.[58] Steady payments were made over the years on account of the trust debt, in varying amounts according to the ability of the junior hong debtors. The balance due was thus reduced, but the condition of the debtors was not materially improved.

In hong debt cases, during the troubled period 1800–1814, foreign creditors thus sought to avoid the Chinese public debt process and having to make claims on the guaranty fund. Whether this is considered simply as an abstention, or rather as an evasion of the system, it did not improve matters. The Consoo Fund enjoyed an initial eight years of relief, from 1801 through 1808, during which no payments were made on foreign claims. The debts of the 1790s had been satisfied, and the *hangyong* tax was going into the fund. Unfortunately, the Chinese government opted to step in and take what foreign creditors did not seem to need. For its part, the state acted in response to its own urgent needs, including piracy in the waters off Canton, which represented a true crisis in the years leading up to 1810. The Consoo Fund was defenseless, with no

56 Ch'en, *Insolvency*, pp. 242–9; Morse, Chronicles, Vol. 3, p. 183, and Vol. 4, pp. 410–1 and 414; Grant, "Failure of the Li-ch'uan Hong," pp. 253–254.

57 Ch'en, *Insolvency*, pp. 245, 335, 340–2, 346, 349 and 355; Morse, *Chronicles, Vol. III*, pp. 233–4.

58 Ch'en, *Insolvency*, pp. 167–8; Morse, *Chronicles, Vol. III*, pp. 195–7.

independent guardian. Many of the hong merchants, the constituency most immediately concerned with the fund, were themselves struggling to survive. Defending the interests of undetermined creditor beneficiaries of the fund that would pay claims arising from the failure of their own firms was no priority of individual members of the outer seas guild.

As always, there was hope for tomorrow. While the claims that were ordered to be paid from the fund over time were large, the foreign wars were over at long last and there was reason to expect a strong rebound in trade.

CHAPTER 6

Years of Rebound and Opium, 1815–1828

The collective guaranty liabilities that were imposed during the period 1815 to 1828 were substantial, but all involved firms which had been in difficult condition in 1815. These failures link the period covered by this chapter with the period covered by the preceding chapter (1800–1814). Four of the five junior hongs that had been put into receivership in 1813 failed in this later period. Conseequa failed in 1823 owing 372,000 taels ($516,336) in foreign debt, which was ordered paid in three annual installments without interest. Pacqua failed in 1826 owing 618,904 taels ($859,589) in government and foreign debt. His foreign debt of 477,216 taels ($662,800) was ordered paid in five annual installments without interest. Poonequa failed in 1827 owing 196,000 taels ($272,222) in government and foreign debt. His foreign debt of 86,000 taels ($119,444) was ordered paid in three equal annual installments without interest. The Fulong hong of the Manhops failed in 1828 owing 1,054,600 taels ($1,464,722) in government and foreign debt. Its foreign debt of 792,000 taels ($1,099,300) was ordered paid in six annual installments without interest.

During this fourteen year period a growing amount of trade, including but not limited to the thriving illegal traffic in opium, was conducted outside of the hong merchant monopoly. Within the guild, winners were becoming more sharply delineated from losers. The hong failures of this period could have been predicted from the start, and no new merchants came in to replace the gaps that opened in the lower ranks of the guild. Excessive risk, including but not limited to collective liability for the imprudence or business losses of colleagues, discouraged entry.

1 The Hong Merchants, 1815–1828

The fourteen year period 1815 to 1828 began with the outer seas guild in a troubled condition. Of its eleven members, seven—almost two thirds of the group—were experiencing financial difficulty. Five remained under the foreign receivership that began in 1813. Kinqua I and Fatqua I had dodged the receivership but were under stress.[1] Chunqua I's hong was stable, although it

1 Ch'en, *Insolvency*, p. 242; Morse, *Chronicles, Vol. III*, p. 247 (the EIC did not reply to the Hoppo's question whether these hongs owed it money).

 | DOI 10.1163/9789004276567_007

had experienced strain during the war years.[2] The firms of the three head merchants were also in good condition. It was said in the 1820s that there were only four hong merchants with whom it was safe to deal.[3]

The Canton officials were concerned about the capitalization of the guild. The retirement of Puankhequa II was revoked in 1815 and he was ordered to resume the business of the Tongwen hong. Puankhequa II, Howqua II and Mowqua II served jointly thereafter as the three head hong merchants, although Howqua II stood as the true head due to his seniority and "reputed wealth."[4] The guild had thus separated, by not later than 1815, into two distinct groups: an upper tier of better capitalized firms, which ran the guild, and a lower tier group of impoverished hongs, which struggled to survive.

Within the upper tier, Howqua II stood at the top. He is often quoted as having estimated his net worth at $26 million as of 1834.[5] It is sometimes said that Howqua was the richest businessman or even the wealthiest man in the world at that time,[6] propositions which are open to question. Howqua II most certainly did not share this estimate of personal resources with the Canton officials. Such indiscretion would have attracted even more and still greater financial demands by the government on him. It is probable that his many assets, said to have included tea plantations in the Wuyi hills, were held in a variety of different names and forms, some with family members and some quite possibly with joint venturers or partners, and that some would have been subject to debt or obligations in the nature of debt. This is normal. It is also reasonable to assume that the wealth held by Howqua II had been gradually built from the original capital and earnings of the Yihe hong founded by his father and run by his brother from 1792 to 1799, and quite likely from capital others provided before and since. Therefore, while it appears that Howqua II personally enjoyed business triumphs and fat earnings in the tricky years of the early nineteenth century, the wealth that is often spoken of as "his" was likely

2 Ch'en, *Insolvency*, p. 357.

3 Greenberg, *British Trade*, p. 86.

4 Ch'en, *Insolvency*, p. 23.

5 Hunter, *Fan Kwae*, p. 48 ("The amount of Houqua's fortune was frequently a subject of debate; but on one occasion, in referring to it in connection with his various investments in rice-fields, dwellings, shops, and the banking establishments known as shroffs, and including his American and English shipments, he estimated it, in 1834, at twenty-six millions of dollars."); Robert Gardella, *Harvesting Mountains: Fujian and the China Tea Trade, 1757–1937* (Berkeley: Univ. of California Press, 1994), p. 35; Sung, "Study of the Thirteen Hongs," pp. 4 and 22–23; White, "Hong Merchants," pp. 83, 94–6 and 108.

6 http://online.wsj.com/public/resources/documents/mill-1-timeline-howqua.htm (accessed 26 March 2014); http://www.encyclo.co.uk/define/Howqua (accessed 26 March 2014).

PLATE 14 *Too big to fail 'with Chinese characteristics.' The senior hong merchant Howqua II (Wu Bingjian), 1769–1843. Oil portrait by Lamqua (Guan Qiaochang), ca. 1840, originally owned by Warren Delano II. (Private collection. Photograph by permission.)*

tangled up with amicable claims or interests of immediate Wu kin. While there is no doubt that Howqua II was the wealthiest hong merchant of his time, the exact amount and components of his personal net worth remain uncertain.

At the bottom of the hong merchant body in 1815, in sharp contrast, the receivership of the four debtors Conseequa, Manhop II, Poonequa and Goqua I was grinding along. Of these firms, only the Dongyu hong of Goqua I would make it to 1828, and it continued in business thereafter under successor family members through 1843.[7] Loqua (Exchin II), the fifth receivership debtor, died on 10 May 1814. The license of his troubled Xicheng hong was renewed in August 1814 in the name of Pacqua (Li Guangyuan) (also known as Exchin III). This caused friction between Loqua's immediate family and the foreign trustees, as the family wanted the firm to be run by Cheequa, a more skilled businessman, but one who unfortunately did not speak English and had had little contact with foreigners. The trustees instead recognized Pacqua, a collateral relative of Loqua, who had been "a frontman in the hong." Pacqua proved a greater risk-taker than Loqua, and the condition of the Xicheng hong did not improve under his management.[8]

No new hong merchants were admitted to the outer seas guild during the period 1815 through 1828. During the same years, four merchants failed and their hongs were closed. This dearth of replacements stands in sharp contrast to the preceding fifteen year period, in which there were nine admissions (1800–1815), and the twenty years before that, in which there had been fifteen (1780–1799).[9] Entry was certainly discouraged by the practice, from at least 1813 to 1829, by which any new hong merchant was required to present a guarantee of financial responsibility for unpaid taxes signed by all of the incumbent hong merchants before he could join the guild. In the crisis year of 1829 the written full commitment rule was relaxed. The written guaranty of two operating firms was all that was thereafter required for admission.[10] The brother of a rich salt merchant is said to have tried in 1828 to form a hong dedicated exclusively to trading with Americans, but that venture was not realized. The hong merchants opposed the effort because they believed that the true purpose of the proposed venture was to act as an agent for outside shopmen who were trading with Americans, facilitating and profiting from that growing business.[11] This was an exceptional case, and it is notable precisely as that. Credible merchants had no interest in joining the outer seas guild. A hong merchant license was seen to involve more burden than potential benefit.

---

7 Ch'en, *Insolvency*, pp. 16–19.

8 Ch'en, *Insolvency*, pp. 341–2; Morse, *Chronicles, Vol. III*, p. 208.

9 Ch'en, *Insolvency*, pp. 39–40 (Tables 1.5 and 1.6).

10 Chang, *Income of the Chinese Gentry*, p. 161.

11 Greenberg, *British Trade*, p. 68; Morse, *Chronicles, Vol. IV*, p. 168; White, "Hong Merchants," pp. 114–5 and 160.

2 The Demands of Government, 1815–1828

Government officials continued to place heavy demands both on the Consoo Fund and individual hong merchants in the period 1815 through 1828. Unlike the period 1805 through 1816, for which detailed records exist, direct evidence for this later period is spotty. In 1815, Hoppo Xiangshao promulgated a regulation requiring the use of three expensive shroffs (money changers) as exclusive sources for the silver required for tax payments. This was understood as an indirect attempt to squeeze yet more fees from the trade, and 66,000 taels ($91,667) was paid to the Hoppo to secure withdrawal of the burdensome regulation.[12]

Early in 1815, financial problems among the hong merchants were reported by a secret informant to an imperial censor. A memorial was sent to the Emperor stating that the junior hong merchants were insolvent. The Governor-General was ordered to investigate, and in response he directed the seven junior hong merchants to provide statements of their foreign debts and of the time required to discharge them. Although the British EIC declined an invitation to corroborate the disclosures made by the seven debtors, the matter was duly concluded. This positive outcome was facilitated by payment of about 100,000 taels ($138,889) to the Hoppo, although an uproar arose when word of the bribe reached the Governor-General (Viceroy). As described in the EIC records,

> Puankhequa informed Mr. Plowden [then at Canton] that the Viceroy was very favorably disposed to settle the question in the desired manner, when some evil intentioned person communicated to the Viceroy that the Merchants had subscribed 100,000 Tales for the purpose of bribing the Officers of Government throwing much suspicion on the Namhai heen and the Quan Choo foo—that this statement had irritated His Exc'y exceedingly and had put a stop to the arrangement taking place.... Altho' there is scarcely any affair that can be arranged in China without the good wishes of the Officer under whose authority the affair may be being previously purchased, still a certain form and shew of justice must be exhibited; and the bribe is neither received openly or avowedly, but is generally arranged thro' the medium of some third person. The Viceroy is stated to be extremely tenacious of these external marks of Purity, altho' it is currently said that he obtains considerable sums.[13]

---

12 Ch'en, *Insolvency*, p. 99.

13 Ch'en, *Insolvency*, pp. 50, 335 and 354–5; Morse, *Chronicles, Vol. III*, pp. 233–4.

While little information survives concerning government exactions during this period, an 1839 memorial to the Emperor provides strong evidence that the supervising officials recognized that the hong merchants had reached a financial limit. The hong merchants had committed in 1819, voluntarily or involuntarily, to pay 600,000 taels ($833,333) for Yellow River flood control work, and then in 1826 to pay another 600,000 taels ($833,333) to support the war in Kashgar. Payment of these pledges, absolute on their face, was then repeatedly deferred on imperial approval through 1839. Twenty years later, 136,151 taels ($189,098) of the 1819 pledge still had not been paid, and none of the 1826 pledge.[14]

It is apparent that by this time the Qing government had, in effect, recognized certain leading hongs as being "too big to fail." In better times, these preeminent firms would have been pressed to all pay taxes and guaranteed foreign debt on or before the payment deadlines that had been set. While these firms still could have been pressed to pay these obligations in full, the officials recognized that a high risk existed that they too would then fail and that, without these leaders, the entire Canton System would grind to a halt (with resulting unemployment, social disorder and disruptions of tax collection). Functional "too big to fail" status protected, notably, the preeminent Yihe hong of the senior hong merchant Wu Bingjian (Howqua II) from heavy government exactions. While this process of restraint worked in the opposite from modern "too big to fail" doctrine, under which state subsidies are extended directly or indirectly to favored firms, it had an identical effect. By not pressing leading firms to pay tax and other debts it otherwise would have demanded, the Chinese government protected those firms it recognized as essential to the functioning of the marketplace.

3 Trading Conditions, 1815–1828

The fourteen year period 1815 through 1828 is characterized by relief and exuberance. The long period of war was over. The silver supply from the United States resumed, and some silver also began to come to Canton through Spanish trade with ports in Mexico and Peru. Credit was freely extended, and international markets soon tested the exuberantly issued paper. Pains felt in distant

14 T. F. Tsiang (Chiang Ting-fu), "The Government and the Co-Hong of Canton, 1839," Chinese Social and Political Science Review, Vol. 15, pp. 602–7 (1932), pp. 606–7.

financial centers were promptly relayed to China, due to the ever increasing reliance of various private traders on financing, notably from London.[15]

The Panic of 1819 was the first disturbance of the period. United States trade with China in 1820 dropped to half what it had been the prior year, and the American portion of the opium trade which had grown significantly after 1815, was reduced to zero in 1820. The 1821 crackdown on opium smuggling by the Chinese government had the effect of moving this illegal commerce just outside the mouth of the Pearl River.[16] Conducted from storeships off Lintin Island, stationary bazaars that were visited by Chinese customers who then did their own smuggling, the opium trade continued in large volume, effectively unhindered. The hong merchants, with rare exceptions which occurred primarily before 1821, had no involvement in this trade. It was conducted far from Canton and they were exposed public figures. It was simply too dangerous.

Throughout the 1820s, the Canton market for Indian cotton was chronically depressed. The stronger hong merchants sought to avoid cotton losses by refusing to purchase on their own account, being willing to accept consignments as brokers only. Those who bought found their capital tied up, as they could not sell other than at a loss. Early in 1822, it was said that "[t]he unprecedented scarcity of money among the Hong merchants is partly caused by the large capitals locked up in cotton."[17] These woes were exacerbated by heavy losses the hong merchants suffered in the great fire of 1–2 November 1822, which destroyed large amounts of warehoused goods.[18]

An international crisis broke in 1825 as the result of an ill-timed decision by the Bank of England to tighten credit. Several important but heavily indebted American China trade houses were brought down by the crisis. The Philadelphia

---

15 Cheong, "Beginnings of Credit Finance," p. 101; Cheong, "China Houses and the Bank of England Crisis of 1825," Business History (Liverpool), Vol. 15, pp. 56–73 (1973), pp. 56, 61–2, 65–7; Cheong, "Trade and Finance in China," p. 41.

16 Downs, "American Merchants and the China Opium Trade"; Greenberg, *British Trade*, p. 121; Stelle, "American Trade in Opium to China, Prior to 1820"; Stelle, "American Trade in Opium to China, 1821–39."

17 Greenberg, *British Trade*, pp. 88–92.

18 Greenberg, *British Trade*, p. 86 (as recorded by Charles Magniac, "Some of the Hong merchants have suffered a terrible loss of property. Howqua has lost about 200,000 taels, Mowqua 350,000 taels, Cheonqua a large sum. Poonqua had a large quantity of woollens, the loss of which will greatly distress him.' He added that he was afraid of the effect of 'the extensive ruin which must have fallen on a number of Chinese dealers and brokers of every description.'"); Patrick Conner, *The Hongs of Canton: Western Merchants in South China, 1700–1900, as Seen in Chinese Export Paintings* (London: English Art Books, 2009), pp. 89–99 (the Great Fire of 1822). The hong merchant losses were uninsured.

firm of Edward Thomson failed in 1825 and the New York and Canton firm of Thomas H. Smith failed in 1827, leaving massive customs debts owing to the United States government, and warehouses of China goods to be sold off into a depressed market. This was also a period of changing consumer taste in the United States, with annual per capita tea consumption falling about fifteen percent in the second half of the 1820s, as the rate of consumption of coffee rose. The American trade with China declined in the 1820s and 1830s, due to over-investment and the attraction of capital into domestic investment opportunities. All the while, various private traders, including Americans, busily continued to bring opium into China. As earnings from drug sales increased, there was less need to bring silver. American imports of specie to Canton declined in the late 1820s and were sharply reduced in the 1830s.[19]

4 The Experience of Conseequa, 1796–1823

The case of Conseequa merits added attention. A prominent example of the new type of hong merchant that did business after 1800, the experiences of Conseequa and his Liquan hong connect the period 1800–1814 (the subject of Chapter Five) with the period 1815–1828 (the subject of this chapter). Conseequa's history illustrates the core problems that tie together these periods: the inadequate capital of the hong merchants; the dominant power of the British EIC as trading partner and as a lender; the extension of credit by hong merchants to foreign debtors, and the problems that could result from it; and the sometimes involved process through which indebted hongs and their foreign creditors sought to avoid resort to the Canton Guaranty System.

A member of the Pan family (Puankhequa), operators of the long-dominant Tongwen hong,[20] Conseequa long enjoyed good working relations with the British EIC. He also worked closely with the new independents, both Americans and country traders. He was bold and a risk-taker, extending massive trade

---

19 Cheong, "China Houses and the Bank of England Crisis," pp. 56, 61–2, 65–7; Downs, *The Golden Ghetto*, pp. 110, 165, 199–201, 358–63 and 425 n.51; Downs, "American Merchants and the China Opium Trade," p. 436; Gibson, *Otter Skins*, p. 103; Latourette, "History of Early Relations," p. 69; Stelle, "American Trade in Opium to China, Prior to 1820," pp. 425 and 442–3; Stelle, "American Trade in Opium to China, 1821–39," pp. 63 and 66–8; *United States v. Three Hundred Fifty Chests of Tea*, 25 U.S. 486 (1827) (Edward Thomson failure).

20 Conseequa was a nephew of Puankhequa I (Pan Wenyen), a cousin of Puankhequa II (Pan Zhixiang) and an uncle of Puankhequa III (Pan Zhengwei). Ch'en, *Insolvency*, p. 330; Cheong, *Hong Merchants*, p. 91.

loans to merchants from the distant United States, and becoming involved in one of the few clearly recorded transactions in which a hong merchant bought opium—nine boxes purchased for $11,972 from Willing & Francis' ship *Bingham* on 28 December 1805.[21]

Conseequa rose rapidly, initially trading without a license in the 1780s and 1790s. Arrested for this offense in December 1796, he was forced to buy a license. The thirty-six year old Conseequa was now proprietor of the Liquan hong, open for regular business.[22] The French thought highly of Conseequa. The American view was more guarded. An agent of Thomas Handasyd Perkins of Boston described him as "very lavish of promises, very shuffling but rich and doing much business. Very liberal credit."[23] The Salem merchant Thomas W. Ward, writing in 1809 as Conseequa's business crumbled, was more blunt. "Rich—roguish—insinuating—polite—sends some excellent cargoes—some bad Cargoes—not attentive enough to business and a man with whom you cannot talk with safely, as he will promise everything & perform what he pleases—not to be seen always."[24]

The new Liquan hong traded with the EIC on a large scale, and also with various other foreign merchants. It often extended credit to American traders, and these loans grew into massive amounts.[25] In 1815 Conseequa told investigating authorities that over $2.5 million was owed to him by American debtors and by the private Armenian country trader Gregory Baboom.[26] American court records show that in April 1808 Conseequa was owed $500,000 by his

---

21 Account of sales of opium from the Ship Bingham dated Canton 28 December 1805, 1805 folder, Willings & Francis Papers, Collection No. 1874, Historical Society of Pennsylvania, reproduced in Jonathan Goldstein, "Resources on Early Sino-American Relations in Philadelphia's Stephen Girard Collection and the Historical Society of Pennsylvania," Ch'ing-shih wen-t'i, Vol. 4 (1980), pp. 114 and 121.

22 Ch'en, *Insolvency*, pp. 330–1 and 338–9; Grant, "Failure of the Li-ch'uan Hong," pp. 244–5; Fu, *Documentary Chronicle*, p. 610 n.166.

23 Carl Seaburg and Stanley Paterson, *Merchant Prince of Boston: Colonel T.H. Perkins, 1764–1854* (Cambridge: Harvard Univ. Press, 1971), p. 101.

24 Thomas W. Ward, "Remarks on the *Canton Trade* and the Manner of Transacting Business," Essex Institute Historical Collections, Vol. 73 (1937), pp. 303 and 307.

25 Grant, "Failure of the Li-ch'uan Hong," p. 244.

26 Ch'en, *Insolvency*, pp. 334–5. For a brief history of Baboom's trade in China, see Carl T. Smith and Paul A. Van Dyke, "Four Armenian Families," Review of Culture, International Edition No. 8, pp. 40–50 (October 2003); Margaret Sarkissian. "Armenians in South-East Asia," Crossroads: An Interdisciplinary Journal of Southeast Asian Studies, Vol. 3, Nos. 2–3, p. 13 (1987).

debtors in the city of Philadelphia alone.[27] A [partial] tabulation of Conseequa's loans, prepared in 1987 from then known records, identifies $420,596 in loans by Conseequa to Americans during the decade 1800–1809.[28]

The source of the funds Conseequa lent is uncertain. As of 1800, he had little free cash. He had been a hong merchant for four years, with seventeen years' prior history as an outside trader. A 50,000 tael ($69,400) smuggling fine levied against the hong that summer forced Conseequa to borrow from the EIC to meet obligations, and left him unable to meet at least one commitment in 1801. That fine was paid, in installments, through the year 1801.[29] As of 1800, his accumulated trading profits do not seem to have been in the range required to support lending on the scale in which the Liquan Hong was becoming engaged. Yet in November 1805, Conseequa told supercargo William Read that he was prepared to make loans of as much as $100,000 to $150,000.[30]

Conseequa obviously borrowed some of the funds he lent. This practice is common today, and can be useful if controlled. When credit is available to customers, they may buy more. Profit may increase as well; a financing seller may make money as a lender, in addition to the profit from the initial sale. It is doubtful that Conseequa originally intended to finance his foreign customers on a large scale. Nor would it seem that he was ever so scientific as to track net gain on the spread between his cost of funds and amounts repaid by his customer debtors. The evidence indicates that his purchase financing started modestly in the late 1700s, and grew in the early 1800s, presumably supported by good repayment experience with early loans.[31] The hong's loan exposure almost certainly then grew beyond Conseequa's intentions and the knowledge of his other creditors. We know that Conseequa was becoming concerned about his exposure in 1805, even as he bragged to William Read about his lending power. A dispute arose that year between Conseequa and the

27 Grant, "Failure of the Li-ch'uan Hong," p. 249.

28 Grant, "Failure of the Li-ch'uan Hong," pp. 259–60. The large dollar amount of promissory notes payable to Conseequa, attached by the Sheriff in Philadelphia on 2 and 4 April 1808 ($500,000), shows that Conseequa's outstanding loans were far greater in amount than can be reconstructed from surviving litigation and archival records. Id., p. 249.

29 Morse, *Chronicles, Vol. II*, pp. 354 and 365; Ch'en, *Insolvency*, pp. 332–3.

30 Grant, "Failure of the Li-ch'uan Hong," p. 248; Letter from William Read (Canton) to Willings & Francis, dated 27 November 1805, 1805 folder, Willings & Francis papers, Collection No. 1874, Historical Society of Pennsylvania, Philadelphia.

31 Grant, "Failure of the Li-ch'uan Hong," pp. 259–60.

supercargo of the ship *Ganges* of Philadelphia, "as to the extent of the credit, which Conseequa said he did not expect would be so large."[32]

The credit purchase of tea carried risk for the buyer, just as the extension of credit to a merchant who lived nearly half a world away involved risk for the too-often financially insecure hong merchant. Great care in judging teas was warranted in any transaction, and it was extremely important when teas were bought on credit late in the Canton season. Much of the best of the annual tea crop had been contracted for by European buyers prior to delivery at Canton, and the rest of the best was sold quickly, usually for cash. In certain years good teas, or better teas of particular varieties, were very scarce;[33] generally, by late in the season, all superior teas were gone.[34] With the best quality not easily distinguished by the visiting supercargo, at least not without the assistance of an expert taster who would require a fee,[35] many of the Chinese merchant lawsuits arose naturally from late season purchases of tea on credit. Stephen Girard, the greatest nineteenth century Philadelphia China trade merchant,[36]

---

32 Grant, "Failure of the Li-ch'uan Hong," pp. 251–2; Deposition of Benjamin C. Wilcocks, Philadelphia, taken on 31 May 1811, in *Consequa v. Willings & Francis*, October term 1809, No. 49, Records of the Circuit Court for the District of Pennsylvania.

33 Deposition of Benjamin C. Wilcocks, undated, in Stephen Girard's records of the lawsuit *Girard v. Biddle* (commenced in the Sept. 1806 term of the Court of Common Pleas of Philadelphia County), Reel 439, Stephen Girard Papers, Estate of Stephen Girard, deceased, microfilm copies on deposit with the American Philosophical Society, Philadelphia; *Cheongwo v. Jones*, 5 F. Cas. 544, 545–546 (C.C.E.D. Pa. 1818) (No. 2,638); *Youqua v. Nixon*, 30 F. Cas. 887 (C.C.E.D. Pa. 1816) (No. 18,189).

34 *Gilpins v. Consequa*, 10 F. Cas. 420, 422 (C.C.E.D. Pa. 1813) (No. 5,452).

35 The failure to use an expert figures in two cases. In *Willings v. Consequa*, 30 F. Cas. 55, 59 (C.C.E.D. Pa. 1816) (No. 17,767), one of the points at issue was the alleged provision of teas "of very inferior quality" to the ship Bingham, which carried them to Amsterdam where they were sold at auction for a poor return. In *Cheongwo v. Jones*, 5 F. Cas. 544, 546 (C.C.E.D. Pa. 1818) (No. 2,638), assertions that the "excellent" teas which the defendant's supercargo believed he had selected at Canton had been switched for the "most infamous" teas that arrived at the warehouses of the Asiatic Company in Amsterdam for auction sale were answered with the testimony of a witness "that he had lived at Canton for ten years, and that it was very difficult for a person who had not, for a period of time, resided in China, to judge of the qualities of teas. That instances had sometimes occurred, of a few chests of teas being changed on board the Hong boats, by the mariners; but that he had never heard of an instance of a cargo being changed by the merchant who had sold it."

36 Jonathan Goldstein, *Stephen Girard's Trade with China 1787–1824: The Norms Versus the Profits of Trade* (Portland, Maine: Merwin Asia, 2011).

doubted that any hong merchant of good reputation would sell teas on credit.[37] On another occasion, Girard stated that in teas

> lies the great deception and I do not believe that a China merchant of good repute & credit who is particular in dealing in the best teas can purchase them even cash in hand as low as any other Chinese whose principal object is to obtain a long credit [T]his last character may possibly purchase teas at the lowest Cash price pay[ab]le. at 2 or 3 years consequently the difference in price will apparently be in his favor but in quality it will perhaps prove to be some fifty to 60 Pr cent worse than the tea purchased by the Chinese merchant of good repute [T]his I have experience[d] at Antwerp in 1804 at the sales of the ship Rousseau's cargo [T]here was a small parcel of Souchong tea purchased at Canton of Eshing which sold upwards of fifty pr cent more than what was furnished by Conseequa.[38]

The experience of William Read, supercargo of the ship *Bingham*, who chose to rely on his own expertise in buying teas from Conseequa on credit late in the season 1805–1806, provides a tragicomic example of the wisdom of Girard's advice. William Read wrote his principal at the time of purchase that he had rejected the 2 percent fee required for the services of Mr. Rabinel the tea examiner as "far beyond what I thought the services to be rendered merited." Read felt confident of his ability to make "such a selection of Teas as will render his assistance of little consequence." A month later he innocently wrote that Rabinel "informs me he has written a letter to his friends in Holland which may be of use in the Sales of the Cargo, and regrets he could not render you the services you wished, and on such terms as would answer your expectations, and consistent with his own and the Interest of the Gentn. his assistants in the Factory." When the *Bingham* reached Amsterdam and its tea cargo was auctioned, the teas William Read had confidently selected at Canton brought a very low price.[39]

---

37 Stephen Girard, "Observations on Mr. Benjamin C. Wilcocks's Deposition," included in Stephen Girard's records of the lawsuit *Girard v. Biddle* (commenced in the Sept. 1806 term of the Court of Common Pleas of Philadelphia County), Reel 439, Stephen Girard Papers, Estate of Stephen Girard, deceased, microfilm copies on deposit with the American Philosophical Society, Philadelphia.

38 Letter, Stephen Girard (Philadelphia) to Edward George and Samuel Nichols, 3 January 1810, Letterbook 11, Stephen Girard Papers, Estate of Stephen Girard, deceased, microfilm copies on deposit with the American Philosophical Society, Philadelphia.

39 *Willings v. Consequa*, 30 F. Cas. 55, 59 (C.C.E.D. Pa. 1816) (No. 17,767); letters, William Read (Canton) to Willings & Francis, 9 Nov. 1805 and 10 Dec. 1805, 1805 folder, Willings & Francis Papers, Collection No. 1874, Historical Society of Pennsylvania, Philadelphia.

Having extended massive amounts of unsecured credit to American debtors, Conseequa—presumably already under pressure himself—grew cross with their delays and excuses. Late in 1807 he handed a group of overdue promissory notes to his friend Benjamin C. Wilcocks at Canton, telling Wilcocks to bring them to America and to see that the debts were collected. The Rhode Island merchant Edward Carrington, later United States Consul at Canton, vividly described Conseequa's resolve in a letter to Samuel Snow, one of Conseequa's debtors. Carrington had explained Snow's situation to the hong merchant, and asked that Snow be allowed one more season to meet his obligations, but "Conseequa pretended to be much disappointed and out of temper in the business." Conseequa

> had given the note [to] Mr. Wilcocks with many others to be sent to Am[eric]a. for collection. I then told him if he would retain it, I would write to you I could secure the money would come next season, he said no it would not do, that the notes must go. I spoke to Wilcocks, who applied to Conseequa on the subject, but without success. Your note, with Bently, B. Dexter and others in Rhode Island are forwarded by this opp[ortunit]y. to Messrs. R.H. Wilcocks & B.C. Wilcocks at Phila[delphia] for Collections. Conseequa is very much out with the Am[eric]a[ns]. in consequence of heavy claims that have been urged against him for bad Goods furnished to them—he has become the most obstinate, pernicious Merch[an]t. of the Hong, & it is almost impossible to move him when he takes a stand. I have been this particular lest you should think I had not attended to your requests.[40]

Wilcocks either traveled with or followed the notes to Philadelphia, where he "made application to" several debtors who provided him with $9,000 for Conseequa. These funds, with other monies due to Conseequa, were sent to Canton, but Wilcocks later testified that he believed a "great part thereof was prevented by capture from getting into Conseequa's hands." Wilcocks

40 Letter from Edward Carrington (Canton) to Samuel Snow, 19 January 1808, Edward Carrington Papers, MSS 333, SG I Series 2, RB.1 F6 Letter Book, China Letterbook F, Rhode Island Historical Society, Providence, Rhode Island. In contrast, the hong merchant Mowqua agreed to hold Snow's notes until the next season. Jacques M. Downs, "A Study in Failure—Hon. Samuel Snow," Rhode Island History, Vol. 25 (1966), pp. 1 and 5. As Snow's firm, Munro, Snow & Munro, had failed over a month before Carrington wrote Snow, it is unlikely that either Conseequa or Mowqua ever fully recovered the amounts Snow owed them.

delivered the remaining unpaid notes to the lawyer Charles Jared Ingersoll for collection.[41] The retention of Ingersoll was at once the natural choice of a leading and well-connected local lawyer and also an inside pick, as Ingersoll was married to Wilcocks' younger sister.[42] Chinese merchant creditors were generally similarly well advised in their debt collection in the United States and commonly retained leading lawyers to represent them in court.[43]

Disaster ensued. Three of Conseequa's debtors, warned of imminent suit against them, filed a preemptive action in the Court of Common Pleas of Philadelphia County seeking to recover damages from Conseequa for poor quality teas allegedly sold to them in 1805. Edward Dunant and Joshua and Thomas Gilpin obtained a court attachment of all of Conseequa's assets in Philadelphia. On 2 and 4 April 1808, the Sheriff attached "all the goods and chattels rights and credits of the said Consequa in the hands of" some twenty-one merchants, namely, notes payable to Conseequa in the total amount of $500,000. This large sum is a dramatic statement of the amount of a single hong merchant's credit to Americans in just one American city early in the nineteenth century.[44] According to Conseequa's later federal court suit against

41 Deposition of Benjamin C. Wilcocks, taken on 5 December 1810, in *Consequa v. Joshua and Thomas Gilpin*, October term 1809, No. 9, Records of the Circuit Court for the District of Pennsylvania.

42 Jean Gordon Lee, *Philadelphians and the China Trade 1784–1844* (Philadelphia: Philadelphia Museum of Art, 1984), p. 45; William M. Meigs, *The Life of Charles Jared Ingersoll* (Philadelphia: J. B. Lippincott Co., 1897), p. 38.

43 Conseequa managed debt collections through George Emlen, Peter Dobell and Benjamin Chew Wilcocks in Philadelphia, through John Jacob Astor in New York City, and in Boston through the lawyer William Sullivan. Where suasion failed and counsel was needed to bring suit, leading local lawyers were hired. Deposition of Benjamin C. Wilcocks, taken on 5 December 1810, in *Consequa v. Joshua and Thomas Gilpin*, October term 1809, No. 9, Records of the Circuit Court for the District of Pennsylvania; Conseequa's Account Current with George Emlen, Gratz Collection, Box 44, Case 14, Historical Society of Pennsylvania, Philadelphia. Similar collection assistance was often extended to other Chinese merchant creditors by the leading American China trade firms. For example, the Samuel Cabot Papers at the Massachusetts Historical Society include several letters from Howqua II to debtors in Philadelphia, Providence, Salem, New York, and Boston, dated at Canton on 28 and 30 January, and 5 February 1814, reciting the "stoppage of the accustomed intercourse between this country and the United States" and Howqua's decision to forward promissory notes to his general agents James & Thomas H. Perkins of Boston for collection free of the uncertainties of shipment by sea in wartime. Grant, "Hong Merchant Litigation," p. 61 n.60.

44 The magnitude of the attachment underscores the great importance of Philadelphia as a center of American trade with China, which has been underappreciated. Downs, *The*

Dunant and the Gilpins, this attachment, which remained in effect through 22 May 1809, prevented the debtors whose promissory notes were attached from paying him.[45] In the meantime, the Embargo of December 1807, which held American shipping idle through March 1809, ruined many of Conseequa's debtors.

Conseequa's collection agent Benjamin Chew Wilcocks is best remembered today as the anonymous, "Mr. W____," the beneficiary of an act of generosity by Howqua II in 1827. His predicament that year, and Howqua's response to it, is described in a famous passage by William C. Hunter:[46]

> An American gentleman, who had resided many years at Canton, and had possessed a considerable fortune, met with serious losses. The hope of regaining it induced him to continue operations, in which he was materially assisted by Houqua. They had been, as was usually said, in the words of the place, 'olo flen.' Time passed, considerable sums were placed at the disposal of Mr. W____, no reference being made to them by the Hong merchant until, at the end of a second or third year, Houqua's and his accounts were compared, and the balance in favor of Houqua was 72,000 dollars. For this amount he took a promissory note and it was locked up in his strong box…

Golden Ghetto, pp. 235 and 377; Lawrence H. Leder, "American Trade to China, 1800–1802: Some Statistical Notes," American Neptune, Vol. 23 (1963), pp. 215 and 218; Lee, *Philadelphians and the China Trade*.

45 The basic facts concerning the lawsuit against Conseequa in the Court of Common Pleas in Philadelphia, the records of which court for this period have not survived, are known through the records of the wrongful attachment actions Conseequa filed against the Gilpins and Dunant in the federal court in Philadelphia (the records of which court have survived). Declarations (complaints) in *Consequa v. Joshua and Thomas Gilpin* (filed 3 March 1810), October term 1809, No. 9, and in *Consequa v. Edward Dunant* (filed 3 March 1810), October term 1809, No. 33, Records of the Circuit Court for the District of Pennsylvania. No newspaper coverage of the Dunant and Gilpins lawsuit against Conseequa has been found in a review of the principal Philadelphia newspapers for this period. It is not known whether Conseequa's federal court actions ever yielded any money from the defendants, or indeed whether these debtors ever made good on their promissory notes.

46 Hunter, *Fan Kwae*, pp. 43–44. The story of the cancellation of Wilcocks' debt, which has doubted by some scholars, should be considered as true. See Philip de Vargas, "William C. Hunter's Books on the Old Canton Factories," Yenching Journal of Social Studies, Vol. 2 (July 1939), pp. 91–117, p. 104 ("The story may or may not be apocryphal, but it has long been taken as symbolic…").

> One day, when on a visit to his Chinese friend, the latter said, 'You have been so long away from your own country, why do you not return?' To which Mr. W____ replied that it was impossible—he could not cancel his note, and this alone would prevent him. Houqua enquired if the bond [note], only, kept him in Canton, and if he had not some means wherewith to provide for a residence at home? The answer was that no other debts existed, and he was not without resources—but the note!! Houqua summoned his purser, and ordered him to bring the envelope containing promissory notes from the treasury. Taking out that of Mr. W____, he said, 'You and I are No. 1, "olo flen;" you belong honest man, only no got chance.' He then tore the note up, and throwing the fragments into the waste-paper basket, added, "Just now hav settee counter, all finishee; you go, you please." That is to say, 'Our accounts are now all settled, you can leave when you like.'

Benjamin Chew Wilcocks left Canton in December 1827.[47]

Wilcocks' $72,000 debt, cancelled by Howqua II in 1827, dates to the failure of William Waln in the Panic of 1819.[48] Waln, Wilcocks' Philadelphia agent, sometime employer, and later father-in-law,[49] also a debtor to Conseequa,[50] failed that summer.[51] According to Hunter, the $72,000 debt was the total sum "placed at the disposal" of Wilcocks by Howqua II over two to three years after Wilcocks suffered serious losses in about 1819. Howqua's original 1819 loan

47 Downs, *The Golden Ghetto*, p. 124; Joan Kerr Facey Thill, "A Delawarean in the Celestial Empire: John Richardson Latimer and the China Trade" (Master's Thesis, University of Delaware, 1973), p. 163.

48 Downs, "American Merchants and the China Opium Trade," p. 434–5 n.59.

49 Downs, "American Merchants and the China Opium Trade," p. 434–5 n.59; Lee, Philadelphians and the China Trade, p. 122 (Waln's daughter Sarah married Wilcocks in 1842).

50 Declarations (complaints) in *Consequa v. Joshua and Thomas Gilpin* (filed 3 March 1810), October term 1809, No. 9, and in *Consequa v. Edward Dunant* (filed 3 March 1810), October term 1809, No. 33, Records of the Circuit Court for the District of Pennsylvania.

51 *Lanfear v. Sumner*, 17 Mass. 110 (1819) (priority dispute among creditors asserting rights in teas shipped from Canton by Benjamin C. Wilcocks to William Waln as consignee and owner, one creditor under a written assignment by Waln at Philadelphia on 2 July 1819 and the other by physical attachment of the teas by the Sheriff in Boston on the same day, 2 July 1819); *Bainbridge v. Wilcocks*, 2 F. Cas. 407, 408 (C.C.E.D. Pa. 1832) (No. 755) (suit by London bankers against Benjamin C. Wilcocks to recover debts for which William Waln had acted as Wilcocks' agent through 1819; among other things, Wilcocks asserted that he had paid Waln the amounts which were due to the plaintiff bankers).

to Wilcocks, and the cancellation of that debt in 1827 were certainly generous acts, but it is an error to view them as acts of charity alone. They are the more understandable when the services are considered, that Wilcocks rendered over many years helping Chinese merchants collect debts in Philadelphia, Providence, New York, and other American cities. Howqua II had good reason to feel gratitude. Among other things, these services helped reduce his potential collective guaranty exposure in the event of failure of his hong merchant creditor colleagues.[52] It is also true that Howqua II and Wilcocks were friends. "You and I are No. 1, 'olo flen;' you belong honest man, only no got chance."

In the midst of his afflictions, several years earlier, Conseequa wrote his friend Peter Dobell in Philadelphia complaining about his financial and legal problems. The 3 April 1813 letter, in pidgin English with an addition by Alexander Pearson, survives in a vandalized condition.

> I have very trouble because all that money America gentlemen owe for me.... I have see hardly any money, now I have very much trouble, owe so much money, no can pay I fear broke. Mr. Ingersoll I know very good man, very good head, only I fear [words deliberately obliterated] talk story so have spoil me too. paper along with this can show how much money, who man owe, I chin chin you look—take care.

Pearson added,

> For the foregoing I have served as an amanuensis to your friend Conseequa. I cannot help thinking that he had met with a great deal of more harsh & ungrateful treatment for such liberality of accommodation (to some whom I hope you will not meet with in America) than it is for the credit of foreigners to this country & of human natives generally, that he should have been subjected to, however I need not amplify on that subject to you.[53]

52 Each dollar collected by Wilcocks for another hong merchant from that merchant's United States debtor, lessened the potential pro rata collective guaranty repayment burden that would be placed on Howqua II, if that hong merchant colleague were to fail.

53 Letter, Conseequa (Canton) to Peter Dobell, 3 April 1813, Breck Family Papers, Library Company of Philadelphia, Collection No. LCP185, on deposit with the Historical Society of Pennsylvania, Philadelphia.

Ten months later, in February of 1814, the frustrated and perplexed hong merchant appealed directly to President James Madison. This letter survives in the National Archives of the United States in its Chinese original, with contemporary English and Portuguese translations. There is no record of action taken in response to the appeal, or that any reply was made to Conseequa's letter, which may be natural enough. The letter was sent in the middle of the War of 1812 between Britain and the United States, and the White House, the official residence of the addressee, was burned by British troops in August 1814, six months after the letter was sent. In "The Petition of Conseequa, a Hong Merchant of the City of Canton in China," Conseequa (Pan Kun) recites the fairness of his dealings, the willingness with which he had granted credit to Americans, and complains that his debtors have evaded and failed to pay him. "Many who do not labour under inability to pay their debts, or who do not acknowledge that they are unable, object to pay them, as he thinks upon frivolous grounds, and involve the Claims upon them in tedious litigation."[54]

> When the American merchants (who owe me money) come to Guangdong and live in Canton, Kun cannot accuse them, because the law of our country prohibits Chinese subjects from accusing the barbarians. This is why Kun must beg Your Excellency, the President of the United States, since Kun hears that the law of your noble country is impartial, and that no matter whether a man is rich or poor, an American or an alien, everyone is equal before the law. Kun is an alien from a remote region and ignorant of the usages and forms proper to presenting his case to your honorable country. Again, because great distance lies between us, I cannot present all my evidence (that the American merchants owe me money) to you. Therefore, your decision on this case may reach me after an interval of several years. The reason for presenting this petition is to appeal to Your Excellency for an impartial judgment.
>
> I hope Your Excellency will not listen to the one-sided story of your dishonest merchants, but judge this issue fairly.... If the American merchants do not return my money, then my whole family will suffer

54 Petition of Conseequa, a Hong Merchant of the City of Canton in China, 10 February 1814 (contemporary English language translation). Despatches of United States Consuls at Canton, Volume I, National Archives, Washington, D.C.; published in File Microcopies of Records in the National Archives, No. 101, Roll 1; Dennett, *Americans in Eastern Asia*, p. 86; Fu, *Documentary Chronicle*, pp. 391–3 (modern translation). No record has been found of any response to Conseequa's petition to President Madison.

> substantially. Not only will I lose my principal for continuing my business, but foreign merchants will not have any faith in me.

Conseequa said that he had asked an English friend to present his petition and evidence, which he hoped the President would act on both for his sake, and in the interest of the reputation of American citizens in China.

> Formerly, I trusted the Americans. I therefore sold goods to them on credit. If they do not return the price of my goods, they will cause the bankruptcy of Kun's family. In the future, who will trade with the subjects of Your Excellency, the President of the United States?

5 The Collective Guaranty of Debt, 1815–1828

During the period 1815 to 1828 the total liability on account of foreign debt that was charged to the hong merchant body under the collective guaranty was 1,725,000 taels ($2,395,833), an average of 123,214 taels ($171,130) annually. The trend of significant increases in average annual liability, evident since the imposition of the collective guaranty in 1780, continued apace. The average annual charge in this fourteen year period was up eight percent (8%) from the prior fifteen years, in which charges averaged 113,733 taels ($157,963) annually (1800–1814). The assessments of that period were up forty percent (40%) on average from the prior twenty years, in which charges averaged 81,050 taels ($112,569) annually (1780–1799). The trend of increases of the average annual amount charged as collective liability for the defaulted foreign debts of members of the outer seas guild during the period 1780 through 1828 is summarized in the following table:

TABLE 3 *Increase in collective liability burden, 1780–1828*

Time Period	Total Liability [Taels/(Dollars)]	Annual Average [Taels/(Dollars)]	Increase in Annual Average from Prior Period [Taels/(Dollars) (Percentage)]
1780–1799	1,621,000/(2,251,388)	81,050/(112,569)	(No prior period.)
1800–1814	1,706,000/(2,369,444)	113,733/(157,963)	32,683/(45,394) (40%)
1815–1828	1,725,000/(2,395,833)	123,214/(171,130)	9,481/(13,167) (8%)

The guaranty burden on the outer seas guild was growing steadily worse. When the New York legislature looked to the Canton Guaranty System as inspiration for proposed banking reform, at the end of this period, it was not made aware of this gradually worsening debt burden.

Collective guaranty liability during the period 1815 through 1828 was limited to the cases of Conseequa, the Manhops, Pacqua (successor to Loqua) and Poonequa. Foreign creditors submitted claims in Chinese debt proceedings, and, again, the Canton officials enforced the collection of foreign loans which were illegal under the Eight Regulations. These "junior" firms failed after their receiverships ended. As of 1818, the receivership trustees for these merchants decided that conditions among them had not improved sufficiently. As recorded by the British EIC,

> The considerate and judicious support, which the Hongs so unhappily circumstanced have received from the Hon'ble Company may be considered to have re-established them; but instead of having employed their restored credit wisely and correctly, we apprehend they have, in this season especially, perverted it to their own Detriment and that of their Creditors.

The EIC resolved to restrict advances to the junior hong merchants to amounts needed for current business only.[55] It ended its practice of nearly a decade of advancing money needed to purchase tea for the coming season. The advances were believed to have driven prices up while discouraging attention to quality, and it had become difficult to track the cash. The EIC noted a "very strong case of necessity" for the change. "[I]t would be impolitic to hazard the Company's Property in a Country where our footing is at all times precarious and where there is no mode of counteracting or of punishing the misconduct of the Merchants on whose behalf the advances may be made, but such as involves the subversion of the system we are desirous to uphold."[56] Termination of the former practice of advancing cash for the use of the weak junior merchants, just as the receivership was nearing its end, did not help their position in the marketplace.

---

55 Morse, *Chronicles, Vol. III*, pp. 311–2.

56 Morse, *Chronicles, Vol. III*, pp. 330 and 332–3; Van Dyke, *Merchants of Canton and Macao*, p. 13.

The trusteeship of Conseequa's Liquan hong came to an end in 1819,[57] but the firm still owed money to the EIC and other foreign creditors. By the end of the 1821–2 season, all of the trust debts (pre-1813 obligations) of the other junior merchants had been paid, except for $200,000 still due from the Xicheng hong (Pacqua [Exchin III] as successor proprietor) and $630,000 owed by the Fulong hong (Manhop I and Manhop II proprietors). The EIC had proposed in each of the two prior years that this residual debt should be paid out of the Consoo Fund, but the hong merchant body repeatedly rejected its proposal.[58]

In the summer of 1822, Pacqua (Exchin III) was petitioned against by Parsi country trader creditors. He was jailed on 18 October 1822. The hong owed about 195,000 taels ($270,833) in government duties and fees, $167,000 to Americans and $330,000 to its Parsi creditors. The government debt was paid with "loans from his friends and a generous donation of forty thousand taels from Howqua and Mowqua."[59] As the duties arrearage had been paid, Governor-General Ruan Yuan and the Hoppo saw no need to close the Xicheng hong. They directed Howqua II as head merchant to work out a settlement with foreign creditors. The EIC supported the effort by agreeing that the debtor hong could retain its two shares of tea business to facilitate payment to foreign creditors, a usual EIC strategy. The Parsis negotiated hard and Howqua II ultimately agreed to pay sixty percent of their debt. With that deal struck, Pacqua was released from jail in December 1822 and allowed to return to business. Management of the two dedicated shares of EIC business, however, was vested by creditor agreement in hong merchant trustees. The trustees were charged to: first, generate profits to pay creditors under the original 1813 junior hong merchant trust; and, second, to pay new creditors as possible. Trustee operations generated $100,000 for 1813 trust creditors, which was paid in the Spring of 1824. Domestic Chinese creditors received nothing. An 1822 petition to the Governor-General by green tea merchants, complaining of 130,000 taels ($180,555) due the from the Xicheng hong, was answered with a directive to the hong merchants to take care of the matter, which accomplished nothing.[60]

For its part, Conseequa's Liquan hong limped forward from trusteeship with unpaid old debt to the EIC, accumulating new liabilities as it did business. Its EIC debt had dropped to $280,169 (201,851 taels) by the end of the trusteeship. In its final years, EIC debt ranged from a high of $579,696 (417,649 taels) to a

57 Ch'en, *Insolvency*, p. 336.

58 Ch'en, *Insolvency*, p. 247.

59 Ch'en, *Insolvency*, pp. 247–8 and 342–5; Morse, *Chronicles, Vol. IV*, pp. 57–8.

60 Ch'en, *Insolvency*, pp. 247–8 and 343–5.

low of $342,630 (246,852 taels).[61] Its asset situation remained difficult, with continuing but declining collections of proceeds of loans made in the early 1800s. Benjamin Chew Wilcocks, for example, had owed Conseequa approximately 300,000 taels ($416,667) as of November 1813.[62] Pursuant to a written release delivered to Wilcocks on 1 April 1820, Conseequa agreed to discharge that debt for a mere $40,000. The settlement seems to have been in the nature of a desperate final deal, and some subsurface grumbling is evident from its text. Much or all of the money paid by Wilcocks was almost certainly taken by the British EIC as Conseequa's dominant creditor. The EIC was represented at the settlement table by James Brabazon Urmston, who signed the release as President of the Select Committee of the EIC and Chief for all Affairs of the British Nation in China. The British EIC even supplied the paper on which the release was prepared.[63] It is no small irony that Urmston himself ended up heavily in debt to hong merchants, and was later removed from office for that very reason.[64]

Conseequa's debt to the EIC had reached the total sum of 400,000 taels ($555,200) by September 1821 when his firm failed again. The other nine hong merchants privately agreed to pay his debt in five annual installments, on EIC insistence (baited by doling out corresponding shares of Conseequa's former

61 Grant, "Failure of the Li-ch'uan Hong," pp. 259–60.

62 Fu, *Documentary Chronicle*, p. 610 n. 166 ("According to a letter dated CC 18:11:4 (26 November 1813) he [Conseequa] lost his fortune because he had lent 300,000 liang of silver to the Wilcocks brothers (this letter is in the Archive of Jardine, Matheson and Company, located in the Anderson Room of the University Library, Cambridge, England.").

63 This release, on laid paper watermarked with the ancient trademark of the EIC, is a remarkable document. Signed by Conseequa in English script, in Chinese characters and marked with a seal of the Liquan hong, before Americans Redwood Fisher and Richard R. Thomson as witnesses, it was witnessed in turn by James Brabazon Urmston, President of the Select Committee of the EIC and Chief for all Affairs of the British Nation in China by his signature and by the application of the EIC's red wax seal. See Frederic D. Grant, Jr., "The April 1820 Debt Settlement between Conseequa and Benjamin Chew Wilcocks," pp. 73–94 in Paul A. Van Dyke, ed., *Americans and Macao: Trade, Smuggling and Diplomacy on the South China Coast* (Hong Kong Univ. Press, 2012).

64 Greenberg, *British Trade*, p. 70 ("Sir James Urmston ... was for many years in debt to several hong merchants on private account. When the latter, headed by Howqua, applied to the Court of Directors to pay off the debts of its Canton President in the same way as the Cohong repaid the debts of 'broke' Hong merchants in all cases, the Court refused and contented itself with removing Urmston from office.").

EIC business to the others).[65] Stripped of its EIC contracts, the hong was mortally wounded.

The third failure of the Liquan hong came two years later, with the 5 August 1823 death of Pan Changyao. Burdened with about 372,000 taels ($516,336) in foreign debt, the hong closed its doors forever. Creditors petitioned Governor-General (and acting Hoppo) Ruan Yuan, seeking payment under the collective guaranty. After considerable proceedings, many creditor objections, and the liquidation of family property in Fujian, the Governor-General ordered the hong merchants to reach an agreement with creditors. The debt was thereafter discharged by the hong merchant body in five equal installments, without interest, with the first two installments being paid to the EIC only. This commitment was eased by continuing recognition by the EIC of the transfer of Conseequa's three shares of EIC business to other hong merchants, with the profits to be used for debt payment, with "a moderate interest." The case was reported to the Emperor. The firm's debts had been contracted by Conseequa, who was dead, and not by his son Pan Ruiqing, who had worked for the firm in its final years. The son was ordered stripped of his purchased official titles, but was not otherwise punished.[66]

The affairs of Pacqua's Xicheng hong were still troubled. In April 1823 Pacqua, Manhop II (Fulong hong) and Poonequa had been jailed for failure to pay monies owed to the government. Early in 1824 Hoppo Dasan approved admission of a shopkeeper as partner of the Xicheng hong, seeking to improve its affairs, without beneficial effect. The hong was petitioned against yet again, found to be insolvent, and was reported to the Emperor in October 1826. The Xicheng hong was found to owe 149,769 taels ($208,012) in duties and other debt to government, 477,216 taels ($662,800) to foreign creditors, and an unknown but substantial debt to Chinese creditors. The sale of firm assets yielded little and the hong merchants were ordered to pay the total balance due, some 618,904 taels ($859,589). The foreign debt was paid in five equal annual installments without interest. Pacqua was ordered banished to Ili, but his departure was delayed for over a year due to frontier wars. He finally left in August 1828, with

65 Ch'en, *Insolvency*, pp. 337–8; Morse, *Chronicles, Vol. IV*, pp. 1 and 8; letter, Samuel Russell (Canton) to Edward Carrington, 13 November 1821, Letterbook I, Container 15, Russell & Co. Papers (Samuel Russell Papers), Library of Congress, Washington, D.C.

66 Ch'en, *Insolvency*, pp. 96 (Table 2.7) and 337–9; Morse, *Chronicles, Vol. IV*, pp. 1, 8 and 73; White, "Hong Merchants," p. 112.

the hong merchant body and the EIC each contributing 1,500 taels to "alleviate the hardships" of his journey and exile.[67]

Although the 1813 trust debts of Poonequa (Mai Jinting of the Tongtai hong) had been fully paid as of 1822, that firm remained on the edge. Poonequa died five years later in January 1827, leaving an insolvent hong. The hong merchants and tea merchant creditors offered to help Poonequa's son run the hong and pay its debts. The son instead chose to immediately flee Canton. Hoppo Wenlian declared the Tongtai hong insolvent, and ordered its assets sold to pay debts. The hong merchants were required to pay 110,000 taels ($152,778) in duty and contribution debt of the failed hong, plus 86,000 taels ($119,444) to its foreign creditors. The foreign debts were thereafter paid in three annual installments without interest, starting in February 1828.[68]

Partial payment in satisfaction of the remaining balance of the receivership debt of the Fulong hong of the Manhops was made in December 1823, under a negotiated compromise with creditors. On account of this over ten year old debt ($630,000), creditors received a lump sum payment of $310,000 (just under 50%). The money came from relatives and friends of the debtors ($60,000), from a loan by the American John Perkins Cushing ($160,000), and from current season EIC profits.[69] The Fulong hong of the Manhops struggled to remain in business but failed five years later in 1828. In a bizarre stroke, the son of its founding partner Inqua materialized in Canton in 1827 like a foreshadowing angel of death, demanding shares of the firm and its recent profits. Seventeen years earlier, in 1810, Inqua the father had run off, abandoning the hong and leaving his partner Manhop I to deal with roughly 700,000 taels ($972,222) in debt to foreign creditors, plus unpaid customs duties as well as debts to Chinese creditors. Inqua's son had since grown up, had served as a minor official in Beijing and was able to wield influence. He severely harassed Manhop II through the Nanhai magistrate and the Hoppo but the matter finally came before the Governor-General who considered and rejected the son's claim.[70]

67 Ch'en, *Insolvency*, pp. 65, 96 (Table 2.7), 248 and 343–5; Morse, *Chronicles, Vol. IV*, pp. 108 and 173. The first installment of Xicheng hong debt paid under the collective guaranty in 1826 included $52,878.28 which was booked by creditors as a final payment of the hong's debt to 1813 trust creditors. Ch'en, pp. 248 and 418 n.73.

68 Ch'en, *Insolvency*, pp. 347–8 and 96 (Table 2.7).

69 Ch'en, *Insolvency*, pp. 248 and 48 (one source of funds was $90,000 in profit earned from EIC transactions that season (two shares)).

70 Ch'en, *Insolvency*, pp. 239–30. William C. Hunter records having seen, after Manhop's failure, a $60,000 promissory note from the hong merchant bearing interest at the extreme

The demise of the Fulong hong followed the no less remarkable disappearance of 30,000 bales of cotton—valued at about 900,000 taels ($1,250,000)—from its warehouses. Safely stored as of November 1827, the massive cotton inventory had vanished as of February 1828. Foreign creditors believed it had gone either to shady secret partners of the firm or in payment to Chinese creditors (the Chinese New Year when debts were required to be settled fell on 15 February 1828). The hong was petitioned against by Magniac & Co. but the Governor-General did not want to act, as he was only the acting Hoppo. On 7 April 1828, Yanlong arrived at Canton as the new Hoppo, and on 10 May 1828 Manhop I was declared insolvent and the case was reported to the Emperor. After asset liquidation, the Fulong hong was found to owe 262,600 taels ($364,722) in duties to the government, and 792,000 taels ($1,099,300) to foreign creditors (Americans and Indian country traders). The Hoppo ordered the hong merchant body to pay the arrears of customs duties, and to pay the foreign debt without interest over eight years. The time payment term was reduced to seven years in response to creditor protest, and finally to six years.[71] Manhop II, the nominal head of the Fulong hong, was ordered banished to Ili. He was rumored to have left Canton with $10,000 and several servants. The EIC sniffed in its records that he had set out on his journey "in a style better suited to the station of a wealthy mandarin than that of a degraded bankrupt merchant about to undergo his punishment."[72]

Burdened by this string of failures, the Consoo Fund remained stressed during the years 1815–1828. The trend of increase of average annual liability continued. It is true that the percentage of annual increase was not as sharp as it had been between the two prior periods, and that all of the failures in this period were junior hongs that had been placed in receivership in the period 1800–1814, but there were otherwise few other reasons for optimism. The guild stood sharply divided between the weak and a few strong hongs. The government continued to draw heavily on the hong merchants for payments to support state needs, but it began to do so more carefully. A policy of deferral of the collection of assessed taxes, implemented on imperial approval in 1819 and continued through the outbreak of war in 1839, demonstrates that the Chinese government understood that the hong merchants had reached the limit of

distress rate of five percent (5%) per month—60% per annum. Greenberg, *British Trade*, p. 65; Hunter, *Fan Kwae*, p. 39.

71 Ch'en, *Insolvency*, pp. 350–1 and 96 (Table 2.7); Forbes, Remarks on China, p. 38 (Manhop I owed $1,125,538 on his failure); Morse, *Chronicles, Vol. IV*, p. 173.

72 Ch'en, *Insolvency*, pp. 350–1; Morse, *Chronicles, Vol. IV*, pp. 150 and 173.

their financial ability. Restraint was in order at Canton, and the guild should not be unusually pressed.

In the winter of 1828–1829, legislators began to consider a proposal for a bank guaranty fund that took its inspiration from the success of the Canton Guaranty System. At Albany, in the State of New York, these legislators were not informed of the precarious financial condition of most of the hong merchant body and of the Consoo Fund. At Canton, in China, the hong merchants were denied the pause and opportunity to rebuild that they so badly needed. In the years that followed, 1829–1842, their collective guaranty liability for the debts of failed colleagues once again soared.

CHAPTER 7

The Last Years of the Canton System, 1829–1842

As of 1829 the British EIC had become deeply concerned about the depleted number and feeble financial condition of the hong merchants. In response, it imposed a five month trade embargo from 1829 into early 1830 in an unsuccessful attempt to force reform of the Canton System. Just four years later, the EIC itself left the Canton trade, its charter terminated as the result of the legislative efforts of British private traders and manufacturing interests which saw bright promise in China. New participants poured into the trade, increasing exports and driving up prices.

The departure of the EIC meant the end of the annual fixed share tea purchase contracts it had long made with the hong merchants, and also the end of the bailout loans the EIC often made as a lender of last resort to keep its hong trading partners in business.[1] The bailout loans had always depended on future revenues the EIC contracts would generate for the hong merchants. The EIC assumed that its hong debtors would be able to repay their loans from the proceeds of its contracts, or that the EIC would be able to simply offset the debt. As the EIC closed down, there was a general realization in the marketplace that the entire Canton Guaranty System had been founded on much the same assumption. Creditors whose claims were being paid over time had assumed that the surviving hongs would be able to pay their guarantor obligations with income from stable tea contracts. As the English private trader W. S. Davidson stated in his 1830 testimony before the Select Committee of the House of Lords:

> I often selected bankrupts to deal with because I could seldom deal with the merchants on fair terms; some of them were satisfied with the certain profits on the Company's business and did not covet other business very much ... They [the bankrupt hongs] gave much better prices; too often (I suspect) they gave higher prices than they could afford to in the actual state of the market.... [He had contracted with them] constantly and in large sums entrusted money to them.... I knew they [i.e., the stronger hongs] had shares in the Company's business and I felt assured they would be able to pay me, which they were.[2]

1 White, "Hong Merchants," p. 120.

2 Greenberg, *British Trade*, pp. 70–1; Basu, "Asian Merchants and Western Trade," p. 348.

 | DOI 10.1163/9789004276567_008

PLATE 15 *The foreign factories at Canton, ca. 1825–1835. Oil painting by an unknown Chinese artist. (Private collection. Photograph by courtesy of the Martyn Gregory Gallery, London.)*

With the EIC contracts terminated, such assumptions could no longer be made. Trade boomed, but under uncertain conditions as the terms of contracting and trading were being worked out on a daily basis. Credit was exceptionally tight. Domestic suppliers to the hong merchants were anxious about how they would be paid and were reluctant to extend more than modest credit. The struggle that ensued between suppliers and hong merchants brought on a number of hong failures, which occurred just as the Panic of 1837 ricocheted around the world from London through to China.

The crisis of 1836–9 exposed the Canton Guaranty System as irreparably damaged. Several hong merchants were found to be insolvent. Creditors wondered how the guild could possibly pay the enormous debts of these hongs. The surviving hongs offered no concrete reason to believe that they would be able to perform their promises to pay, and they sought long repayment terms to boot. In this crisis of confidence, foreign creditors increasingly looked to the Chinese government, which had imposed and long enforced the collective guaranty, to pay these private debts. In a February 1838 letter to Lord Palmerston, Charles Elliot, British Superintendent of Trade at Canton, stated that the Chinese government had in effect guaranteed payment of the hong merchant foreign debts as the *quid pro quo* for the privations the foreigners were forced to suffer in abiding by the restrictive rules of the Canton System.[3] The failure to pay hong merchant debts—which a London pamphleteer spoke of as a transfer of British capital to Chinese citizens[4]—became a bloody shirt that British traders waved as they sought war against China in 1839.

1 The Hong Merchants, 1829–1842

The pressing problem in 1829 was whether the hong merchants had the financial ability to conduct the trade that was being done. In the wake of the massive Manhop II failure of the year before (involving 1,054,600 taels—$1,464,722—in debt owed to foreigners and the government), the guild had shrunk to seven merchants.[5] Of this number, only three—Goqua II, Howqua II, and Puankhequa III—were believed to be truly solvent.[6] Yet even Goqua had sought an EIC loan to pay taxes in June 1828, as he had done often before. He pleaded "deficient capital" and told the EIC that "no one will help me with a loan."[7] The hong of Chunqua III was on the edge, and that of Mowqua II was

3 R. Randle Edwards, "Ch'ing Legal Jurisdiction," pp. 237–8.

4 "These debts constitute a transfer of British capital to the Chinese Hong-merchants of about three millions of dollars, which the creditors require, surely not unreasonably, to be repaid within that time in which that capital would double itself by compound interest at the usual market rate of twelve per cent., which time is about six years; whereas the Chinese propose to liquidate the debts in nine years, beginning with next year, which, in the case of Hingtae, would be ten and a half years from the date of adjustment of account, and a still longer time in the case of Kinqua." Anonymous [Robert Harry Inglis], *The Chinese Security Merchants in Canton and their Debts* (London: J. M. Richardson, 1838), p. 43.

5 Ch'en, *Insolvency*, p. 17.

6 Greenberg, *British Trade*, p. 53; Morse, *Chronicles, Vol. IV*, pp. 166 and 209; White, "Hong Merchants," p. 116.

7 Basu, "Asian Merchants and Western Trade," pp. 351–2 ("I have hitherto been benefited by loans from your Company so that I was able to meet the payment of government duties ... the Viceroy has ordered that all the Hongs no later than the twentieth of this month remit the [gongjia] (tribute to the Court) and the [sengjia] (ginseng duty). The total ginseng duty of this year is 68,712.2 taels and my share is 6,247.2 taels. As for [gongjia] the total is 61,400 taels and my share is 2,707.8192 taels. My total remittance thus amounts to 8,955 taels. I thought it over and over but could not find a way to raise the sum. My business is small in scale and being often deficient in capital, no one will help me with a loan ... normally since your Company already helped me several times to pay off my duties, I should not have made this appeal again. Although I think hard, I can find no way out. In recent years, I have been relying on your Company for loans to pay off my share of duties, I therefore appeal to you gentlemen once more ...").

tottering.[8] Kinqua I and Fatqua II were known to be heavily in debt, but were believed to be able to meet current commitments.

The British EIC and other foreign traders feared that the imminent failures would reduce the number of hongs to the point that the survivors could easily control prices against EIC interest, i.e., that they might combine and exert monopoly force in opposition to its own. New foreign trade merchants were needed, but the EIC understood that the financial burdens of the collective guaranty and official exactions discouraged entry. Reform was therefore seen as badly needed, for without changes to the system itself qualified merchants would never enter the guild. The EIC could see that the officials had been unable to attract new merchants: "the Hoppo was said to have reduced his fee from 70,000 to 10,000 taels, the Viceroy had been authorized to waive the requirement that all the old Hong Merchants should jointly guarantee the new, the old Hongists all professed their eagerness to obtain new colleagues—and yet none came forward."[9] These concerns generated intense debate within the Canton Committee of the EIC, which finally voted to withhold its trade and to press hard for an improvement of trading conditions at Canton.

The EIC sought sweeping free trade reforms in communications to the Canton officials which began in September 1829,[10] but it received nothing more

---

8 Ch'en, *Insolvency*, p. 41.

9 Morse, *Chronicles, Vol. IV*, pp. 199 and 201–2; White, "Hong merchants," pp. 115–8.

10 Eight propositions, which "were calculated to upset the entire system under which the officials of Canton had battened on the foreign trade, and which had been developed during a century of exploitation," were presented by the EIC to the hong merchants on 5 October 1829 for transmittal to the Governor-General: "1st. The Tungsheng Hong (Chunqua) must not be allowed to fall; but Lew Chingshoo (the elder Chunqua) must return bringing money with him. 2nd. The new merchants for foreign trade, whether twenty or fifty houses, were not to be liable for the debts of others; this would restrict their credit since they could not be called upon to make good the deficiency of bankrupts' estates. 3rd. The old Hong Merchants would in future not be liable for the debts of others; they must at once liquidate their debts, or declare the amounts of those outstanding. 4th. The liquidation of bankrupt estates now proceeding should be continued, the money being collected from new and old Hong Merchants alike, and the installments are to be paid as now arranged; when the present debts are paid off, no further sums shall be collected for the purpose. 5th. The import duties were to be assessed daily and paid within five days; the same with the export duties. 6th. Foreign merchants were to be free to hire warehouses and keep them under their own management; there need be no Security Merchant for the foreigners; and the foreigners must pay the duties in cash without the intervention of a Hong Merchant or a Linguist. 7th. None of the Hongs for Foreign Trade should be required to act as Security for foreign ships, the reason ceasing to exist when duties are paid in cash; and 'Since the Security Merchants really cannot control the actions of Foreigners, the Law requiring Security Merchants, only assists the Hoppo's

than acceptance of some small changes in exchanges with Governor-General Li Hongbin over the following six months. All the while, the EIC kept its vessels and their inbound cargoes out of port. The Governor-General "issued a mandate to the merchants, expressing his surprise that they had not produced others to act as their colleagues, and offering to remit all fees payable in the interval before the arrival of the new Hoppo."[11] The Governor-General then ordered the hong merchants "to find out among their intimate friends substantial people to undertake the situation."[12] The EIC knew perfectly well that this would accomplish nothing. "It never can be expected while the obnoxious Regulations exist which make a Hong Merchant a slave for life to the Govt. and render him liable for debts incurred by others, and responsible for the conduct of men over whom he has no control, that any Person of Common Sense will expose himself to ignominy, and his Family and Property to Ruin, for the sake of at best a very precarious hope of advantage."[13] In its records for 1829, the EIC noted two concrete reasons no qualified candidate would come forward.

> First, because the Hong Merchants are often subjected to insult, extortion and vexatious detentions at the Hoppo's office, by the King Ching [*Jingcheng*] Secretary, the attendants, the clerks, and to a degree that it is difficult for the human feelings to bear. Therefore people are unwilling to become Hong Merchants. A rich merchant's son[14] has been heard to say, '[*ningwei yizhi kou, buwei yangshang zhishou*]' (Shall rather be a dog than a Hong Head Merchant). Secondly, according to the old regulations, when once a man entered the Hong, he became a prisoner for life. Although by the toil and labor of many years, he had attained affluences, was now old and his health declining, and owed no one anything, he

office to make pretexts and extort money, so that both Natives and Foreigners are vexatiously hindered and distressed by minute interference.' Further the commanders of ships should be free to select their own compradors and to buy their supplies for ready money. 8th. 'For the entrance of Foreign Ships into the Port, the charges at present exacted by all sorts of Officers must be diminished, after which those remaining to be paid should be in proportion to the size of the Ship.' In the future the port might expect an influx of small ships, to which the present system was unfair." Morse, *Chronicles, Vol. IV*, pp. 206–7.

11 Ch'en, *Insolvency*, pp. 209–10; Morse, *Chronicles, Vol. IV*, pp 199–221 (quotation at p. 208). The incumbent Hoppo had died on 8 August 1829. The new Hoppo arrived on 18 December 1829, during the Embargo. Morse, *Chronicles, Vol. IV*, pp. 204 and 214.

12 Ch'en, *Insolvency*, p. 257.

13 Morse, *Chronicles, Vol. IV*, p. 208.

14 Shinqua (Pan Zhengheng), the eldest son of Puankhequa II.

> was not allowed to retire and return home. A Hong Merchant[15] has said: 'I would willing[ly] give eight tenths of my property to government, if they would allow me to retire, go home, and enjoy the remaining two tenths.' This being the case, how can an Invitation succeed in bringing any to purchase the hateful responsibility of a Hong Merchant?[16]

Nonetheless, the EIC recognized that the "peremptory and urgent tone" of the mandate from the Governor-General "may possibly compel the merchants to induce their relatives and friends to enter into the foreign trade."[17]

The standoff between the EIC and the Canton officials further damaged the already weakened hongs. In a letter sent on 30 December 1829 the hong merchants reminded the EIC that they had contracted for black teas, and made advances on green teas, in reliance on promises to buy that the EIC had not performed. The Chinese New Year was imminent, no money was coming in, and the squeeze threatened to put them "in a deplorable position."[18] The EIC coldly replied that the merchants "must endure the consequences of the refusal of the Chinese authorities to admit the justice of the Committee's contention, and to remedy the grievances from which the Company's trade suffered."[19] Yet within two months, without any material change on the Chinese side, the EIC quietly folded, returning to Canton in February 1830 and bringing its vessels in to conduct the season's now long-delayed trade.[20]

The fulminating servants of the EIC realized in the end that the Company depended as much on the continuance of its enormous trade as did China, although the effects of the fruitless embargo fell most immediately and harshly on citizens of China. In November 1829, William Jardine noted the distress prevailing at Canton. The tea merchant and silk weaver suppliers, in particular, had become "very discontented."[21] The embargo improved nothing and, instead, unsettled the trading community. The alarm it raised among suppliers to the hongs, in particular, soon bore bitter fruit.

In 1829, the Hoppo sent a memorial to the throne which stated that the reason the foreigners were misbehaving was because there were too few hong merchants to control them. Liberalized rules for hong licensing were proposed

---

15 Wu Bingjian (Howqua II).

16 Ch'en, *Insolvency*, pp. 254–6 and 420.

17 Ch'en, *Insolvency*, p. 257.

18 Morse, *Chronicles, Vol. IV*, p. 215.

19 Morse, *Chronicles, Vol. IV*, pp. 215–6.

20 Morse, *Chronicles, Vol. IV*, pp. 220–1.

21 Greenberg, *British Trade*, p. 43.

and implemented on imperial approval. Under new rules effective in 1830, hong licenses became available on a one or two year provisional basis. If the new merchant proved able to "trade fairly, maintain good credit, pay all taxes, and not go bankrupt" within that period, then a permanent license would be issued for which only two incumbent hong merchants would be required to serve as financial guarantors.[22] The new rules provided a mechanism for admission of the weak candidates who came forward in response to the Governor-General's mandate.

Six merchants joined the outer seas guild in 1830. Four were admitted early in the year, timed to the period of British pressure,[23] and the last two in September. These admissions briefly brought the hong merchant body up to thirteen, but membership had fallen to ten by year end, after the August 1830 failure of the Dongsheng hong of Chunqua III and the near instant collapse of both of the September hongs.[24] The six new hong merchants, the first new merchants to join the guild in almost twenty years, were:[25] Mingqua (Minqua),[26] Hingtae, Saoqua,[27] Pwanhoyqua (Punhoyqua),[28] Chingqua and Tuckune. William Jardine grumbled in March 1830:

> We have now four or five new Hongs, one conducted by a Tea merchant, one or two men from Macao, who have some money and some character but who have been engaged in the opium trade—and one of them has visited the cold country passage free [i.e., been banished to Ili]. The others are mere adventurers without money and without character—or rather with so very so-so character—broken down opium brokers, dismissed

22 Chang, *Income of the Chinese Gentry*, p. 161; Morse, *Chronicles, Vol. IV*, p. 208; White, "Hong Merchants," p. 117.

23 Morse, *Chronicles, Vol. IV*, pp. 219 and 221.

24 Ch'en, *Insolvency*, p. 17.

25 Ch'en, *Insolvency*, p. 40 (Table 1.6).

26 Pan Wentao, proprietor of the Zhonghe hong, was known as Minqua (or Mingqua). Ch'en, *Insolvency*, pp. 17–8, 21 and 40 (Table 1.6). He is said to have been the son of a tea merchant, Ch'en, p. 154 (Table 4.6), and to have been a brother of the Renhe hong merchant Pan Wenhai. White, "Hong Merchants," p. 151.

27 Ma Zuoliang, proprietor of the Shuntai hong, was known as Saoqua. He had traded with foreigners in Macao, and his partner was an opium dealer. Ch'en, *Insolvency*, pp. 17–8, 21, 40 (Table 1.6) and 154 (Table 4.6).

28 Pan Wenhai, proprietor of the Renhe hong, was known as Pwanhoyqua (or Punhoyqua). Ch'en, *Insolvency*, pp. 17–8, 21 and 40 (Table 1.6). He is said to have been the son of a clerk in the Hoppo's office, Ch'en, p. 154 (Table 4.6), and to have been a brother of the Zhonghe hong merchant Pan Wentao. White, "Hong Merchants," p. 151.

> Hoppo's pursers, etc. What is to become of this newfangled nonsense I know not.[29]

Although all the new hong merchants had thin backgrounds and thin capital, Hoppo Zhongxiang charged each handsomely for the privilege of entry. Minqua, Hingtae and Saoqua are said to have paid 42,024 taels ($58,367) each for their licenses.[30] Another source estimates that fees of from $30,000 to $50,000 per admission went to the Hoppo personally, plus another $30,000 to his subordinates.[31]

Of the new hongs, the Xingtai ("Hingtae") hong of the brothers Yan Qiqang (titular head) and Yan Qixiang (active manager) was the most important. Their new hong went up like a rocket over the Canton marketplace in the early 1830s but blew up spectacularly in the crisis of 1836–7.[32] The brothers were young, described as having been boys or adolescents at the time their father died in the late 1820s. The father, a shroff or goldsmith who did business under the prominent name Sunshing, left an inheritance of $50–$60,000 that his sons used to start the Xingtai hong. The firm was also known as Sunshing, due to its association with the father.[33] The brothers were hungry for business and enjoyed apparent success, transacting a fourth or a fifth part of Canton's entire legal foreign trade at their peak.[34] Beneath the veneer of success, however, the firm had no capital to fall back on. Its licensing fees, alone, had exhausted the Sunshing inheritance. As Yan Qixiang explained in a 19 April 1837 letter to William Jardine, his largest creditor:

> In 1830, I began business with a limited capital; after deducting expenses of hanging out my signboard, beginning business, and buying packing houses and furniture, not a *cash* remained to me. In that year on account of the English ladies coming up to Canton, I was confined to prison for more than a month and found myself minus a lac of dollars [$100,000]. In the fifth year happened Lord Napier's affair. I was detained several

29 Greenberg, *British Trade*, p. 66.

30 Ch'en, *Insolvency*, pp. 123, 159 and 366; Morse, *Chronicles, Vol. IV*, p. 372 (detailed list of fees for opening a new hong in 1829).

31 Basu, "Asian Merchants and Western Trade," p. 341.

32 Ch'en, *Insolvency*, pp. 17–18, 20, 37 (Table 1.4), 40 (Table 1.6) and 365–7.

33 Basu, "Asian Merchants and Western Trade," p. 340; Ch'en, *Insolvency*, pp. 154 (Table 4.6), 157 and 365–7; Chinese Repository, Vol. 3, p. 440 (Jan. 1835) ("Journal of Occurrences … liberation of Sunshing").

34 Basu, "Asian Merchants and Western Trade," p. 341; Ch'en, *Insolvency*, p. 366.

> months in prison and did little business. My expenses at the offices of the Viceroy and the Hoppo and other places were not less than another lac [$100,000].[35]

Chingqua and Tuckune, the last two hong inductees of 1830, were especially weak and did not survive the year. Shortly after he opened the Maosheng Hong, Chingqua (Lin Yingkui) was appointed security merchant for a ship commanded by a Captain Yales. When Chingqua failed to pay the 2,500 taels ($3,472) in measurement and other fees that were due for that ship, his license was revoked and the other hong merchants were ordered to pay the customs debt. The other September admittee was the Tuckune (Teyuan) hong. Its licensed proprietor was Tam Hoanfun, who operated in partnership with a silk goods trader known as Lawune (Luo Yuan). A gift of three pairs of gold watches was made to the Hoppo on behalf of the Tuckune hong soon after it opened, but Lawune failed to inform the recipient that the valuable gift had not been paid for. When the vendor Mr. Just petitioned the Hoppo to compel the Tuckune hong to pay $990 due for the gift that the Hoppo had in his own hands, the embarrassed Hoppo immediately revoked the hong's license.[36]

The Canton authorities continued to try to rebuild the membership of the hong merchant body after 1830. Samqua and Tungqua (also known as Fuksune) (Wang Datong of the Fuquan hong)[37] were admitted in 1832, bringing the number of hongs up to twelve. Samqua (Wu Tianyuan), the proprietor of the Tongshun hong, had the local nickname of "Maiji Shuang" (chicken-seller Shuang) because he (Shuang) formerly sold chickens.[38] The 1835 admissions of Footae and Lamqua briefly brought membership to a 1780–1842 period high of fourteen. Footae (Yi Yuanchang) had been an outside shopman His Futai hong was effectively shut down within two years when foreign creditors seized its stock in trade, estimated to have been worth $10,000. The firm was revived by bringing in a partner, the son of a trader of birds and other goods with a less than pristine history ("Tommy Birdman"), and it survived as a minor hong.[39] Lamqua (Luo Futai), unrelated to the Canton artist who used the same

35 Greenberg, *British Trade*, pp. 66–7; Ch'en, *Insolvency*, p. 159.

36 Ch'en, *Insolvency*, pp. 359–61.

37 Ch'en, *Insolvency*, pp. 17–8, 21, 37 (Table 1.4), 40 (Table 1.6), 154 (Table 4.6) and 361–2.

38 Ch'en, *Insolvency*, pp. 17–8, 21 and 40 (Table 1.6); Sung, "A Study of the Thirteen Hongs," p. 28. Samqua was the brother of a compradore employed by Magniac & Co., and his partner was a tea merchant. Ch'en, p. 154 (Table 4.6).

39 Ch'en, *Insolvency*, pp. 18–9, 40 (Table 1.6), 154 (Table 4.6) and 161–2; Basu, "Asian Merchants and Western Trade," p. 342.

business name, also suffered from inadequate capitalization. His Dongchang hong was sanctioned for a smuggling incident and quietly went out of business in 1837, with the arrears it owed to the Consoo Fund ordered assumed by the surviving hong merchants.[40] Takqua (Rung Yuguang), admitted as the proprietor of the Anchang hong in about 1836, has the distinction of being the last hong merchant ever licensed. His firm was ordered closed just three years later in 1839 by Lin Zexu for allowing outside merchants to sell tea to foreigners under its cover.[41] The new admissions did not improve the ability of the hong merchant body to handle the trade that was being done. Writing in May 1834, Joseph Coolidge of the American firm Russell & Co. rightly anticipated that "[m]any of the hongs must fail. Several... are not worth one cash."[42]

The Canton officials promulgated two new regulations concerning hong debts during this period. On 27 April 1830 the Hoppo issued a mandate to the hong merchants requiring the immediate disclosure of all debts due to foreigners, and stating that debts not so declared would not be recognized in Chinese debt proceedings.[43] Five years later, in 1835, Governor-General Lu Kun announced a new approach to hong debts. The hong merchants would be required to fully report all of their foreign debts as of the end of each trading season, and to pay such debts as far as practicable. Unreported debts would be treated as illegal loans and would not be enforceable or covered by the Consoo guaranty.[44] These regulations were not enforced and they had no effect on the payment of debts of hongs which failed after their promulgation.

Hong admission regulations were tightened in the international financial crisis year 1837 by Governor-General Deng Tingzhen. No new members would be allowed to come in except to replace retiring, insolvent or deceased hong merchants. When a new member was selected as qualified, all the incumbent hong merchants would be required to sign a financial guaranty bond, as in the old days. These regulations might be said to have had some effect. No new members thereafter joined the outer seas guild.[45]

---

40 Ch'en, *Insolvency*, pp. 18, 20, 40 (Table 1.6), 153, 154 (Table 4.6) and 365. This merchant is unconnected with the well-known artist who produced portraits and paintings at Canton in the same period and used the same business name.

41 Ch'en, *Insolvency*, pp. 18, 21, 37 (Table 1.4), 40 (Table 1.6), 154 (Table 4.6) and 367–8; White, "Hong Merchants," pp. 144–5.

42 White, "Hong Merchants," p. 122.

43 Morse, *Chronicles, Vol. IV*, p. 230.

44 Basu, "Asian Merchants and Western Trade," pp. 335–6; White, "Hong Merchants," p. 123.

45 White, "Hong Merchants," p. 143.

2 Trading Conditions, 1829–1842

Difficult trading conditions continued to plague the hong merchants in the early 1830s. The market for imported cotton remained flat, as in the 1820s. In 1829 some hong merchants still held cotton they had purchased two years earlier.[46] Then a series of unusually cold years, beginning in 1831, destroyed the late harvests and reduced agricultural production. Guangdong and neighboring provinces experienced food shortages. As the regional economy suffered demand for imported goods fell in turn.[47]

The hong merchants were also sharply affected by changes which followed the abolition of the China trade monopoly of the British East India Company. The British trade, legal and illegal, was enormous. Much of it was illegal, with opium constituting two-thirds of the value of all British imports into China in the period 1833 through 1842.[48] The balance was legal, and had been conducted through 1834 on an orderly contractual basis with the licensed hong merchants. The Canton community learned quickly that the British Parliament had voted late in the Summer of 1833 to terminate the EIC monopoly effective as of the Spring of 1834. This major looming change and its consequences were warily anticipated by the market.[49] One fundamental change was termination of the role of the British EIC as bulk purchaser of tea, and the end of the relatively stable long term fixed share contracts it had long made with the hong merchants.

With the huge EIC tea business thrown open, new British traders rushed in. There was a sharp increase in demand for teas for export, and prices soared. The EIC, withdrawn from direct involvement, still strongly influenced the trade. In England it held large quantities of its teas in warehouses, supporting high prices. At Canton it acted as a banker, with some $2 million in its treasury. Through its China Agency, the EIC financed tea purchases by the new entrants. The hong merchants happily received its cash, in preference to the Indian cotton or British manufactured goods brought in by the incumbent private traders and agency houses. Responding to high prices for tea, the hong merchants sent much of this cash upcountry to increase production. As the price of Chinese export goods rose, the price of imports—other than opium—fell. Competition forced these imports out onto the market and, as the Canton Agency recorded, "'the readiest buyers were the neediest Hong Merchants, who purchased them

46 Morse, *Chronicles, Vol. IV*, p. 186.

47 Marks, *Tigers, Rice, Silk, and Silt*, pp. 217–9.

48 Greenberg, *British Trade*, p. 50.

49 Peter Ward Fay, *The Opium War 1840–1842* (Chapel Hill: Univ. of North Carolina Press, 1975), p. 67.

at long credits to resell them immediately among their countrymen for cash."[50] Much of the Hingtae debt was for credit purchases of this character.[51]

As the prices of export goods increased, domestic Chinese suppliers grew increasingly worried about the credit risks they were running. From the early days of the trade, inland suppliers had placed implicit reliance on the British EIC as stable ultimate purchaser as a source of repayment.[52] The bulwark of reliable long term sale contracts with the British EIC was now gone, and instability was in the air. Suppliers of the black teas favored in England pressed the hong merchants for prompt payment. As of 1836 the "black tea men" refused to deliver even previously contracted teas without first receiving cash or some form of security in advance.[53] Similar pressure came from other suppliers, such as vendors of silk piece goods, the prices for which had tripled between 1833 and 1838.[54]

In 1835, Puankhequa III was suspended from trading for failing to pay 32,000 taels ($44,444) in duties.[55] The condition of the formerly eminent Guangli hong of Mowqua II (Lu Wenjin) sharply darkened the same year. The firm had barely survived crunches in 1829 and again in 1832, paying 12% interest on some $1.5 million in loans from Chinese and foreign creditors out of thin trading profits and the 6%–8% estimated annual return on its large landholdings.[56] Mowqua II lived well and put up a good front. Those appearances were over by 1835. He was imprisoned for debt in December 1835, and died soon after his release early in 1837, the result of judicial beatings and mistreatment while in prison. The Guangli hong was found to owe more than $600,000 to foreign creditors, and a larger amount to domestic creditors.[57]

The crisis of confidence of 1836–9 broke in this precarious context. Willing lenders could no longer be found, and credit was frozen. The hong merchants and certain foreign traders responded by trying to negotiate a program for the

---

50 Basu, "Asian Merchants and Western Trade," pp. 337 and 340.

51 Basu, "Asian Merchants and Western Trade," pp. 337 and 340.

52 See Hanser, "British Private Traders," p. 208 (George Smith [of Madras], writing to Henry Dundas in 1787, noted that upcountry tea suppliers to the hong merchants placed their ultimate confidence in the "liberty, integrity and honor of the English East India Company" as a source of repayment).

53 Weng Eang Cheong, *Mandarins and Merchants: Jardine Matheson & Co., a China Agency of the Early Nineteenth Century* (London: Curzon Press Ltd., 1979), p. 197; Greenberg, *British Trade*, pp. 189 and 197.

54 Cheong, *Mandarins and Merchants*, p. 196.

55 Cheong, *Mandarins and Merchants*, p. 196.

56 Ch'en, *Insolvency*, pp. 20 and 116–7; Greenberg, *British Trade*, p. 63.

57 Cheong, *Mandarins and Merchants*, pp. 196–7 and 251.

PLATE 16 *The hong merchant Mowqua II (Lu Wenjin). Oil portrait by Lamqua (Guan Qiaochang), 1830s. Described as "a debauchee" by a British observer, Mowqua II was imprisoned for debt in December 1835 and died soon after his release in 1837 as the result of beatings and mistreatment while in prison. (Private collection. Photograph by courtesy of the Martyn Gregory Gallery, London.)*

restoration of strictly short term credit with foreign suppliers. As agreed, hong purchasers would be able to discount the payment of imported goods at the rate of 1% per month plus a ten day grace period, after which the hong merchant could be petitioned against for debt. Domestic Chinese cotton dealers disrupted the new system by using inferior silver to pay for cotton imports the hong merchants sold them.[58]

The credit crisis broke the Xingtai (Hingtae) hong, against which foreign creditors submitted $2,738,768 in claims. The Tianbao hong of Kinqua (Kingqua) (Liang Chengxi) was also exposed as insolvent, owing foreigners $1 million.[59] Writing in February 1837, William Jardine described the bleak conditions at Canton and the danger that these failures could bring down all of the hong merchants.

> I am convinced that not one of the recently made Hongs are free from debt, and except Howqua and Puankhequa there is now not one hong with $20,000. If we break one, we may break the whole; and if we do break the whole, the *Hoppo* will quickly make six or eight more, charging them 40,000 taels each for the privilege. These would of course be men of no property and little character who would in a few years break in their turn. This is a gloomy picture but it is a true one.[60]

The large number and size of claims made it impossible to offsets debts with credits. The balance of the Consoo Fund was inadequate, and there was no practical way to collect credit balances due to the fund from individual hong merchants. The EIC had formerly held such credits on its books on behalf of individual merchants, but those days were over.[61] The international financial crisis of 1837 made the rapid recovery of debts desirable, but there was little hope.

58 Cheong, *Mandarins and Merchants*, p. 199.

59 Cheong, *Mandarins and Merchants*, p. 198.

60 Greenberg, *British Trade*, p. 190. Cheong provides a slightly different quotation: "if we break one, we may break the whole; and if we break the whole, the Hoppo will quickly make up 6 or 8 more charging them 30,000 to 40,000 taels each for the privilege. They will be non-propertied and will use the first assignment of order to pay off the Hoppo and in a few years, they in turn will be broke" Cheong, *Mandarins and Merchants*, p. 198.

61 Cheong, *Mandarins and Merchants*, p. 198.

TABLE 4 *Hong Merchant Collective Guaranty Liability for Foreign Debt, 1780–1842*

Year of Failure	Name of Debtor	Foreign Debt Assumed (in Taels)*	No. (and Average Amount) of Annual Installments	Tax Debt Assumed (In Taels)
1780	Yngshaw and Kewshaw	600,000	10 (60,000)	Amount Unknown[62]
1784	Seunqua	166,000	10 (16,600)	None
1790	Eequa	255,000	6 (42,500)	None
1795	Gonqua	600,000	6 (100,000)	None
1809	Fonqua	259,000	3 (86,333)	None
1810	Ponqua and Gnewqua II	1,447,000	10 (144,700)	Amount Unknown[63]
1823	Conseequa	372,000	5 (74,400)	None
1826	Pacqua	475,000	5 (95,000)	None
1827	Poonequa	86,000	3 (28,667)	110,000[64]
1828	Manhop	792,000	6 (132,000)	262,600[65]
1830	Chunqua	418,000	3 (139,333)	$41,226[66]
1835	Fatqua II	None	None	300,000[67]
1837	Hingtae	1,656,000	8 (207,000)	Unknown[68]
1838	Kinqua	720,000	10 (72,000)	None

* Amounts given in round numbers.
Source of the data in the first four columns of this table: Ch'en, *Insolvency*, p. 96, Table 2.7, "Foreign Debts Assumed by the Body of Hong Merchants, 1760–1843."

62 Kuo-tung Ch'en and Weng Eang Cheong agree that Yngshaw and Kewshaw had unpaid customs duties but disagree as to the amount and whether such debt was or was not satisfied from asset sales. Ch'en, *Insolvency*, p. 206 (150,000 taels, partially satisfied from asset sales, the balance paid by the hong merchants); Cheong, *Hong Merchants*, pp. 152 and 186 n.103 (175,000 taels [$243,055], recovered by the state from asset sales, information attributed to Henri Cordier without further citation).

63 Ponqua owed 88,000 taels in duties, Gnewqua II 89,000 taels in duties, and the two jointly owed another 30,000 taels for piracy control at the time of their failure. It is unclear whether these debts were satisfied from asset sales. Morse, *Chronicles*, Vol. III, p. 150 and Vol. IV, p. 83; Cheong, *Hong Merchants*, pp. 92 and 123 n. 49 (Ponqua owed 80,000 taels in duties and Gnewqua II owed $89,000 in duties)

64 Ch'en, *Insolvency*, pp. 347–8.

65 Ch'en, *Insolvency*, p. 351.

66 Ch'en, *Insolvency*, p. 359.

67 Ch'en, *Insolvency*, p. 364.

68 The Xingtai hong owed customs and other tax debts, which the hong merchants were ordered to pay. Ch'en, *Insolvency*, p. 367.

3 The Collective Guaranty of Debt, 1829–1842

The thirteen year period 1829 to 1842 saw massive hong failures and large amounts of debt thrown onto the hong merchant body. The hong merchants were ordered to assume and pay the largest foreign debts ever experienced by the guild, at a time when the guild collectively was in a very weak condition. The 1830 failure of the Dongsheng hong of Chunqua III produced a 418,000 tael ($580,555) charge, directed to be paid over three years. The 1837 failure of the Xingtai hong (Hingtae) produced a 1,656,000 tael ($2,261,439) charge, ordered to be paid over eight years. Last came the Kinqua (Kingqua) failure of 1838 and the 720,000 tael ($1,000,000) liability it exposed, which was ordered to be paid over ten years.[69]

The total collective guaranty liability that was charged to the hong merchant body between 1829 and 1842 was 2,794,000 taels ($3,880,555), which averages out to 186,266 taels ($258,703) annually over these thirteen years.[70] These assessments represent another forty percent (40%) increase from the prior period. The trend of large increases of the average annual hong merchant collective liability for foreign debts during the period 1780 through 1842 is summarized in the following table:

TABLE 5 *Increase in collective liability burden, 1780–1842*

Time Period	Total Liability [Taels/(Dollars)]	[Taels/(Dollars)] Annual Average	Increase in Annual Average from Prior Period [Taels/(Dollars) (Percentage)]
1780–1799	1,621,000/(2,251,388)	81,050/(112,569)	(No prior period.)
1800–1814	1,706,000/(2,369,444)	113,733/(157,963)	32,683/(45,394) (40%)
1815–1828	1,725,000/(2,395,833)	123,214/(171,130)	9,481/(13,167) (8%)
1829–1842	2,794,000/(3,880,555)	186,266/(258,703)	63,052/(87,573) (40%)

69 Ch'en, *Insolvency*, p. 96 (Table 2.7).

70 Ch'en, *Insolvency*, p. 96 (Table 2.7).

This data is examined in Table Four and Chart One. Table Four, entitled "Hong Merchant Collective Guaranty Liability for Foreign Debt, 1780–1842," sets out the dates and amounts of the liabilities that were imposed. Chart One, entitled "Collective Guaranty Liability, 1780–1842, By Year," is a bar chart showing the average liability imposed annually over this sixty-two year period. Chart One, which is another treatment of the percentages of increase shown in the preceding summary table, demonstrates that the average annual burden increased significantly over the course of this period. Table Four sets out the source data with which the summary table and Chart One were prepared. It also shows that the annual assumption burden on the hong merchants was even worse than is shown in those tables. In addition to defaulted foreign debt (the subject matter of Chart One), the hong merchants were also required to pay taxes left unpaid by failed colleagues.

Unfortunately, much of the tax assumption data has not survived. The fifth column of Table Four sets out the amounts of tax debt ordered to be assumed, where that information is known. These three tables demonstrate that there were steady heavy increases over time in the average annual burden of collective liability. Table Four indicates that tax debt was a significant—if inadequately known—part of this burden. The tables and chart show that the liabilities that were charged to the hong merchants in the last years of the Canton System, 1829–1842, were unprecedentedly large. They placed a severe burden on the hong merchants at a time when they were struggling to survive.

Tax collections by the Chinese government from the hong merchants were also failing in the years after 1829. Extensions of tax obligations to the government dating back to 1819, and other current accommodations, are recorded in detail in a memorial presented jointly to the Emperor by Governor-General Deng Dingjin and Hoppo Yugun on 29 April 1839. As of that date, the total arrearage owed by the hong merchants to the government stood at 1,464,282.732 taels ($2,033,726).[71] The details in this memorial are especially important as information on the hong merchants becomes scarce in official records of the last years of the Canton System. The opium problem and its ramifications crowded out customary official recordkeeping.[72] On the Western side, the EIC had exited the trade and stopped its pen. As the Canton officials and their supervisors in Beijing had long paid close attention to hong finances and ability to pay, tax collection leniency and extensions, on approval from Beijing, provides strong proof that the hong

71 Tsiang, "Government and Co-Hong," pp. 602–7.

72 White, "Hong Merchants," pp. 121–2.

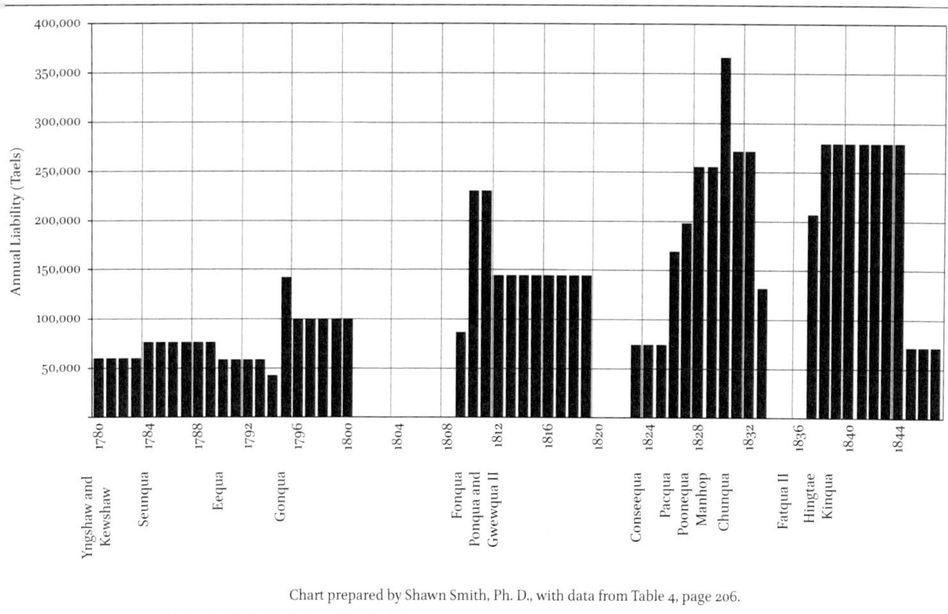

CHART 1 *Collective Guaranty Liability, 1780–1842, By Year.*

merchants' diminished financial capacity was genuine. The entire hong merchant body was at the edge, and the officials at Canton and in Beijing knew it. Despite these conditions, there is no evidence of any attempt to measure foreign debt risk subject to the collective guaranty, or to adjust the amount of the *hangyong* tax on the trade in accordance with anticipated risk, during this or indeed in any earlier period.

The joint memorial sent to the Emperor on 29 April 1839 demonstrates that tax payment punctuality was no longer the rule as of 1839, and that it had not been for many years. An 1819 hong merchant commitment to advance 600,000 taels ($833,333) to pay for Yellow River works had been repeatedly deferred. As the hong merchants were unable to pay the pledge when it was made in 1819, the funds were drawn from the provincial treasury, subject to repayment by the hong merchants. Despite successive deadline extensions, all duly reported, some 136,151 taels ($189,098) of the original 1819 pledge remained to be repaid twenty years later in 1839.[73] The hong merchants made a further 600,000 tael ($833,333) pledge to support the war in Kashgar in 1826. Payment of that now thirteen year old promise had been deferred until after

73 Tsiang, "Government and Co-Hong," pp. 603 and 606.

the 1819 Yellow River works obligation was paid in full.[74] That entire amount remained due in 1839. In 1835 the hong merchants were assessed 60,000 taels ($83,333) for reconstruction of the Bocca Tigris forts, of which sum 39,162 taels ($54,392) had not yet been paid.[75] They had also been ordered to pay 316,613 taels ($439,740) in tax and other obligations due to the government from the Maosheng (Chingqua) and Wanyuan (Fatqua II) hongs, which had failed in 1831 and 1835 respectively, on account of which nothing had been paid.[76] As of 1839, the hong merchants had recently been ordered to pay tribute and ginseng assessments due to the Court for the years 1836–9, and other debts, totaling another 534,978 taels ($743,025), but had failed to pay the full sum, leaving 372,357 taels ($517,162) still due.[77] The memorial details arrearages due from individual hong merchants, item by item. "We pray your Majesty to set them the limit of one year. If after the time limit they fail to pay up, they should all be sent to the district prison, as a warning."[78] The hong merchant Kinqua II was singled out for immediate punishment.

> His failure to pay in spite of numerous pressings shows that he purposely plays with the matter. It is inconvenient to protract our leniency. We therefore pray for Imperial sanction to put Liang Chen-hsi of Tienpao Hong into the prison of Nanhai Hsien, and to allow him one more year for the payment of all that he owes to the Government. In case of failure after the time limit is up, he should be exiled and whatever debts remaining to be paid should be assigned to the other merchants of the Co-Hong on the pro-rata basis.[79]

The other hong merchants, however, needed more time to pay. The memorial states plainly that the time for payment of all of the listed debts—save the deferred Kashgar war pledge of 1826—"has arrived. However, if we collect the debts together with the current revenue, it would be too heavy a burden for the merchants." The officials accordingly requested further extensions and deferrals.[80] Professor Chiang Ting-fu, who located and published this memo-

74 Tsiang, "Government and Co-Hong," pp. 605 and 606.

75 Tsiang, "Government and Co-Hong," pp. 605–6.

76 Tsiang, "Government and Co-Hong," pp. 605–6; Ch'en, *Insolvency*, p. 37 (Table 1.4).

77 Tsiang, "Government and Co-Hong," pp. 603 and 606.

78 Tsiang, "Government and Co-Hong," pp. 604–5.

79 Tsiang, "Government and Co-Hong," p. 604.

80 Tsiang, "Government and Co-Hong," p. 606 ("May we pray for the grace of Your Majesty to allow them to pay first the debts with a one year time limit, and afterwards the con-

rial in 1932, rightly observes that "the mere fact that such enormous debts existed and tended to increase was a sure sign that some disease was eating away the vitals of the Co-Hong not long before the Treaty of Nanking officially pronounced its demise."[81]

The first to fall in the final act of the Canton System drama was the Dongsheng hong of the Chunquas. This was a venerable firm by hong licensing standards. It had been founded in about 1787 by Chunqua I (Liu Dezhang) and was first licensed in 1794.[82] The founder had engaged in sharp practices and exploited his Beijing connections, which may explain why his firm lasted so long. When Chunqua I died in December 1824, management passed to Chunqua II (Liu Chengshu) who traded for three seasons, sold his interest to Inqua (a tea merchant) for 100,000 taels ($138,888), and left Canton. The firm became a three member partnership, with Liu Dong (Chunqua III), younger brother of Chunqua II), as its official head. Outside partner Inqua soon found that he had been defrauded. Assets had been exaggerated and large debts had been kept secret from him. In the summer of 1829 the hong's insolvency became public. Unable to pay its tea merchant suppliers, the firm surrendered title deeds to some of its property to them. Foreign creditor alarm about the insolvency of this important hong, and efforts to have Chunqua II brought back to Canton (rumor had it that he had made off with $600,000), form the backdrop to the five month EIC trade embargo of 1829–30. Debt proceedings were commenced and the Dongsheng hong was officially declared insolvent on 19 August 1830. Its debts were found to be slightly under 648,000 taels ($900,000), which was reduced to 418,000 taels ($579,193) through the liquidation of its remaining assets. The hong merchant body was directed to pay this sum in three annual installments, without interest, and also to pay $41,226 in customs duties due to the government. Chunqua III was imprisoned and beaten. He hanged himself in jail in 1831. In 1830 Chunqua II briefly returned to Canton, without any funds, and was gone again by the summer.[83] He thereafter remained at large, seeming

tributions and assigned debts according to the agreed schedules—the Bocca Tigris forts contribution of Taels thirty-nine thousand and the Kashgar War contribution of Taels six hundred thousand first, then the assigned debt of Taels 316,612.865. No further delay should be allowed so that all sums would be paid step by step.").

81 Tsiang, "Government and Co-Hong," pp. 606–7.

82 Ch'en, *Insolvency*, pp. 15, 19–21 and 352.

83 Ch'en, *Insolvency*, pp. 119, 122 and 352–9; Morse, *Chronicles, Vol. IV*, pp. 221, 230 and 255–6; The Asiatic Journal and Monthly Register for British and Foreign India, China, and Australasia, Vol. 6 (New Series) (Sept.–Dec. 1831) (London: Parbury, Allen and Co., 1831), p. 71.

to have achieved—at the dear expense of Inqua—as close to a secure retirement from the trade as had been achieved in many years.

The Wanyuan hong of the Fatquas, a chronically weak firm run by the son of its founder, failed in 1835. Licensed in 1808 by Fatqua I (Li Xiefa), the hong had long been in financial difficulty and is known to have borrowed money at very high interest rates. Fatqua I was assisted at times by loans from Mowqua II, a relative, and the British EIC. When the father died on 25 April 1822, Fatqua II (Li Yinggui) succeeded as head of the hong, but he found himself saddled both with unpaid customs duties and large fees the Hoppo charged for a successor license. Withdrawal of the EIC in 1834 posed a mortal challenge, as the hong had limited itself to EIC trade since about 1817. Foreign creditors had nothing to complain about in its failure, as the Wanyuan hong had no foreign debt. Its failure was a matter of great woe to the hong merchants, as the firm owed about 300,000 taels ($416,667) in unpaid customs duties. This arrearage was ordered to be assumed by the hong merchants and paid in two years, but, as of 1839, it had not been fully paid. There is no record of punishment of Fatqua II, if any.[84]

The crisis of confidence of 1836 brought on the most famous hong failure, the Xingtai (Hingtae) hong of Yan Qiqang and Yan Qixiang. The brothers had aggressively built up their business in the six year span of its existence, and were deeply involved in importations and other ventures with Jardine, Matheson & Co. Jardines was the hong's largest creditor, owed about $2 million.[85] Yan Qiqang said that his fall was the result of over-trading, market miscalculations, and excessive draw for family expenses, but the more true causes were undercapitalization of the firm and excessive payments taken by the Canton officials. The firm had overinvested in cotton supplied by Jardines, on which it was said to be losing $500,000 annually.[86] In the wake of the Xingtai failure, William Jardine reassured Hollingsworth Magniac in London as to the stability of their own firm by pointing out that the Consoo Fund was legally bound to pay the Xingtai debt. Michael Greenberg, the author of an invaluable study of early nineteenth century British trade with China, calls Jardine's appeal "to the despised laws of China ... an ironic instance of the devil having a use for the Scriptures."[87]

84 Ch'en, *Insolvency*, pp. 16–9, 37 (Table 1.4), 40 (Table 1.6), 122 (Table 3.1), 154 (Table 4.6), 176 and 363–4; Tsiang, "Government and Co-Hong," pp. 605–6.

85 Cheong, *Mandarins and Merchants*, pp. 198 and 251; Greenberg, *British Trade*, p. 66.

86 Greenberg, *British Trade*, p. 66; White, "Hong Merchants," p. 124.

87 Greenberg, *British Trade*, p. 70.

Unable to extend or to refinance its enormous debt, the Xingtai hong stopped payment at the end of 1836. Debt proceedings were commenced by foreign creditors on 21 April 1837.[88] Governor-General Deng Tingzhen appointed a committee of three senior hong merchants and three foreigners, who met at the Consoo House, to examine and then administer the payment of claims against the insolvent hong. This procedure was revolutionary in at least two respects. For the first time, foreigners became involved together with Chinese in the evaluation of claims against a hong debtor. Second, also for the first time, the Cohong's account books were opened for review and inspection by foreign creditors.[89]

Of a total of $2,738,768 in submitted claims, the committee recommended their allowance in the reduced amount of $2,470,332 (90%) as claims against the debtor. Hard negotiations then ensued concerning payment, which took much of the year (amid worldwide depression, the Panic of 1837). The hong merchants initially proposed a twenty year repayment period, but the time allowed was gradually brought down to eight (effectively nine) years.[90] The committee was granted control of the assets of the Xingtai hong on 30 November 1837,[91] and on 3 December 1837 the hong merchant body was formally ordered to pay foreign debt in the assessed amount of 1,656,000 taels ($2,261,439) in eight annual installments without interest.[92] The joint Chinese-foreign committee for the administration of the Xingtai claims finally closed its account book in 1844, when the debts had been fully paid.[93]

During the 1837 proceedings before the Governor-General on the Xingtai debts, creditors demanded that their claims against the Tianbao hong of Kinqua (Kingqua) (Liang Chengxi) should be included. Founded in 1808 and able to support a large extended clan at its peak, the Tianbao hong had long since fallen on hard times and had become involved in high interest rate

88 Ch'en, *Insolvency*, pp. 96 (Table 2.7), 210–1 and 367; Cheong, *Mandarins and Merchants*, p. 251.

89 Basu, "Asian Merchants and Western Trade," p. 346; Ch'en, *Insolvency*, pp. 210–1.

90 Basu, "Asian Merchants and Western Trade," p. 344; Ch'en, *Insolvency*, pp. 366–7; Cheong, *Mandarins and Merchants*, pp. 198–9.

91 Basu, "Asian Merchants and Western Trade," p. 347; White, "Hong Merchants," p. 126 ("as late as October of 1837, all that was known in Peking of the Hsing-t'ai Hong was that its owner was behind in the payments on a contribution for public works. The emperor ordered that Yen Ch'i-ch'ang's rank and title be temporarily removed, to be granted again only after he had paid the required amount.").

92 Ch'en, *Insolvency*, pp. 96 (Table 2.7), 210–1 and 366–7.

93 Basu, "Asian Merchants and Western Trade," p. 347.

borrowing that worsened its problems.[94] In 1831, a British observer stated that "Kinqua has dipped deep into barter with Americans, parsees, and free-traders generally. He has been on the verge of ruin for years, and is only saved by the good management of an honest, intelligent, shopkeeper, whom he has taken into partnership.[95] The withdrawal of the EIC, the firm's lack of capital, and the credit crisis of 1836–9 left the Tianbao hong struggling to pay its debts, which were estimated at 720,000 taels ($1,000,000). As the hong was still able to do business, it was permitted to continue trading, but the hong merchant body was ordered to assist the Tianbao hong by paying its $1 million in old foreign debt over ten years, with six percent (6%) interest (an unprecedented concession).[96]

Foreign creditors also pressed Governor-General Deng Tingzhen for similar treatment of their overdue claims against the Guangli hong of Mowqua III (Lu Jiguang). Known as the most opulent of the hongs during the time of Mowqua I (Lu Guanheng) (1792–1812), the firm had been ruined in the following twenty years. Excessive debt and spending had been the subject of struggle within the Lu family.[97] A British observer stated in 1831 that "Mowqua [II], the hong merchant, is a debauchee. His brother, who conducts the business of the hong, is a respectable man; but his credit has not been good for some time past, and he is only kept up by Howqua's assistance."[98] Mowqua II was imprisoned for debt in December 1835, and died soon after his release early in 1837, as the result of judicial beatings and mistreatment in prison. He owed more than $600,000 to foreign creditors, and a larger amount to domestic creditors. Investigation showed that the assets of the Guangli hong exceeded its debts. The Canton officials arranged for the continuation of the hong under Mowqua III, a son or third brother.[99] While these debts remained unpaid in 1837, the officials were wary of the consequences of directing the hong merchants to pay the debts of

94 Ch'en, *Insolvency*, pp. 16–8, 20, 25, 38, 40 (Table 1.6), 41, 122 (Table 3.1), 154 (Table 4.6), 158–9, 176 and 210–1; Hummel, *Eminent Chinese*, pp. 501–2; Mazumdar, *Sugar and Society in China*, p. 116; White, "Hong Merchants," pp. 144–5.

95 The Asiatic Journal and Monthly Register for British and Foreign India, China, and Australasia, Vol. 6 (New Series) (Sept.–Dec. 1831) (London: Parbury, Allen and Co., 1831), p. 71.

96 Ch'en, *Insolvency*, pp. 16–8, 20, 25, 38, 40 (Table 1.6), 41, 122 (Table 3.1), 154 (Table 4.6), 158–9 and 210–1; White, "Hong Merchants," pp. 144–5.

97 Ch'en, *Insolvency*, pp. 15–8, 20, 41, 116, 122 (Table 3.1), and 210–1.

98 The Asiatic Journal and Monthly Register for British and Foreign India, China, and Australasia, Vol. 6 (New Series) (Sept.–Dec. 1831) (London: Parbury, Allen and Co., 1831), p. 71.

99 Cheong, *Mandarins and Merchants*, pp. 196–7 and 251.

another firm that was still able to transact business. Foreign creditor attempts to force the hong merchants to pay the accumulated debts of the Guangli hong were accordingly rebuffed.

British creditors did not confine their efforts to Canton. At London, they actively sought government assistance in hong debt collection, by distributing pamphlets such as *The Chinese Security Merchants in Canton and their Debts* (1838) and by the active lobbying of government representatives. These efforts were a major part of domestic British efforts to initiate war with China, which propagandists preferred to frame as an effort to recover defaulted debts and to seek redress for diplomatic indignities than as a major military deployment in aid of the sale of illegal narcotic drugs.[100] Creditors expressed the fear that unless the Chinese government (as implicit guarantor) was compelled by Great Britain to make good on the hong debts, they "will either never be paid, or else liquidated at so remote a period as to amount to a total loss of their immediate trading capital."[101] One indication of awareness in England of the "Chinese Debts" crisis that war propagandists stirred in 1838–39 is a satirical print, "The Broken Hong Merchant or the Empty Tea Chest," that was published in London in November 1838. The print lampoons the professed financial plight of His Royal Highness Prince Augustus, the Duke of Sussex (1777–1843) (the sixth son of King George III), who complained that his allowance was inadequate to cover the cost of his Royal Society membership, by reference to the hong merchants. The print portrays the obese Duke in robes as a Chinese merchant, destitute, with nothing but the empty tea chest that he holds in his right hand. (Plate 17.)

Only a small part of the amounts due on account of the Xingtai and Kinqua (Kingqua) debts had been paid as of the outbreak of the Opium War. In accordance with the British Treaty of Nanking, $3 million in hong merchant debt repayment was delivered to the British consul at Canton on 23 July 1843. Of this sum, $1,266,102 was applied to Xingtai (Hingtae) debts, $922,432 went to Kinqua (Kingqua) debts, and $354,692 went to debts of the Guangli hong (Mowqua III).[102] It had taken a war for British private traders to get the foreign debts of the failed hong merchants paid in full.

100 See Dilip K. Basu, "Chinese Xenology and the Opium War," to be published in the Journal of Asian Studies, August 2014.

101 Anonymous, *The Chinese Security Merchants*, p. 4.

102 Ch'en, *Insolvency*, pp. 96 (Table 2.7), 210–1 and 367; Hosea Ballou Morse, *The International Relations of the Chinese Empire, Vol. 1, The Period of Conflict, 1834–1860* (London: Longmans, Green, 1910), p. 165 n. 81 ("To this settlement Howqua contributed $1,000,000; Footae, $90,000; Mowqua, $60,000; Pwankhequa, $130,000; Kinqua, $70,000; Samqua and Gouqua,

PLATE 17 *"The Broken Hong Merchant or the Empty Tea Chest." British print satirizing the professed financial plight of His Royal Highness the Duke of Sussex by reference to the financial condition of the hong merchants of Canton. A. Ducôté lithographer, published by T. M. McLean, London 18 November 1838.* (*Private collection. Photograph by permission.*)

The thirteen year period following its adoption as a model by the State of New York were the last years of the Canton Guaranty System. At the end of this final act, it was terminated, abolished together with the Canton System by the Treaty of Nanking in 1842. Ironically, in New York, the legislature observed the thirteen year anniversary of the Safety Fund—also battered by the worldwide depression of 1837—by amending the statute to limit liabilities of the fund.

In its final scene, at Canton, the Consoo Fund stood silent. A series of massive debts were ordered paid out of the fund in the mid-1830s, but it did not have assets to pay any material part of these claims, nor *hangyong* tax revenue adequate to pay them for years to come. The fund had never had any independent existence, nor a disinterested defender, nor had any effort ever been made to anticipate, adjust premiums for, or to maintain reserves sufficient to pay claims. When the predictable storm hit, the fund failed. The imprudent activi-

$100,000 each; Punhoyqua, $70,000; Mingqua, $20,000; Saoqua about $20,000. The balance it is supposed came out of the Consoo fund.—Chin. Rep., Aug. 1843.")

ties that led to these claims were probably obvious to the other hong merchants who did business at Canton. The severe risks arising from this trading almost certainly would have been revealed had any independent scrutiny been carried out for the benefit of the Consoo Fund. Nothing was unforeseeable about the calamity, even if the timing of the final crisis was perhaps accelerated by financial difficulties worldwide in the period 1834 through 1837 and thereafter.

The hong merchant guild, as guarantors, were unwilling to commit to pay the collective liability for these huge losses except over many years, and there was doubt whether the hong merchants could meet even a negotiated payment schedule. War followed, and these liabilities presently became a demand obligation of the Chinese government as some private British creditors had demanded. Although China tendered the payment in July 1843, the final burden of a large part of these charges fell on the last few apparently successful hongs. They presumably raised the necessary funds demanded by the Chinese state as direct obligor by asset liquidations on a massive scale at a time of financial distress. It may not be pure coincidence that Howqua II (Wu Bingjian) died on 4 September 1843, just six weeks after the $3 million was delivered to the British.[103] In the last scene of the tragedy, not even "too big to fail" entities were spared from loss.

103 Hummel, *Eminent Chinese*, p. 877.

CHAPTER 8

From Safety Fund to Bank Deposit Insurance

The Safety Fund statute of the State of New York, the first bank deposit insurance law ever enacted,[1] was conceived and drafted late in the year 1828 by Joshua Forman. He initially circulated the proposal to several leading bankers in New York City and Albany, and seemingly received their approval in principle before he presented the plan to Martin Van Buren,[2] newly elected as Governor in November. The unlimited guaranty program he proposed had no precedent. As David A. Moss explains, "Forman recommended a radical plan for mandatory bank liability insurance, the first of its kind in America and probably the world.... Forman's scheme was extraordinary because it aimed to manage money risk through an unprecedented combination of compulsory *risk spreading* (bank insurance) and *risk reduction* (ongoing bank supervision), a surprisingly modern approach for the 1820's."[3]

As Joshua Forman explained, the Safety Fund had been inspired by Chinese government regulation of the hong merchant monopoly of Canton.

> The propriety of making the banks liable for each other was suggested by the regulation of the Hong merchants in Canton, where a number of men, each acting separately, have by the grant of the government the exclusive right of trading with foreigners, and are all made liable for the debts of each in case of failure. The case of our banks is very similar; they enjoy in common the exclusive right of making a paper currency for the

1 Hammond, *Banks and Politics in America*, p. 445; Randall S. Kroszner and William R. Melick, "Lessons from the U.S. Experience with Deposit Insurance," in Ash Demirgüç-Kunt, Edward J. Kane and Luc Laeven, eds., *Deposit Insurance Around The World: Issues of Design and Implementation* (Cambridge: MIT Press, 2008), p. 193.

2 Robert E. Chaddock, *The Safety Fund Banking System in New York, 1829–1866* (National Monetary Commission, 61st Cong., 2nd sess., Senate Document No. 581) (Washington, D.C., U.S. Government Printing Office, 1910), p. 260.

3 David A. Moss, *When All Else Fails: Government as the Ultimate Risk Manager* (Cambridge: Harvard Univ. Press, 2002), p. 100 (emphasis in the original); Carter Golembe, "The Deposit Insurance Legislation of 1933," Political Science Quarterly, Vol. 75, pp. 181–200 (1960), p. 183 ("There seems to have been no American precedent for the proposed insurance plan.... The examination proposal was hardly less novel, since it contemplated regular examination by salaried officials empowered to investigate the condition of the banks fully—in short a degree of supervision almost unthinkable at the time.").

 | DOI 10.1163/9789004276567_009

> people of the state, and by the same rule should in common be answerable for that paper. This abstractly just principle, which has stood the test of experience for seventy years, and under which the bond of a Hong merchant has acquired a credit over the whole world, not exceeded by that of any other security, modified and adapted to the milder features of our republican institutions, constitutes the basis of the system.[4]

In the foregoing passage, Joshua Forman does not simply look to Canton as the source of the idea of a guaranty fund. The business community of the State of New York was already familiar with the concept of guaranty or insurance in various forms. Forman instead directly linked the requirement that such a fund must be maintained to the enjoyment of rights or privileges granted by government. At Canton, the hong merchants were licensed by the Chinese government and were granted monopoly rights. As a condition of this exercise of sovereignty in their favor, the hong merchants were required to guarantee the debts of other merchants within the monopoly. The case of the New York banks, in Forman's view, was "very similar." The banks existed by virtue of a charter granted by the New York legislature, and had been granted "in common the exclusive right of making a paper currency for the people of the state," itself an exercise of the sovereign power of issuing money. It was just that this exercise of sovereignty in favor of the banks should be conditioned on the maintenance of a fund to assure that all of this currency was sound. In Forman's words, "by the same rule [the banks] should in common be answerable for that paper." This connection between monopoly privileges granted by government and the conditioning of such grants on advantages to the state or to society has roots in the mercantilistic system of colonial America.[5] Since all banks profited from the use by the public of banknotes they issued pursuant to governmental authority, the banks should guarantee that the public would suffer no loss from the use of these notes.[6]

4 Van Buren, *Message of His Excellency Gov. Van Buren on the Subject of Banks*, p. 23; Howard Bodenhorn, *State Banking in Early America: A New Economic History* (Oxford: Oxford Univ. Press, 2003), p. 158; Hammond, *Banks and Politics in America*, p. 557; Golembe, "Deposit Insurance Legislation," p. 183; Allen Johnson and Dumas Malone, eds., *Dictionary of American Biography* (New York: Charles Scribner's Sons, 1931), Vol. 6, pp. 525–526 (biography of Joshua Forman by H.T.).

5 Charles W. Calomiris, *U.S. Bank Deregulation in Historical Perspective* (Cambridge: Cambridge Univ. Press, 2000), p. 44.

6 Hammond, *Banks and Politics in America*, p. 557.

The preceding four chapters reviewed the experience of unlimited collective responsibly for debt among the hong merchants of China during the years 1780 to 1842. This chapter considers the experience of this transplant in the United States of America, taking the idea from its introduction in 1829 through to the 1933 adoption of national bank deposit insurance. The reception by a society that was already recognized as strongly individualistic of a Chinese practice that imposed liability on a collective basis is itself notable.[7] The history begins with Joshua Forman, proponent of the Safety Fund, the person who recognized and transplanted the Chinese idea in 1829. The New York State legislature enacted a bank guaranty fund law that year, but it did not adopt the Canton Guaranty System. While the Chinese example was understood to have been a success, it was nonetheless "modified and adapted to the milder features of our republican institutions." The New York Safety Fund was thus established as a separate institution, unlike the example at Canton. It had distinct employees and officers and maintained its own accounts. New York also provided for ongoing scrutiny of the insured banks by the commissioners of the fund, another important difference. The Safety Fund offered unlimited coverage, as did the Chinese model, but did not mandate participation by all of the New York banks. It ended up paying all of the claims that were made against the fund, but needed considerable time to pay these claims, as had typically happened at Canton. Although the Safety Fund failed, the idea of a guaranty fund remained attractive, and a series of states enacted their own bank guaranty statutes in the course of the following century. Each offered unlimited coverage, each tended to require all banks to participate, and each failed in its turn. Proponents began to press for the adoption of national bank deposit insurance, especially in the wake of the Panic of 1907, to be structured so as to avoid the problems experienced by the state guaranty funds. It was believed that the idea required only certain further modifications and national implementation to make it entirely successful. After years of effort, national deposit insurance found its moment in the banking crisis of 1933 and was enacted into law. Deposit insurance has remained in effect in the United States since then, and has inspired bank deposit insurance in many other countries, a complicated history that is outlined in the following Chapter Nine.

7 See Alexis de Tocqueville, *Democracy in America* (George Lawrence, tr., J. P. Mayer, ed., Garden City, N.Y.: Anchor Books, 1969), pp. 506–13.

1 Joshua Forman

Energetic and curious, Joshua Forman (1777–1848) is a solid example of the type of entrepreneur who pursued land development in the United States in the early 1800s. Tall, friendly and well-connected, a skilled orator and a conversationalist, Forman was an effective proponent both of projects to improve the State of New York and of his own development efforts. He impressed others with the depth of his applied knowledge, and repeatedly reached out to gather information from far away. This willingness to gather helpful information from disparate and distant sources is evident in Forman's interests in canals, salt production and banking.[8]

Born in Dutchess County in 1777, Joshua Forman graduated from Union College in 1798, studied law in Poughkeepsie and New York City, and moved with his wife in 1800 to Onondaga County, then almost a wilderness. In the course of his life he wore many hats—variously lawyer, judge (Court of Common Pleas of Onondaga County from 1813 to 1823), member of the New York Assembly (elected in 1806 for one term), and a merchant—but his core occupation was always in real estate development. In 1808, as a newly elected member of the New York Assembly, Forman introduced and carried a resolution to develop a canal between the tidewaters of the Hudson River and Lake Erie. In framing the proposal and pressing for construction of the Erie Canal, Forman drew on direct knowledge of the region and his research into canal development in Europe. Although he is not known to have worked directly in banking, Forman's real estate and trade experiences seem to have contributed to a practical understanding of the need for sound currency in areas in the process of development.[9]

In 1819 Forman moved to the site of the City of Syracuse, of which he is recognized as a founder, and began to develop some 250 acres at the heart of the present city which he then controlled. Forman was active in commerce,

8 Johnson and Malone, *Dictionary of American Biography*, Vol. 6, pp. 525–526; William S. Powell, ed., *Dictionary of North Carolina Biography* (Chapel Hill: Univ. of North Carolina Press, 1986), Vol. 2, pp. 220–1 (biography of Joshua Forman by C. Sylvester Green); Ellen E. Dickinson, "Joshua Forman, the founder of Syracuse," Magazine of American History, Vol. 8 (1882), pp. 400–7; Joshua Victor Hopkins Clark, *Onondaga; or Reminiscences of Earlier and Later Times* (Syracuse: Stoddard and Babcock, 1849), Vol. 2, pp. 69–83.

9 Johnson and Malone, *Dictionary of American Biography, Vol. 6*, pp. 525–526; Powell, *Dictionary of North Carolina Biography, Vol. 2*, pp. 220–1; Dickinson, "Joshua Forman," p. 400 (Forman's family had emigrated from Holland); Clark, *Onondaga, Vol. 2*, pp. 69–83.

PLATE 18 *Joshua Forman, 1777–1848, the father of bank deposit insurance. Oil portrait by an unknown artist. (Collection of the Onondaga Historical Association Museum and Research Center, Syracuse, New York. Photograph by permission.)*

but always in ways that supported or benefited from his development efforts. He variously owned a tavern, an inn, and grist mills, and organized a plaster company and saltworks to utilize gypsum deposits and salt resources near Syracuse. Forman was a pioneer in the production of salt by solar evaporation in America, and sought out and engaged technical assistance from New Bedford, Massachusetts.[10]

Shortly before he advanced the proposal for Safety Fund legislation, in about 1826, Forman suffered serious reverses in his real estate investments. These stresses, in the context of the international economic crisis of the years 1825–26, seem to have focused his active mind on issues of banking stability and credit. Forman was under so much strain that he applied for a public job for the income he needed to pay his bills and stay in Syracuse, but was turned down. The disappointed, perchance embittered, founder of Syracuse moved of necessity to New Brunswick, New Jersey where he had an interest in a copper mine. The banking crisis thus deepened in the State of New York while Joshua Forman was in the State of New Jersey trying to rebuild his fortune. The guidance he provided on banking reform came on visits from New Jersey to New York, with Forman said to have spent most of the Winter of 1828–29 in Albany at the request of Governor Van Buren, working with legislators and others on plan issues. Forman's wife Margaret died in New Jersey in 1828. His fortunes had recovered sufficiently by the Safety Fund year of 1829 that he was able to purchase about 300,000 acres of land in Rutherfordston, North Carolina to which he moved. Forman supported himself developing and selling that tract, remarried, and became a leading member of his new community, among other things serving as vice president of the temperance society. Joshua Forman suffered a stroke in about 1844 and died in North Carolina in 1848.[11]

---

10 Johnson and Malone, *Dictionary of American Biography, Vol. 6*, pp. 525–526; Powell, *Dictionary of North Carolina Biography, Vol. 2*, pp. 220–1; Dickinson, "Joshua Forman," pp. 400–7; Clark, *Onondaga, Vol. 2*, pp. 69–83.

11 Johnson and Malone, *Dictionary of American Biography, Vol. 6*, pp. 525–526; Powell, *Dictionary of North Carolina Biography, Vol. 2*, pp. 220–1; Dickinson, "Joshua Forman," pp. 400–7; Clark, *Onondaga, Vol. 2*, pp. 69–83; Bruce E. Stewart, "Distillers and Prohibitionists: Social Conflict and the Rise of Anti-Alcohol Reform in Appalachian North Carolina, 1790–1908" (Ph.D. diss., Univ. of Georgia, 2007), p. 59.

2 The Power of Suggestion

The source of Forman's knowledge of Chinese foreign trade regulation is an enigma. In his reform proposal, he states that the bank guaranty plan "was suggested by the regulation of the Hong merchants in Canton." His capsule description of that system is accurate, if incomplete. Forman's information source was good, as far as it went. Contemporary comment confirms that Chinese inspiration of the banking reform was understood by his audience. Yet Joshua Forman was primarily engaged in inland real estate development. He had little (if any) direct connection with merchants engaged in foreign trade by sea. How did Forman acquire the information that "suggested" the Safety Fund Act of 1829?

Joshua Forman speaks of hong merchant regulation and practices as if they were common knowledge. "[T]he bond of a Hong merchant has acquired a credit over the whole world, not exceeded by that of any other security." No source had to be identified, as his audience understood the topic. Some may have possessed this knowledge, but it was not common knowledge.[12] Forman wrote in a manner framed as a compliment to an educated audience, in this case the honorable elected members of the legislature of the State of New York. He "assumed" their knowledge of Chinese trade regulations, as one might speak to an educated audience of elegant wines or of refined teas. Some might understand references to "2005 Château Margaux" or to "Pu'er tea packed in the 1950s," and some might not, but all would feel respected by address as being included among the elite group that is familiar with such matters. Coming

12 Negligible information on the hong merchants of Canton was found in an extensive review of published contemporary sources available in New York, both newspapers and books. A review of articles in the Albany Argus newspaper in late 1828 and the early months of 1829 (when it covered the debate on the Safety Fund legislation), found no mention of the hong merchants or of the Chinese inspiration for the reform proposal. This review, of microfilm records, was done on two separate occasions. A review of the large number of New York State newspapers included in the Readex "America's Historical Newspapers" database (period 1790 to 1842), by a search for "hong Merchant," yielded few articles, most of which would today be considered to be in the nature of "filler" content. To guard against database overlap error, this search was conducted of the entire newspaper database, and also individually of the majority of the New York State newspapers in such database for this time period. In addition, major books available to American audiences in this period, as identified by the late A. Owen Aldridge in *The Dragon and the Eagle: The Presence of China in the American Enlightenment* (Detroit: Wayne State University Press, 1993), were reviewed. Little about hong merchants, and nothing concerning the regulation of the hong merchant body, was found in these books.

from Joshua Forman, a former member of the legislature and a man known to have studied and drawn carefully from foreign sources, every indication was that this information could be trusted.

New York was the center of knowledge in the United States about commercial practices at Canton, as London was the center of British knowledge about trade with China. As of the late 1820s, the port of New York had established a position of clear dominance over United States trade with China. Hundreds of New Yorkers invested in Canton voyages, and many New York firms were prominent in the trade. John Jacob Astor stood as a leader among this group.[13] At the Port of New York, as in the City of London, knowledge about the China trade was proprietary. It had been developed, generally at private expense, to be used in commerce for private advantage. A working knowledge of the regulations that constituted the Canton System, and of how to interact with the Canton officials, was a key component of this body of knowledge.[14] This understanding, which was as important to Western traders who came and went as to the licensed and regulated hong merchants who resided at Canton, was a principal marker of success on both sides. In the West, such working knowledge was uncommon. When Henry Dundas began the process of planning a British embassy to China in London in the 1780s, he found knowledge of the China

13 Robert G. Albion, *The Rise of New York Port* [1815–1860] (New York: Charles Scribner's Sons, 1939), pp. 200–3; Downs, *Golden Ghetto*, pp. 67–8, 201 and 377; Walter Barrett (pseudonym for Joseph A. Scoville), *The Old Merchants of New York City* (New York: Carleton, 1863–70, Thomas Knox, 1871–85) (5 vols.); Conrad E. Wright, "Merchants and Mandarins: New York and the Early China Trade," pp. 17–54 in David S. Howard, *New York and the China Trade* (New York: The New-York Historical Society, 1984), pp. 27 and 30. In his 1997 study of American trade with China, Jacques Downs observed that "New York City, oddly enough, needs more exploring." Downs, *Golden Ghetto*, p. 377.

14 One example of this knowledge is a manuscript, "Observations on the manner of trading at Canton," prepared by John Gibson in Philadelphia, Pennsylvania and dated 13 November 1807 (Collection of Cornell University, Kroch Library Rare and Manuscript Department) (32 pages). Written in response to specific questions about trade navigation posed by a party intending to depart soon for Canton, this document offers precise detail on customs procedures, declarations and expenses, how to proceed whether engaged in smuggling or not, provides information on the cohong and individual merchants and outside shopmen, and includes advice on particular articles of trade and market conditions. This was private and valuable advice. It relates, for example, to detailed instructions provided by United States principals to their representatives engaged in trade in China, as for example the instructions to supercargoes found in the papers of Stephen Girard. Why this document survived is unclear. It is dated six weeks before President Jefferson signed the Embargo Act. This "letter of advice" might perhaps have survived because the voyage for which it was intended was canceled.

trade to be scarce, and often affected by private interest.[15] There is no reason to believe that specialist knowledge of the Canton trade regulations was any more common in New York State in 1829 than it was in London during the decade of the 1780s. The content of the information known to Joshua Forman shows that it came from a knowledgeable source. The incomplete nature of this information may suggest bias, or limits to knowledge, but that is pure speculation. Evidence concerning precisely what information was given to Forman, from whom, and when, may survive in some public or private cache of documents, another diamond lost in the archival haystack. Pending the discovery of such evidence, the source of Forman's knowledge of Chinese foreign trade regulation must remain an enigma.

3 The Banking Crisis in the State of New York

The banking crisis experienced in the State of New York in the years leading up to 1829 had its roots in a currency shortage. There was simply not enough coined United States currency to meet demand. Americans of the era relied on a hodgepodge of foreign coins which were accepted as legal tender. Nor was there enough silver coin to meet the demands of commerce. Paper banknotes made due. Printed in large numbers, banknotes represented the bulk of the money supply in the early United States. Banknotes are estimated to have constituted between seventy and eighty percent of circulating currency in the 1820s and 1830s. Hard coin may have represented as little as eleven percent of the money supply by 1835.[16]

---

15 Jessica Hanser, "Mr. Smith Goes to China: British Private Traders and the Interlinking of the British Empire with China, 1757–1793" (Ph.D. diss., Yale University, 2012), pp. 104, 110–4, 128 (George Smith [of Canton] "possessed something rare and valuable at the time: on the ground knowledge of and experience in China."), 131–2 ("George Smith [of Canton] was one of a limited number of people in London, who possessed first-hand knowledge of the China trade."), 133 and 136. As further evidence of the limited availability of knowledge in London at this time, another informal advisor to Dundas, George Smith [of Madras], recommended in 1783 that "Dundas should contact certain China experts then resident in London. Thomas Lockwood of Mortimer Street Cavendish Square, Thomas Fitzhugh of Portland Place and James Flint of Kent had all resided in China for decades and could offer Dundas their expert knowledge on the China trade." Hanser, p. 214.

16 Howard Bodenhorn, *A History of Banking in Antebellum America: Financial Markets and Economic Development in an Era of Nation-Building* (Cambridge: Cambridge Univ. Press, 2000), pp. 16–7; Bodenhorn, *State Banking in Early America*, p. 95; Bruce D. Smith and

This flood of banknotes was entirely generated by private banks. There was no paper United States currency, and the United States Constitution prohibited the states from producing money.[17] The depreciated state and federal paper of the revolutionary era—still remembered in the expression "not worth a Continental"—had left a bitter aftertaste. Paper currency was produced by banks, which were individually chartered in various states. Colonial era reservations about the chartering of banking corporations had been overcome,[18] and the number of private banks had increased rapidly. There were three chartered commercial banks in 1790. That number was up to 28 as of 1800, had climbed to 212 by 1815, stood at 328 in 1820, and had reached a total of 584 chartered commercial banks in the United States as of 1835—"and that despite a war, an embargo, and a deep recession in the late 1810s and early 1820s."[19]

"Bank currency," as Howard Bodenhorn explains, "was the lifeblood of commerce in early America and nowhere was its animating influence more profound than in areas of recent settlement."[20] Paper currency served economic development in at least two ways. First, it facilitated investment, in all forms and places. Second, off in the countryside, it fostered commerce by minimizing the inefficiencies and constraints of barter transactions.[21] This lifeblood—paper currency—was badly needed, and it was generally accepted. While there was wariness about paper of distant or questionable origin, which was discounted accordingly, the rapid growth of the medium stands as evidence of popular confidence in the issuing private banks. Americans can be trusting people. The promise to pay embodied in all early banknotes was supported by the handwritten ink signatures of two bank officers.[22] There was an expectation that specie or other good collateral sat in the vaults to back up the

---

Warren E. Webber, "Private Money Creation and the Suffolk Banking System," Journal of Money, Credit and Banking, Vol. 31, No. 3, Part 2 (1999), p. 627 n. 6.

17 United States Constitution, Art. I, § 10 ("No State shall ... coin Money; emit Bills of Credit; [or] ... make any Thing but gold and silver Coin a Tender in Payment of Debts ..."); Jane Kamensky, *The Exchange Artist: A Tale of High-Flying Speculation and America's First Banking Collapse* (New York: Viking, 2008), pp. 15–6.

18 Calomiris, *U.S. Bank Deregulation*, p. 43.

19 Bodenhorn, *Banking in Antebellum America*, p. 10; Kamensky, *Exchange Artist*, pp. 16–7.

20 Bodenhorn, *Banking in Antebellum America*, p. 17.

21 Bodenhorn, *Banking in Antebellum America*, p. 17; Robert E. Wright, "The First Phase of the Empire State's 'Triple Transition': Banks' Influence on the Market, Democracy, and Federalism in New York, 1776–1838," Social Science History, Vol. 21, pp. 521–58 (1997), p. 532.

22 Kamensky, *Exchange Artist*, p. 15; Q. David Bowers, *Obsolete Paper Money Issued by Banks in the United States 1782–1866* (Atlanta: Whitman Publishing LLC, 2006).

paper notes, and that the promises to pay of most bankers—typically leading citizens—were good and reliable.

The year 1809 saw the first failure of a private bank in the independent United States, together with the first string of bank failures. This debacle, vividly described by Jane Kamensky in *The Exchange Artist*, was set in motion in Boston, Massachusetts in 1806. An ambitious young man, Andrew Dexter, Jr., used connections and financial legerdemain to build up a network of interconnected banks, in places such as Pittsfield (Massachusetts), Gloucester (Rhode Island), Keene (New Hampshire), Bucksport (Maine) and Detroit (in the pre-statehood Michigan Territory). Dexter's banks were invariably sited in inconvenient or distant locales, as part of a calculated effort to retard the redemption of their paper for silver.[23] The coterie of Dexter banks issued and circulated among themselves a vast number of banknotes with minimal backing throughout 1807 and 1808.[24] The first to fail, the Farmers' Exchange Bank of Gloucester, Rhode Island, had issued over $600,000 in banknotes in the prior year but held only $86.48 in specie on its closing in 1809.[25] Dexter used much of the paper his banks produced to construct a seven-story building in Boston, Massachusetts, the Exchange Coffee House. Unfortunately, the Embargo imposed by President Jefferson in December 1807 stalled the coastal economy into early 1809 and Boston real estate was blighted. The project failed and large numbers of common workers and merchants ended up ruined, the embarrassed final holders of bad paper generated by the Dexter banks.[26] This complex and costly banking fraud became national news when it was exposed in 1809.[27] As Jane Kamensky relates, the wave of failures of Dexter banks in 1809 gave rise to "an acute loss of confidence not just in banknotes, but in confidence itself."[28]

As private banks grew in number, the use of the paper currency they printed became ever more complicated. Even on the best of days, every user had to cope with a web of uncertainties and discounts relating to the financial condition, distance from source, and even forgery of the various banknotes issued

---

23 Kamensky, *Exchange Artist*, pp. 59 and 140–2.

24 Kamensky, *Exchange Artist*, pp. 9, 62–70, 93, 109–10, 128–35, 144 and 153–62.

25 Kamensky, *Exchange Artist*, pp. 9 and 158–60.

26 Kamensky, *Exchange Artist*, pp. 129 and 165–217.

27 Kamensky, *Exchange Artist*, pp. 1–4, 162–4 and 168–73. It generated headlines again a decade later when the underutilized building burned to the ground in a spectacular fire.

28 Kamensky, *Exchange Artist*, p. 168.

by many bank suppliers.[29] Not every day was the best. Private banknotes were supposed be redeemable in coin, but redemption could be, and was, suspended during periods of crisis,[30] or might be frustrated by fraud of the Dexter type. On the worst of days, one or more issuing banks failed. Bank failure meant currency failure. As bank failures often occurred in the context of a panic or an economic downturn, the timing of the loss of use of paper money tended to be horrific. Good tender and acceptable one day, the paper of a failed bank became useless the moment that bank stopped payment of its obligations. This risk was profoundly frightening. The chance that a now useless banknote might be partially paid, years later, from the proceeds of liquidation of assets of a failed issuing bank provided little solace to the public.

The State of New York had been experiencing banking strain for over a decade when Martin Van Buren was sworn into office as Governor on 1 January 1829. Several banks had failed during the Panic of 1819, which affected the availability of all forms of currency, specie and banknotes.[31] Conditions remained difficult through the turbulent 1820s, which brought more bank failures. Corruption became an urgent public concern, as the state directly (and individual legislators covertly) were believed to have been using the licensing of financial institutions as an opportunity to exact fees that affected their supervisory judgment.[32] As David A. Moss relates, "[t]he sensational 'conspiracy trials' of 1826 (in which several well known and highly regarded New York

---

29 Davis R. Dewey, *State Banking Before the Civil War* (National Monetary Commission, 61st Cong., 2nd sess., Senate Document No. 581) (Washington, D.C., U.S. Government Printing Office, 1910), pp. 100–4 (methods of evading redemption); David A. Moss and Sarah Brennan, "Managing Money Risk in Antebellum New York: From Chartered Banking to Free Banking and Beyond," Studies in American Political Development, Vol. 15, pp. 138–62 (Fall 2001), p. 140; Bowers, *Obsolete Paper Money*, p. 177; Bodenhorn, *State Banking in Early America*, p. 95; Kamensky, *Exchange Artist*, pp. 17–8, Smith and Webber, "Suffolk Banking System," p. 625; Gary B. Gorton, *Slapped by the Invisible Hand: The Panic of 2007* (Oxford: Oxford Univ. Press, 2010), p. 5.

30 Bodenhorn, *State Banking in Early America*, p. 155 ("Systemwide suspensions occurred during the panic of 1819 and the depression of the early 1820s, during the panics of 1837 and 1839 (lasting through 1842), and during the panic and recession of the late 1850s.").

31 Bodenhorn, *State Banking in Early America*, p. 8; Moss, *When All Else Fails*, pp. 95–100; Wright, "Banks' Influence," p. 539; Anonymous, *An Examination of Some of the Provisions of the "Act to Create a Fund for the Benefit of the Creditors of Certain Monied Corporations, and for Other Purposes," Passed April, 1829; Particularly as to its Effects on the City of New-York. By a Stockholder* (New York: Ludwig & Tolefree, 1829), p. 4.

32 Bodenhorn, *State Banking in Early America*, pp. 156–7; Chaddock, *Safety Fund Banking System*, p. 242; Moss and Brennan, "Managing Money Risk," pp. 145–6; Wright, "Banks' Influence," p. 536.

City residents were tried for financial fraud), along with a new round of bank and insurance company failures in 1827, reignited public hostility against the 'moneyed institutions' and set the stage for major new reforms of New York's banking system."[33] Alarmed about the condition of the banks, the legislature denied all applications for new or renewed bank charters in 1827 and again in 1828. As of 1829, the charters of the majority of the state's banks were up for renewal within the next two or three years, and there was deep concern that some banks were in an unsafe and unsound condition.[34] The public was anxious about the currency they issued.[35] Banking matters were a prime concern of the legislature and reform became a top priority of the new Governor.

4 The 1829 New York Safety Fund Statute

The Safety Fund proposal would seem to have been presented to Martin Van Buren by Joshua Forman in December of 1828. On Tuesday, 6 January 1829, five days after being sworn in as Governor, Van Buren delivered a message on the banking crisis to the New York Senate and Assembly. He had received a reform plan, which would soon be submitted to them for consideration. In the view of the Governor, currency stability was vitally important.

> we should keep constantly in view the important consideration, that the solvency of the banks, and the consequent stability of their paper, is the principal and almost the only point, in which the public has much interest.... Our chief duty in this respect, is, to see that the farmer, when he exchanges his produce or estate—the mechanic his wares—the merchant his goods—and all other classes of the community their property or services for bank paper,—may rest contented as to its value.

33 Moss, *When All Else Fails*, p. 97; Anonymous, *An Examination*, p. 13 ("During the session of 1824 and 1825, the legislature chartered several moneyed institutions for this city, under the denomination of loan companies, who issued their bonds and passed them off as money, to a large amount. This large addition to the circulating paper of the city, was, in a measure, one of the causes, which led to the great cotton speculations of 1826, and which broke down so many of our citizens, and finally broke down the companies also."); Q. David Bowers, *Obsolete Paper Money*, pp. 123–4 and 128–9.

34 Bodenhorn, *State Banking in Early America*, p. 158; Moss, *When All Else Fails*, p. 100; Moss and Brennan, "Managing Money Risk," p. 148.

35 Chaddock, *Safety Fund Banking System*, pp. 248–51; Charles W. Calomiris, "Is Deposit Insurance Necessary? A Historical Perspective," The Journal of Economic History, Vol. 50, pp. 283–295 (1990), p. 284.

"The idea" upon which the reform plan was based, the Governor stated, while novel, "is not entirely new to the commercial world, although it has not heretofore been applied in this form." The Governor believed that the currency of the New York banks ("our paper") would derive a competitive advantage from the proposed reform. New York banknotes would achieve new power at home and in the nation—"the consequent high character and correspondent circulation it would give to our paper—the expulsion from circulation of the doubtful paper which now engrosses it, and the substitution in its place of that issued by banks in full credit."[36] The 1829 "Safety Plan" program to strengthen the New York banks and their currency was thus strategic, implemented as part of an ongoing contest for economic primacy between the adjacent states of New York and Pennsylvania.[37] The stronger New York could make its banks and currency, the stronger the state's development prospects and future were apt to be.

On 24 January 1829, Joshua Forman presented the Governor with a letter, his reform plan, and a detailed list of objections and answers. The package was provided to the legislature two days later, with a message of support from the Governor. In this final formal presentation, which was printed in the newspapers and reprinted as a forty-two page pamphlet,[38] the competitive advantages of the proposed system for the state were emphasized. According to Forman, the Safety Fund, if enacted, "would at once give to our state as high a credit and respectability in her monied concerns, as she stands pre-eminent in commercial rank among the states of the Union."[39]

Despite the prior outreach to bankers that had been made by Joshua Forman and Martin Van Buren, legislation calling for a tax on and ongoing supervision of the state's banks proved highly controversial. The city banks, in particular, objected that the tax would fall too heavily on them and that such problems as existed largely concerned the smaller country banks. An anonymous pamphlet, which came out after the Act had become law, doubted that adequate

36 Journal of the Senate of the State of New-York at their Fifty-Second Session (Albany: E. Croswell, 1829), p. 10; Journal of the Assembly of the State of New-York at their Fifty-Second Session (Albany: E. Croswell, 1829), p. 13; Albany Argus, 7 January 1829, p. 2.

37 Moss, *When All Else Fails*, p. 101; Moss and Brennan, "Managing Money Risk," p. 139; Hammond, *Banks and Politics in America*, pp. 445 and 559; Frank Otto Gatell, "Sober Second Thoughts on Van Buren, the Albany Regency, and the Wall Street Conspiracy," The Journal of American History, Vol. 53, pp. 19–40 (1966), p. 20.

38 Journal of the Assembly of the State of New-York (1829), p. 186.

39 Van Buren, *Message of His Excellency Gov. Van Buren on the Subject of Banks*, p. 13.

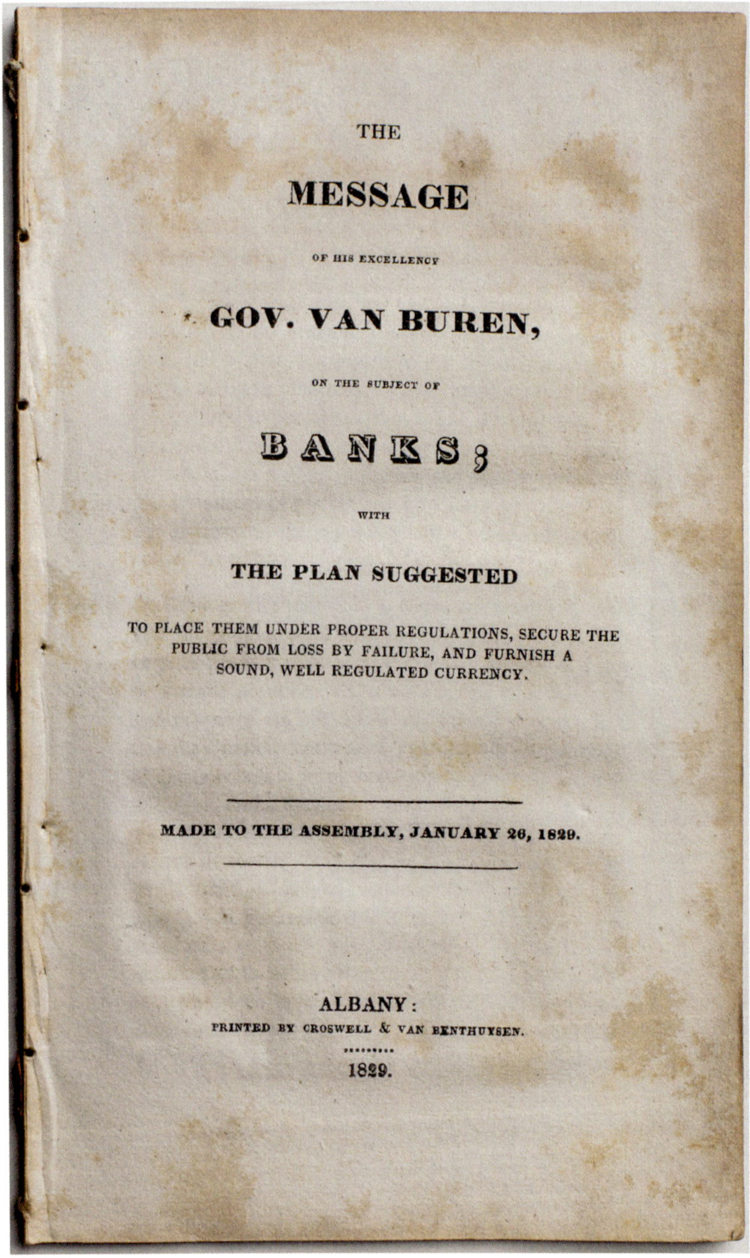

THE

MESSAGE

OF HIS EXCELLENCY

GOV. VAN BUREN,

ON THE SUBJECT OF

BANKS;

WITH

THE PLAN SUGGESTED

TO PLACE THEM UNDER PROPER REGULATIONS, SECURE THE PUBLIC FROM LOSS BY FAILURE, AND FURNISH A SOUND, WELL REGULATED CURRENCY.

MADE TO THE ASSEMBLY, JANUARY 26, 1829.

ALBANY:
PRINTED BY CROSWELL & VAN BENTHUYSEN.

1829.

PLATE 19 *Cover of the pamphlet containing Joshua Forman's proposal for the adoption of bank liability insurance, as presented to the New York legislature on 26 January 1829. (Private collection. Photograph by permission.)*

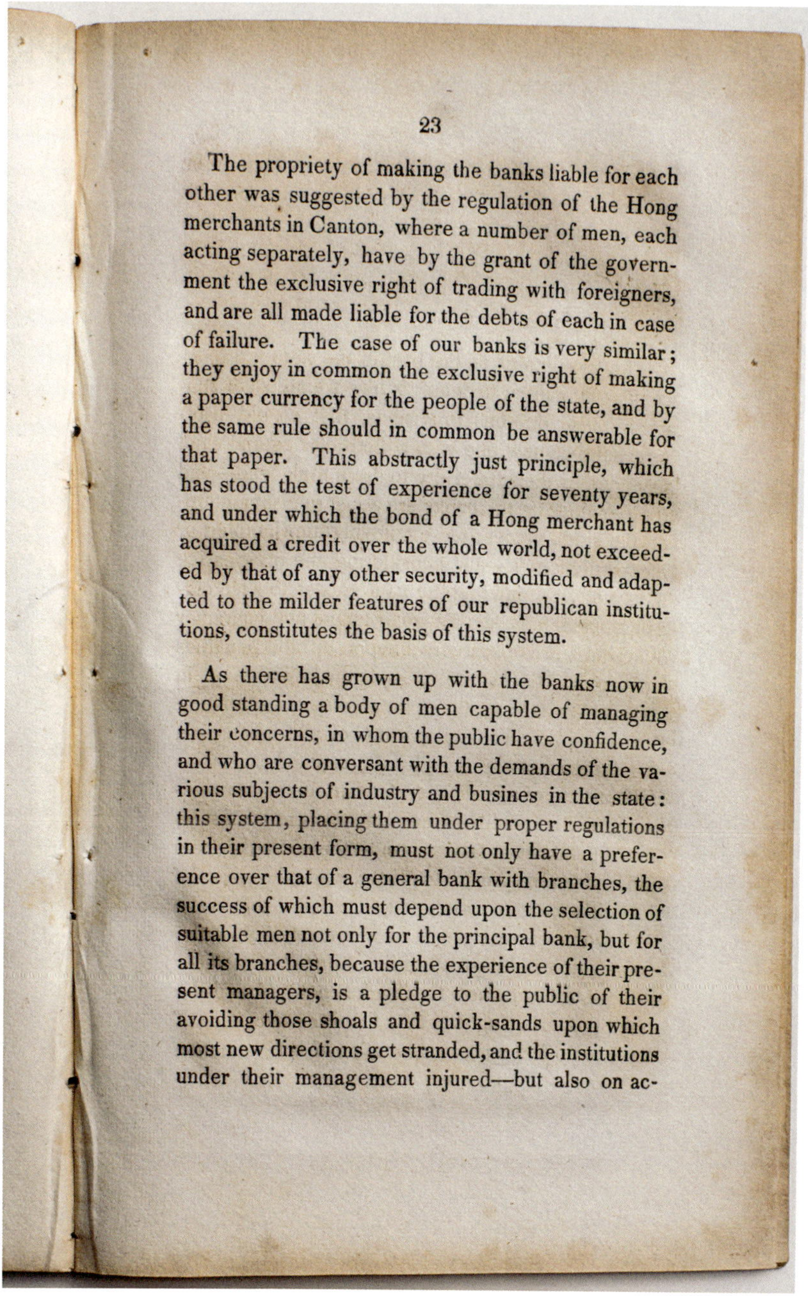

23

The propriety of making the banks liable for each other was suggested by the regulation of the Hong merchants in Canton, where a number of men, each acting separately, have by the grant of the government the exclusive right of trading with foreigners, and are all made liable for the debts of each in case of failure. The case of our banks is very similar; they enjoy in common the exclusive right of making a paper currency for the people of the state, and by the same rule should in common be answerable for that paper. This abstractly just principle, which has stood the test of experience for seventy years, and under which the bond of a Hong merchant has acquired a credit over the whole world, not exceeded by that of any other security, modified and adapted to the milder features of our republican institutions, constitutes the basis of this system.

As there has grown up with the banks now in good standing a body of men capable of managing their concerns, in whom the public have confidence, and who are conversant with the demands of the various subjects of industry and busines in the state: this system, placing them under proper regulations in their present form, must not only have a preference over that of a general bank with branches, the success of which must depend upon the selection of suitable men not only for the principal bank, but for all its branches, because the experience of their present managers, is a pledge to the public of their avoiding those shoals and quick-sands upon which most new directions get stranded, and the institutions under their management injured—but also on ac-

PLATE 20 *The page of the Safety Fund Act proposal, in which Joshua Forman states that inspiration for this banking reform came from "the regulation of the Hong merchants in Canton."* (*Private collection. Photograph by permission.*)

supervision could be accomplished and challenged the justice of holding only banking corporations responsible for each others' debts.

> The author of this novel system, Mr. J. Forman, has told us, in his expose to the governor, that "the propriety of making the banks liable for each other, was suggested to him by the regulation of the Hong merchants of Canton, where a number of men, each acting separately, have, by the grant of government, the exclusive right of trading with foreigners, and are all made liable for the debt of each, in case of failure." Now, upon this principle, all the other corporations of this state ought to be made liable for the debts of each other in case of failure, as well as the banks. The fire and marine insurance companies; the turnpike, rail road, and canal companies, and particularly the manufacturing companies. They all enjoy exclusive privileges, as well as the Hong merchants or the New-York banks; and it would be just as reasonable to pass an act, compelling each of these corporations, transacting a like business, to pay an annual per centage on their capital, as a fund to indemnify their creditors from loss, in the event of their failure, as it is to compel the banks to do it. Would such a proposition be sustained by the legislature? We think not.[40]

After much debate, key concessions, and political wrangling, all within the short time period of six weeks, the Safety Fund Act was passed by the New York Assembly with a large margin on 18 March 1829, and by the New York Senate two weeks later. As with the adoption of deposit insurance at the federal level a century later, bank reform legislation that imposed liability on a collective basis enjoyed strong popular support and moved rapidly. As Martin Van Buren had in the meantime resigned as Governor to become Secretary of State under President Andrew Jackson, the Safety Fund bill was signed into law by the state's new Governor, Enos T. Throop, on 2 April 1829.[41]

Under the enacted statute, the Safety Fund was funded through the contribution by each participating bank of a total of three percent of its paid-in capital. Payments were to be made in six annual installments of one-half of one percent. If the fund was depleted, banks were made subject to emergency assessments not to exceed one-half of one percent of paid-in capital per

---

40 Anonymous, *An Examination*, pp. 6–7. See *Noble State Bank v. Haskell*, 219 U.S. 104, 112 (1911) (O.W. Holmes, J.) ("It is asked whether the state could require all corporations or all grocers to help to guarantee each other's solvency, and where we are going to draw the line. But the last is a futile question, and we will answer the others when they arise.").

41 Moss, *When All Else Fails*, p. 103; Hammond, *Banks and Politics*, pp. 557–9.

year, until the fund was replenished. All newly chartered banks, and all banks renewing old charters, were required to participate in the fund. All creditors, banknote holders and depositors alike, were entitled to be paid in full from the fund to the extent the proceeds of liquidation of a failed bank proved inadequate. Administration was placed in the hands of three commissioners who were charged with conducting a quarterly inspection and audit of each bank, and given powers to seek court injunctions if any violation of statutory standards was detected.[42] Its provisions for a common fund, for mandatory supervision, and even its name, were all new in American law.[43]

Passage of the Safety Fund Act brought the former charter issuance backlog to an end, and the New York legislature eagerly licensed many new banks. While criticism of the statute continued,[44] the city banks, which had initially been reluctant, decided that they would—or must—participate. The Safety Fund operated smoothly for about a decade, but experienced a profound shock with the Panic of 1837. Many of its member banks had made loans to western land speculators, and the three (3) commissioners who were supposed to supervise these ninety (90) banks had variously missed or failed to confront numerous problems.[45] Regulatory forbearance was exposed in the Panic of 1837 to have created a class of "zombie banks." These banks had been

---

42 Bodenhorn, *State Banking in Early America*, pp. 160, 161 and 166–169.

43 One measure of the novelty of New York's 1829 experiment is that the term "Safety Fund" was newly created. Dictionary research finds no use of the term before 1829, and when it is found, it is in older sources, or dictionaries of Americanisms, tied to the system of 1829. Mitford M. Mathews, ed., *A Dictionary of Americanisms* (Chicago: Univ. of Chicago Press, 1951), Vol. 2, p. 1442; William A. Craigie and James R. Hulbert, eds., *A Dictionary of American English* (Chicago: Univ. of Chicago Press, 1944), Vol. 4, pp. 2001–2002; Isaac K. Funk, ed., *A Standard Dictionary of the English Language* (New York: Funk & Wagnalls Co., 1935), Vol. 2; *Webster's New International Dictionary* (1925), p. 1867. The term has been carried over into the American insurance industry, where it has had an independent life with at least two meanings, such as a common fund created by contract, Joseph A. Joyce, *A Treatise on the Law of Insurance of Every Kind* (2d ed., Rochester: Lawyers Co-operative Publishing Co., 1917), § 1287, p. 3:2427, or a non-compulsory law permitting an insurance company to accumulate from profits a fund to be used to meet emergency claims. Lewis E. Davids, *Dictionary of Insurance* (6th rev. ed., Totowa, N.J.: Rowman & Allanheld, 1983), p. 271; H. R. Hayden, ed., *The Annual Cyclopedia of Insurance of the United States 1894–1895* (Hartford: H. R. Hayden, 1895), pp. 506–507 (listing states with such laws).

44 Anonymous, "Bank of the United States," North American Review, Vol. 32 (April 1831), p. 56; Albert Gallatin, *Considerations on the Currency and Banking System of the United States* (Philadelphia: Carey & Lea, 1831), p. 70.

45 Howard Bodenhorn, "Zombie Banks and the Demise of New York's Safety Fund," Eastern Economic Journal, Vol. 22, pp. 21–33 (1996), pp. 23–4, 28 and 30.

allowed to trudge slowly along and to do business although they were deeply insolvent—"avoid[ing] the finality of death through the black magic of blanket liability guarantees."[46] As Howard Bodenhorn relates:

> As promising an idea as the Safety Fund was, it failed to bring any real stability to new York's banking system. Its first (and only) test came during the panic of 1837 when the failure of just eleven members effectively bankrupted the system. Reimbursements to creditors of failed banks exceeded $2.5 million, while the fund realized only about $150,000 on assets forfeited by those banks. More importantly, creditor claims were disbursed so slowly that many frustrated creditors, mostly banknote holders, sold their claims at cents on the dollar. Despite its promise, the Safety Fund failed to protect the payments system or bank creditors individually.[47]

When New York adopted free banking as an alternative in 1838 and permitted licensed free banks to leave the Safety Fund, many did. Free banks were required to back their total issue of circulating banknotes with bonds and mortgages to an equal value on deposit with state officials.[48] An amendment to the Safety Fund statute in 1842 which restricted coverage to banknotes (it was claimed that there was uncertainty whether deposit liabilities were

46 Bodenhorn, "Zombie Banks," p. 27 ("Edward Kane called the latter zombie banks because they enjoyed an 'unnatural life-in-death experience, in that if they had not been insured, the firm's creditors would have taken control from the stockholders once it had become clear that their enterprise's net worth was exhausted'"), citing Edward J. Kane, *The S & L Insurance Mess: How Did It Happen?* (Washington, D.C.: The Urban Institute Press, 1989). "Ten of 16 member-bank failures prior to 1842 (the period when insurance was still perceived as effective) were traceable to fraud or unsafe practices. Moreover, such problems were not detected until after they had imposed large losses on the fund." Calomiris, "Is Deposit Insurance Necessary?," p. 287; Charles W. Calomiris, and Eugene N. White, "The Origins of Federal Deposit Insurance," in Claudia Goldin and Gary D. Libecap, eds., *The Regulated Economy: A Historical Approach to Political Economy* (Chicago: Univ. of Chicago Press, 1994), p. 149, and also in Charles W. Calomiris, *U.S. Bank Deregulation in Historical Perspective* (Cambridge: Cambridge Univ. Press, 2000), pp. 167–8.

47 Bodenhorn, *Banking in Antebellum America*, pp. 38–9; Hammond, *Banks and Politics in America*, pp. 560–2; Moss, *When All Else Fails*, p. 367 n.98; Moss and Brennan, "Managing Money Risk," pp. 150–151; Calomiris, *U.S. Bank Deregulation*, p. 69; Calomiris, "Is Deposit Insurance Necessary?," p. 286; Bowers, *Obsolete Paper Money*, pp. 218–23 and 535–8.

48 Golembe, "Deposit Insurance Legislation of 1933," p. 186; Calomiris, *U.S. Bank Deregulation*, pp. 44–5 and 70; Calomiris, "Is Deposit Insurance Necessary?," p. 286.

covered under the original banknote-focused law)[49] provided internal relief by reducing liabilities chargeable to the fund.[50] The fund struggled on until its last member bank charters expired in 1866, and ultimately paid all of its liabilities, albeit after extended delay.[51] Banking historian Howard Bodenhorn provides its epitaph: "Adverse selection and moral hazard ultimately undid the Safety Fund, but they were assisted by ineffectual supervision, ineffective to nonexistent portfolio restrictions, everything from marginally legal activities to outright fraud, and some politically motivated regulatory forbearance. The mixture was combustible, and it led to the Safety Fund's failure."[52]

5 Early State Bank Guaranty Programs

The safety fund concept—the idea that a guaranty fund could ease the pain of failure for noteholder or depositor members of the public—has had a lasting influence in American banking thought. The New York model was copied, with some revisions and adaptations, by other states in the nineteenth century and again by other states and then by the United States government in the twentieth century. Of the contemporary guaranty programs, several had periods of success, but all ultimately failed. In addition to the New York program (1829–1866), safety funds were employed in the states of Vermont (1831–1866), Indiana (1834–1866), Michigan (1836–1842), Ohio (1845–1866) and Iowa (1858–1865).[53] The Vermont and Michigan statutes were fairly direct copies of

49 Golembe, "Deposit Insurance Legislation," pp. 189–90; Moss, *When All Else Fails*, p. 371 n. 117; Harry E. Miller, *Banking Theories in the United States Before 1860* (Cambridge: Harvard Univ. Press, 1927), p. 151; Thomas Bruce Robb, *The Guaranty of Bank Deposits* (Boston: Houghton Mifflin, 1921), p. 12.

50 Golembe, "Deposit Insurance Legislation," p. 190; Calomiris, *U.S. Bank Deregulation*, p. 70; Calomiris, "Is Deposit Insurance Necessary?," pp. 286–7.

51 Moss, *When All Else Fails*, p. 367 n. 98; Moss and Brennan, "Managing Money Risk," p. 154 n. 129; Calomiris, *U.S. Bank Deregulation*, p. 70; Calomiris, "Is Deposit Insurance Necessary?," p. 286; Hammond, *Banks and Politics in America*, p. 561.

52 Bodenhorn, *State Banking in Early America*, pp. 181–182 and 183.

53 Golembe, "Deposit Insurance Legislation," pp. 184–186 and 191; Calomiris, *U.S. Bank Deregulation*, pp. 70–1; Hammond, *Banks and Politics in America*, p. 563; Federal Deposit Insurance Corporation, *Federal Deposit Insurance Corporation: The First Fifty Years: A History of the FDIC 1933–1983* (Washington, D.C.: Federal Deposit Insurance Corporation, 1984), pp. 16–7.

the New York Safety Fund, with only minor changes having been made.[54] The other statutes varied in details from but took their inspiration from the New York model.[55] The primary objective of these early statutes was the protection of the value of banknotes issued by state-chartered banks. This need was reduced by the rise of free banking, which provided another means of protecting banknotes. The need was then effectively eliminated by the introduction of national banknotes during the Civil War. Under the National Banking Act of 1863, federal banknotes were protected both by the deposit of United States government bonds to equal value with the U.S. Treasury and by an explicit federal government guarantee. The imposition in 1865 of a heavy national tax on the banknotes of state banks brought the colorful and chaotic era of their use to a close.[56] In the years that followed, deposits with American banks grew rapidly and soon far exceeded banknotes in their significance. As of the year 1870, the amount of deposits stood at about twice, and by the end of the 1800s exceeded by seven times, the amount of banknotes in circulation.[57]

The shock of the Panic of 1907, at the outset of the twentieth century, had a number of effects on American banking.[58] At the national level, Congress responded in 1913 by establishing the Federal Reserve System. The twelve Federal Reserve banks, operating under the supervision of the Federal Reserve Board in Washington, D.C., became the first American central bank since the demise of the Second Bank of the United States in the 1830s.[59]

---

54 Golembe, "Deposit Insurance Legislation," p. 184; Dewey, *State Banking Before the Civil War*, pp. 130 and 193.

55 Golembe, "Deposit Insurance Legislation," pp. 184–6; Chaddock, *Safety Fund Banking System*, p. 387.

56 Calomiris, *U.S. Bank Deregulation*, p. 166 n. 2; Golembe, "Deposit Insurance Legislation," p. 187; Moss, *When All Else Fails*, p. 115; Moss and Brennan, "Managing Money Risk," p. 161; Allan H. Meltzer, *A History of the Federal Reserve, Vol. 1* (1913–1951) (Chicago: Univ. of Chicago Press, 2003), pp. 66 n. 2 and 69; Kroszner and Melick, "Lessons from the U.S. Experience," p. 193.

57 Golembe, "Deposit Insurance Legislation," p. 187.

58 Gary Gorton asserts that the international panic of 2007 was similar to that of 1907. Gorton, *Slapped by the Invisible Hand*, pp. 2–3.

59 Moss, *When All Else Fails*, p. 116. The banking industry sympathies of Frederic A. Delano (1863–1953), Franklin D. Roosevelt's uncle, resulted in his being appointed a member and Vice Chairman of the first Federal Reserve Board. Delano served as a member of the Federal Reserve Board from 1914 to 1918 and as a director of the Federal Reserve Bank of Richmond in the early 1930s. Meltzer, *History of the Federal Reserve, Vol. 1*, pp. 73–4; Rik W. Hafer, *The Federal Reserve System: An Encyclopedia* (Westport, Conn.: Greenwood Press, 2005), pp. 433 and 437; Gabriel Kolko, *The Triumph of Conservatism: A Re-interpretation of American History, 1900–1916* (New York: The Free Press, 1977), p. 249 ("To take the place of

Interest in bank deposit insurance at the federal level was renewed in the wake of the Panic of 1907. It repeatedly came before Congress in draft legislation that then stalled. Starting in 1886, and continuing through adoption of the National Banking Act of 1933, some 150 bills were introduced in Congress to implement a national program of deposit insurance.[60] As summarized by Carter Golembe:

> During the first decade of the new century forty-five additional bills were introduced in Congress, most of them in the 60th Congress in 1907–9. Deposit insurance was included in the original Federal Reserve Act as passed by the Senate, but was omitted from the bill passed by the House and eliminated in the Conference report. From two to eight proposals for deposit insurance or guaranty were submitted in each Congress from the 61st in 1909–11 to the 71st in 1929–31. In the 72nd Congress twenty-one separate bills were introduced, reflecting the impact of the depression, and one of these was passed by the House of Representatives in 1932. In the first ten weeks of the 73rd Congress in 1933, fifteen more such bills were submitted.[61]

Among the states, the losses and dislocations of the Panic of 1907 impelled action. Over the following ten years, eight states adopted deposit insurance programs which were generally compulsory for state-chartered banks. The state programs were funded by assessments on bank deposits, and the interests of depositors were protected without a maximum coverage limit per depositor.[62] These programs built on the legacy of the nineteenth century

---

one of these rejections, Frederic A. Delano, a railroad administrator and a former director of the National Citizens' League, was given the job.... In all, the banking community and those close to it were given three of the five board seats."). The author is a great-grandson of Frederic A. Delano.

60 Golembe, "Deposit Insurance Legislation," pp. 187–8; James Grant, *Money of the Mind: Borrowing and Lending in America from the Civil War to Michael Milken* (New York: Farrar Straus Giroux, 1992), pp. 137–40; Calomiris, and White, "Origins of Federal Deposit Insurance," in Goldin and Libecap, *Regulated Economy*, pp. 150 and 152 ("Of these 150 bills, 147 never emerged from the House or Senate committees that were given the responsibility of considering them."), and also in Calomiris, *U.S. Bank Deregulation*, pp. 171–2.

61 Golembe, "Deposit Insurance Legislation," pp. 188 and 195.

62 Golembe, "Deposit Insurance Legislation, pp. 187–8; A History of the FDIC 1933–1983, pp. 25–7; Kroszner and Melick, "Lessons from the U.S. Experience," p. 194; Moss, *When All Else Fails*, p. 117; Moss and Brennan, "Managing Money Risk," p. 161. In *Noble State Bank v. Haskell*, 219 U.S. 104, 109 (1911), the Supreme Court described the Oklahoma deposit

safety fund laws, which also generally provided unlimited coverage. In 1911, the United States Supreme Court rejected a Constitutional challenge to the first of the eight programs, the Oklahoma statute of 17 December 1907 (enacted one month after the State of Oklahoma was admitted to the Union). Justice Oliver Wendell Holmes, writing for the Court, stated that "the device [of bank deposit insurance] is a familiar one. It was adopted by some states the better part of a century ago, and seems never to have been questioned until now."[63] The early twentieth century state deposit insurance programs suffered large losses during the 1920s. All had ended up insolvent or inoperative as of 1933, their failures being variously ascribed to the cyclical hazards of agricultural finance, excessive risk taking by bank lenders, or neglect by officials charged with supervising the insured banks.[64]

6 Implementation of National Deposit Insurance in the United States

The year 1933 found the United States in the midst of the Great Depression, gripped by a banking panic that reached its peak early in March. Just four

insurance law as follows: "This act creates the Board and directs it to levy upon every bank existing under the laws of the state an assessment of one percent of the bank's average daily deposits, with certain deductions, for the purpose of creating a Depositors' Guaranty Fund. There are provisos for keeping up the fund, and by an act passed March 11, 1909, since the suit was begun, the assessment is to be five percent. The purpose of the fund is shown by its name. It is to secure the full repayment of deposits. When a bank becomes insolvent and goes into the hands of the Bank Commissioner, if its cash immediately available is not enough to pay depositors in full, the Banking Board is to draw from the Depositors' Guaranty Fund (and from additional assessments if required) the amount needed to make up the deficiency. A lien is reserved upon the assets of the failing bank to make good the sum thus taken from the fund." See Kroszner and Melick, "Lessons from the U.S. Experience," pp. 193–7 (analysis of the Oklahoma deposit insurance program in operation).

63 *Noble State Bank v. Haskell*, 219 U.S. 104, 112 (1911) (O. W. Holmes, J.); Golembe, "Deposit Insurance Legislation," pp. 191–2; Kroszner and Melick, "Lessons from the U.S. Experience," p. 193. "In 1910, practically all of Oklahoma's brand-new deposit-guarantee fund was tied up in a single bank failure, and The New York Times chose to caption its editorial on the Holmes decision (and on state deposit insurance in general), 'Constitutional, But Worthless.'" Grant, *Money of the Mind*, p. 137.

64 Golembe, "Deposit Insurance Legislation," pp. 187–8; Calomiris, *U.S. Bank Deregulation*, pp. 72–5; Calomiris, and White, "Origins of Federal Deposit Insurance," in Goldin and Libecap, *Regulated Economy*, pp. 149–50, and also in Calomiris, *U.S. Bank Deregulation*, pp. 168–9; Kroszner and Melick, "Lessons from the U.S. Experience," pp. 197–8; Grant, *Money of the Mind*, pp. 135–7.

months earlier, on 8 November 1932, Franklin Delano Roosevelt had been elected President by a landslide, carrying forty-two states as against the six that favored Herbert Hoover. His election was spurred by popular suffering and demands for reform in the wake of the stock market crash of October 1929. Banking reform was urgently demanded. Some 4,000 banks had ceased operations by March 1933. The number of closures soared to 9,000 by year end, resulting in depositor losses of about $1.3 billion. Notices that checks drawn on out of town banks could not be honored greeted inaugural guests on arrival at hotels in Washington, D.C. As of 4 March 1933, Inauguration Day, every state in the Union had declared a bank holiday.[65]

Urgent consideration of bank issues and banking reforms occupied the early days of the Franklin Roosevelt administration. Two days after his inauguration, the President declared a national bank holiday, ordering the nations' banks closed as a first step to breaking the panic. A series of reforms and measures to restore financial order were then brought through Congress, and some—but not all—of the shuttered banks were gradually permitted to reopen. Among proposed reforms that were considered but rejected in these early hours was bank deposit insurance. The idea had many strong opponents including the President himself. Yet on 16 June 1933 Roosevelt directed the nationwide implementation of deposit insurance by signing the Banking Act of 1933, which he called "the second most important banking legislation enacted in the history of the country." Writing in 1960, Carter Golembe rightly called the Act "the only important piece of legislation during the New Deal's famous 'one hundred days' which was neither requested nor supported by the new administration." In 2009, Charles Calomiris described deposit insurance as "the main surviving legacy of the banking legislation of the New Deal—a stark reminder of the power of crises to change the course of banking regulation."[66] Just as in New York State in 1829, public outrage over banking conditions had reached the point at which fundamental changes to the banking system had become politically possible.[67]

65 *A History of the FDIC 1933–1983*, pp. iii, 3 and 38; Helen M. Burns, *The American Banking Community and the New Deal Banking Reforms 1933–1935* (Westport, Conn.: Greenwood Press, 1974), pp. 31 and 39–41; Grant, *Money of the Mind*, pp. 222 and 225–7.

66 Golembe, "Deposit Insurance Legislation," pp. 181–2; Susan Estabrook Kennedy, *The Banking Crisis of 1933* (Lexington: The Univ. Press of Kentucky, 1973), p. 222; Charles Calomiris, "Banking Crises and the Rules of the Game" (Cambridge, Ma.: National Bureau of Economic Research, Working Paper No. 15403, 2009), p. 15, see: "http://www.nber.org/papers/w15403" (accessed 29 January 2012).

67 Golembe, "Deposit Insurance Legislation," p. 199.

While deposit insurance had popular support, the drive to see it made law came from members of the United States Congress. By the 1930s, the introduction of deposit insurance legislation had become something of an annual tradition in Washington, D.C., much like watching the cherry trees blossom. Momentum for deposit insurance built with the banking crisis. In April of 1932, before the election, Representative Henry Steagall of Alabama—a leading proponent—is said to have told House Speaker John Nance Garner: "You know, this fellow Hoover is going to wake up one day soon and come in here with a message recommending guarantee of bank deposits, and as sure as he does, he'll be re-elected." Garner is said to have replied: "You're right as rain, Henry, so get to work in a hurry. Report out a deposit insurance bill and we'll shove it through." The Steagall bill, H.R. 11362, was passed by the House of Representatives on 25 May 1932 but went no further. Henry Steagall found himself unable to convince Senator Carter Glass to include deposit insurance in banking reform legislation then pending before the Senate.[68] During the Presidential campaign of 1932, Franklin Roosevelt showed no enthusiasm for deposit insurance. In correspondence, he called the guaranty plan "quite dangerous." "It would lead to laxity in bank management and carelessness on the part of both banker and depositor. I believe that it would be an impossible drain on the Federal Treasury to make good any such guaranty."[69]

John Nance Garner was carried by the Democratic Party election victory from the position of Speaker of the House to Vice President of the United States. Garner pushed for deposit insurance in conversations with Roosevelt before their inauguration, but got nowhere. "It won't work, Jack," the President-elect replied. "The weak banks will pull down the strong."[70] In office, Garner's first disagreement with Franklin Roosevelt was on this subject. "You'll have to have it, Cap'n," said Garner, "or get more clerks in the Postal Savings banks. The people who have taken their money out of the banks are not going to put it back without some guarantee."[71] Roosevelt remained firm in opposition.

---

68 Kennedy, *Banking Crisis of 1933*, p. 214; Mark D. Flood, "The Great Deposit Insurance Debate," The Federal Reserve Bank of St. Louis Review, Vol. 74, pp. 51–77 (July/August 1992), p. 63 and n.79, see: "http://research.stlouisfed.org/publications/review/92/07/Deposit_Jul_Aug1992.pdf" (accessed 26 January 2012). In his last days as President, Herbert Hoover is said to have pressed the Federal Reserve to agree to implement a bank deposit insurance program. R. Gordon Hoxie, "Hoover and the Banking Crisis," Presidential Studies Quarterly, Vol. 4/5, Vol. 4, no. 3/4–Vol. 5, no. 1, pp. 25–28 (Summer/Fall, 1974–Winter, 1975), p. 28.

69 Anonymous, "Roosevelt 'Won' to Bank Insurance," *The New York Times*, 27 October 1936.

70 Adam Cohen, *Nothing to Fear: FDR's Inner Circle and the Hundred Days that Created Modern America* (New York: The Penguin Press, 2009), p. 278.

71 Kennedy, *Banking Crisis of 1933*, p. 214.

PLATE 21 *Franklin Roosevelt with Warren Delano II—a China trader who did business with Howqua II and was in Canton during the Opium War—and twelve of his Delano first cousins. Photograph taken at Algonac, Newburgh, New York, September 1897. The future President, then fifteen years old, leans casually on his grandfather's wheelchair. The author's grandmother, Catherine Delano, is standing at left rear. (Photograph by courtesy of the Franklin Roosevelt Presidential Library and Museum.)*

The President's aversion to deposit insurance was neither ideological nor the product of interest group pressure. He was familiar with the policy debate and the arguments pro and con and doubted the proposed reform due to the high risk of loss indicated by a historical record of failure.[72] Roosevelt had direct experience with the subject matter. He had been employed from 1921 to 1928 as a Vice President with the Fidelity and Deposit Company of Maryland, the fourth largest surety bonding company in the nation.[73] He had a

72 Golembe, "Deposit Insurance Legislation," p. 198 n.23; Kennedy, *Banking Crisis of 1933*, p. 214.

73 Geoffrey C. Ward, *A First-Class Temperament: The Emergence of Franklin Roosevelt* (New York: Harper & Row, 1989), pp. 560–3, 623 n. 19, 650–5, 732–3 (the company had become third largest by 1923); Kenneth S. Davis, *FDR: The Beckoning of Destiny, 1882–1928* (New York: Random House, 1971), pp. 627, 629, 673, 697–8 and 708; Flood, "Great Deposit

working knowledge of guaranty risk which had been developed over his years of employment with the F&D (as he called the company). That facility is evident in the President's response to a question posed at his first press conference on 8 March 1933, four days after he was sworn into office.

> Q: Can you tell us anything about guaranteeing of bank deposits?
>
> THE PRESIDENT: I can tell you as to guaranteeing bank deposits my own view, and I think that of the old Administration. The general underlying thought behind the use of the word "guarantee" with respect to bank deposits is that you guarantee bad banks as well as good banks. The minute the Government starts to do that the Government runs into a probable loss. I will give you an example. Suppose there are three banks in town: one is 100 percent capable of working out, one 50 percent and another 10 percent. Now, if the Government assumes a 100 percent guarantee, it will lose 50 percent on one and 90 percent on the other. If it takes on a 50 percent guarantee, it will lose nothing on the first and second, but will lose a lot on the 10 percent solvent bank. Any form of general guarantee means a definite loss to the Government. The objective in the plan we are working on can be best stated this way: There are undoubtedly some banks that are going to pay one hundred cents on the dollar. We all know it is better to have that loss taken than to jeopardize the credit of the United States Government or to put the United States Government further in debt. Therefore, the one objective is going to be to keep the loss in the individual banks down to a minimum, endeavoring to get 100 percent on them. We do not wish to make the United States Government liable for the mistakes and errors of individual banks, and put a premium on unsound banking in the future.
>
> Q: That is off the record?
>
> THE PRESIDENT: Yes.[74]

Insurance Debate," p. 61 n. 58. In addition, Franklin Roosevelt's uncle Frederic A. Delano, with whom he was close, had banking industry ties and had long served on the Federal Reserve Board. See p. 201 n. 58 above. Of all of the input he was receiving from banking industry proponents in various quarters, Roosevelt quipped at one point, "They'll make a banker of me yet." Kennedy, The *Banking Crisis of 1933*, p. 168.

74 Franklin D. Roosevelt, *The Public Papers and Addresses of Franklin D. Roosevelt, Vol. 2* (New York: Random House, 1938), p. 37 (first press conference, 8 March 1933).

In the early months of 1933 an intense debate raged among supporters and opponents of bank deposit insurance. Opponents included the President, his Treasury Secretary, the Federal Reserve, and the larger banks and banking organizations.[75] Rome C. Stephenson, President of the American Bankers Association, said that the very mention of the topic could induce "every sign of incipient apoplexy" in a banker. The bankers fought the proposal to the last ditch.[76] All of the arguments and historical evidence on the subject of deposit insurance, which had been accumulating since 1829, were advanced. Leading proponents included Representative Henry Steagall of Alabama (a Democrat), who was associated with unit bankers, and Senator Arthur H. Vandenberg of Michigan (a Republican), also a champion of the small banks. The proponents were buoyed, and ultimately carried the day, by mounting support from a populace outraged by the banking crisis and news headlines of disclosures of bank abuses revealed in investigatory hearings conducted by the U.S. Senate Committee on Banking and Currency.[77] As Mark Flood concludes in his examination of the 1933 debate about deposit insurance, "[o]ne of the casualties of the [prevailing] anti-banker sentiment was the bankers' battle against deposit insurance."[78]

Proponents of the proposed legislation emphasized the existence of coverage ceilings in the bill, as opposed to the unlimited guarantees which had contributed to the failure of the state systems.[79] Proponents rejected the applicability of historical examples of guaranty fund failure,[80] arguing that these had involved only narrow risk pools, such as excessive agricultural loan exposure. They insisted that the proposed reform would comply with the fundamental principle of insurance that there must exist wide and general distri-

---

75 Moss, *When All Else Fails*, p. 118; Kennedy, *Banking Crisis of 1933*, pp. 214–8; Calomiris, "Banking Crises and the Rules of the Game," pp. 12–14; Flood, "Great Deposit Insurance Debate," p. 59.

76 Howard H. Preston, "The Banking Act of 1933," The American Economic Review, Vol. 23, pp. 585–607 (1933), pp. 599–600; Flood, "Great Deposit Insurance Debate," pp. 59 and n. 48 (citing Rome C. Stephenson, "Providing Safety for Future Banking," Bankers Magazine (May 1931), pp. 591–94) (the footnote shows the hint of truth in Stephenson's hyperbole).

77 Golembe, "Deposit Insurance Legislation," pp. 197–8; Kennedy, *Banking Crisis of 1933*, pp. 203–4 and 212; Calomiris, and White, "Origins of Federal Deposit Insurance," in Goldin and Libecap, *Regulated Economy*, p. 176, and also in Calomiris, *U.S. Bank Deregulation*, pp. 199–200; Flood, "Great Deposit Insurance Debate," p. 66.

78 Flood, "Great Deposit Insurance Debate," p. 60.

79 Flood, "Great Deposit Insurance Debate," p. 62.

80 Preston, "Banking Act of 1933," pp. 597–8.

bution and diversification. Opponents, for their part, denied that the "deposit insurance" proposal was "insurance" at all.

> Insurance involves an old and tried principle. The essence of insurance is the payment by *the insured* of premiums in *actuarial relation to the risk involved.* Under the terms of the permanent plan, however, the costs or premiums are not charged according to the risk.[81]

Missing from the proposed legislation was the principle of "selected risk," i.e., that insured parties are differentiated by risk and charged different premia in accordance with their risk classification. One opponent accordingly warned that an "inexcusable" scrambling of terminology was involved. "Guarantee is where you make the good bank pay for the poor one. Insurance is where you make those who get the benefit pay for it."[82] Professor Edwin W. Kemmerer of Princeton University, speaking to the Savings Bank Association of Massachusetts in September 1933 after the bill had become law, summarized this argument and drew it to a moral hazard conclusion.

> For it is to be remembered that the weak banks get the same insurance as the strong ones, and, unlike the situation in other kinds of insurance, the bad risk pays no more for its insurance than the good one. This means competition among banks in slackness in the granting of loans. The bank with the loose credit policy gets the business and the bank with the careful, cautious credit policy loses it. The slack banker dances and the conservative banker pays the fiddler. If the conservative banker protests, the slack one invites him to go to a warmer climate. Soon all are dancing and the fiddler, if paid at all, must collect from the depositors or from the taxpayers.[83]

On 1 May 1933 Senator Glass introduced a new bill, proposing the creation of the Federal Deposit Insurance Corporation, which came before the Senate for debate two weeks later. Senator Vandenberg proposed an amendment to immediately insure deposits of up to $2,500, and the bill, thus amended, was passed with only six votes in opposition on 25 May 1933. Legislation proposed

---

81 Flood, "Great Deposit Insurance Debate," p. 58 (quoting from "Guaranty of Bank Deposits," Association of Reserve City Bankers, Commission on Banking Law and Practice, Bulletin No. 3 (Chicago, November 1933), p. 27 [emphasis in the original]).

82 Flood, "Great Deposit Insurance Debate," p. 57 n.29.

83 Flood, "Great Deposit Insurance Debate," pp. 57–60.

by Representative Steagall had been passed by the House of Representatives on 23 May by a vote of 262 to 19, and both bills now went to conference committee. There they sat stalled in the face of Presidential opposition, notably to the prospect of a 100 percent guarantee. At a cabinet meeting on 23 May 1933, Franklin Roosevelt said he would veto the entire banking bill if deposit insurance was not removed. Such a veto would have come at a heavy political cost, for the bill had strong Congressional support, and Huey Long claimed that if the bill was vetoed there were enough votes to override. Senator Glass told Roosevelt that, if insurance was not put into the administration bill, Congress would include it anyway. Glass had now yielded to public opinion because "Washington does not remember any issue on which the sentiment of the country has been so undivided or so emphatically expressed as upon this." In correspondence dated in early June 1933, FDR stated that he was trying to make the draft bill "as sound as possible" and that he was "doing everything possible to correct it." Roosevelt had decided that the time had come to reach a deal. On 12 June he agreed to accept a capped and delayed program, under which deposit insurance would not become operative until 1934. The bill was reported out of the committee and on 13 June, after brief debate, both the House and the Senate voted to accept the conference report and approve the bill. Three days later, on 16 June 1933, Franklin Roosevelt signed the Banking Act of 1933 into law.[84]

The new law provided for the implementation of deposit insurance in two stages. The first stage was a temporary program of six months only, effective 1 January 1934, under which deposits were insured for up to $2,500 for any one depositor. The second stage was a distinct permanent plan, slated to take effect by 1 July 1934. The temporary plan was then extended, and the permanent plan delayed, by the Banking Act of 16 June 1934. The Banking Act of 1935 then revised the permanent plan, so that it resembled the temporary plan, and it became effective on 23 August 1935 as so revised.[85] As Mark Flood notes,

84 Kennedy, *Banking Crisis of 1933*, pp. 219–222; Burns, *American Banking Community*, pp. 90–2; Calomiris, and White, "Origins of Federal Deposit Insurance," in Goldin and Libecap, *Regulated Economy*, p. 174, and also in Calomiris, *U.S. Bank Deregulation*, p. 197; Cohen, *Nothing to Fear*, p. 278; Preston, "Banking Act of 1933," pp. 585, 589 and 597; Grant, *Money of the Mind*, p. 113; Flood, "Great Deposit Insurance Debate," pp. 52 and 67.

85 Golembe, "Deposit Insurance Legislation," pp. 193–4; Preston, "Banking Act of 1933," pp. 591–2; Flood, "Great Deposit Insurance Debate," pp. 52 n. 3; Calomiris, "Banking Crises and the Rules of the Game," p. 14.

PLATE 22 *President Franklin Delano Roosevelt signing the Banking Act of 1933, 16 June 1933. Standing behind the President, from left to right, are: Senator Allen Barkley, Senator Thomas Gore, Senator Carter Glass, Comptroller of the Currency J. F. T. Connors, Senator William G. McAdoo, Representative Henry S. Steagall, Senator Duncan U. Fletcher, Representative Alan Goldsborough and Representative Robert Luce. (Photograph © Bettmann/CORBIS.)*

Under the temporary plan, coverage ceilings were conservative, the insurance corporation was emphatically segregated from the federal taxpayer, chartering standards for national banks were raised, and supervisory authority was broadly increased. These characteristics were retained under the permanent plan of the Banking Act of 1935. As such, deposit insurance, as construed in the Banking Acts of 1933 and 1935, succeeded in simultaneously protecting the small depositor and leaving the banker answerable to both supervisors and large depositors for the quality of his management.[86]

86 Flood, "Great Deposit Insurance Debate," p. 73.

Under the extensions of the temporary plan, the insurance limit was raised to $5,000 per depositor, which had been found to provide full coverage to 98 percent of depositors. The Banking Act of 1935 maintained this coverage limit. Insured banks would now be charged a premium of one-twelfth of one percent of their deposits, payable twice annually, which was a sharp reduction from the one half percent charged under the temporary plan. The 1935 Act expanded the supervisory powers of the Federal Deposit Insurance Corporation (FDIC), and required all member banks of the Federal Reserve System to insure their deposits with the FDIC. Nonmember banks with deposits of under $1 million could obtain insurance with FDIC approval, but had to agree to submit to examination.[87] While deposit insurance became mandatory in the United States for all federally-chartered banks and savings institutions, as is evidenced by the FDIC coverage sticker that is commonly seen at American banks, insurance coverage is not universal, as among certain state-chartered banks.

Having given in and decided that he would support the deposit insurance plan, as modified, Franklin Roosevelt became its proud parent. He congratulated Carter Glass for the success of the legislation but also took credit for himself (to the amusement or outrage of various observers). Raymond Moley, a key adviser, wrote that "Roosevelt at first endured and then embraced it.… I am convinced that finally he made himself believe he had favored it from the beginning."[88] On one such occasion, Vice President Garner winked and commented, "I see Roosevelt is claiming credit for the guarantee of bank deposits."[89] The Republican party made a political point of this, insisting that the Republicans deserved credit for the popular reform, not FDR. In 1936 the Republican National Committee issued a press release publicizing an October 1932 letter in which Franklin Roosevelt had sharply criticized deposit insurance, stating that for "a number of reasons of sound government finance, such a plan would be quite dangerous." According to an article in The New York Times, the Republican National Committee "declared that Federal deposit insurance was put through by Senator Arthur H. Vandenberg, Republican, 'in the face of the strongest opposition from Franklin Delano Roosevelt

87 Golembe, "Deposit Insurance Legislation," pp. 193–4; Calomiris, and White, "Origins of Federal Deposit Insurance," in Goldin and Libecap, *Regulated Economy*, p. 176, and also in Calomiris, *U.S. Bank Deregulation*, pp. 199–200; *A History of the FDIC 1933–1983*, p. 5.

88 Burns, *American Banking Community*, p. 92; Cohen, *Nothing to Fear*, p. 279.

89 Kennedy, *Banking Crisis of 1933*, p. 222 and n.57.

and from the banks almost as a unit.'"[90] It is possible that the idea of deposit insurance had yet struck a chord with the President, despite his strong reservations about the notion of unlimited bank guaranty. The idea came from New York, originated during the governorship of Martin Van Buren, another New Yorker of Netherlands heritage who later became President of the United States, and was inspired by Canton hong merchants with whom his grandfather had done business.[91]

The bank deposit insurance program that was implemented in the United States in the 1930s is significantly different from the collective guaranty program that was enforced among the hong merchants of Canton between 1780 and 1842. The concept had evolved in the course of its transplantations. The United States and Chinese programs each concerned businesses operated under government license. Each involved a fund, maintained with the proceeds of a form of tax, that was intended to pay the claims of creditors against members of the licensed group. One program was local, and the other national. The imperial Chinese system lacked independent management, existence, or accounts. The modern United States program involves independent administration, distinct accounts and accounting, and government oversight of the program itself. At Canton, the Consoo Fund was heavily drawn on by the government for other purposes, with the result that adequate liquid funds were never available to pay claims when losses occurred. In the United States, the Federal Deposit Insurance Corporation and other deposit insurers have always held their insurance funds free from government draw, although funds on hand have not always been adequate to pay losses that have arisen. Under the Chinese program, the risks that were taken by members of the insured guild were not subject to regulatory scrutiny. As a result, some of the hong failures, and the scale of the losses involved, came as a surprise. The United States program involves ongoing examiner scrutiny of the risks taken by insured banks, with the objective that losses and bank failures ought not to come as

---

90 Anonymous, "Roosevelt 'Won' to Bank Insurance," The New York Times, 27 October 1936.

91 Downs, *The Golden Ghetto*, p. 179. One can easily imagine Franklin Roosevelt taking an interest in the origins of bank deposit insurance. There was much in the topic to perk his interest. The innovation came out of New York State, then under the another Governor of Netherlands origin (Martin Van Buren), who also went on to become President of the United States. The hong merchant origins of the idea received publicity in 1931 when Volume Six of the Dictionary of American Biography was published. It is tempting to imagine the article on Joshua Forman, which mentions the hong merchant connection, being brought to the attention of Roosevelt or his circle as the deposit insurance debate raged in 1932–33. The author is unaware of any evidence that ever happened.

a surprise. In the United States, in 1933, the liability of the deposit insurance fund was limited. This was a key objective of President Roosevelt. At Canton, the liability of the Consoo Fund was unlimited. While the modern United States bank insurance program thus differs in key respects from the structure of the Canton program, its experiences after 1933, the subject matter of the following chapter, yet echo other aspects of its Chinese prehistory.

CHAPTER 9

Eighty Years of Bank Deposit Insurance

This work set out to answer certain questions about the transplantation of a Chinese idea to the State of New York and the further progress of that idea through the adoption of national bank deposit insurance in the United States. The preceding chapters have taken the idea through Manchu officials at the port of Canton, the New York State legislature, and on to Washington, D.C. at the moment of the banking crisis of 1933. This short chapter takes the story forward from then. It is a sketch. The worldwide history of bank deposit insurance is enormously complex. It is also the matter of headlines. The international financial crisis of 2007–2008, which at first seemed to simply be an emergency involving securitized American mortgages, broke as work on this study began. That crisis moved into a new phase, casting a shadow over European public finance, banking and the Euro currency, as this chapter was being written. An international history of bank deposit insurance is thus not only outside of the scope of this study, but it is probably premature as well. That eighty year history—dull at the outset, and dramatic in its more recent phases—is outlined in the following pages. This sketch frames the context for consideration of the original questions posed in this study in the next and final chapter.

National bank deposit insurance in the United States celebrated its eightieth anniversary in 2013. The federal deposit insurance program has now operated for a longer time period than both the New York Safety Fund (1829–1866), which lasted for thirty-seven years, and the Canton Guaranty System (1780–1842), which expired in its sixty-second year. This is ripe old age by any standard, and for much of this period the United States experienced a remarkable calm in the affairs of its insured banks. Starting in the 1960s, and more rapidly in the 1990s and thereafter, many nations have adopted bank deposit insurance programs. The earliest programs were inspired by success in the United States. The accelerating implementations of more recent years have tended to be in response to program initiatives, or market conditions, such as the perceived need to implement bank deposit insurance lest bank deposits take flight from uninsured to insured locales.

An enormous scholarly literature and large amounts of learned journal, newspaper and online commentary have developed regarding bank deposit insurance. Much of this material is technical, concerned with the implementation or operation of deposit insurance programs, or is focused on deposit insurance in the context of economic theory. Some is polemical, produced, for

 | DOI 10.1163/9789004276567_010

example, in response to the American savings and loan crisis of the 1980s or the international financial crisis that began in 2007. Some history of deposit insurance appears in this literature, but usually only to address or illustrate current operating problems. No general history of bank deposit insurance in the United States has been written. Important early contributions were made by scholars such as Carter Golembe (1960) and Bray Hammond (1957),[1] but most of the history of federal deposit insurance has taken place since those works were published. Much of the work needed for a general history has been done, by scholars such as Charles W. Calomiris and David A. Moss. Their work is primarily found in scholarly journals or in essay collections such as *U.S. Bank Deregulation in Historical Perspective* (2000).[2] The Federal Deposit Insurance Corporation produced a useful company history to mark its fiftieth anniversary in 1984, but even that official history is now almost thirty years old.[3] The adoption of deposit insurance programs in many nations worldwide is an important further development that also calls for a general history, but it too remains to be written. All of this experience may simply be too young and too much in flux for a useful general history to be written at this time. Valuable work toward an understanding of the international experience with deposit insurance has nonetheless been produced in various languages and formats, some of which is cited below. Perhaps the most useful book produced to date is *Deposit Insurance Around The World: Issues of Design and Implementation* (2008).[4]

1 Federal Deposit Insurance in the United States

The federal deposit insurance law was popular at the time of its adoption and for a long time it had excellent press. This period of calm ran well into the 1960s, carrying with it a generally sunny view of the effects of the 1933 statute. In 1963 deposit insurance was pronounced by leading economists to be "the

1 Carter Golembe, "The Deposit Insurance Legislation of 1933," Political Science Quarterly, Vol. 75, pp. 181–200 (1960); Bray Hammond, *Banks and Politics in America from the Revolution to the Civil War* (Princeton: Princeton Univ. Press, 1957).

2 Charles W. Calomiris, *U.S. Bank Deregulation in Historical Perspective* (Cambridge: Cambridge Univ. Press, 2000).

3 Federal Deposit Insurance Corporation, *Federal Deposit Insurance Corporation: The First Fifty Years: A History of the FDIC 1933–1983* (Washington, D.C.: Federal Deposit Insurance Corporation, 1984).

4 Ash Demirgüç-Kunt, Edward J. Kane and Luc Laeven, eds., *Deposit Insurance Around The World: Issues of Design and Implementation* (Cambridge: MIT Press, 2008).

most important structural change in the banking system to result from the 1933 panic," and "the structural change most conducive to monetary stability since state bank notes were taxed out of existence immediately after the Civil War."[5]

With the United States enjoying relative calm after the Great Depression and World War II, and the deposit insurance system appearing to function well, coverage limits gradually crept up. As noted above, the original limit was $2,500 under the temporary plan of 1933, but was promptly raised to $5,000 effective 30 June 1934. The coverage limit was raised to $10,000 in 1950, to $15,000 in 1966, to $20,000 in 1969, and to $40,000 in 1974. The coverage limit was next raised to $100,000 in 1980, and then to $250,000 on 3 October 2008.[6] These figures, which marched ahead of the inflation rate, are somewhat illusory. First, it was always possible to multiply FDIC coverage through simple structuring, even within a single bank.[7] Second, even in the calm early years of deposit insurance, the FDIC was already trying to give 100 percent coverage to all depositors (i.e., coverage in excess of stated limits). The 'no depositor loss' objective was often achieved through some type of merger or purchase and assumption transaction, in which the failed bank was combined with a healthy successor. Depositors were entirely satisfied but the final accounting was necessarily somewhat opaque. Senator Fulbright challenged this policy in Congressional hearings in 1951, asserting that Congress had never intended for the FDIC to provide above limits coverage and that a failure of cost calculation was obviously involved.[8]

It was a short leap from an undeclared policy of seeking to provide 100 percent coverage to all depositors, to an implicit policy of too big too fail. Under a too big to fail policy, all creditors of those select large financial institutions which are considered to be somehow vital to the economy or society are paid in full by the insurer (or by government, i.e., the taxpayer, as a last resort).[9]

5 Kennedy, *Banking Crisis of 1933*, p. 214 (quoting Milton Friedman and Anna Jacobson Schwartz, *A Monetary History of the United States, 1867–1960* (Princeton: Princeton Univ. Press, 1963), p. 434).

6 *History of the FDIC 1933–1983*, p. 69; Grant, *Money of the Mind*, pp. 238–9, 255–7 and 364; Robert Pozen, *Too Big to Save? How to Fix the U.S. Financial System* (Hoboken, N.J.: John Wiley & Sons, Inc., 2010), p. 179; Demirgüç-Kunt, Kane and Laeven, "Deposit Insurance Design and Implementation," pp. 18–9.

7 Pozen, *Too Big to Save?*, p. 180.

8 Gary H. Stern and Ron J. Feldman, *Too Big to Fail: The Hazards of Bank Bailouts* (Washington, D.C.: Brookings Institution Press, 2004), p. 152; Grant, *Money of the Mind*, pp. 256–7 and 367.

9 One consequence of "too big to fail" policies is that the favored institutions have tended to grow still larger. This increase in scale, combined with indications that management has not been able to effectively control the risks taken in large-scale complex transactions, has given

In the United States, this doctrine rose out of the wreckage of the Continental Illinois National Bank in 1984. Then the seventh largest bank in the United States, and considered indispensable, the bank was allowed to fail only in the sense that its ownership and management were changed. It became an 80 percent owned investment of the FDIC. This very generous treatment was seen as setting a new precedent. Questioning the Comptroller of the Currency in congressional hearings, an exasperated Congressman McKinney said that with this transaction,

> We have a new kind of bank. And today there is another type created. We found it in the thrift institutions, and now we have given approval for a $1 billion brokerage deal to Financial Corporation of America. Mr. Chairman, let us not bandy words. We have a new kind of bank. It is called too big to fail. TBTF, and it is a wonderful bank.[10]

Now embraced worldwide, and especially in the course of the financial crisis that began in 2007, the "too big to fail" doctrine has been defined as involving grants of "discretionary government support [to] a bank's uninsured creditors who are not automatically entitled to government support."[11] The result has been, per James Grant, that "the government's credit, in the estimation of the average public depositor, [had] superseded the credit of the bank that kept his money. By the 1980s, with the evolution of the doctrine that some banks were too big to fail, the government [has thus] become the silent partner of even uninsured depositors."[12]

As Congressman McKinney indicated in his questioning of the Comptroller of the Currency, a long period of banking calm in the Unites States was spectacularly undone in the savings and loan (thrift) bank crisis of the 1980s. Deregulated, and given a green light to move heavily into speculative real estate and other lending far removed from their traditional home mortgage lending business, the "thrifts" ended up massive losers when real estate values

rise to concern that some institutions have grown so complicated that they simply cannot be safely managed. See Gillian Tett, "How 'too big to fail' banks have become 'too complex to exist,'" Financial Times, 8 June 2012, p. 20.

10 Grant, *Money of the Mind*, p. 367; Stern and Feldman, *Too Big to Fail*, p. 13.

11 Stern and Feldman, *Too Big to Fail*, p. 1; Demirgüç-Kunt, Kane and Laeven, "Deposit Insurance Design and Implementation," p. 3 ("Every country offers implicit insurance because, during banking crises, the pressure on government officials to rescue at least some bank stakeholders becomes difficult to resist.").

12 Grant, *Money of the Mind*, pp. 238–9, 255–6 and 364.

fell. Large numbers of savings and loan institutions failed, and their deposit insurance fund was wholly inadequate. Policies of regulatory forbearance, which permitted insolvent institutions to continue as (what have become known as) "zombie" banks, motivated to employ risky strategies with which to try to return to solvency, only made matters worse. The final bill to the United States government for losses associated with the savings and loan disaster was $153 billion, or about 2 percent of United States gross domestic product, which was raised from taxpayers and the banking industry.[13]

The rise of the Federal National Mortgage Association (Fannie Mae) and the Federal Home Loan Mortgage Association (Freddie Mac) tracked the decline of the savings and loan industry. These quasi-public corporations, which had been active for many years in support of American home ownership, became increasingly active in buying up residential mortgages in and after the 1980s. Enjoying a set of privileges typically enjoyed only by federal agencies, but actually owned by private shareholders, they could sell bonds and raise money at interest rates significantly less than their private competition. Fannie Mae and Freddie Mac packaged the hundreds of billions of dollars of mortgages they acquired as mortgage-backed securities, and sold them, guaranteeing these mortgages against default. Together with another federal mortgage guarantee program called the Government National Mortgage Association (Ginnie Mae), these corporations owned or guaranteed nearly half of all United States mortgages by the year 2003. Banks became heavily involved with the mortgage related activities of Fannie Mae, Freddie Mac, and Ginnie Mac, which collectively supported a large amount of United States mortgage debt. The close association of these corporations with the United States government and enjoyment of privileges associated with government status led investors to believe that their guarantee enjoyed the implicit backing of the United States Treasury.[14]

This assumption was tested in the financial crisis of 2007–8 when Fannie Mae and Freddie Mac reported crippling losses on guarantees of subprime

13 The inadequately capitalized fund of the Federal Savings and Loan Insurance Corporation (FSLIC) was exhausted by the crisis and FSLIC was abolished in 1989. Kroszner and Melick, "Lessons from the U.S. Experience," pp. 199 and 204–8; Stern and Feldman, *Too Big to Fail*, pp. 23–4; Pozen, *Too Big to Save?*, pp. 184 and 198; Flood, "Great Deposit Insurance Debate," p. 51.

14 Pozen, *Too Big to Save?*, pp. 27 and 30; Grant, *Money of the Mind*, p. 352; Gretchen Morgenson and Joshua Rosner, *Reckless Endangerment: How Outsized Ambition, Greed, and Corruption Led to Economic Armageddon* (New York: Times Books, 2011), pp. 13, 18–9, 21 and 239.

mortgage loans. They were placed in federal receivership on 6 September 2008 and holders of existing common and preferred stock were largely wiped out. In conservatorship, the claims of bondholders—which included financial institutions worldwide—were honored with payment in full due to U.S. government concern about the potential risks to the global financial system posed by their threatened default. "Thus," in the view of Robert Pozen and many other seasoned observers, "the bailout vindicated the widely held perception that the bonds of Fannie Mae and Freddie Mac were indeed the moral obligations of the federal government."[15] While the rescue was not performed by a deposit insurance fund, it supported government interests in keeping deposit insurance solvent, for a failure or a material loss of confidence in these corporations might have had severe effects on mortgages held as collateral by insured banks. The United States Treasury has since provided massive capital support to Fannie Mae and Freddie Mac in conservatorship. As the full extent of their losses depends on the default rates of outstanding mortgage loans, the value of which remains uncertain, the amount of the bill that taxpayers will have to pay is unknown. Total United States government losses from the failures of Fannie Mae and Freddie Mac were estimated as of 2010 in the amount of not less than $160 billion and possibly as much as $1 trillion.[16] In addition, in the financial crisis of 2007–8, the FDIC guaranteed for a period of up to three years 100 percent of over $300 billion in the debts of banks, thrifts, and their holding companies. The final out of pocket cost of these accommodations, and of myriad other extensions of governmental support to financial institutions worldwide in and after these troubled years, is unknown.[17]

2 The International Progress of Bank Deposit Insurance

Since its introduction as a national program in the United States in 1933, bank deposit insurance has swept the world. The first national deposit insurance programs, after the United States, were introduced in India and in Norway in 1961. During the long period of bank insurance calm that prevailed in the United States from the 1930s through the 1960s, deposit insurance made slow

15 Pozen, *Too Big to Save?*, p. 38.

16 Pozen, *Too Big to Save?*, pp. 27–8; Lorraine Woellert and John Gittelsohn, "Fannie-Freddie Fix at $160 Billion With $1 Trillion Worst Case," Bloomberg News, 13 June 2010 7:00 PM ET, see: "http://www.bloomberg.com/news/2010-06-13/fannie-freddie-fix-expands-to-160-billion-with-worst-case-at-1-trillion.html" (accessed 26 March 2014).

17 Pozen, *Too Big to Save?*, pp. xvii, 155 and 169.

progress elsewhere.[18] As of 1980, only twenty nations had explicit bank deposit guaranty programs. That number stood at forty-nine by January 1995, had increased to eighty-seven by the end of 2003, and now exceeds one hundred nations. Deposit insurance programs were first implemented in European countries in the 1970s and 1980s, and are now required within the European Union.[19] The EU Directive on deposit-guarantee schemes, adopted in the wake of the 1991 failure of the Bank of Credit and Commerce International and amended in 2009, requires the insurance of individual bank accounts up to a coverage limit of €100,000.[20] Ironically, it was only recently, and just as the bank deposit insurance programs in the originating United States were being wrenched by the budget-busting excesses of the savings and loan crisis and then the subprime mortgage debacle, that the adoption of bank deposit insurance accelerated worldwide.

---

18 Demirgüç-Kunt, Kane and Laeven, "Deposit Insurance Design and Implementation," pp. 4 (Figure 1.1, bar graph showing slow progress toward adoption of deposit insurance programs), 6–7 (Figure 1.2, world map showing countries that have adopted deposit insurance) and 18; Ash Demirgüç-Kunt, Edward J. Kane and Luc Laeven, "Adoption and Design of Deposit Insurance," in Demirgüç-Kunt, Kane and Laeven, *Deposit Insurance Around The World*, pp. 34–9 (Table 2.2, "Explicit deposit insurance system at year-end 2003"); Calomiris, and White, "Origins of Federal Deposit Insurance," in Goldin and Libecap, *The Regulated Economy*, p. 145, and also in Calomiris, *U.S. Bank Deregulation* in Historical Perspective, p. 164 ("... until recently it [bank deposit insurance] was strictly an American phenomenon. Many countries adopted deposit insurance in imitation of the United States, ...").

19 Demirgüç-Kunt, Kane and Laeven, "Adoption and Design of Deposit Insurance," p. 29; Jessica Cariboni, Karlien Vanden Branden, Francesca Campolongo and Manuela De Cesare, "Deposit Protection in the EU: State of Play and Future Prospects," Journal of Banking Regulation, Vol. 9, pp. 82–101 (2008), p. 84; Gillian Garcia and Henriëtte Prast, "Depositor and Investor Protection in the Netherlands: Past, Present and Future," De Nederlandsche Bank, Occasional Studies, Vol. 2, No. 2 (2004), pp. 8 (The Netherlands was among the first European countries to introduce deposit insurance) and 18–26; Andrew G. Haldane and Piergiorgio Alessandri, "Banking on the State," BIS [Bank for International Settlements] Review 139/2009, pp. 4 and 16 (Chart 6), see: "http://www.bis.org/review/r091111e.pdf" (accessed 19 January 2012).

20 Cariboni, Vanden Branden, Campolongo and De Cesare, "Deposit Protection in the EU," pp. 83 and 86; Harry Huizinga, "The EU Deposit Insurance Directive: Does One Size Fit All?," in Demirgüç-Kunt, Kane and Laeven, Deposit Insurance Around The World, pp. 253–79; Directive 94/19/EC of the European Parliament and of the Council of 30 May 1994 on deposit-guarantee schemes, see: "http://eur-lex.europa.eu/LexUriServ/LexUriServ.do?uri=CELEX:31994L0019:EN:HTML" (accessed 2 September 2012); Directive 2009/14/EC, amending Directive 94/19/EC, see: "http://ec.europa.eu/internal_market/bank/docs/guarantee/200914_en.pdf" (accessed 2 September 2012).

Deposit insurance has powerful and well-intentioned friends. Since the 1990s, the International Monetary Fund has recommended deposit insurance as part of its crisis management advice. The World Bank supports the introduction of national deposit insurance programs, through advice and by providing adjustment loans for the initial capital of funds in certain countries.[21]

Details of the many deposit insurance programs that have been adopted worldwide vary greatly. Typically, membership is compulsory for chartered banks.[22] Coverage limits differ, but averaged as of 2003 at $20,660 per deposit in all countries, ranging from a low of $120 in the Ukraine to a high of $243,520 in Norway. Limits tend to be higher in more developed countries.[23] Coverage limits have soared worldwide in response to the financial crisis that began in 2007. In The Netherlands, for example, the limit was raised from €20,000 to €40,000 in 2007, after the failure of Van der Hoop bankiers N.V., and to €100,000 in turn as of 7 October 2008, in response to international conditions.[24] Limits within the EU were raised generally to €100,000 under the 2009 amendment to the EU Directive on deposit-guarantee schemes, cited above, which also reduced the permissible delay before funds had to be paid out to depositors. National boundaries mean less in an era of capital fluidity. Weak banks offering high interest rates, in jurisdictions with high amounts of insurance coverage, may draw deposits away from more solvent banks in less heavily insured jurisdictions. The adoption of bank deposit insurance, and increases in the amounts of insurance coverage, have been advocated as means of preventing capital flight.

Explicit deposit insurance programs are not universal. They are not found in the People's Republic of China, Israel, or in many African countries. Asian countries have been slow to adopt deposit insurance. It has existed in India since 1961, in Japan since 1996, and in the Republic of China (Taiwan) since 1985. In China, deposit insurance exists in practice, but it is implicit only.

---

21 Demirgüç-Kunt, Kane and Laeven, "Deposit Insurance Design and Implementation," pp. 3 and 21; Garcia and Prast, "Depositor and Investor Protection," pp. 21–4.

22 Demirgüç-Kunt, Kane and Laeven, "Deposit Insurance Design and Implementation," p. 11.

23 The cited averages are in United States dollars. Luc Laeven, "Pricing of Deposit Insurance," in Demirgüç-Kunt, Kane and Laeven, *Deposit Insurance Around The World*, p. 111; Cariboni, Vanden Branden, Campolongo and De Cesare, "Deposit Protection in the EU," pp. 85–9.

24 Cariboni, Vanden Branden, Campolongo and De Cesare, "Deposit Protection in the EU," pp. 86–7; Garcia and Prast, "Depositor and Investor Protection," pp. 42–7 (detailed description of depositor protections in The Netherlands as of 2003); De Nederlandsche Bank, Factsheet, "Obligations Investor-Compensation Scheme and Deposit-Guarantee Scheme, accessed 15 February 2012, see: http://www.toezicht.dnb.nl/en/2/51-224859.jsp (accessed 26 March 2014).

Protection has been extended by the Chinese government to retail depositors on a case by case basis. Australia, New Zealand and Hong Kong held out through the financial crisis of 2007–8, after which each adopted deposit guarantee programs. Hong Kong imposed a blanket guarantee of all bank deposits with the goal of preventing capital from moving to other, perhaps safer, venues. Many previously adopting countries—over forty—responded to the 2007–8 international crisis either by sharply increasing coverage limits, or by removing them entirely (said to be on a temporary basis).[25] This spirit proved highly contagious. In Europe, as Robert Pozen writes, "Ireland jumped out ahead of the European Union by quickly announcing a blanket guarantee of all bank deposits. In order to prevent local deposits from moving to Ireland, soon afterward many of the larger European countries like England and Germany offered higher or blanket guarantees of deposits at their banks."[26]

The cost of these extensive guarantees has yet to be tallied. As of early 2012, losses from explicit bank guaranty programs in Asia have been minimal. European guaranty losses may be significant, as the result of the subprime loan crisis that began in 2007, the subsequent Euro debt crisis, and application of too big to fail policies. Ireland will be a big loser, as the state has provided a blanket guaranty of bank debt. The extent of the property-related losses of the Irish banks are unknown, but could be in the range of €106 billion euros ($10.6 trillion.) Of this liability, Michael Lewis recently wrote: "Ireland gave its promise. And the promise sank Ireland."[27] In Iceland, the failure of the tiny nation's three leading banks produced outsized losses reckoned in the range of $100 billion.[28] The amount of private bank and public guaranty fund losses that will result from the financial problems of Greece, Spain, Italy, Portugal and France are unknown. The estimates are disheartening and have tended to grow.

---

25 Demirgüç-Kunt, Kane and Laeven, "Deposit Insurance Design and Implementation," p. 5; Pozen, *Too Big to Save?*, p. 185; Stern and Feldman, *Too Big to Fail*, p. 100; Jang-Bong Choi, "Structuring a Deposit Insurance System from the Asian Perspective," in Rising to the Challenge in Asia: A Study of Financial Markets, Vol. 2 (Special Issues) (Manila: Asian Development Bank, 1999), p. 73, see: "http://www.aric.adb.org/pdf/aem/external/financial_market/Special_Issues/Volume2b.pdf" (accessed 26 March 2014); Haldane and Alessandri, "Banking on the State," p. 4 ("And more than forty countries have increased the coverage limits of their existing schemes, including in the UK, US and Germany. In a few countries, deposit insurance limits have temporarily been removed—for example, in Germany and Ireland. In many others, they have been removed implicitly.").

26 Pozen, *Too Big to Save?*, p. 185.

27 Michael Lewis, *Boomerang: Travels in the New Third World* (New York: W. W. Norton & Co., 2011), pp. 84–5 and 114.

28 Michael Lewis, *Boomerang*, pp. 3 and 23.

China has its own domestic banking problems—and not just the recent growth of a shadow banking sector seeking to serve underbanked parts of its populace. The Chinese people are remarkably thrifty,[29] and that is a virtue. Their banks however have incurred staggering losses, for example in bad real estate loans and in loans made to advance public policy objectives. As of 2008, China had, in effect, recapitalized its four leading banks in the amount of about $350 billion. In the words of Patrick Honohan, "The recapitalization of China's big banks has already entailed one of the largest fiscal or quasifiscal outlays for any banking system in history."[30] Yet this is hardly the end of China's banking problems. The nation's stimulus response to the global financial crisis of 2007–8 saddled provinces and cities with RMB 10.7 trillion ($1.7 trillion) in bank debts which they were not able to pay within a few years as originally planned. Chinese banks were instructed as of February 2012 to undertake a massive rollover of these loans, extending maturities by as much as four years, in order to avoid a wave of defaults.[31]

China has long offered implicit deposit insurance protection[32] The magnitude of the protection extended to its leading banks may be seen as an extension of that policy. At the individual level, household depositors have been protected thus far, but even that protection is not unlimited. The central government, which has used state funds to support the obligations of insolvent institutions under its control, has signaled that failures of local institutions are to be the responsibility of local governments.[33]

Debate has gone on inside China for years concerning the adoption of explicit bank deposit insurance. Although deposit insurance rules are said to have been prepared by the People's Bank of China, the concept remains

---

29 Juann H. Hung and Rong Qian, "Why Is China's Savings Rate So High?: A Comparative Study of Cross-Country Panel Data" (Washington, D.C.: Congressional Budget Office, Working Paper No. 2010-07) (November 2010), see: "http://www.cbo.gov/sites/default/files/cbofiles/ftpdocs/119xx/doc11958/2010-07-chinasavingrate.pdf" (accessed 30 April 2012).

30 Patrick Honohan, "Protecting Depositors in China: Experience and Evolving Policy," in Demirgüç-Kunt, Kane and Laeven, *Deposit Insurance Around The World*, pp. 335, 337, 342 and 346.

31 Simon Rabinovitch, "Beijing to roll over provinces' loan terms," Financial Times, 13 February 2012, p. 1.

32 Lou Jianbo, "Introducing a Deposit Insurance System Into China," Peking Univ. Journal of Legal Studies, Vol. 1, pp. 233–54 (2008), p. 239.

33 Honohan, "Protecting Depositors in China," pp. 337 and 348.

controversial.[34] China, which provided the regulatory example that inspired American deposit insurance in the nineteenth century, has proven reluctant to explicitly set out on the same road. Its reluctance is somehow fitting. Bank deposit insurance programs—which have been billed as both "modern" and "American"—actually carry embedded within them traces of collective responsibility and imperial monopoly regulation from China's own pre-revolutionary past. China is wrestling today with whether this innovation properly belongs in the dustbin of history or whether it might have a role in assuring the orderly continuance of its modern economic miracle.

---

34 Honohan, "Protecting Depositors in China," pp. 348–9 (proposed coverage limits); Chen Jia, "Time to Launch Deposit Insurance, Economists Say," China Daily, 12 January 2012, p. 13; Wang Xiaotian, "Freeing Up of Rates Not on Agenda for this Year," China Daily, 7 February 2012, see: "http://news.xinhuanet.com/english/business/2012-02/07/c_131395812.htm" (accessed 26 March 2014).

CHAPTER 10

Epilogue

The hong merchants have long had a reputation as wealthy men. In the late 1600s, the poet Chu Dajun wrote of silver "piling up" in the thirteen hongs. Customs taxes collected from their trade were a key part of the revenues of the imperial Court in Beijing, representing 38% on average of the so-called "surplus quota" taxes that were directed to the Imperial Household Department (*neiwufu*) during the period 1796 to 1821. The Department viewed Canton as a "rich" post, and sent indebted officials there as an opportunity to restore their fortunes and pay off debts to the state. The hong merchants lived well. Some supported large extended families, had magnificent houses and gardens, and collected books and art,[1] practices which caused foreign creditors to sputter. Summarizing the Canton scene, a French trader stated that "The Mandarins wanted tranquility in their nation and the [hong] merchants opulence in their homes."[2]

The hong merchant of the port of Canton, China was one of the first great international brands. That brand was marketed both as an image and as a reputation for value and creditworthiness. The image is familiar today, in the form of the august portraits of Chinese businessmen that were brought home by or were sent to trading partners worldwide, and in anecdotal accounts of the munificence of hong merchants. Through the years 1780 to 1842, the trend in hong merchant portraiture is toward grandeur. The austere style of earlier portraits gives way to a more luxurious, magnificent and colorful presentation. The actual trend of hong merchant fortunes in this period was instead one of decline, with the notable exception of Howqua II, who was growing more wealthy. The trend in portraiture runs contrary to economic reality. The portraits are somewhat misleading—or perhaps the appropriate word is aspirational. They present grand images of hong merchants in the success they hoped they would attain, but largely did not.

To Western traders in the eighteenth and nineteenth centuries, these painted images were of almost no consequence. Hong merchants built up their high standing with trading partners through commercial reliability and daily

1 Ch'en, *Insolvency*, pp. 107–111.

2 "Les Mandarins veulent la tranquilité dans leur pays, et les marchands l'opulence dans leurs maisons." Letter from Michel à Rothe dated 31 December 1760, quoted in Dermigny, *La Chine et L'Occident, Vol.* 2, p. 835 n.2.

 | DOI 10.1163/9789004276567_011

PLATE 23 *An example of an early hong merchant portrait. Portrait of a hong merchant who traded with the Philadelphia merchant Stephen Girard, ca. 1787–1824. Oil on canvas, by an unknown Chinese artist. Compare with Plates 13 (an early hong merchant portrait) and 14 (a later portrait of Howqua II). Jonathan Goldstein, scholar of Girard's trade with China, believes that this is an early portrait of Howqua II, with whom Girard did considerable business. Goldstein,* Stephen Girard's Trade, *p. 62. (Collection of Girard College, Philadelphia, Pennsylvania. Photograph by courtesy of Girard College History Collections.)*

practices which assured that value was delivered to the customer. The Canton trade functioned efficiently, as a whole, and on those rare occasions when teas turned out to be bad on delivery in the West, hong merchant sellers gave full credit to foreign buyers, even years after the original sale. The collective guaranty by the entire hong merchant body of the foreign debts of its members, in particular, was important to the Western trading community. It meant that for many years any hong merchant's promise to pay was rock solid. The commitment of a hong merchant could be relied upon anywhere. As Joshua Forman stated in 1829, "the bond [i.e., the promise to pay] of a Hong merchant has acquired a credit over the whole world, not exceeded by that of any other security." For all the value the foreign traders found in the collective guaranty, it was not a promotional feature that the hong merchant guild either sought or desired. It was imposed, and strictly enforced, by the Chinese government as part of a regulatory system that sought to maintain security in and tax revenue flow from an enormous foreign trade upon which China had become dependent. The Canton Guaranty System assured that the licensed hong merchants of Canton paid their foreign debts in full and made good for any problems in trade.

The Canton Guaranty System yielded significant benefits for the parties involved. The collective guaranty raised foreign confidence in the ability of the hong merchants to perform their commitments. This served both Chinese and foreign interests in stabilizing the foreign trade from Canton. In modern times, similarly, the public good is seen as advanced by bank deposit insurance, which encourages the deposit in banks and the efficient circulation of funds, and also by automobile insurance guaranty funds, which decrease uninsured driving.

In daily practice, the Canton program was understood to mean that the financial commitments of guild members would be fulfilled. This contributed to an international brand image of equal strength—and honor—among all of the hong merchants. For the Chinese state, and for foreign creditors, it minimized the amount of effort that had to be devoted to debt collection disputes and thus made the trade more efficient. As designed, it advanced the Confucian ideal of maintaining harmony in trade. It may have accomplished this objective in some cases in the short term, but over time the growing amount of undischarged debt damaged many surviving firms and yielded a final bounty of disharmony. The system had a funding mechanism—the *hangyong* tax—that might have covered creditor claims had the Chinese state abstained from taking these tax revenues from the Consoo Fund. Without independent existence, or interested local parties able and willing to defend it, the fund proved powerless to protect its assets from the needs of the state and of the guild members who ran the fund. By helping the most frail perform their imprudent contracts, and fostering a global image of equal creditworthiness ("not exceeded by that of any other security"), the collective guaranty contributed to a misleading appearance of hong merchant wealth. The hong merchants had good commercial reasons to join in building that image, as the appearance of strength gave them status in the marketplace and attracted foreign customers. Opulent lifestyles, plus grand images in portraits sent to the West, supported a gilded image. Unfortunately, in many cases the image of wealth was founded on little more than the equation of (a) being able to pay large expense bills on a regular basis with (b) being rich.

The economic reality of hong merchant existence was utterly different. In his study of hong insolvencies, Kuo-tung Ch'en concludes that most of the hong merchants "labored under incessant financial difficulties."[3] Their situation was "particularly bad" between 1760 and 1843. As he states,

> During that period, thirty-seven Hong merchants closed business.... Of that thirty-seven, only two retired with substantial fortunes. Four disappeared from all accounts without notice. Eight were closed down by the local authorities on account of their incompetence or infringement of laws. Three stopped business upon their death. The remaining twenty merchants were publicly declared bankrupt. These bankrupts were always heavily indebted to the foreign traders, the government, as well as to their own countrymen who either provided merchandise for them or lent them money.[4]

Hong merchant insolvency was "not only common but also perennial."[5] Ch'en set out to find its causes, examining, among other things, the profitability, capitalization, borrowing and expenses of hong firms. During the nineteenth century, by Ch'en's estimate based on British EIC records, the total import and export business of the entire hong merchant body averaged more than ten million taels ($13,888,889) annually, or roughly one million taels ($1,388.889) per hong.[6] His examination of each of the principal lines of hong merchant

3 Ch'en, *Insolvency*, p. 251.
4 Ch'en, *Insolvency*, pp. 36–8 and Table 1.4.
5 Ch'en, *Insolvency*, p. 41.
6 Ch'en, *Insolvency*, p. 152.

business—their trades in tea, woolens and cotton—indicated basic profitability in these areas,[7] but also a nagging problem of capitalization.[8]

Few of the hong merchant firms had the money they needed to do business on the scale in which they were engaged. They took high interest rate loans from foreigners, or found other precarious ways to raise funds, out of necessity because credit was not available from domestic sources.[9] Ch'en finds that, on average, the hong merchants carried heavy expenses in running their businesses, in making the deposits for tea purchases required by inland suppliers, in supporting extended families, in high living, in paying the debts of failed hong merchants, and in paying frequent demands for money by the Canton officials.[10] While these averaged expenses largely consumed the merchants' averaged profits, Ch'en found exactions by the Canton officials to have been particularly harmful.[11]

Continual *ad hoc* demands by Chinese governmental bodies and officials for the payment of discretionary fees, known as *kejuan zashui*, are familiar throughout Chinese history. These exactions have attained recent prominence as part of an answer to a question posed by William C. Kirby in 1995—Why have mainland Chinese been so reluctant to do business in the form of a corporation with statutory limited liability?[12] In their solution to the "Kirby Puzzle," J. Ray Bowen II and David C. Rose pointed to government exactions as the primary cause. As they explain,

> the practice of *kejuan zashui* has the effect of making the government, and not the firm owner, the residual claimant on any private firm's income. This makes public trading of privately owned shares too risky, effectively depriving PPCs [privately owned, publicly traded corporations] of their principal advantage over other firm governance structures in China. As a result, all significant economic activity is driven into either state-affiliated enterprises or highly secretive family firms.[13]

7 Ch'en, *Insolvency*, pp. 43–88, 102–3 and 251.

8 Ch'en, *Insolvency*, p. 152.

9 Ch'en, *Insolvency*, pp. 162–177.

10 Ch'en, *Insolvency*, pp. 103–150.

11 Ch'en, *Insolvency*, pp. 136, 138 ("In the dissipation of the Hong merchants' profit, the rapacious demand of officials in fact played a more important part."), 139 and 251–2.

12 Kirby, "China Unincorporated," pp. 57–9.

13 Ray J. Bowen II and David C. Rose, "On the Absence of Privately Owned, Publicly Traded Corporations in China: The Kirby Puzzle," Journal of Asian Studies, Vol. 57, pp. 442–52 (1998), p. 450.

A climate in which exactions by government were uncertain, or, worse yet, increased when the firm seemed to be doing well, trained generations of Chinese business owners to be cautious when dealing with government. Scholarship has related these demands to an "obsession with secrecy" in the Chinese family firm, to business activity tending to be coordinated by relationships rather than by contracts which might require government involvement, and to a preference for business operation in family form.[14] The record shows that the hong merchants were frequently required to pay discretionary fees, in the nature of *kejuan zashui*, and also that there was little trade information that they could keep secret from the government. To the extent they engaged in legitimate trade, for example in allotted shares of the tea contracts of the British EIC, the Canton officials could easily track their business, and officials were able to adjust their "expectations" to the conditions of the moment.[15]

At Canton, the expenses analyzed by Ch'en outstripped the operating profits and capital of most of the hongs. While records indicating the original capital of the hongs are rare, such records as have been found indicate that such capital tended to be meagre.[16] Once a hong merchant found himself in need of money, as Ch'en explains, he

> was in fact thrown into a vicious cycle, in which he was constantly compelled to raise funds with all kinds of methods detrimental to his own interest. When his indebtedness increased and his imminent need grew, he was obliged to engage in the detrimental practices in a much more extensive way than before. The insolvency of a Hong merchant then became chronic.[17]

The ultimate causes of the many hong merchant insolvencies, according to Ch'en, were a lack of sufficient capital, poor financial management and official exactions. This toxic mix destroyed many of the hongs and discouraged new merchants from joining the guild. The hong merchants became "a group of reluctant people whose capital and ability were always insufficient to carry on

14 Bowen and Rose, "The Kirby Puzzle," pp. 445–6.

15 Cheong, *Hong Merchants*, p. 228 (discussing how the increased profits of the decade of the 1780s resulted in a "steep increase" in official exactions).

16 Ch'en, *Insolvency*, pp. 153 and 157; Van Dyke, *Merchants of Canton and Macao*, p. 177 (while "Chinese merchants kept detailed records of all their transactions, just like the foreigners, ... none of the Chinese records have survived.").

17 Ch'en, *Insolvency*, p. 177.

the enormous volume of their business. Their insolvency and ultimate failure, no doubt, was but a matter of course."[18]

This insolvency analysis is incomplete, as Kuo-tung Ch'en admits. It is primarily based on British EIC records. These are only part of a commercial whole, of which the remaining records are largely missing. While Ch'en carefully probes various categories of hong revenues and expenses, his study necessarily relies on selected data. Business skill, experience, and luck varied considerably from merchant to merchant, and from year to year. Furthermore, trading results during the period 1780 through 1842 often depended on wars and international economic downturns over which the hong merchants had no control and of which they typically had little or no warning. Under these conditions, average data can be misleading. Just as the British EIC did two centuries earlier, Ch'en faults the hong merchants for poor management, but he fails to identify any corrective measures which, if taken, would have saved any number of hongs from insolvency. The "incessant financial difficulties" under which the hong merchants labored from 1760 through 1842 indicate problems of a systemic character. Solving these problems—within the rules of the Canton System—exceeded the skills of virtually all of the hong merchants. These were experienced traders and some had considerable business talent. Accomplishing the revival of a financially troubled hong firm, within this system (including the scarcity and high cost of credit), would represent a challenge even to a modern business school graduate or turnaround management consultant.

Kuo-tung Ch'en identifies lack of capital as a chronic problem among the hong merchants, and there is abundant evidence that he is correct. Inadequate business capital was a problem from the early days of the hong merchant system through to its final years, in which several merchants found that they had no working capital left as of the first day they did business. In analyzing the financial plight of the hongs, however, Ch'en does not factor in the repayment expectations of domestic sources of capital. This might follow from the fact that records of original or later investments in hong businesses are scant, but a paucity of investment evidence is not good cause to omit consideration of repayment. As Ch'en discusses,[19] and as Paul Van Dyke details in his new study of the eighteenth century hong merchants, family alliances, joint ventures and partnerships were in common use among the hong merchants to conduct their growing trade with the West. While the details of such arrangements in the early nineteenth century remain unclear, there is no doubt that

18 Ch'en, *Insolvency*, p. 258.

19 Ch'en, *Insolvency*, pp. 160–2.

they existed. They may have been common. Whether characterized as equity or debt, or viewed as some hybrid of the two, or if the combination involved jointly held lineage property, the person or persons who advanced assets to a hong expected a financial return. To the extent such capital came from family or kinship sources, these demands weighed heavily on the affected merchants. If there was indeed no net income left after expenses, these hong merchants were in grave trouble already, for there were never going to be funds to provide a return on investment for sources of capital, let alone cash to set aside to save the business in an hour of need.

The Ch'en analysis avoids singling out particular culprits for the hong merchant insolvencies. He calculates profit on average, tallies up the various expenses of the hongs on average, and concludes that little if anything remained after expenses in the average case. This analysis is accurate as far as it goes. It is certainly in accord with the limited available evidence. The Xingtai hong merchant Yan Qixiang thus explained, after the 1836 failure of his firm, that "In 1830, I began business with a limited capital; after deducting expenses of hanging out my signboard, beginning business, and buying packing houses and furniture, not a *cash* remained to me. In that year on account of the English ladies coming up to Canton, I was confined to prison for more than a month and found myself minus a lac of dollars [$100,000]."[20] The hong opened for business with no capital, and then, as if by a snap of the fingers, its net worth was transformed into negative $100,000. So it was with the weakened hongs of the later years. For these marginal firms, any material expense could become the straw that broke the proverbial camel's back. The problem, therefore, seems to lie on the expense side of the ledger.

With but one exception, the categories of hong firm expenses Ch'en reviewed and averaged are current expenses. Business operating cost, household expenses, and even ostentatious living, were all expenses that were paid in the year in which they were incurred. Taxes assessed by government, exactions demanded from individual hongs by the Canton officials, and advances as security for future purchases of tea, were all, for the most part,[21] payments of current year charges. Payments by hong merchants as their collective responsibility for the debts of failed hongs, alone, represented the current payment of debts which had been incurred in the past. The fact that they were channeled

20 Greenberg, *British Trade*, pp. 66–7; Ch'en, *Insolvency*, p. 159.

21 Payment of substantial sums due to the Chinese government was deferred, starting in 1819, on Imperial approval, due to hong merchant inability to pay. The total arrearage owed to the state by the hong merchant body stood at 1,464,282.732 taels ($2,033,726) as of 29 April 1839. Tsiang, "Government and the Co-Hong of Canton, 1839."

through the Consoo Fund, and currently paid to foreign creditors from that source, does not alter the status of these payments as the weight of the past. Ch'en averages the total cost to the guild of collective responsibility for foreign debt at about 150,000 taels ($208,333) annually.[22] This figure understates the true guaranty burden as the guild was also forced to pay the tax debts of failed hongs to the state, much of which are unknown.[23] See Chapter Seven, Table Four (list of debt assumptions including the amounts of unpaid taxes also required to be assumed, where known). In this instance the use of an annual average becomes truly misleading, for, as is detailed in Chapters Four through Seven above, the average annual burden of collective liability for foreign debt had increased steadily during the period 1780 to 1842. The initial average foreign debt assumption burden of the years 1780 to 1799 was 81,050 taels ($112,569) annually. That average rose to 113,733 taels ($157,963) annually between 1800 and 1814 (a 40% increase), to 123,214 taels ($171,130) annually in 1815–1828 (an 8% increase), and then soared to 186,266 taels ($258,703) annually in the *derniers jours* of 1829–1842 (another 40% increase). This increase trend is shown as a bar chart in Chapter Seven, Chart One.

The dead weight burden of the old foreign debt and tax obligations of failed hongs steadily increased precisely as the overall financial health of the hong merchant body gradually declined. It may well be that thin capitalization and inadequate access to credit were ultimate causes of many hong merchant insolvencies, but it was the mounting burden of collective liability that pushed these firms over the edge. Ch'en fingers official exactions as an accelerant,[24] and rightly so, but it was the steady growth of the guaranty burden that undid the barely profitable economics of the hong merchant order. The old debts became combustible. The cash required to feed this mounting fire deprived the hong merchants of the money they needed to operate in the present and fund the future. The collective guaranty carried the debt conflagration into the surviving hongs and many of them were consumed by it in their own turn.

Chapter One introduced the Canton Guaranty System in the context of the parallel financial crises of the year 1829. In that year, a collective liability regulation that was applied locally among the hong merchant guild at Canton became the inspiration for bank guaranty fund legislation that was enacted in the State of New York. The idea had been transplanted before, within China into the regulated salt and ginseng trades, and even in the thirteenth century from China into Russia. It was then transplanted again, from New York State to

22 Ch'en, *Insolvency*, p. 147.

23 Ch'en, *Insolvency*, p. 95 ("the precise figures are rarely available").

24 Ch'en, *Insolvency*, p. 138.

Washington, D.C., where it inspired national deposit insurance in the United States, and in turn from the United States across the world as large numbers of nations followed and adapted this 'American' innovation to meet local conditions.

The remarkable journey of this legal idea conforms with the model introduced by Alan Watson in 1974 in *Legal Transplants*. Watson states that "foreign law can be influential even when it is totally misunderstood."[25] In this case, the basic Chinese rule was understood, but its record in China was totally misunderstood. The New York legislature knew nothing of the troubled history of the Canton Guaranty System. As Joshua Forman states, the structure of the Chinese system was "modified and adapted" for use in New York. In other words, he found parts of the Chinese system unsatisfactory. This also conforms with Watson's model. "[A] time of transplant is often a moment when reforms can be introduced," as happened in New York. Watson quotes Jeremy Bentham:

> I would venture to lay down the following propositions: 1st, That the English law is a great part of it of such a nature, as to be bad everywhere: 2nd, But that it would not only be, but appear worse in Bengal than in England: 3rd, That a system might be devised, which, while it would be better for Bengal, would also be better, even for England.[26]

Each stage of the reception of this venerable idea has proven to be, and has been taken as, the occasion for reform and adaptation to its new purpose. Watson also posits that "reception is possible and still easy when the receiving society is much less advanced materially and culturally."[27] New York State was a raw growing commercial power in the United States in 1829. Joshua Forman himself was a developer, and his banking reforms were motivated in large part by development concerns. It may be argued that Canton was less advanced in 1780. However that may be, the conditions that existed in the Chinese ginseng business in 1739 (less than a century after the Manchu conquest) were certainly primitive. At every stage, as Watson teaches, the adoption of a legal transplant was eased because it was shown to have come from an authoritative source.[28] In 1829, the banking reform was based on a practice that was

25 Watson, *Legal Transplants* (2d ed.), p. 99.

26 Watson, *Legal Transplants* (2d ed.), p. 35.

27 Watson, *Legal Transplants* (2d ed.), pp. 51 (importance of "the lack of a strong native law and the absence of system.") and 99.

28 Watson, *Legal Transplants* (2d ed.), pp. 88 and 99.

said to have achieved seventy years of success in imperial China and worldwide. The innovation was significant, involving the reception of an idea that sought to impose liability on a collective basis by a society that was already recognized as highly individualistic. As of 1933, it had been tested in numerous American states, and wanted only, so it was said, national implementation and a few more adjustments to operate with complete success. Since 1933, the idea of deposit insurance has been adopted in large numbers of countries, due, for the most part, to years of success enjoyed by the system in other nations. At each stage, the system was validated by its association with perceived success (or near success) in a context respected by the adopting society. At its source, collective responsibility for debt among the hong merchants of Canton was terminated in 1842, and its demise was mourned by no Chinese and by few if any foreigners. A century and a half later, a far more advanced system of risk sharing that grew out of this idea—bank deposit insurance—is thriving in transplanted and adapted form in many countries worldwide.

Three questions were posed in Chapter One about the idea that first inspired bank deposit insurance in the United States. First, was the Chinese idea of collective legal responsibility for debt accurately transmitted to the New York legislature in 1829? Second, was the actual experience of the Canton Guaranty System accurately transmitted to the New York legislature in 1829? Third, do either the Chinese idea of collective legal responsibility for debt or the experience of the Canton Guaranty System offer any lessons for contemporary bank deposit insurance? It was also asked, who won under the Canton Guaranty System, who lost, and why?

As noted above, question one is answered in the affirmative. The Chinese idea of collective legal responsibility for debt was accurately transmitted to the New York legislature. Joshua Forman provided a correct description of the basic practice of collective financial responsibility at Canton. His three sentence description is incomplete, but the missing details had no bearing on the idea that served as Forman's model. The security and tax collection duties of the hong merchants were omitted, but these components had no part in the Safety Fund Forman proposed. It is also possible, as Forman suggests, that some members of his educated audience already knew the basic structure of the Canton System.

Question two is answered in the negative. The actual experience of the Canton Guaranty System for hong merchant creditors was not accurately transmitted to the New York legislature in 1829. It was certainly the view of some foreign creditors, in 1829, that the Canton Guaranty System was then a success—that it had stood the test of experience for many years, and that under it "the bond [i.e., promise to pay] of a Hong merchant has acquired a credit over the whole world, not exceeded by that of any other security." Forman's bright view of the Canton Guaranty System contained two errors, one technical, the second profound. First, the Chinese system was not even fifty years old, as opposed to the seventy year pedigree Forman gave it.[29] Second and more fundamentally, Forman failed to report the terrible financial condition of the hong merchants to the New York legislature in 1829. It is likely that he did not know of the crisis of that year, and newspaper evidence indicates that this news did not reach the general American public. There was some newspaper coverage of hong failures, and of payments of hong debts under the collective guaranty, but only a *creditor's* lesson was drawn from this news. The other hong merchants were paying old debts under the guaranty, and, by inference, all was well on the Canton waterfront. Joshua Forman was unaware of the degree to which the Canton Guaranty System contributed to the hong firm failures. This is an excusable oversight. Information on hong merchant finances was closely guarded in his time. The understanding we now have of the negative effects of the collective guaranty of debts is the fruit of modern scholarship, using source material which was largely confidential when these events occurred.

The third question is answered in the affirmative. Many of the tribulations experienced under the Canton Guaranty System are immediately familiar today. While the parallels to present day regulatory experience are imperfect, they can be telling:

> (A) At Canton, the state-enforced collective guaranty system failed to anticipate, reserve for, or tax adequately to cover the foreign debt default risk that it was supposed to cover. For its part, modern bank deposit insurance has been criticized since its inception as not representing "true" insurance at all. This charge is based both on the fact that premiums are not assessed in actuarial relation to the risks involved and because collected premiums have proven inadequate to cover losses incurred.

> (B) At Canton, a reserve fund—the Consoo Fund—was created but it was soon depleted and was then regularly drawn on by government for other purposes with the result that funds were not available to cover losses when hong failures occurred. While modern bank deposit insurance has not, to date, accumulated reserve balances in amounts large

29 Comprehensive regulations of the Canton trade were introduced in 1760, but collective responsibility for debt among the hong merchants only began in 1780.

enough to attract the notice of government, these funds have often been depleted by losses, as in the Savings and Loan crisis in the United States, with the result that governments have had to advance additional monies to prevent deposit insurance funds themselves becoming insolvent.

(C) In China, as discussed in Chapter Three above, strict protective laws were enacted in order to prevent loan losses that would have to be paid from the Consoo Fund under the collective guaranty. It was illegal for foreigners to make and for hong merchants to accept foreign loans. These protective laws were not enforced. Today, it is a popular if controversial view that many insured bank losses have resulted from illegal conduct. Prosecutions for violations of law that led to losses suffered in the financial crisis of 2007–8, for example, have been few.

(D) At Canton, as analyzed in Chapter Three above, systemic disincentives existed which discouraged official enforcement of the existing protective laws. In modern times, disincentives to the enforcement of protective laws are more subtle, as in the existence of the "revolving door," whereby key persons are influenced by the prospect of subsequent employment by financial institutions, consulting firms, or even governments.

(E) Two centuries ago, as reviewed in Chapters Four through Seven above, foreign lenders made risky and imprudent loans to Chinese hong merchants, confident that the collective guaranty would protect them from the consequences. For their part, hong debtors repeatedly took desperate risks in the vain hope of returning to profitability. Today, such conduct may be recognized as examples of "moral hazard," i.e., excessive risks taken when insurance coverage shields parties from the economic consequences of their actions.[30] Contemporary examples of moral hazard include the imprudent behavior of some weak banks, which have attracted deposits by offering abnormally high interest rates or have made high interest rate loans to dubious borrowers, and also the laxity of bank customers when their deposits are fully insured.

---

30 "In the insurance literature where the term has its roots, moral hazard is defined as a situation where the provision of insurance increases the probability of the event being insured against, due to diminished incentives for the insured party to take preventive actions." Jun Il Kim, "Unconditional IMF Financial Support and Investor Moral Hazard," IMF [International Monetary Fund] Working Paper No. WP/07/104 (May 2007), p. 3.

(F) At Canton, when losses loomed, attempts were made to dodge the guaranty system. Such evasions, as in the Gnewqua II and Ponqua receivership of 1810, invariably ended badly. The Canton Guaranty System ended up bearing heavier losses accrued through the time of exposure. Some critics see attempts to evade bank capital requirements and national guaranty schemes in certain of the increasingly complex structures used in modern international banking. If that is true, such evasions ended badly in the financial crisis of 2007–8.

(G) Furthermore, something in the nature of a "too big to fail" policy was observed at Canton during the period 1780 to 1842. Its objective, as under the modern doctrine, was the protection of key firms whose continued operation was believed to be vital to the economy and to society. The Qing government, however, did not bail out firms that it believed were vital to the economy. To the contrary, "too big to fail" status (the modern term was not used) protected fortunate key hongs from excessive exactions by government (*kejuan zashui*). The existence of a well recognized limit on how much money the state or its officials could extract from the hongs is evidenced, for example, by the deferral from 1819 through 1839 on imperial approval of large amounts of taxes that were due to Beijing from the hong merchants. The government could easily have demanded payment of these taxes in full from the senior hong firms, but it avoided doing so out of concern that they would fail, and that the entire Canton System would fail along with them.

In sum, a number of parallels exist between the experiences of the Canton Guaranty System and those of the modern bank deposit insurance programs.

The context is certainly very different between the foreign trade that was conducted at Canton in the eighteenth and nineteenth centuries and that of the operations of insured banks in the present day. Nonetheless, some problems experienced under the Canton Guaranty System anticipate, to a remarkable degree, problems of bank deposit insurance systems today. While the Canton system experienced heavy losses, and those losses are instructive, at least two factors that restrained risk taking in the 1700s and 1800s are largely absent today. First, debts under the Canton Guaranty System were incurred and were largely paid in the form of silver coin. Currency was valuable metal, not printed paper founded on public credit and subject to added production in accordance with state needs. Hard currency could not be easily multiplied. Second, with the exception of the British East India Company, none of the parties who were involved in transactions covered by the Canton Guaranty System were limited liability entities. Almost all of the parties involved were individuals or partnerships subject to unlimited personal risk. Unlimited exposure operated as a restraint on risk taking. In the modern era, transactions that are covered by bank deposit insurance are often made among entities organized as one of any number of types of limited liability entities, often organized under the law of remote foreign jurisdictions. These barriers, which further separate the parties taking economic risk from the consequences of such risk, are seen as encouraging risk taking by financial institutions. The Canton Guaranty System operated in a radically different environment.[31]

Despite all of these differences, the historical record of the Canton experience offers valuable lessons to the modern world. These include: (1) that the tax that supports a deposit insurance fund must be based on an assessment of the risk of loss that the fund has undertaken to pay; (2) that the fund and its insureds must be subject to strong independent supervision; (3) that laws enacted to avoid risk contingencies must be enforced, with care taken to avoid any disincentives to enforcement of those laws; and (4) that both corruption and the diversion of premium revenues intended for the fund must be strictly prohibited. None of these controls were observed at Canton between 1780 and 1842. Perhaps most important, (5) bank deposit insurance funds must avoid the unlimited commitment to pay losses that was made under the Canton system. Unlimited coverage impaired the economic incentives for insureds to protect themselves. The mounting burden of unlimited liability for losses brought the Canton Guaranty System and those exposed under it to the point of ruin.

With respect to the last question posed at the outset of this study, it is easiest to identify losers. The hong merchants lost, weakest to strongest, from bottom to the top. The weight of old debt, undischarged and demanding full payment, was rolled forward by the guaranty and contributed to the failure of many surviving hongs. There can be no doubt that various factors, such as official exactions, contributed to the large number of hong merchant insolvencies, but the ever increasing burden of collective liability for debt stands out as a leading cause of failure. It is difficult to conceive even of the "too big to fail" hongs as winners, for at the end they were tapped to pay hong debts and other obligations after the Opium War. The details of how these funds were raised are unclear, but it is doubtful for example that the $3 million that was paid to the British on 23 July 1843 had been held by the hong merchants as ready cash

31 See James Grant, "Requiem for the Dollar," Wall Street Journal, 5 December 2009 (discussing both of the factors discussed at the end of this paragraph), see: "http://online.wsj.com/article/SB10001424052748704342404574575761660481996.html" (accessed 26 March 2014).

at that time. The asset liquidations that were necessary to raise these funds must have been painful even for the "successful" firm that was forced to raise cash at this difficult moment.

It might be said that foreign creditor firms, the guarantee beneficiaries, were the clear winners under the Canton Guaranty System. With respect to the imprudent creditors, that is certainly the case. Some foreign creditors courted enormous losses and were spared from ruin by the collective guaranty. It seems remarkable enough that William Jardine exposed over $2 million of assets of his own firm and its constituents in credit extended to the frail young Xingtai Hong. Yet more remarkable is the note of calm with which Jardine assured his London partner that this enormous sum would be paid under the collective guaranty.[32] Jardine was absolutely right, and his claims were paid in full. As for the other foreign firms at Canton, including those firms which were more prudent extending credit, the answer whether they were "winners" is less clear. The British EIC had understood, from the dawn of the Canton Guaranty System, that a guaranty is never free. To the extent that creditor claims would be paid, payment necessarily came out of the trade, driving up costs, potentially narrowing profits, and increasing the ultimate cost to consumers in the West. Furthermore, capital that might have been profitably used elsewhere was locked up during the time period over which hong debts were repaid, without interest. These were not reasons to fail to take advantage of the system when it existed, to file and to demand full payment of claims, but they narrowed the creditor's advantage at the end of the day.

In the 1930s, banker opponents feared that the adoption of deposit insurance in the United States would result in the entire banking industry being dragged down by careless practices. Shortly after the National Banking Act of 1933 became law, Professor Edwin W. Kemmerer of Princeton University warned of its consequences. In the new era,

> The bank with the loose credit policy gets the business and the bank with the careful, cautious credit policy loses it. The slack banker dances and the conservative banker pays the fiddler. If the conservative banker protests, the slack one invites him to go to a warmer climate. Soon all are dancing and the fiddler, if paid at all, must collect from the depositors or from the taxpayers.[33]

32 Greenberg, *British Trade*, p. 70.

33 Flood, "Great Deposit Insurance Debate," p. 60.

Kemmerer's words were prescient in substance and in metaphor. The professor anticipated a now infamous statement by an American banker, made as the crisis of 2007–2008 set in. Citigroup was going to stay in the market for United States subprime loans. It intended to dance on. Chuck Prince, chief executive of Citigroup, stated in July 2007 that "When the music stops, in terms of liquidity, things will be complicated. But as long as the music is playing, you've got to get up and dance. We're still dancing."[34]

The quotation from Kemmerer also provides a fitting epitaph for the hong merchants under the Canton Guaranty System. They failed in droves. Collective responsibility cast the debts of failed merchants onto survivors, many of whom failed in turn. The end of the China monopoly of the British EIC triggered a crisis of confidence in 1834, with foreign and domestic creditors wondering alike how the fiddler could ever be paid. Foreign eyes turned to the Chinese government, which had enforced the system of collective guaranty since 1780, to pay the massive sum the Consoo Fund and the hong merchants seemed unable to pay as implicit state guarantor. The Opium War followed soon thereafter, an awful echo of the British gunboat diplomacy that caused the Canton Guaranty System to be adopted in 1780, resulting in payment in full of all outstanding hong debts in July 1843. The metaphorical fiddler was paid by the Chinese state, which drew heavily from one firm that had been considered, until this point, as too big to fail.

Loss can be painful, as can be the recognition of loss. An unlimited guaranty can be painful as well, and its ramifications potentially disastrous. An unlimited guaranty delays or prevents the recognition of loss. More fundamentally, it delays or prevents the education—the market discipline—that should follow from every instance of loss. Where undischarged, debt accrues interest and grows. Where an unlimited guaranty exists, that ever increasing burden is shifted to the guarantor. President Franklin Roosevelt expressed concern in 1932, at the dawn of bank deposit insurance, that the unlimited guaranty of bank deposits might prove "an impossible drain" on the national treasury. In the too big to fail era, unlimited guarantees of debt threaten to drag down banks, guaranty funds, and even national treasuries, the prudent with the imprudent. Professor Kemmerer saw the fiddler being paid, "if paid at all," ultimately by depositors or taxpayers. This has begun to occur. If private parties

34 Michiyo Nakamoto and David Wighton, "Citigroup chief stays bullish on buy-outs," Financial Times, 9 July 2007, see: "http://www.ft.com/intl/cms/s/0/80e2987a-2e50-11dc-821c-0000779fd2ac.html#axzz278Oae11X" (accessed 26 March 2014) (registration required).

are not made to bear some material part of the burden of losses arising from their own insured transactions, then this process will continue. It is right to be concerned that at some future point, as unrecognized losses continue to be passed through to governments and taxpayers under state commitments of unlimited guaranty, that this burden will test mathematical possibility.

Appendices

Appendix 1

The Original Five Regulations (1760)

Modern Translation, Full text of the New Regulations Made to Control Foreign Merchants," dated 29 January 1760, as translated by Lo- shu Fu, *A Documentary Chronicle of Sino-Western Relations (1644–1820)* (Tucson: Univ. of Arizona Press, 1966), pp. 224–6, quoted with permission of the Association for Asian Studies, Inc., see: www.asian-studies.org:

> The ministers of the grand council deliberated and reported: "The Viceroy of Liang-Kwang, Li Shih-yao, in a memorial suggested regulations to control and restrain the foreign barbarians as follows:
>
> "(1) The barbarian merchants should be prohibited from passing the winter in the provincial capital: On investigation, the viceroy found that originally foreign trade had been limited to a fixed period, namely, from the time that the foreign ships put into port until their subsequent departure. Foreigners were not allowed to remain secretly in the Interior. Recently, the fact that in some cases hong merchants owed them money which they did not pay gave the barbarians a pretext for remaining in the provincial capital. Inevitably there would arise intrigues between the foreign and the Chinese merchants which might lead to trouble. Consequently the viceroy now petitioned that in the future after the foreign merchants sell out their goods and collect their money, they should return to their own country according to our time limit. Even if they have not liquidated their debts with our hong merchants, they ought to live in Macao temporarily. They should hand their goods over to the hong merchants as their agents to sell the goods. The following year they can collect their money and return to their own country.
>
> "This legislation is intended to prevent the barbarians from living in the Interior. We should approve what the viceroy has petitioned, but we are afraid that when the corrupt hong merchants hear that the foreign merchants cannot stay long in the Interior they will purposely delay the sale of their goods. If such a thing happens and an accusation is made, the local magistrates must punish the treacherous hong merchants according to law. They should not be spared!
>
> "(2) When the foreigners arrive in Kwangtung they must reside in the factories of the hong merchants and be under their control and supervision: On investigation the viceroy found that when the barbarian merchants came to Kwangtung and lived in the factories of the hong

 | DOI 10.1163/9789004276567_012

[*start Documentary Chronicle page 225*]

merchants, they were not allowed to come and go as freely as they pleased. If they are not ordered to live in the factories of the hong merchants who had been officially registered, we shall have difficulty in knowing whether they engage in intrigue and when they come and go. Again, if their business is not managed by the hong merchants, there will be more abuses.

"This regulation should also be approved as the viceroy has petitioned. Hereafter we order foreign merchants to reside at the factories of the hong merchants who are under our strict jurisdiction. If their rooms and houses are not large enough to house the foreigners, then we should order that the hong merchants rent houses and send men to take care of them. We do not allow traitors to enter and depart at will, to trade privately with them. However, the hong merchants should not exploit them by raising their rent as they see fit, now that we have the situation really under control. We order the local magistrates to watch carefully and sternly prohibit such abuse.

"(3) We should forbid Chinese merchants from borrowing capital from the foreign barbarians and we should forbid the foreigners from hiring Chinese as their servants: On investigation, the viceroy found that the barbarian merchants who always came to Kwangtung are allowed to sell out the goods they bring and purchase other goods to take back to their own countries. No contraband should be secretly exported. Recently, the hong merchants and people of the Interior borrowed money mostly from the barbarians in order to do their business and to share their profits.

"We should approve what the viceroy has petitioned and order the hong merchants who had borrowed foreign money to report the truth. We should set a time limit within which they should be required to pay off their debts. Then they will be no longer subject to further investigation. Hereafter, if anyone violates the prohibition and borrows money from the foreigners and engages in intrigue with them, he should be punished according to the law by which we punish criminals who communicate with a foreign country, borrow money or hold their goods or money without payment. The money which they borrow should be confiscated by the government.

"Originally the foreigners brought their own boys to serve them because they were not allowed to hire people of the Interior. Hereafter, if any shameless Chinese (with the exception of interpreters and agents) are so greedy for money that they are willing to be hired, they should strictly be prohibited from this practice by the local magistrates. If the local magistrates let them enjoy indulgences, then they, too, should be punished.

"(4) We should strictly prohibit the old abuse, namely, the hiring of our people by foreign merchants to transmit their news and letters: On investigation, the viceroy found that the barbarians coming from afar and

[*start Documentary Chronicle page 226*]

going to the hongs to trade, should not be allowed, under the pretext of gathering news, to hire coolies for the transmission of news, and thus communicate with the treacherous merchants of the Interior.

"We should approve what the said viceroy has petitioned and order the hong merchants and coolies to show everything they carry for the foreigners to the local magistrates for their scrutiny and investigation. If any disobey this order, we should forthwith punish the men who, acting on behalf of the foreigners, look for and hire the coolies. We should also punish the men who transmit letters for the foreigners.

"When the Westerners living in Macao have official business and desire to send a letter to the Imperial Board of Astronomy, the foreign chief should petition our maritime sub-prefect to forward it to the viceroy and respectively communicate with the Board of Astronomy and the throne. This regulation should also be approved as the viceroy has petitioned.

"(5) We should consider detaching officers from other garrisons to send them to the places where foreign ships anchor in order to examine and control their ships: On investigation the viceroy found that whenever the foreign ships anchor, unfortunate incidents occur because they bring in their crews, men of cruel and violent character. Moreover, traitors and the tankas may secretly win over these men to their plots.

"The said viceroy reported that at Kwangtung we used to have one garrison regiment of one officer and twelve soldiers to maintain order, but that was not enough. We should allow the said viceroy to select a candidate of the rank of major under command of the viceroy's brigade to be specially stationed there to supervise the officers of the guard houses both for defense and for patrol."

The Emperor approved this memorial.

Appendix 2

The Original Five Regulations (1760)

Contemporary Translation, Full text of the "Regulations for the Control of Trade at Canton, 1760," as set out in Hosea Ballou Morse, *The Chronicles of the East India Company Trading to China 1635–1834* (Oxford: Clarendon Press, 1929), Vol. V, pp. 94–98 (Appendix AK):

The merchants seperately received a Chop from the Tsongtou which is said to be published by the Emperors Order in Consequence of the Representation under Him by the above mentioned Magistrate.

The following is a Translation of the Chop wch. came from Court.

FOU Minister of State and Accounts presents this Memorial in obedience to your Majestys Orders given to the Council called Kiunki, to deliberate on the Memorial of Ly Tsongtou of the Provinces of Canton and Quangsi who proposes some regulations regarding Foreigners.

1st. He represents the Residence of Foreigners at Canton in the Absence of the Ships, and demands that it may be forbid. He says the Foreigners commonly arrive in the Fifth and Sixth Month, and return about the Ninth or Tenth Month. If any of them are under the necessity of staying on their affairs, the Custom formerly was that they should go to Macao, Now many of them under the pretence of their Affairs not being finished live secretly at the Capital, and it is difficult to avoid bad consequences happening from it, which may be the occasion of much trouble. He demands that after they have loaded their Ships, they may be ordered to return home at the usual time, and if there be any who have not settled their Affairs with the Hongists, that they are obliged to go [to] Macao, and that their unsold goods be left with the Hongist to sell for them in their Absence, that in the following Monsoon they may return to their respective Kingdoms &c.

There is then a fixed certain time for the European Vessells to come and return. The Custom is that none should remain secretly in the Interior parts of this Kingdom. At present because the Merchants have not paid their Debts, and that they have not finished their affairs with them, the Foreign Merchants make this pretence to live at the [provincial] Capital, endeavor to know the prices of Goods, and to buy them at Cheap rates to make a Profit on them. The People of the Country intrigue with them and are guilty of base Tricks. At present the

 | DOI 10.1163/9789004276567_013

Tsontou demands, that after the Foreign Merchants have finished their affairs, they return to their respective Ships. That they should have no pretence to remain in the Interior parts of the Country,

[*start Chronicles page 95*]

To have comers & goers occasions irregularities and disorders, wch are against the good Rules and Orders of the Country. The Merchants or Hongists must settle all their accounts justly by the time of the departure of the Ships, and punctually pay what they are indebted, If any Merchandize or Goods are unsold, the Merchants must among them bring affairs to a Conclusion, and must not prolong their Debts from Year to Year. Both parties must act with Sincerity and fidelity, and not occasion losses, and oblige the Mandarines to assert their Authority. The Foreign Merchants should return at their usual time, They deliver their Goods to the Hongists to sell for them, If there be any who abuse the Credit given them, and are Guilty of Rogueries, and it should come to the Knowledge of the Mandarines, they shall be severely Judged according to the laws of the Country, and punished without any Grace.

If the Foreigners should not have finished their Affairs, and they will in the mean time live at Macao, They will in this case do as they Judge convenient to themselves, it is not necessary to oblige them to return to Europe, by which they must suffer great difficulties & Losses.

2nd. He represents the necessity of Ordering the Hongists to watch the Foreigners who live in their Hongs with the Strictest Attention. The Custom is for Foreigners on their arrival to take apartments in the Hongs. At present there are Vagabonds who build Handsome houses to allure Strangers for which they receive great Rents, who let them do many bad things, who come and go, occasion trouble, carry on illicit trade, defraud the Customs, and commit several such like disorders. Hereafter none but the approved Hongists must be permitted to lodge, and trade with the Europeans. If the Foreign Merchants commit disorders, and Violate the Laws, and the lower Mandarines do not prevent it they shall be broke, and rendered incapable of Serving &c. The Hongist must carefully watch, and keep in order, the Foreign Merchants who live in their Hongs. If the appointed Hongists, and the Linguists are in Collusion with them to commit Villanies, The Tsontou demands that hereafter the Guilty should be punished, That they will not be allowed to dispose of the houses at their pleasure, that all abuses be suppressed, and that the Foreign Merchants should not suffer Losses.

3rd. He represents, concerning the money lent by Foreigners, and the Chinese who are in their Service, And he demands that these abuses be forbid. At present numbers of Foreigners lend their Money that remains unemployed in trade, to the Merchants

[*start Chronicles page 96*]

of this Country, who go into other Provinces to trade, they make Contracts with them, and make use of them for sundry purposes. If the people of this Country do hereafter on any pretence whatsoever take up money of Foreigners, he requires that they should be severely punished. Foreign Merchants are allowed only to sell their Merchandizes they bring with them. And to purchase what they have occasion to carry away, any other Trade has been long since prohibited, they are not permitted to send their Goods into other Provinces for their Accounts, At present there are many Peoples of the Country who trade with the Europeans Capital. It is by such like Intrigues that Lieou- Ya-Pien has occasioned so much trouble. And this prohibition is of great Consequence to the Country. He demands that the Hongists be obliged to finish all their Accounts, and affairs, before the return of the Ships; If they act contrary to such Orders, if they don't settle their Accounts, and if they are guilty of any Rogueries, that they be severely punished, and that all the Goods also of those who borrow money be Confiscated.

Foreigners also bring with them Servants sufficient for their use, formerly they could only take few of the people of this Country into their Service. Hereafter none but the established Linguists and Compradores are allowed of, and if any others presume to enter into the Service of the Europeans, the Inferior Mandarines must be acquainted with it, That it be ordered the Linguists take care this Prohibition be strictly observed, and if there be any who Act contrary to it they shall be strictly punished.

4th. He represents that the Foreigners hire people to carry Lettrs into the Country, and demands that this Abuse be totally forbid. There are many Foreigners who to carry on their trade send Peoples into the Province of Nankin, Chet-kiang and others, and even hire Post Horses to inform themselves of the price of Goods, as Hong- shing-y did when the Mandarines sent expresses to Seize the Criminals, the said Criminals received Intelligence before the arrival of the Orders by which means they Evaded them and fled from Justice, Lieou-Song-Ling of the Tribunal of Mathamaticks has twice given Intelligence that Que-Gan, Kouening, Fang-Cheou-Y and others desired to be called to Court to be employed in the service of the Emperor, and that it was by Lettrs he received from Macao, which gave him information thereof. These Lettrs were brought by Chinese and this is what must for ever be forbid &c. Foreigners take Hongs to trade in but under pretence of informing themselves of the price of Goods, they must not hire people to carry Lettrs

[*start Chronicles page 97*]

or otherwise have such Connections with the Country People; this is an Abuse that must be entirely Abolished. The Tsongtou requires that the said Lettr carriers be severely punished, that if it is necessary to communicate any affairs, the Report be made to the Mandarines, in Order for them to judge what is requisite to be done. If after these Orders there be any who undertake to carry Letters, that those who are employed in these affairs and the Letter Carriers be severely punished. As to the Foreigners of Macao, if they have any affairs, for the Service of the Emperor, to communicate to the Tribunal of Mathematicks, the Procurator must give information to the Mandarine called Hany-Fang-Tong-Tchy [the Kunming Fu] who will make his report to the Tsongtou, and he will accordingly as he may think proper send the necessary advices to Court, He demands that it should be the Tsongtou to treat on these affairs.

5th. He represents that some Mandarines of War should be stationed to watch and keep the Foreign Ships in Order. The Foreign Ships enter into the River and anchor at the place called Whampo, each Ship Crew consists of 100 to 200 Men. The Custom has hitherto been for a Mandarine of the Corps called Hie-Piao to be there with Soldiers to keep a good watch and prevent Disorders. But this force is not sufficient, He therefore demands that a Reinforcement of a Mandarine called Cheou-Pei [Shou-pei] be added, that every thing be well looked after, and for the support of the said Augmentation, that Eight Tales per Month be taken out of the Receipt of the Customs. That the Body of Guards in the Neighbourhood to appoint a Vessell with Soldiers to pass backwards and forwards, and that they keep a strict look out, which is to be continued until the departure of the Ships. The Foreign Ships have a great number of People, many of them are of a wild brutish Nature, and may easily occasion trouble, The Villainous Boat Men connect themselves wth them, wch occasions continual disturbances. The Tsontou desires besides the Mandarines who according to the antient Custom are on Duty, another be appointed with the Command of 100 or 200 Men, which will with difficulty be sufficient to keep the Foreigners in Order. There must then be another Mandarine called Cheou-Pei of the Corps call Tou-Piao who must always be on Guard, prevent Disorders, and from time to time give all necessary Intelligence for the Expence and Charges of those on Duty according to the

Ancient Custom Eight Tales per Month is allowed. To defray the Expense of this Reinforcement Eight Tales must also be allowed, and the whole force must be on Duty until the Departure of the

[*start Chronicles page 98*]

Ships, and if they do not diligently do their Duty, the Superior Mandarines must break the Inferior Ones.

We have examined and deliberated on all of Above mentioned Articles, and judge it necessary they be complied with, for which purpose we present this Memorial to your Majesty, Humbly imploring your most gracious Light, and through your profound Penetration to receive your Instructions, that your Orders may be communicated to the Tribunal, to be by them transmitted to the Tsongtou, that he may conform thereto, and Effectually see them observed.

The Emperors answer was, that it be done according to their Request.

Appendix 3
The Eight Regulations (1831)

Contemporary Translation, Full text of the "Eight Restrictions on Foreigners," as set out in Hosea Ballou Morse, *The Chronicles of the East India Company Trading to China 1635–1834* (Oxford: Clarendon Press, 1929), Vol. IV, pp. 293–301 (Appendix AB) (footnotes in the original, have been renumbered):

Order from the Governor [Viceroy], communicated by the Namhaeheen on the subject of Eight Restrictions on Foreigners. Dated 12th, received 20th May, 1831.

Puan, the Namhaeheen, etc. hereby issues an order to the Hong Merchants with which they are required to make themselves fully acquainted. A Communication has now been received from the Kwangchowfoo, which being opened is as follows:

'On the 19th day of the 2d Moon of the 11th Year of Taoukwang (March 9, 1831) a communication was received from Kwae the Poochingsze, stating that on the 9th day of the 2d moon of the 11th year of Taoukwang (February 27) he had received the following communication from Le the Cabinet Minister and Governor.

'It appears that on the 6th day of the 2d moon of the 11th year of Taoukwang (Feby 24th) I, the Governor, united with Choo, the Fooyuen and Chung the Hoppo, in sending a respectful Memorial to the Emperor, explaining old regulations, intended to guard against outside barbarians, and deciding on the circumstances that required modification by addition or diminution. Besides waiting til the Vermillion Pencil's reply be received, when it shall respectfully be recorded and communicated, I also take the original of the memorial to his Majesty and communicate it forthwith. When sent to the Sze, let him pass it to the Foo, to deliver to the Hien, that he may make it known to the local civil and military officers, and may also order the Hong Merchants to act in obedience to it. Oppose not.' Accompanying is a Copy of the original Memorial.

I, the Namhaeheen, having received this forthwith issue a copy of it, for obedience thereto. When it reaches the said Merchants, let them immediately obey, and act according to the tenor thereof. Oppose not. A special order—

Annexed is a copy of the original Memorial.

© KONINKLIJKE BRILL NV, LEIDEN, 2014 | DOI 10.1163/9789004276567_014

Dated Taoukwang 11th Year 4th moon 1st day.

May 12th 1831.

Regulations to guard against foreigners proposed to the Emperor by Governor Le, Deputy Governor Choo and Hoppo Chung, in Council. February 24th 1831, Communicated to foreigners by

[*start Chronicles page 294*]

an order of Government dated May 12th. Received at Macao May 20th.

A memorial to explain old regulations intended to guard against outside barbarians, and also certain deliberations to modify them by additions and diminutions, that the same may be obeyed and kept. Looking up we pray for the sacred glance at the business.

Canton Provincial City being near the Coast and the place where foreign ships go and come, it is extremely fitting that the guard against them and watch over them should be perfectly complete and close.

During the reign of Kienlung the English foreign merchants having violated the prohibitions of the Celestial Empire, the then Governor Le-she-yaou[1] proposed to the Emperor and had enacted five regulations to guard against outside barbarians which were available to keep them under control: **but through length of days they have gradually been neglected and the execution of them relaxed.**

In the 9th year of Taoukwang the English foreign merchants having long deferred entering the Port because they solicited a diminution of the Port charges and again last year having secretly taken foreign women to live in the Factories, and by stealth conveyed them to Canton, which things were reported to the Emperor at the time, although the said foreigners repented and did not end as they had begun with perverted opposition; still the disposition of Barbarians being deceitful and crafty, it is absolutely necessary to carry into effect with severity the inhibitory orders and to strengthen the guards against them.

1 Tradition says that this Governor had a share in Puankhequa's house.

But as to the old regulations that were enacted, **present and former circumstances are different; and there are some points which require consideration and modification to suit the times**, and then the whole may be obeyed and kept.

We, calling to our aid the Treasurer and Judge with the old regulations [and] deliberated on the modifications which the times require—and have charged the civil and Military Officers; the soldiers and police to exert themselves in keeping up a constant patrol and guard. And have required the Hong Merchants and Linguists to be faithful in examining and searching into what is going on. Thus when strictness inside has become a habit—or established customs inside are enforced with strictness—disturbances fro outside barbarians will be eradicated: and, seemingly the principles of a good Charioteer in restraining and soothing his horse will be more thoroughly carried into effect.

Having reverently associated with us the Hoppo Chung, we unitedly present with profound respect this Memorial, and send

[*start Chronicles page 295*]

a fair Copy of the Eight regulations which have been deliberated on for the Emperor's inspection—prostrate praying for His Majesty's Sacred perusal and instructions.

A Copy of the original regulations to guard against foreigners, together with the alterations which have now been made and arranged under eight topics is hereby reverently presented for His Majesty's perusal.

1st. Foreign Merchants must not remain over the Winter at Canton. This is an old regulation that should be modified to keeping up at all times a guard against them.

When this regulation was originally framed the foreign Ships came to Canton and anchored during the 5th and 6th moons; during the 9th or 10th they returned to their respective Countries, they were not allowed to remain in Canton City to find out the price of goods; to make purchases and acquire profit; and to go backwards and forwards having intercourse with Native Chinese, which originated traitorous connexions. If the goods in their Hongs were not all sold, and they wished for the time being to live at Macao they were permitted to suit their convenience.

On searching it is found that in the time of Kienlung the foreign vessels which came to Canton did not exceed 30 or 40, but now they amount to 70 or 80, or even 100.

Of late years the English Company's Barbarian Ships have arrived in succession during the 7th or 8th moons, and having exchanged their Cargoes, have left the Port in the 12th moon, or onward to the 1st and 2nd moons of the ensuing Year.

The said Nation's Company's Chief and foreign merchants, after the Company's ships were gone and affairs completed requested permits to go to Macao and reside there, till the 7th or 8th moons when the said Nation's merchant ships came to Canton Province and then they requested permits to go up to Canton City to superintend the Commerce.

Exclusive of these, there are the several Nations of India and America whose foreign ships come to Canton. Their trade is coming and going at uncertain intervals, by no means like the English Company's. Of these under one Man's name there may be one or two ships in a Year that come to Canton; or three or four ships, or an individual may have no ship at all, but only goods consigned to him to sell in some other ship. These foreign Merchants all remain at Canton to manage their affairs. As the foreign ships are now double what they were formerly, and the time of their anchoring is uncertain—beside, as they have remained at Canton, transacting their Commercial Affairs, for many years with mutual tranquility, it is doubtless unnecessary

[*start Chronicles page 296*]

to restrict them positively to the 9th or 10th moon to return to their own country.

Hereafter if foreign Merchants do indeed arrive early at Canton City and all their goods be sold, then according to the old regulations, let them reverse their oar at the appointed time, but if they arrive late on the 8th or 9th moons, and require time to sell their goods, let the Hong Merchants be charged to keep a strict oversight and control over the Foreign Merchants residing in Canton. At the same time dealing justly to make haste to pay the price of things; **not being allowed to contract debts** and persist in delaying.

Let the foreign Merchants of all Nations when their goods are sold and business finished—whatever the time may be go home with their Ships or go down to Macao and reside there; they must not intentionally delay their departure. By this modification, foreigners will all be prevented from lingering long in Canton, and traitorous Natives will rarely have a pretext for forming illegal connexions.

2nd. Borrowing foreign Merchants money—it is right to eradicate the evil of contracting debts.

When the regulations were originally established native merchants violated prohibitions by borrowing money of foreign Merchants, and strung on, being led by hooked connexions. **At that time their offences were punished according to the law for 'Forming connexions with foreign nations and borrowing money to defraud.' The money borrowed was prosecuted for and confiscated.**

This old law against Hong Merchants' borrowing money of foreign Merchants was long strictly acted on. But the Hong Merchants when foreign Merchants left the port, **eventually made a vague statement (whether they were indebted for balances or not) that affairs were concluded. These are unworthy of credit and the gloss should be done away with.**

Hereafter beside prosecuting and punishing according to law the Hong Merchants who borrow money of foreigners and string on and are led by hooked connexions with them—the foreign Merchants who trade with Hong Merchants must be made every year, when their affairs are concluded, **to give in to the Hoppo, a voluntary written declaration, for his examination, whether there be any outstanding claims or not**. Then should the Hong Merchant fail, the foreign claims which have been previously reported will be paid by instalments, those that have not been reported, even if prosecuted for, will not receive any attention from Government.

And it must be ordered that all balances due by Hong Merchants **must be paid within three months.** Procrastination will

[*start Chronicles page 297*]

not be permitted and when they are paid the foreign Merchant's receipt must be presented to Government and preserved on record. **If payment be not made within the limited period, it is allowed to the foreign merchant to prosecute.** If he does not choose to prosecute he may do as he pleases; but if he prosecute after the period has expired, Government will pay no attention to his claims. This is to eradicate the trick of old and new claims being made to radiate upon each other.

3rd. The original interdict was to prevent foreign Merchants having Natives to serve them. This requires a little modification. The original regulations ran thus. That foreign Merchants living in the factories were strictly interdicted from employing any other Natives than Linguists and Compradores.

It is found by research that of the Natives who have been given to foreigners to serve, there had heretofore been a class denominated Shawan[2] (quasi dicat Sand Literate) these have long been interdicted and it is right, still to act according to the old prohibitions, and severely interdict them. But recently the foreign Merchants of various Nations who have come hither have much increased. They continually require people to look after their goods; to watch their gates; to carry water and to carry goods, and the black demon Slaves which the foreign Merchants bring are by nature very stupid and fierce; if they (the foreign Merchants) be compelled to use entirely black demon slaves, it is really apprehended that there will be such a large collection of them, that in going out and in they will wrangle with the natives, and the arrangement turn out to be the creation of disturbance.

It is right to request that hereafter the people necessary in the foreign factories, for taking care of Cargo, keeping the gate, carrying water, and carrying goods be hired by the Compradore from among Natives, and he shall report their names and surnames to the Hong Merchants, who, with the said Factory's Compradore, shall be made responsible for searching into what they do and controlling them.

Should any of these people instruct and seduce the foreign Merchants to act traitorously, let the Hong Merchants and Compradore report them to Government and request that they might be prosecuted.

4th. After the foreign Merchants enter the port and anchor, let there be at that place as heretofore Military Officers and soldiers appointed to search and examine. In the Hong Merchants factories where foreigners live—let them be under the restraint and control of the Hong Merchant, to prevent disturbances.

The regulations originally enacted were, that when the foreign

[*start Chronicles page 298*]

2 Shawan is the Chinese mode of pronouncing the English word 'servant.'

ship had entered the Port and anchored at Whampoa, Military Officer and twelve soldiers should be sent from the Kwangheep; these were to construct a mat shed and keep guard. A Military Officer was also to be selected sent from the Suhpeaou, to search and examine—And from the adjacent Military Station a row boat was to be sent, to unite with another boat sent from the left wing of the middle division in searching and examining. After the Ship left the Port they were to be recalled. In these arrangements there is no occasion to make any change. But from length of days these orders are considered mere form. It is right to make continually a secret search, and if the Military become remiss and steal repose, to punish them severely forthwith.

As to foreign Merchants lodging in Hong Merchants factories, it has heretofore been the duty of Hong Merchants to govern and control them. **The purchases of goods made by them must pass through the hands of a Hong Merchant.** This was originally designed to guard against the traitorous Natives misleading them, teaching them and egging them on. Hereafter the foreign Merchants dwelling in the Hong Merchants Factories, must not be allowed to presume of their own accord to go out and in, lest they should Trade and carry on clandestine transactions with traitorous Natives.

The boats on Canton river in which they go must not be allowed to set sail and go fast; lest they rush against Native boats on the River and wrangle and quarrel. They must not be allowed to wander about the Villages and Market places near Canton in order that bloody affrays may be prevented.

5th. Foreigners clandestinely taking foreign females to dwell in the factories, at Canton, their ascending to sit in shoulder chariots (sedan chairs) must both be interdicted.

It is found on enquiry that the foreigners of every Nation bringing wives and women servants to Canton City to dwell has long been strictly interdicted; but last year the English Chief violated the laws and brought them. They have already been expelled and driven back to Macao. It is found out that the woman he brought to Canton, was brought by the said foreign Merchant from his own Country. The women servants who followed them were Portuguese of Macao hired to serve.

Hereafter it is right to issue strict orders to the Chief foreign Merchants of every Nation disallowing them bringing foreign women to Canton to reside. If they are wilfully to disobey **then trade will be forthwith stopped**, and they immediately sent under escort to Macao. At the same time let it be made the duty of Custom house Cruizers, officers and soldiers in the event of meeting foreigners carrying females to Canton to intercept them and send them back.

[*start Chronicles page 299*]

Further let orders be given to the Tungche of Macao to transmit orders to the Portuguese foreign Headman Weileto, and the Fanchae (or foreign 'Envoy) that hereafter other foreigners hiring women to serve are allowed to reside at Macao only—it is not allowed to the Macao Authorities to permit them being taken to Canton. If there be disobedience to this Order—Weileto alone will be responsible.

As to foreigners using chairs in Canton, it all arose from traitorous vagabonds giving them, and chair-bearers coveting gain. Besides ordering foreigners of every Nation to Yield obedience and that hereafter they must not at Canton City ascend the shore in Sedan Chairs; let it be strictly interdicted for traitorous Merchants to give chairs to, or hire chair bearers for foreigners. And if chairmen scheming to obtain gain dare to disobey this order as soon as it is discovered let them be seized and severely prosecuted.

6th. It is right to make it a duty of Custom House Cruizers officers and soldiers, with more strictness and care to interdict and prevent foreigners from conveying musketts and guns to Canton.

The interdict against foreigners bringing muskets or guns with them to Canton was originally very strict; but last year there was a foreigner who suddenly and by stealth conveyed muskets and guns to a foreign factory in Canton, violating in an extreme degree old regulations. Hereafter let it be the duty of Custom house Cruizers Officers and soldiers, to be faithful in endeavoring to find out such attempts; or if; still worse, should they know of them and connive at them, let the said Officers and men be immediately brought up, tried and sentenced.

7th. In case of English Company's Captains[3] going backwards and forwards in boats; and foreign Merchants cargo vessels receiving clearances to quit the Port, it is right to obey the standing regulations.

---

3 Skippers.

Of the foreign ships that trade the Company's Captains, when it occurs they have public business to attend to, go backward and forward in San pan boats, to interdict and stop which is difficult. It is right to allow them as heretofore to go in boats. If they carry contraband goods, let the Custom house officers and soldiers examine strictly and report for the management of the Affair. But heretofore, there must be a foreign headman or Captain in her before a Sanpan boat is allowed to go with a flag

[*start Chronicles page 300*]

set. If there be no headman or ship Captain in her it must not be allowed, irregularly to sail a boat with flag—Still let the old regulation be adhered to [to] prevent confusion.

In going from Macao to Whampoa and Canton and from Canton to Whampoa and Macao, let a permit[4] be requested. They must not go and come when and as they please. Doing so will be an offence that will be enquired into.

As to foreign Merchants Cargo Vessels receiving a Red Chop (or Clearance) to quit the Port, heretofore application has been made to the Custom House. Let it still be the duty of the Custom House to inform the forts on every such occasion, that they may examine and let go, and so stoppages and disturbances be prevented.

8th. It is necessary to make arrangements concerning foreigners presenting Petitions: whether a distinction would not be made in Affairs of importance, and it be settled when they must be presented for them and when they themselves may present them.

There must be explicit and fixed regulations determining whether the Hong Merchants are to present Petitions for foreign Merchants or they are to present them themselves; then a confused way of acting, and one exceeding what is proper may be prevented. Let an order be issued to the English and other foreign Merchants requiring their obedience thereto,—that hereafter, if any very important affair occur, which it is absolutely necessary to convey to the Governor's Office, let the Petition be delivered to the Senior Hong Merchant or Security Merchant to present it for them. It is not allowed that foreigners should presume to go the City Gate and deliver it to the Military Officer on Guard. When they

4 A Red Chop.

present a Petition one or two foreigners only are allowed to proceed with it. They are not allowed to take a number of men with them to blazon abroad the Affair.

If the business be of a common place nature, and the Hong Merchants have not refused to present it for them; or the topic be one which it was improper to present; then the foreigner who shall perversely offend and take a number of people to the City Gate to present a Petition, **that foreign Merchants trade shall forthwith be stopped** one Month, and he be disallowed to buy or sell any goods, thereby to chastise his disrespect.

Petitions concerning ordinary topics of Trade, must be presented at the Hoppo's Office; and ordinary Petitions

[*start Chronicles page 301*]

concerning local occurrences must be presented to the Macao Tungche, or the Heangshan Hien; or the Macao Tsotang—in all which cases it is allowed to appeal

as usual.

Appendix 4

The Eight Regulations (1835)

"*The new regulations for foreigners*, which were prepared by their excellencies the governor, fooyuen, and hoppo, on the 28th of the 1st moon of the 15th year of Taoukwang, (Feb. 25th, 1835) have received the approbation of his majesty, with solemn injunctions that thenceforth they be strictly obeyed. Copies of these regulations, with the hoppo's seal stamped upon them, have recently been circulated among the residents in Canton. The regulations are eight in number; for a translation of them the reader is referred to the third volume of the Repository, pages 580–584." Chinese Repository, Vol. 4, page 199 (August 1835).

Contemporary Translation. Full text of the "Eight Regulations," promulgated 8 March 1835, with their official transmittal, as published in the Chinese Repository, Vol. 3, pages 579–584 (April 1835):

Document from the hoppo, containing a memorial from the Canton government to the emperor, with eight regulations restrictive of foreign trade.

Pang, by imperial appointment, superintendent of the maritime customs of Canton, &c. &c., issues this order to the hong-merchants, requiring their full acquaintance with the contents thereof. I have received the following communication from the governor:—

"Whereas I the governor united, on the 28th day of the first moon, in the 15th year of Taoukwang, with your excellency the hoppo, and Ke, the lieutenant-governor of Kwangtung, in framing a respectful memorial concerning restrictive regulations decided on for the direction of the trade and of barbarians: We must now await the receipt of a reply in vermilion [i.e., in the imperial handwriting], when the same shall be reverently recorded and communicated to you.

"A communication is at the same time addressed to the governors of the metropolitan provinces [Chihle and Keangnan], and of Minche [Chekeang and Fuhkeen], and to the lieut-governors of the provinces of Keangsoo, Chekeang, and Fuhkeen, requesting that they will issue general orders to all civil and military officers along the coast within their jurisdiction, strictly to command that the merchant ships, hereafter, when resorting to Canton to purchase foreign goods, shall one and all repair to the chief custom-house of Canton, and request

 DOI 10.1163/9789004276567_015

a stamped manifest, enumerating the goods and their quantities; likewise to disallow private purchases; and also to maintain strict investigation, that if any vessels from the sea, bringing home transmarine goods, be found on examination to be without the stamped manifest of the custom-house, such goods may be immediately regarded as contraband, and examination made and punishment inflicted, according to the regulations.

"Instructions also are given to the tungche of Macao, for him immediately to give strict orders to the pilots, the compradors, and so forth, that they may obey and act accordingly. Hereafter, they are imperatively required to adhere to the regulations established by memorial to the emperor; they are to be careful in piloting vessels; and they must not unlawfully combine (with foreigners) to smuggle; if the barbarian ships go out or come in contrary to the regulations, or if the barbarians clandestinely go about in small boats to places along the coast, rambling about the villages and farms, the said pilots are to be assuredly brought with strictness to an investigation: if there be any sale or purchase of contraband goods, or stealthy smuggling of goods liable to duty, and the compradors do not report according to the truth, they also are to be immediately punished with rigor; and are decidedly to have no indulgence shown to them.

"Instructions are likewise given to the poochingsze and anchasze to examine and act in accordance with the tenor of the copy of this memorial; and immediately to transmit directions to the civil and military officers along the coast (of the province) to act in obedience thereto; also to command the hong-merchants and linguists to enjoin orders on the barbarian merchants of every nation, for them to obey and act accordingly."

This coming before me the hoppo, I unite the circumstances, and issue this order. When the order reaches the said merchants, let them act in obedience to the tenor of the copy of the memorial, and enjoin orders on the barbarian merchants of every nation, that they may pay obedience thereto. Oppose. An to special order. Annexed is a paper containing a fair copy of the memorial, as follows:—

"A reverent memorial concerning restrictive regulations determined on for the direction of the trade and of barbarians, is hereby presented, imploring the Sacred Glance to be cast thereon. With reference to barbarians from beyond the outer seas coming to Canton to trade, since the time when, the in 25th year of Keenlung [1760], restrictive enactments were fixed by a representation (to the throne), there have also been further regulations from time to time determined on; viz., in the 14th year of Keaking [1810], and in the 11th year of Taoukwang

[*start Chinese Repository page 580*]

[1831], by several former governors and lieut.-governors; and on representation (to the throne) the same have been sanctioned, obedience has been paid to them, and they have become established laws. These have been complete and effectual. But during the length of days they have been in operation, either they have in the end become a dead letter, or there have gradually sprung up unrestrained offenses. Last year, the English Company was ended and dissolved. The said nation's merchants come at their own option to trade. There is none having a general control. Although commands have been issued to the said nation's barbarian merchants to send a letter home to their country, to continue the appointment of a taepan, who shall come to Canton for the direction and control (of affairs); yet as the merchants are now many, and individuals are mingled together, while affairs are under no united jurisdiction, it is necessarily required that regulations should be enacted and published, that they may be obeyed and adhered to. But the affairs of time have variations of present and past; and since the English barbarians' Company is dissolved, the attendant circumstances of commerce are also slightly different from what they were formerly.

"Besides those old regulations, respecting which it is unnecessary further to deliberate, but which may all, as formerly, continue to be distinctly enumerated in plain commands; and besides the regulations regarding the management of barbarian debts, and regarding the strict seizure of smugglers, which have already been specially represented; there are still regulations which require to be reconsidered, for the purpose of adding or altering. These we, your majesty's ministers, calling into council with us the poochingsze and the anchasze, have fully deliberated upon. The rules of dignified decorum should be rendered awe-striking in order to repress overstepping presumption; the bounds of intercourse should be closely drawn, in order to eradicate Chinese traitors; the restraints on egress and ingress should be diligently enforced; the responsible task of investigation and supervision should be carefully attended to: then surely in the restrictive enactment, there will be unceasingly displayed minute care and diligence. At the same time the hong-merchants should be strictly commanded to deal fairly and equitably; each regarding highly his respectability in order that all the foreigners, thoroughly imbewed with the sacred dew of favor, may universally quake with awe, and be filled with tender regard. Looking upwards, to aid our sovereign's extreme desire to soothe into subjection the far-coming barbarians, and to give weight and attention to the maritime guard: we respectfully join these expressions in a reverent and duly prepared memorial; and also take the eight regulations which we have determined on, and making separately a fair copy thereof, respectfully offer them for the imperial eye: prostrate, supplicating our sovereign to cast the sacred glance thereon, and to impart instruction. A respectful memorial. Taoukwang, 15th year, 1st moon, 28th day. (Feb. 25th, 1833.)

"We respectfully take eight additional and altered regulations, restrictive of the barbarians, whereon we have deliberated and decided, and have attentively made a fair copy thereof, we with reverence offer them for the imperial perusal:"

1. The outside barbarians' ships of war convoying goods are not permitted to sail into the inner seas. It is requisite to enforce with strictness the prohibitory commands, and to hold the naval force responsible for keeping them off.

On examination it appears, that the trading barbarians may bring ships of war to protect their goods themselves. This has been the case for a long time past. But the regulation hitherto existing, only permits them to anchor in the outer seas, there waiting until the cargo vessels leave the port, and then sailing back with them. They are not allowed to presume to enter the maritime port. From the period of the reign of Keaking onwards, they have gradually failed to pay implicit obedience to the old rule; and last year there was again an affair of irregularly pushing in through the maritime entrance. Although the said barbarians, sailing into the shallow waters of the inner river, can effect nothing in the least; yet restrictive measures always should be perfect and complete. With regard to the line of forts at the Bocca Tigris, there are now some additional erections and some removals in progress: and at the same time more cannon are being cast, and measures of preparation and defense are being determined on. It is, besides this, requisite to enforce with strictness the regulations and prohibitions.

[*start Chinese Repository page 581*]

Hereafter, if a ship of war of any nation convoying goods presumes to enter either of the maritime ports of Cross Harbor or the Bocca Tigris, the barbarians merchants' cargo vessels shall have their holds altogether closed, and their trade stopped, and at the same time the (ship of war) shall be immediately driven out. The naval commander-in-chief also shall be held responsible, whenever he meets with a ship of war of the outside barbarians anchored in the outer seas to give commands immediately to all officers and men of the forts, that they apply themselves to the object of keeping up preventive measures against the same; also to lead forth in person the naval squadron, to cruize about with them in guard of all the maritime entrances, and to unite their strength to that of the forts, for the purpose of guarding against (any such ship of war). Should the officers or soldiers be guilty of negligence and indolence, they shall be reported against with severity. It is imperatively necessary that the power of the naval and land forces should be exerted in unbroken concert, that the barbarian ships may have no way of irregularly pushing through.

2. When barbarians stealthily transport muskets and cannon, or clandestinely bring up foreign females or foreign sailors, to the provincial city, the hong-merchants shall be held responsible in all points for investigating the matter.

It appears on examination, that barbarians may carry with them one sword, one rapier, and one gun each; this the regulations do not prohibit. But if they presume, besides this, to bring cannon and muskets or other military weapons, or foreign females, up to the provincial city, the fixed regulations hold the officers and men of the guard-houses responsible for finding out and stopping them. The guard-stations have indeed the responsible task of searching and discovering; but the barbarian merchants at Canton, dwelling in the outside barbarians' factories, the apartments which they occupy are all rented by them from the hong-merchants. The said merchants' ears and eyes are close to them: they certainly cannot be ignorant (of anything they do); it is evidently befitting that they should, on all points, be held responsible for investigating and finding out (whatever is done).

Hereafter, the barbarians of every nation shall be altogether disallowed bringing up muskets, cannon or other military weapons, or foreign females or sailors, to the provincial city. If any should clandestinely bring them up, the hong-merchant from whom their factory is rented, shall be held responsible for discovering and preventing it, and for disallowing them to be brought into the factory; and for at the same time repairing to the local magistrate to present a report (of any such attempt). Should he suffer, connive at, and conceal such attempt the said hong-merchant shall be punished according to the law against clandestine intercourse with outside nations. The officers and men of the guard-stations who fail to discover such misdemeanors shall also be severally tried and rigorously punished, as guilty of 'failing to investigate and willfully conniving.'

3. Pilots and compradors of barbarian ships must have licenses from the tungche of Macao; it must not be allowed that they should be privately hired.

It is found on examination that in the office of the tungche of Macao, there have hitherto been appointed 14 pilots: and whenever a barbarian ship arrives in the sea outside the Bocca Tigris, a report should be made to the said tungche, that he may command a pilot to take the ship into port. For the provisions and necessaries required by the barbarian merchants on board the ship, a comprador should be employed; who is also selected from among men conspicuous in their native place for substance and property, and is appointed by the said tungche to fill the station. Of late, there has constantly been a set of vagabonds in the outer seas, falsely acting in the capacity of pilots; who artfully make away with the goods of barbarians, and then run off. There has also been a class of vagabonds who craftily assume the name of compradors, and unlawfully combine for the purpose of smuggling and other illegalities. When the thing is discovered, and search is made for them, their names and surnames having been falsely assumed, there are no means of finding and bringing them to trial.

Hereafter, the tungche of Macao, when appointing pilots, shall ascertain fully their age and outward appearance, their native place and habits of life, and shall give them a place on the list (of pilots), and a sealed and signed waist-war-

[*start Chinese Repository page 582*]

rant.* A list also shall be kept of them, and a full report respecting them sent to the office of the governor and to the custom-house, to be there preserved. When a barbarian ship is to be piloted in, a sealed license shall be given to them, stating explicitly the names and surnames of the pilot and master of the ship, which when the guard-stations have verified, they shall let the ship pass on. Any men without the sealed and signed waist-warrant, the barbarian ships must not hire or employ. With regard to the compradors required by the barbarian ships, when anchored at Macao or Whampoa, they must all have waist-warrants given to them by the said tungche; and must be subject at Macao to examination by the said tungche, and at Whampoa, to examination by the Pwanyu heen magistrate. If the barbarian ships come in or go out contrary to the regulations, or if the barbarians go about clandestinely in small boats, to places along the coast, rambling among the villages and farms, the pilots shall be brought to a strict investigation. And if there be any trading in contraband goods, or any stealthy smuggling of goods subject to duty, and the compradors do not report the same according to the truth, the offense shall be rigorously punished.

4. With regard to hiring and employing natives in the barbarian factories, there must be limits and rules clearly settled.

On examination it appears, that it was formerly the regulation, that the trading barbarians should not be permitted to hire and employ any natives except linguists and compradors. In the 11th year of Taoukwang, it was, on representation (to the throne), permitted, that in the barbarian factories, for gatekeepers, and for carriers of water and carriers of goods, natives might be hired for (foreigners) by the compradors. But the silly populace earnestly gallop after gain, and possess but little shame. And adjoining the provincial city, are many persons who understand the barbarian speech. If the barbarians are allowed to hire them at their own pleasure, it will be difficult to prevent unlawful combinations and traitorous procedure. It is evidently befitting that a limit and rule should be fixed, and that a special responsibility should be created.

Hereafter, in each barbarian factory, whatever be the number of barbarians inhabiting it, whether few or many, it shall be permitted only to employ two gatekeepers and four water-carriers; and each barbarian merchant may hire one man to keep his goods. It shall not be permitted to employ any more than this limited number. The comprador of the barbarian factory shall be held responsible for hiring these men; the linguists shall be held responsible for securing, and filling up the places of the compradors; and the hong-merchants shall be held responsible for securing and filling up the places of the linguists. (This will be) a shutting up rule, extending through progressive grades. If there be any illicit combination or breach of law, only the one who hired and stood security shall be answerable. At the same time commands shall be given to the superintending hong-merchant, to make out monthly a fair list of the names and birthplaces of the compradors and coolies under each barbarian's name, and hand it in to the district magistrate, to be kept in the archives, ready at any time to be examined. As to the carriers of goods, the linguists shall be commanded to hire them miscellaneously, when the time comes (that they are required); and when the business is finished to send them back. With regard to natives being hired to become the menial attendants of barbarian merchants, under the name of shawan [servants], it shall still be for ever prohibited. Should merchants hire coolies beyond the limited number, or clandestinely hire shawan as menial attendants, the linguists and hong-merchants shall both receive punishment.

5. With regard to barbarians sailing vessels about in the inner rivers, there should be reductions and limitations severally made, and the constant practice of idly rambling about should be prohibited.

It appears on examination, that the barbarian trading vessels, when they enter the port, anchor at Whampoa. In going to and fro between Canton and Macao, the English Company's skippers only have hitherto been permitted to travel in flag-bearing sampan boats. This kind of sampan is a boat with a rather large hull, and a deck over it; rendering it easy to carry in it military weapons and

[*start Chinese Repository page 583*]

contraband goods. Now that the Company has been dissolved, all the flag-bearing sampan vessels should be done away with. As to the barbarians residing in the foreign factories, they are not permitted to presume to go in and go out at their own pleasure. In the 21st year of Keaking [1816], when governor Tseang was in office, it was arranged, that on three days, viz., the 8th, 18th, and 28th of every month, they should be permitted to ramble about once, in the neighborhood. Of late years, the barbarians have continually disobeyed the old regulations; it is imperatively necessary to enforce powerfully the prohibitory commands.

Hereafter, all the barbarians, when their ships reach Whampoa, if they have any business requiring them to go to and fro between Canton and Macao, or to interchange letters, are only permitted to use uncovered small sampans; they may not again use flag-bearing sampan vessels. When the small sampans pass the custom-houses, they must wait until they are searched; and should they have in them contraband goods, or cannon or other military weapons, they must be immediately driven out. The barbarians residing in the factories shall only be allowed to ramble out on the 8th, the 18th, and the 28th, three days of each month, in the neighboring flower gardens, and the Haechwang sze temple [on Honan]. Each time there must not be more than ten individuals; and they must be limited to the hour of five in the evening to return to their factories. They must not be allowed to remain out to sleep, or drink liquor. If, when it is not the day that they may receive permission, they should go out to ramble, and they exceed the number of ten individuals, or if they go to other villages, hamlets, or market-places, to ramble about, the hong-merchants and linguists shall both receive punishment.

6. When barbarians petition on any subject, they should in all cases petition through the medium of the hong-merchants, in order that the dignity of government may be rendered impressive.

On examination it appears, that the written characters of outside barbarians and the central flowery people are not of the same nature. Among them [the former], there are some who have a rough idea of Chinese characters; but they are unacquainted with style and god diction, and are ignorant of the rules required for maintenance of dignity. When they petition on affairs, their expressions are devoid of intelligent signification, and there is always much that is difficult to explain. They also, in an irregular manner, adopt epistolary forms, and confusedly proceed to present papers themselves; greatly infringing the dignity of government. Moreover, that for one and the same barbarian affairs, petitions should be presented, either through the medium of the hong-merchants, or by barbarians themselves, is an inconsistent mode of acting.

Hereafter, on every occasion of barbarians making petitions on any affair, they must always have the hong-merchants to petition, and state the circumstances for them. It is unnecessary that they should themselves frame the expressions of the petitions. If there be accusations to be brought against a hong-merchant on any affair, and the hong-merchants may, perhaps, carry it oppressively, and refuse to petition for them, then the barbarians may be allowed to go themselves to the offices of the local magistrates and bring forward their charges; and the hong-merchants shall be immediately brought to examination and trial.

7. In securing barbarian ships by hong-merchants, there should be employed both securities by engagement and securities by rotation, in order to eradicate clandestine illegalities.

It is found on examination, that when barbarian ships come to Canton the old rule is, that they should be secured by all the hong-merchants in successive rotation; and that if they transgress the laws, the security-merchant shall alone be responsible. Afterwards, it was apprehended, that securing by rotation was attended with offenses of grasping and oppressive dealing; and all the keang keo barbarian [i.e., country] ships were permitted themselves to invite hongs to secure them. Now, the Company has been dissolved; and the barbarian ships that come are scattered, and without order; if the responsibility of being secured by the hong-merchants in rotation be again enforced, as formerly, it is apprehended that offenses of extortionate oppression will arise. And yet if suffered themselves to choose their securities, it is difficult to insure that there will not be acts of unlawful combination.

[*start Chinese Repository page 584*]

Hereafter, when the barbarian ships arrive at Canton, they shall still as formerly, be permitted to invite hongs in which they have confidence , to become their engaged securities; and all the trade in goods, the requesting of permits, the payment of duties, and the transaction of public affairs, shall be attended to by the engaged security-merchant. In the payment of duties, the tariff regulations shall be conformed to; it shall not be allowed to make the smallest fractional addition. At the same time, to each vessel shall be appointed a security by rotation, the duty of which, each hong-merchant shall fulfill in his successive routine. It shall be his special duty to examine and investigate affairs. If the engaged security-merchant join with the barbarian to make sport of legal practices and traitorous machinations, or secretly add to the amount of duties, or incur debts to the barbarians, the security-merchant by rotation shall be held responsible for giving information thereof, according to the facts, that the other may be brought to an investigation, and that the debts may be reclaimed. If the security by rotation connive, he shall also, on discovery, be brought to an investigation.

8. If barbarian ships on the seas, clandestinely sell goods chargeable with duty, the naval forces should be held responsible for finding out, and seizing the same. Also communications should be sent to all the seaboard provinces, to examine and investigate.

It appears on examination, that when the barbarian ships of every nation bring goods to Canton, it is reasonably required that they should enter the port, pay measurement charges and duties, and sell off through the medium of the hong-merchants. But the said barbarian vessels continually cast anchor in the outer seas, and delay entering the port; and some even do not at all enter the port, but return and sail away; not only storing up and selling opium, but also, it is feared, clandestinely disposing of foreign goods. We, your majesty's ministers, on every occasion of such being reported to us, have immediately replied, by strict directions to the naval forces to urge and compel them to enter the port, or if they will not enter the port, to drive them instantly away, and not permit them to loiter about. We have also appointed officers at the various maritime entrances, to seize with strictness smuggling vagabonds. In repeated instances, men and vessels going out to sea to sell opium have been seized, and on investigation, punishment has been inflicted. But the province of Canton has a line of coast continuous along the provinces of Fuhkeen, Chekeang, Keangsoo, and Teentsin [Chihle]. Traitorous vagabonds of the several provinces sail in vessels of the sea on the outer ocean, and clandestinely buy and sell goods, dealing with the barbarians, and then carry back (their purchases) by sea. This class of traitorous dealers, neither entering nor leaving any of the seaports of Canton, there are no means of guarding against or seizing them. And the foreign goods having a divided consumption, the amount that enters the port is gradually lessened; the consequences of which on the duties are great.

Hereafter, the naval commanders-in-chief should be held responsible for giving commands to the naval vessels to cruize about in the outer seas in a constant course; and if there be any dealers approaching the barbarian ships, clandestinely to purchase foreign goods, immediately to seize them and give them over for trial and punishment. Also, regulations should be established that vessels of the sea, of whatever province, when wanting to purchase foreign goods, shall all repair to the chief custom-house of Canton, and request a sealed manifest, enumerating the goods and their quantities; and that none should be permitted to make private purchases. Communications should be sent to the provinces of Fuhkeen, Chekeang, &c., that general orders may be issued requiring obedience to be paid to this, and that strict search may be maintained in all the seaports, that if any sea-going vessel bring back foreign goods, and it appears that she has not the sealed manifest of the custom-house, they shall be immediately regarded as contraband, and, on legal investigation, the vessel and cargo confiscated.

Taoukwang, 15th year, 2d moon, 10th day. [March 8th, 1835.]

- This is a piece of wood with characters cut thereon, to be carried about the person; hence called a waist-warrant.

Appendix 5

The Eight Regulations (*Per W.C. Hunter*)

Contemporary Translation. Full text of the "Eight Regulations," in an undated version, from William C. Hunter, *The 'Fan Kwae' at Canton Before Treaty Days 1825–1844* (London: Kegan Paul, Trench & Co., 1882), pp. 28–30 (italics and footnotes in the original) (footnotes renumbered):

> The authorities framed eight regulations for the especial government and control of these divers people from afar. They date from the year 1760, and are curious enough to recall. Never having been abrogated, they were assumed to be in force always. They were confirmed by an edict of the Emperor Kea-King [the Jiaqing Emperor] in 1819, after a revision in 1810. Some of them came to be disregarded by the foreign community, particularly those referring to the Gardens, the Honam Temple, and pulling in their own boats on the river; but so far as regards women entering the Factories, an infringement of them in this essential particular took place in 1830, as will be seen hereafter. The chief sufferers in the event of a disregard of any important item of the regulations would of course be the Hong merchants. The 'Eight Regulations' were now and then brought to the Factories by a Linguist, as an intimation that they were not to be considered a 'dead letter.' Translated into English they read thus—
>
> *Regulation* 1.—All vessels of war are prohibited from entering the Bogue. Vessels of war acting as convoy to merchantmen must anchor outside at Sea till
>
> their merchant-ships are ready to depart, and then sail away with them.
>
> *Regulation* 2.—Neither women, guns, spears, nor arms of any kind can be brought to the Factories.
>
> *Regulation* 3.—All river-pilots and ships' Compradores must be registered at the office of the 'Tung- Che'[1] at Macao. That officer will also furnish each one of them with a licence, or badge, which must be worn around the waist. He must pro-
>
> [*start Fan Kwae page 29*]

1 An assistant-magistrate. Up to 1848 Macao was under the joint government of the Portuguese and Chinese.

 | DOI 10.1163/9789004276567_016

duce it whenever called for. All other boatmen and people must not have communication with foreigners, unless under the immediate control of the ships' Compradores; and should smuggling take place, the Compradore[2] of the ship engaged in it will be punished.

Regulation 4.—Each Factory is restricted for its service to 8 Chinese (irrespective of the number of its occupants), say 2 porters, 4 water-carriers, 1 person to take care of goods ('godown coolie'), and 1 ma-chen (intended for the foreign word 'merchant'), who originally performed all the duties of the 'House Compradore,' as he is styled to-day.

Regulation 5—prohibits foreigners from rowing about the river in their own boats for 'pleasure.' On the 8th, 18th, and 28th days of the moon 'they may take the air,' as fixed by the Government in the 21st year of Kea-King [Jiaqing] (1819). All ships' boats passing the Custom-houses on the river must be detained and examined, to guard against guns, swords, or firearms being furtively carried in them. On the 8th, 18th, and 28th days of the moon these foreign barbarians may visit the Flower Gardens and the Honam Joss-house,[3] but not in *droves* of over ten at one time. When they have 'refreshed' they must return to the Factories, not be allowed to pass the night 'out,' or collect together to carouse. Should they do so, then, when the next 'holiday' comes, they shall not be permitted to go. If the ten should presume to enter villages, public places, or bazaars, punishment will be inflicted upon the *Linguist* who accompanies them.

Regulation 6.—Foreigners are not allowed to present petitions. If they have anything to represent, it must be done through the Hong merchants.

Regulation 7.—Hong merchants are not to owe debts to foreigners. Smuggling goods to and from the city is prohibited.

Regulation 8.—Foreign ships arriving with merchandise must not loiter about outside the river; they must come direct

[*start Fan Kwae page 30*]

2 At this time the ships' Compradores were engaged at Macao, and not at Whampoa.

3 Buddhist Temple.

to Whampoa. They must not rove about the bays at pleasure and sell to rascally natives goods subject to duty, that these may smuggle them, and thereby defraud His Celestial Majesty's revenue.

Bibliography

1 Primary Sources

1.1 *Unpublished Primary Sources*

American Philosophical Society, Philadelphia, Pennsylvania.

Stephen Girard Papers, Estate of Stephen Girard, deceased, microfilm copies on deposit with the American Philosophical Society.

Deposition of Benjamin C. Wilcocks, undated, in Stephen Girard's records of the lawsuit Girard v. Biddle (commenced in the Sept. 1806 term of the Court of Common Pleas of Philadelphia County).

Stephen Girard, "Observations on Mr. Benjamin C. Wilcocks's Deposition," in Stephen Girard's records of the lawsuit Girard v. Biddle (commenced in the Sept. 1806 term of the Court of Common Pleas of Philadelphia County).

Letter, Stephen Girard (Philadelphia) to Edward George and Samuel Nichols, 3 January 1810, Letterbook 11.

Franklin Roosevelt Library, Hyde Park, New York.

Delano Family Papers, Edward Delano Correspondence.

Letter from Edward Delano to Franklin Hughes Delano, dated Canton 24 September 1841.

Historical Society of Pennsylvania, Philadelphia, Pennsylvania.

Breck Family Papers, Library Company of Philadelphia, Collection No. LCP185, on deposit.

Letter from Conseequa (Canton) to Peter Dobell, 3 April 1813.

Gratz Collection, Collection No. 0250B, Box 44, Case 14.

Conseequa's Account Current with George Emlen.

Willings & Francis Papers, Collection No. 1874, 1805 folder.

Letters from William Read (Canton) to Willings & Francis, 9 Nov. 1805 and 10 Dec. 1805.

Letter from William Read (Canton) to Willings & Francis, dated 27 November 1805.

Statement of Gregory Baboom, dated 28 December 1805.

Library of Congress, Washington, D.C.

Russell & Co. Papers (Samuel Russell Papers).

Letter from Samuel Russell (Canton) to Edward Carrington, 13 November 1821, Letterbook I, Container 15.

Rhode Island Historical Society, Providence, Rhode Island.

Edward Carrington Papers, MSS 333, SG I.

Letter from Peter W. Snow (Canton) to Edward Carrington, 11 August 1811, Series 1, Box 13.

Letter, Edward Carrington (Canton) to Samuel Snow, 19 January 1808, Series 2, RB.1 F6 Letter Book, China Letterbook F.

United States National Archives, Washington, D.C.

Despatches of United States Consuls at Canton, Volume I.

Petition of Conseequa, a Hong Merchant of the City of Canton in China, 10 February 1814, published in File Microcopies of Records in the National Archives, No. 101, Roll 1.

1.2 *Published Primary Sources*

Dzengseo (Nicola di Cosmo, tr.). *The Diary of a Manchu Soldier in Seventeenth-Century China*. Abington: Routledge Books, 2006.

Fu, Lo-shu. *A Documentary Chronicle of Sino-Western Relations (1644–1820)*. Tucson: Univ. of Arizona Press, 1966, quoted with permission of the Association for Asian Studies, Inc., see: www.asian-studies.org.

Van Buren, Martin. *The Message of His Excellency Gov. Van Buren on the Subject of Banks; with the Plan Suggested to Place them Under Proper Regulations, Secure the Public from Loss by Failure, and Furnish a Sound, Well Regulated Currency; Made to the Assembly, January 26, 1829*. Albany, N.Y.: Croswell & Van Benthuysen, 1829.

1.3 *Published Constitutions, Laws, Regulations and Legislative Materials*

Directive 94/19/EC of the European Parliament and of the Council of 30 May 1994 on deposit-guarantee schemes, see: "http://eur-lex.europa.eu/LexUriServ/LexUriServ.do?uri=CELEX:31994L0019:EN:HTML" (accessed 2 September 2012).

Directive 2009/14/EC of the European Parliament and of the Council, amending Directive 94/19/EC, see: "http://ec.europa.eu/internal_market/bank/docs/guarantee/200914_en.pdf" (accessed 2 September 2012).

Journal of the Assembly of the State of New-York at their Fifty-Second Session (Albany: E. Croswell, 1829).

Journal of the Senate of the State of New-York at their Fifty-Second Session (Albany: E. Croswell, 1829).

United States Constitution, Art. I, § 10.

1.4 *Published Court Decisions*

Bainbridge v. Wilcocks, 2 F. Cas. 407, 408 (C.C.E.D. Pa. 1832) (No. 755).

Cheongwo v. Jones, 5 F. Cas. 544 (C.C.E.D. Pa. 1818) (No. 2,638).

Chomqua v. Mason, 5 F. Cas. 649 (C.C.D.R.I. 1812) (No. 2,693).

Consequa v. Fanning, 3 Johns. Ch. 587, 603, 605 (N.Y. 1818).
Gilpins v. Consequa, 10 F. Cas. 420, 422 (C.C.E.D. Pa. 1813) (No. 5,452).
Lanfear v. Sumner, 17 Mass. 110 (1819).
Noble State Bank v. Haskell, 219 U.S. 104 (1911).
United States v. Three Hundred Fifty Chests of Tea, 25 U.S. 486 (1827).
Willings v. Consequa, 30 F. Cas. 55 (C.C.D. Pa. 1816) (No. 17,767).
Youqua v. Nixon, 30 F. Cas. 887 (C.C.E.D. Pa. 1816) (No. 18,189).

1.5 *Unpublished Court Records*

Federal Archives and Records Center, Waltham, Massachusetts, U.S.A.
Records of the Circuit Court of the United States for the District of Rhode Island.
File of Exsching Looqua v. Dexter, June term 1815.
Federal Archives and Records Center, Philadelphia, Pennsylvania, U.S.A.
Records of the Circuit Court of the United States for the District of Pennsylvania.
File of Consequa v. Joshua and Thomas Gilpin, October term 1809, No. 9, Deposition of Benjamin C. Wilcocks, taken on 5 December 1810.
File of Consequa v. Edward Dunant (filed 3 March 1810), October term 1809, No. 33.
File of Consequa v. Willings & Francis, October term 1809, No. 49, Deposition of Benjamin C. Wilcocks, Philadelphia, taken on 31 May 1811.
File of Keetshing v. Wells, Apr. term 1822, No. 36.
File of Kingling v. Read, Apr. term 1805, No. 68.
File of Namshing v. Coe, Apr. term 1826, No. 25.
File of Pacqua v. Pleasants, Apr. term 1822, No. 4.
File of Thonching v. Coe, Apr. term 1826, No. 28.

2 Secondary Sources

2.1 *Books and Articles*

Albion, Robert G. *The Rise of New York Port [1815–1860]*. New York: Charles Scribner's Sons, 1939.
Aldridge, A. Owen. *The Dragon and the Eagle: The Presence of China in the American Enlightenment*. Detroit: Wayne State University Press, 1993.
Anonymous. *An Examination of Some of the Provisions of the "Act to Create a Fund for the Benefit of the Creditors of Certain Monied Corporations, and for Other Purposes," Passed April, 1829; Particularly as to its Effects on the City of New-York. By a Stockholder*. New York: Ludwig & Tolefree, 1829.
Anonymous. "Bank of the United States." *North American Review*, Vol. 32 (April 1831), p. 56.
Anonymous. "Chinese Pirates." *Chinese Repository*, Vol. 3, pp. 62–83 (June 1834).

Anonymous [Inglis, Robert Harry]. *The Chinese Security Merchants in Canton and their Debts*. London: J. M. Richardson, 1838.

Anonymous. "Journal of Occurrences ... liberation of Sunshing." *Chinese Repository*, Vol. 3, p. 440 (Jan. 1835).

Anonymous. News article. *Albany Argus*, 7 January 1829, p. 2.

Anonymous. News article. *The Asiatic Journal and Monthly Register for British and Foreign India, China, and Australasia*, Vol. 6 (New Series), p. 71 (Sept.–Dec. 1831). London: Parbury, Allen and Co., 1831.

Anonymous. "Roosevelt 'Won' to Bank Insurance." The New York Times, 27 October 1936.

Ashton, Richard James. *The Merchant Shipping Activity of South China 1644–1860*. M.A. Thesis. Honolulu: Univ. of Hawaii, 1967.

Balleisen, Edward J. *Navigating Failure: Bankruptcy and Commercial Society in Antebellum America*. Chapel Hill: Univ. of North Carolina Press, 2001.

Basu, Dilip K. *Asian Merchants and Western Trade: A Comparative Study of Calcutta and Canton 1800–1840*. Ph.D. dissertation. Berkeley: Univ. of Calif., Berkeley, 1975.

Blussé, Leonard. *Strange Company: Chinese Settlers, Mestizo Women and the Dutch in VOC Batavia*. Dordrecht, Foris Publications, 1986.

———. *Visible Cities: Canton, Nagasaki, and Batavia and the Coming of the Americans*. Cambridge, Mass.: Harvard Univ. Press, 2008.

Bodenhorn, Howard. *A History of Banking in Antebellum America: Financial Markets and Economic Development in an Era of Nation-Building*. Cambridge: Cambridge Univ. Press, 2000.

———. *State Banking in Early America: A New Economic History*. Oxford: Oxford Univ. Press, 2003.

———. "Zombie Banks and the Demise of New York's Safety Fund." *Eastern Economic Journal*, Vol. 22, pp. 21–33 (1996).

Bodde, Derk. "Henry A. Wallace and the Ever-Normal Granary." *Far Eastern Quarterly*, Vol. 5, pp. 411–426 (1946).

———. "The State and Empire of Ch'in," in Twitchett, Denis and Loewe, Michael, eds., *The Cambridge History of China*, Vol. 1, The Ch'in and Han Empires, 221 B.C.–A.D. 220. Cambridge: Cambridge Univ. Press, 1986, pp. 20–102.

Bowen, Ray J., II and Rose, David C. "On the Absence of Privately Owned, Publicly Traded Corporations in China: The Kirby Puzzle." *Journal of Asian Studies*, Vol. 57, pp. 442–52 (1998).

Bowers, Q. David. *Obsolete Paper Money Issued by Banks in the United States 1782–1866*. Atlanta: Whitman Publishing LLC, 2006.

Bowra, E. C. "The Manchu Conquest of Canton" (Part One). *China Review*, Vol. 1, pp. 86–96 (1872).

Burns, Helen M. *The American Banking Community and the New Deal Banking Reforms 1933–1935*. Westport, Conn.: Greenwood Press, 1974.

Burts, Robert. *Around the World: A Narrative of a Voyage in the East India Squadron*. New York: Charles S. Francis, 1840, Vol. II.

Butterfield, Lyman H. "Bostonians and their Neighbors as Pack Rats." *The American Archivist*, Vol. 24, pp. 141–159 (1961).

Calomiris, Charles W. "Banking Crises and the Rules of the Game." *National Bureau of Economic Research, Working Paper No. 15403*. Cambridge, Mass., 2009), see: "http://www.nber.org/papers/w15403" (accessed 29 January 2012).

———. "Is Deposit Insurance Necessary? A Historical Perspective." *The Journal of Economic History*, Vol. 50, pp. 283–295 (1990).

———. *U.S. Bank Deregulation in Historical Perspective*. Cambridge: Cambridge Univ. Press, 2000.

Calomiris, Charles W. and White, Eugene N. "The Origins of Federal Deposit Insurance," in Goldin, Claudia and Libecap, Gary D., eds., *The Regulated Economy: A Historical Approach to Political Economy*. Chicago: Univ. of Chicago Press, 1994. Also in: Calomiris, Charles W., *U.S. Bank Deregulation in Historical Perspective*. Cambridge: Cambridge Univ. Press, 2000.

Cariboni, Jessica, Vanden Branden, Karlien, Campolongo, Francesca and De Cesare, Manuela. "Deposit Protection in the EU: State of Play and Future Prospects." *Journal of Banking Regulation*, Vol. 9, pp. 82–101 (2008).

Chaddock, Robert E. *The Safety Fund Banking System in New York, 1829–1866*. National Monetary Commission, 61st Cong., 2nd sess., Senate Document No. 581. Washington, D.C., U.S. Government Printing Office, 1910.

Chang, Chung-li. *The Income of the Chinese Gentry*. Seattle: Univ. of Wash. Press, 1962.

Chang Te-ch'ang. "The Economic Role of the Imperial Household in the Ch'ing Dynasty." *Journal of Asian Studies*, Vol. 31, pp. 243–74 (1972).

Chen, Chin chih. "The Japanese Adaptation of the *Pao-Chia* System in Taiwan, 1895–1945." *Journal of Asian Studies*, Vol. 34, pp. 391–416 (1975).

Chen Jia. "Time to Launch Deposit Insurance, Economists Say." *China Daily*, 12 January 2012, p. 13.

Ch'en, Kuo-tung Anthony. *The Insolvency of the Chinese Hong Merchants 1760–1843*. Nankang: Institute of Economics, Academia Sinica, 1990.

Cheong, Weng Eang. "The Beginnings of Credit Finance on the China Coast: The Canton Financial Crisis of 1812–1815." *Business History* (*Liverpool*), Vol. 13, pp. 70–92 (1971).

———. "China Houses and the Bank of England Crisis of 1825." *Business History* (*Liverpool*), Vol. 15, pp. 56–73 (1973).

———. *The Hong Merchants of Canton: Chinese Merchants in Sino-Western Trade*. Richmond, Surrey: Curzon Press, 1997, © Nordic Institute of Asian Studies.

———. *Mandarins and Merchants: Jardine Matheson & Co., a China Agency of the Early Nineteenth Century*. London: Curzon Press Ltd., 1979.

———. "Trade and Finance in China: 1784–1834, A Reappraisal." *Business History (Liverpool)*, Vol. 7, pp. 34–56 (1965).

Chirot, Daniel. "The Rise of the West." *American Sociological Review*, Vol. 50, pp. 181–195 (1985).

Chiu, Pengsheng. "The Discourse on Insolvency and Negligence in Eighteenth-Century China," in Hegel, Robert E. and Carlitz, Katherine, eds., *Writing and Law in Late Imperial China: Crime, Conflict, and Judgment*. Seattle: Univ. of Washington Press, 2007, pp. 125–42.

———. "Refining Legal Reasoning from Precedents: Economic Crimes and Rhetoric in Ming-Qing Casebooks." Unpublished paper prepared for Annual Meeting of the Association for Asian Studies, New York City, 2003, see: "http://idv.sinica.edu.tw/pengshan/OnEcoLegalReasoningdraft.pdf" (accessed 3 June 2012).

Choi, Jang-Bong. "Structuring a Deposit Insurance System from the Asian Perspective," in *Rising to the Challenge in Asia: A Study of Financial Markets*, Vol. 2 (Special Issues) (Manila: Asian Development Bank, 1999), p. 73, see: "http://www.aric.adb.org/pdf/aem/external/financial_market/Special_Issues/Volume2b.pdf" (accessed 26 March 2014).

Clark, Joshua Victor Hopkins. *Onondaga; or Reminiscences of Earlier and Later Times*. Syracuse: Stoddard and Babcock, 1849, Vol. 2.

Coates, Austin M. *Macao and the British, 1637–1842: Prelude to Hong Kong*. Hong Kong: Hong Kong University Press, 2009.

Cohen, Adam. *Nothing to Fear:* FDR*'s Inner Circle and the Hundred Days that Created Modern America*. New York: The Penguin Press, 2009.

Cohen, Jerome Alan. "Chinese Mediation on the Eve of Modernization." *California Law Review*, Vol. 54, pp. 1201–26 (1966).

Collingwood, Cuthbert. *Rambles of a Naturalist on the Shores and Waters of the China Sea*. London: John Murray, 1868.

Conner, Patrick. *The Hongs of Canton: Western Merchants in South China, 1700–1900, as Seen in Chinese Export Paintings*. London: English Art Books, 2009.

Cordier, Henri. "Les Marchands Hanistes de Canton" *T'oung pao* (2d ser.), Vol. 3, pp. 282–315 (1902).

Cranmer-Byng, J. L. *An Embassy to China: Lord Macartney's Journal, 1793–1794 (1962); rpt.,* Patrick J. N. Tuck, Britain and the China Trade 1635–1842. London: Routledge, 2000.

Crosby, Alfred. *The Columbian Exchange: Biological and Cultural Consequences of 1492*. Westport, Conn.: Praeger, 2003.

Cushman, Jennifer. "Duke Ch'ing-fu Deliberates: A Mid-Eighteenth Century Reassessment of Sino-Nanyang Commercial Relations." *Papers on Far Eastern History*, Vol. 17, pp. 137–56 (1978).

———. *Fields from the Sea: Chinese Junk Trade with Siam during the Late Eighteenth and Early Nineteenth Centuries*. Ithaca: Cornell Southeast Asian Program, 1993.

Dai, Yingcong. "Yingyun Shengxi: Military Entrepreneurship in the High Qing Period 1700–1800." *Late Imperial China*, Vol. 26, No. 2 (2005).

Davis, Kenneth S. *FDR: The Beckoning of Destiny, 1882–1928*. New York: Random House, 1971.

Davis, Nancy Ellen. *The American China Trade, 1784–1844: Products for the Middle Class*. Ph.D. dissertation. Washington, D.C.: The George Washington University, 1987.

Demirgüç-Kunt, Ash, Kane, Edward J. and Laeven, Luc, eds. *Deposit Insurance Around The World: Issues of Design and Implementation*. (Cambridge, Mass.: MIT Press, 2008.

Deng, Kent G. "Development and Its Deadlock in Imperial China, 221 B.C.–1840 A.D." *Economic Development and Cultural Change*, Vol. 51, pp. 479–522 (2003).

Dennerline, Jerry. "The Shun-chih Reign," in Peterson, Willard J., ed., *The Cambridge History of China*, Vol. 9, The Ch'ing Dynasty to 1800, Part I. Cambridge: Cambridge Univ. Press, 2002, pp. 73–119.

Dennett, Tyler. *Americans in Eastern Asia*. New York: The MacMillan Co., 1922.

Dermigny, Louis. *La Chine et L'Occident: Le Commerce A Canton Au XVIIIe Siècle 1719–1833*. Paris: Service de Vente des Publications Officielles de l'Education Nationale, 1964 (4 Vols.).

De Tocqueville, Alexis (George Lawrence, tr., J. P. Mayer, ed.). *Democracy in America*. Garden City, N.Y.: Anchor Books, 1969.

De Vargas, Philip. "William C. Hunter's Books on the Old Canton Factories." *Yenching Journal of Social Studies*, Vol. 2 (July 1939).

Dewey, Davis R. State Banking Before the Civil War. National Monetary Commission, 61st Cong., 2nd sess., Senate Document No. 581. Washington, D.C., U.S. Government Printing Office, 1910.

Dewey, Horace W. "Russia's Debt to the Mongols in Suretyship and Collective Responsibility." *Comparative Studies in Society and History*, Vol. 30, pp. 249–270 (1988).

Dickinson, Ellen E. "Joshua Forman, the founder of Syracuse." *Magazine of American History*, Vol. 8 (1882).

Downs, Jacques M. "American Merchants and the China Opium Trade, 1800–1840." *Business History Review*, Vol. 42, pp. 418–442 (1968).

———. "A Study in Failure—Hon. Samuel Snow." *Rhode Island History*, Vol. 25 (1966).

———. *The Golden Ghetto: The American Commercial Community at Canton and the Shaping of American China Policy, 1784–1844*. Bethlehem: Lehigh Univ. Press, 1997.

Eberhard, Wolfram. *A History of China*. Berkeley: Univ. of Calif. Press, 4th ed., 1977.

———. *Social Mobility in Traditional China*. Leiden: E.J. Brill, 1962.

Edwards, R. Randle. "Ch'ing Legal Jurisdiction Over Foreigners," in Cohen, Jerome A., Edwards, R. Randle, and Chang Chen, Fu-mei, eds., *Essays on China's Legal Tradition*. Princeton: Princeton Univ. Press, 1980, pp. 222–269.

———. “The Old Canton System of Foreign Trade,” in Li, Victor H., ed., *Law and Politics in China’s Foreign Trade*. Seattle: Univ. of Washington Press, 1977, pp. 360–378.

Elliott, Mark C. *The Manchu Way: The Eight Banners and Ethnic Identity in Late Imperial China*. Stanford: Stanford Univ. Press, 2001.

Fairbank, John K. *Trade and Diplomacy on the China Coast: The Opening of the Treaty Ports 1842–1854*. Cambridge, Mass.: Harvard Univ. Press, 1953, Vol. 1.

Farmer, Edward L. “James Flint Versus the Canton Interest,” *Papers on China*, Vol. 17, pp. 38–66. East Asian Research Center, Harvard University, 1963.

Faure, David. *Emperor and Ancestor: State and Lineage in South China*. Stanford: Stanford Univ. Press, 2007.

Fay, Peter Ward. *The Opium War 1840–1842*. Chapel Hill: Univ. of North Carolina Press, 1975.

Federal Deposit Insurance Corporation. *Federal Deposit Insurance Corporation: The First Fifty Years: A History of the* FDIC *1933–1983*. Washington, D.C.: Federal Deposit Insurance Corporation, 1984.

Fichter, James R. *So Great a Proffit: How the East Indies Trade Transformed Anglo-American Capitalism*. Cambridge, Mass.: Harvard Univ. Press, 2010.

Flood, Mark D. “The Great Deposit Insurance Debate.” *The Federal Reserve Bank of St. Louis Review*, Vol. 74, pp. 51–77 (July/August 1992), see: “http://research.stlouisfed.org/publications/review/92/07/Deposit_Jul_Aug1992.pdf” (accessed 26 January 2012).

Forbes, John D. “European Wars and Boston Trade, 1783–1815.” *New England Quarterly*, Vol. 11, pp. 709–730 (1938).

Forbes, Robert Bennet. *Remarks on China and the China Trade*. Boston: Samuel M. Dickinson, 1844.

Gaastra, Femme S. *The Dutch East India Company: Expansion and Decline*. Zutphen: Walburg Pers, 2003.

Gallatin, Albert. *Considerations on the Currency and Banking System of the United States*. Philadelphia: Carey & Lea, 1831.

Garcia, Gillian and Prast, Henriëtte. “Depositor and Investor Protection in the Netherlands: Past, Present and Future.” *De Nederlandsche Bank, Occasional Studies*, Vol. 2, No. 2 (2004).

Gardella, Robert. *Harvesting Mountains: Fujian and the China Tea Trade, 1757–1937*. Berkeley: Univ. of California Press, 1994.

Gatell, Frank Otto. “Sober Second Thoughts on Van Buren, the Albany Regency, and the Wall Street Conspiracy.” *The Journal of American History*, Vol. 53, pp. 19–40 (1966).

Gibson, James R. *Otter Skins, Boston Ships, and China Goods: The Maritime Fur Trade of the Northwest Coast, 1785–1841*. Seattle: Univ. of Washington Press, 1992.

Goldstein, Jonathan. “*Resources on Early Sino-American Relations in Philadelphia’s Stephen Girard Collection and the Historical Society of Pennsylvania*.” Ch’ing-shih wen-t’i, Vol. 4 (1980).

———. *Stephen Girard's Trade with China 1787–1824: The Norms Versus the Profits of Trade*. Portland, Maine: Merwin Asia, 2011.

Golembe, Carter. "The Deposit Insurance Legislation of 1933." *Political Science Quarterly*, Vol. 75, pp. 181–200 (1960).

Gordon, Stewart. *When Asia was the World.* Philadelphia: Da Capo Press, 2008.

Gorton, Gary B. *Slapped by the Invisible Hand: The Panic of 2007*. Oxford: Oxford Univ. Press, 2010.

Graeber, David. *Debt: The First 5,000 Years*. Brooklyn, N.Y.: Melville House Publishing, 2011.

Grant, Frederic D., Jr. "The April 1820 Debt Settlement between Conseequa and Benjamin Chew Wilcocks," in Paul A. Van Dyke, ed., *Americans and Macao: Trade, Smuggling and Diplomacy on the South China Coast*. Hong Kong: Hong Kong Univ. Press, 2012, pp. 73–94.

———. "The Failure of the Li-ch'uan Hong: Litigation as a Hazard of Nineteenth Century Foreign Trade." *American Neptune*, Vol. 48, pp. 243–60 (1988).

———. "Hong Merchant Litigation in the American Courts." *Proceedings of the Massachusetts Historical Society*, Vol. 99, pp. 44–62 (1987).

Grant, James. *Money of the Mind: Borrowing and Lending in America from the Civil War to Michael Milken*. New York: Farrar Straus Giroux, 1992.

———. "Requiem for the Dollar." *Wall Street Journal*, 5 December 2009, see: "http://online.wsj.com/article/SB10001424052748704342404574575761660481996.html" (accessed 26 March 2014).

Greenberg, Michael. *British Trade and the Opening of China 1800–42*. Cambridge: Cambridge Univ. Press, 1951.

Haldane, Andrew G. and Alessandri, Piergiorgio. "Banking on the State." BIS [*Bank for International Settlements*] *Review*, 139/2009, see: "http://www.bis.org/review/r091111e.pdf" (accessed 19 January 2012).

Hammond, Bray. *Banks and Politics in America from the Revolution to the Civil War*. Princeton: Princeton Univ. Press, 1957.

Hanser, Jessica. *Mr. Smith Goes to China: British Private Traders and the Interlinking of the British Empire with China, 1757–1793*. Ph.D. dissertation. New Haven: Yale University, 2012.

Ho Ping-ti. "The Salt Merchants of Yang-Chou: A Study of Commercial Capitalism in Eighteenth-Century China." *Harvard Journal of Asiatic Studies*, Vol. 17, pp. 130–69 (1954).

Hoxie, R. Gordon. "Hoover and the Banking Crisis." *Presidential Studies Quarterly*, Vol. 4/5, Vol. 4, no. 3/4—Vol. 5, no. 1, pp. 25–28 (Summer/Fall, 1974–Winter, 1975).

Hsiao, Kung-chuan. *Rural China: Imperial Control in the Nineteenth Century*. Seattle: Univ. of Washington Press, 1960.

Huc, Evariste Régis. *A Journey Through the Chinese Empire*. New York: Harper & Brothers, 1856, Vol. 1.

Hummel, Arthur, ed. *Eminent Chinese of the Ch'ing Period.* Washington, D.C.: U.S. Govt. Printing Office, 1943.

Hung, Juann H. and Qian, Rong. "Why Is China's Savings Rate So High?: A Comparative Study of Cross-Country Panel Data." *Congressional Budget Office, Working Paper No. 2010-07* (Washington, D.C., November 2010), see: "http://www.cbo.gov/sites/default/files/cbofiles/ftpdocs/119xx/doc11958/2010-07-chinasavingrate.pdf" (accessed 30 April 2012).

Hunter, William C. *Bits of Old China.* Shanghai: Kelly and Walsh Ltd., 1911.

———. *The 'Fan Kwae' at Canton Before Treaty Days 1825–1844.* London: Kegan Paul, Trench & Co., 1882.

Jacobs, Els M. *Merchant in Asia: The Trade of the Dutch East India Company During the Eighteenth Century.* Leiden: CNWS Publications, 2006.

Jing Junjian. "Legislation Related to the Civil Economy in the Qing Dynasty," in Bernhardt, Kathryn and Huang, Philip C.C., eds., *Civil Law in Qing and Republican China.* Stanford: Stanford University Press, 1994, pp. 42–84.

Jones, Susan Mann and Kuhn, Philip A. "Dynastic Decline and the Roots of Rebellion," in John K. Fairbank, ed., *The Cambridge History of China,* Vol. 10, Late Ch'ing, 1800–1911, Part I. Cambridge: Cambridge Univ. Press, 1978, pp. 107–62.

Jones, William C., tr., *The Great Qing Code.* Oxford: Clarendon Press, 1994. By permission of Oxford University Press.

Jörg, C. J. A. *Porcelain and the Dutch China Trade.* The Hague: Martinus Nijhoff, 1982.

Joyce, Joseph A. *A Treatise on the Law of Insurance of Every Kind.* Rochester: Lawyers Co-operative Publishing Co., 1917, 2d ed.

Kamensky, Jane. *The Exchange Artist: A Tale of High-Flying Speculation and America's First Banking Collapse.* New York: Viking, 2008.

Kane, Edward J, *The S & L Insurance Mess: How Did It Happen?* Washington, D.C.: The Urban Institute Press, 1989.

Kaske, Elisabeth. "Fund Raising Wars: Office Selling and Interprovincial Finance in Nineteenth-Century China." *Harvard Journal of Asiatic Studies,* Vol. 71, pp. 69–141 (2011).

———. "The Great 1830 Forgery Case: Metropolitan Clerks and Venality in Qing China." Unpublished paper presented at The Fairbank Center for Chinese Studies, Harvard University, October 24, 2008.

Kato Shigeshi. "On the Hang or the Associations of Merchants in China." *Memoirs of the Research Dept. of the Toyo Bunko,* pp. 45–83 (1936).

Keay, John. *The Spice Route: A History.* Berkeley: Univ. of California Press, 2006.

Kennedy, Susan Estabrook. *The Banking Crisis of 1933.* Lexington: The Univ. Press of Kentucky, 1973.

Kessler, Lawrence D. *K'ang-hsi and the Consolidation of Ch'ing Rule 1661–1684.* Chicago: Univ. of Chicago Press, 1976.

Kim, Jun Il. "Unconditional IMF Financial Support and Investor Moral Hazard." IMF [International Monetary Fund] Working Paper No. WP/07/104 (May 2007).

King, Frank H. H. *Money and Monetary Policy in China 1845–1895*. Cambridge, Mass.: Harvard Univ. Press, 1965.

Kirby, William C. "China Unincorporated: Company Law and Business Enterprise in Twentieth- Century China." *Journal of Asian Studies*, Vol. 54, pp. 43–63 (1995).

Kishimoto-Nakayama, Mio. "The Kangxi Depression and Early Qing Local Markets." *Modern China*, Vol. 10, pp. 227–56 (1984).

Kolko, Gabriel. *The Triumph of Conservatism: A Re-interpretation of American History, 1900–1916*. New York: The Free Press, 1977.

Koninckx, Christian. *The First and Second Charters of the Swedish East India Company (1731–1766)*. Kortrijk, Belgium: Van Ghemmert Pub. Co., 1980.

Kroszner, Randall S. and Melick, William R. "Lessons from the U.S. Experience with Deposit Insurance," in Ash Demirgüç-Kunt, Edward J. Kane and Luc Laeven, eds., *Deposit Insurance Around The World: Issues of Design and Implementation*. Cambridge, Mass.: MIT Press, 2008.

Lach, Donald F. and Van Kley, Edwin J. *Asia in the Making of Europe*. Chicago: Univ. of Chicago Press, 1965–1993 (three volumes and nine books).

Landes, David S. "Why Europe and the West? Why Not China?" *The Journal of Economic Perspectives*, Vol. 20, pp. 3–22 (2006).

Latourette, Kenneth S. "The History of Early Relations Between the United States and China." *Transactions of the Connecticut Academy of Arts and Sciences*, Vol. 22, pp. 1–209 (1917).

Leder, Lawrence H. "American Trade to China, 1800–1802: Some Statistical Notes." *American Neptune*, Vol. 23 (1963).

Lee, Jean Gordon. *Philadelphians and the China Trade 1784–1844*. Philadelphia: Philadelphia Museum of Art, 1984.

Leonard, Jane Kate. *Wei Yuan and China's Rediscovery of the Maritime World*. Cambridge, Mass.: Harvard Univ. Press, 1984.

Lewis, Michael. *Boomerang: Travels in the New Third World*. New York: W. W. Norton & Co., 2011.

Li, Gertrude Roth. "State Building Before 1644," in Willard J. Peterson, ed., *The Cambridge History of China*, Vol. 9, The Ch'ing Dynasty to 1800, Part I (Cambridge: Cambridge Univ. Press, 2002, pp. 9–72.

Li Tana Van Dyke, Paul A. "Canton, Cancao, and Cochinchina: New Data and New Light on Eighteenth-Century Canton and the Nanyang." *Chinese Southern Diaspora Studies*, Vol. 1, pp. 1–28 (2007).

Liang Jiabin. *Guangdong Shisan Hang Kao*. Shanghai: Commercial Press for the State Institute of Compilations and Translations, 1937; revised edition, Taipei, 1960.

Lin, Justin Yifu. "The Needham Puzzle: Why the Industrial Revolution Did Not Originate in China." *Economic Development and Cultural Change*, Vol. 43, pp. 269–292 (1995).

Lind, Abram Jr. *A Chapter of the Chinese Penal Code*. Leiden: E.J. Brill, 1887.

Little, Reg. "Confucian Reconstruction of Global Economics and Finance." *Culture Mandala: Bulletin of the Centre for East-West Cultural & Economic Studies*, Vol. 8, pp. 62–73 (2009).

Liu Yong. *The Dutch India Company's Tea Trade with China, 1757–1781*. Ph.D. dissertation. Leiden: Leiden University, 2006.

———. "The VOC Business Culture in China: How the VOC Did Business in Canton in the Eighteenth Century," in Groenendijk, Evert, Vialle, Cynthia and Blussé, Leonard, eds., *Canton and Nagasaki Compared 1730–1830: Dutch, Chinese, Japanese Relations*. Leiden: Institute for the History of European Expansion, 2009, pp. 235–248.

Lou Jianbo. "Introducing a Deposit Insurance System Into China." *Peking Univ. Journal of Legal Studies*, Vol. 1, pp. 233–54 (2008).

MacSherry, Charles W. *Impairment of the Ming Tributary System as Exhibited in Trade Involving Fukien*. Ph.D. dissertation. Berkeley: Univ. of California, 1952.

Mann, Bruce. *Republic of Debtors: Bankruptcy in the Age of American Independence*. Cambridge, Mass.: Harvard Univ. Press, 2002.

Marks, Robert B. "Rice Prices, Food Supply, and Market Structure in Eighteenth-Century South China." *Late Imperial China*, Vol. 12, pp. 64–116 (1991).

———. *Tigers, Rice, Silk, and Silt: Environment and Economy in Late Imperial South China*. Cambridge: Cambridge Univ. Press, 1998.

Mazumdar, Sucheta. *Sugar and Society in China: Peasants, Technology and the World Market*. Cambridge, Mass.: Harvard Univ. Press, 1998.

McElderry, Andrea. "Guarantors and Guarantees in Qing Government-Business Relations," in Leonard, Jane Kate and Watt, John R., eds., *To Achieve Security and Wealth: The Qing Imperial State and the Economy*. Ithaca: Cornell Univ. Press, 1991, pp. 119–37.

Meigs, William M. *The Life of Charles Jared Ingersoll*. Philadelphia: J.B. Lippincott Co., 1897.

Meltzer, Allan H. *A History of the Federal Reserve*. Chicago: Univ. of Chicago Press, 2003, Vol. 1 (1913–1951).

Metzger, Thomas A. "Ch'ing Commercial Policy." *Ch'ing-shih Wen-t'i*, Vol. 1, pp. 4–10 (1966).

———. "The Organizational Capabilities of the Ch'ing State in the Field of Commerce: The Liang huai Salt Monopoly, 1740–1840," in Willmott, W. E., ed., *Economic Organization in Chinese Society*. Stanford University Press, 1972, pp. 9–45.

Miller, Harry E. *Banking Theories in the United States Before 1860*. Cambridge, Mass.: Harvard Univ. Press, 1927.

Morgenson, Gretchen and Rosner, Joshua. *Reckless Endangerment: How Outsized Ambition, Greed, and Corruption Led to Economic Armageddon*. New York: Times Books, 2011.

Morse, Hosea Ballou. *The Chronicles of the East India Company Trading to China, 1635–1834*. Oxford: Oxford Univ. Press, 1926–1929 (5 Vols.).

———. *The International Relations of the Chinese Empire*, Vol. 1, The Period of Conflict, 1834–1860. London: Longmans, Green, 1910.

Moss, David A. *When All Else Fails: Government as the Ultimate Risk Manager*. Cambridge, Mass.: Harvard Univ. Press, 2002.

Moss, David A. and Brennan, Sarah. "Managing Money Risk in Antebellum New York: From Chartered Banking to Free Banking and Beyond." *Studies in American Political Development*, Vol. 15, pp. 138–62 (Fall 2001).

Murray, Dian H. *Pirates of the South China Coast 1790–1810*. Stanford: Stanford Univ. Press, 1987.

Myers, Ramon H. and Wang, Yeh-chien. "Economic Developments, 1644–1800," in Peterson, Willard J., ed., *The Cambridge History of China*, Vol. 9, The Ch'ing Dynasty to 1800, Part I (Cambridge: Cambridge Univ. Press, 2002), pp. 563–645.

Nakamoto, Michiyo and Wighton, David. "Citigroup chief stays bullish on buy-outs." *Financial Times*, 9 July 2007, see: "http://www.ft.com/intl/cms/s/0/80e2987a-2e50-11dc-821c-0000779fd2ac.html#axzz278OaeuX" (accessed 26 March 2014) (registration required).

Ng Chin-keong. "Gentry-Merchants and Peasant-Peddlers—The Response of the South Fukienese to the Offshore Trading Opportunities 1522–1566." *Nanyang Univ. Journal*, Vol. 7, pp. 161–174 (1973).

———. *Trade and Society: The Amoy Network on the China Coast 1683–1735*. Singapore: Singapore Univ. Press, 1983.

Ng, On-cho. Ch'ing Management of the West: A Study of the Regulations, Homicide Cases and Debt Cases, 1644–1820. M.A. Thesis, Univ. of Hong Kong, 1979, see: "http://hub.hku.hk/bitstream/10722/32944/1/FullText.pdf" (accessed 10 May 2012).

Phipps, John. *A Practical Treatise on the China and Eastern Trade*. London: William H. Allen, 1836.

Pollan, Michael. *The Botany of Desire: A Plant's Eye View of the World*. New York: Random House, 2001.

Pozen, Robert. *Too Big to Save? How to Fix the U.S. Financial System*. Hoboken, N.J.: John Wiley & Sons, Inc., 2010.

Preston, Howard H. "The Banking Act of 1933." *The American Economic Review*, Vol. 23, pp. 585–607 (1933).

Pritchard, Earl H. "Anglo-Chinese Relations During the Seventeenth and Eighteenth Centuries." *Univ. of Ill. Studies in the Social Sciences*, Vol. 17, Nos. 1–2 (March–June 1929).

———. "The Crucial Years of Early Anglo-Chinese Relations, 1750–1800." *Research Studies of the State College of Washington*, Vol. 4, Nos. 3–4 (Washington: Pullman, 1936), © Washington State University Press.

Quincy, Josiah. *The Journal of Major Samuel Shaw, The First American Consul at Canton*. Boston: William Crosby & H. P. Nichols, 1847.

Rabinovitch, Simon. "Beijing to roll over provinces' loan terms." *Financial Times*, 13 February 2012, p. 1.

Robb, Thomas Bruce. *The Guaranty of Bank Deposits*. Boston: Houghton Mifflin, 1921.

Roosevelt, Franklin D. *The Public Papers and Addresses of Franklin D. Roosevelt.* New York: Random House, 1938, Vol. 2.

Rowe, William T. *China's Last Empire: The Great Qing.* Cambridge, Mass.: Belknap Press of Harvard University Press, 2009.

———. "Domestic Interregional Trade in Eighteenth-Century China," in Blussé, Leonard and Gaastra, Femme, eds., *On the Eighteenth Century as a Category of Asian History: Van Leur in Retrospect*. Aldershot, England: Ashgate Publishing Ltd., 1998, pp. 173–192.

Sarkissian, Margaret. "Armenians in South-East Asia." *Crossroads: An Interdisciplinary Journal of Southeast Asian Studies*, Vol. 3 (1987).

Schottenhammer, Angela. "The East Asian Maritime World, 1400–1800: Its fabrics of power and dynamics of exchanges—China and her neighbors," in Schottenhammer, Angela, ed., *The East Asian Maritime World, 1400–1800: Its Fabrics of Power and Dynamics of Exchanges*. Wiesbaden: Harrassowitz Verlag, 2007, pp. 1–83.

Seaburg, Carl and Paterson, Stanley. *Merchant Prince of Boston: Colonel T.H. Perkins, 1764–1854*. Cambridge, Mass.: Harvard Univ. Press, 1971.

Smith, Bruce D. and Webber, Warren E. "Private Money Creation and the Suffolk Banking System," *Journal of Money, Credit and Banking*, Vol. 31, No. 3, Part 2 (1999).

Sorkin, Andrew Ross. "Why the Bailout in Spain Won't Work." *The New York Times*, 12 June 2012, pp. B1 and B5.

Smith, Carl T. and Van Dyke, Paul A. "Four Armenian Families." *Review of Culture, International Edition*, No. 8, pp. 40–50 (October 2003).

Spence, Jonathan D. "The K'ang-hsi Reign," in Peterson, Willard J., ed., *The Cambridge History of China*, Vol. 9, The Ch'ing Dynasty to 1800, Part I. Cambridge: Cambridge Univ. Press, 2002, pp. 120–229

———. *Ts'ao Yin and the K'ang-hsi Emperor, Bondservant and Master*. New Haven, Conn.: Yale University Press, 1966.

Spuler, Bertold. *The Mongols in History*. New York: Praeger Publishers, 1971.

Staunton, George Thomas. *Ta Tsing Leu Lee; Being the Fundamental Laws, and a Selection from the Supplementary Statutes of the Penal Code of China*. London: T. Cadell and W. Davies, 1810.

Stelle, Charles C. "American Trade in Opium to China, Prior to 1820." *Pacific Historical Review*, Vol. 9, pp. 425–444 (1940).

———. American Trade in Opium to China, 1821–39." *Pacific Historical Review*, Vol. 10, pp. 57–74 (1941).

Stern, Gary H. and Feldman, Ron J. *Too Big to Fail: The Hazards of Bank Bailouts*. Washington, D.C.: Brookings Institution Press, 2004.

Stewart, Bruce E. *Distillers and Prohibitionists: Social Conflict and the Rise of Anti-Alcohol Reform in Appalachian North Carolina, 1790–1908*. Ph.D. dissertation. Athens, Georgia: Univ. of Georgia, 2007.

Sung, An-un. *A study of the Thirteen Hongs of Kuangtung; A Translation of Parts of the Kuangtung Shih-San-Hang Kao of Liang Chia-Pin*. M.A. thesis. Chicago: Univ. of Chicago, 1958.

Symons, Van Jay. *Ch'ing Ginseng Management: Ch'ing Monopolies in Microcosm*. Tempe, Arizona: Arizona State Univ. Press, 1981.

Tett, Gillian. "How 'too big to fail' banks have become 'too complex to exist.'" *Financial Times*, 8 June 2012, p. 20.

Thill, Joan Kerr Facey. *A Delawarean in the Celestial Empire: John Richardson Latimer and the China Trade*. Master's Thesis. University of Delaware, 1973.

Torbert, Preston M. *The Ch'ing Imperial Household Department: A Study of its Organization and Principal Functions, 1662–1796*. Cambridge, Mass.: Harvard Univ. Press, 1977.

Tsai, Simon Yang-chien. *Trading for Tea: A Study of the English East India Company's Tea Trade with China and the Related Financial Issues, 1760–1833*. Ph.D. dissertation. Leicester: University of Leicester, 2003.

Tsiang, T. F. (Chiang Ting-fu). "The Government and the Co-Hong of Canton, 1839." *Chinese Social and Political Science Review*, Vol. 15, pp. 602–607 (1932).

Van der Sprenkel, Sybille. *Legal Institutions in Manchu China: A Sociological Analysis*. London: The Athlone Press, Univ. of London, 1962, © Berg, by permission of Bloomsbury Publishing Plc.

Van Dyke, Paul A. *The Canton Trade: Life and Enterprise on the China Coast, 1700–1845*. Hong Kong: Hong Kong Univ. Press, 2005.

———. "Description of Price and Wage Data from Canton and Macao 1704–1833" (unpublished paper dated 4 March 2008), p. 5, see: "http://www.iisg.nl/hpw/canton .pdf" (accessed 9 September 2012).

———. *Merchants of Canton and Macao: Politics and Strategies in Eighteenth-Century Chinese Trade*. Hong Kong: Hong Kong Univ. Press, 2011.

———. "Tan Suqua and Family: Merchants of Canton 1716–1778," ARI [*Asia Research Institute, National University of Singapore*] *Working Paper*, No. 50, Sept. 2005, see: "http://www.ari.nus.edu.sg/docs/wps/wps05_050.pdf" (accessed 17 November 2008).

Wakeman, Frederic, Jr. "The Canton Trade and the Opium War," in Fairbank, John K., ed., *The Cambridge History of China*, Vol. 10, Late Ch'ing, 1800–1911, Part 1. Cambridge: Cambridge Univ. Press, 1978, pp. 163–212.

———. *The Fall of Imperial China*. New York: The Free Press, 1975.

———. *The Great Enterprise: The Manchu Reconstruction of Imperial Order in Seventeenth-Century China*. Berkeley: Univ. of Calif. Press, 1985.

———. *Strangers at the Gate: Social Disorder in South China, 1839–1861*. Berkeley: Univ. of California Press, 1966.

Waley-Cohen, Joanna. "Collective Responsibility in Qing Criminal Law," in Turner, Karen G., Feinerman, James V. and Guy, R. Kent, eds., *The Limits of the Rule of Law in China*. Seattle: Univ. of Washington Press, 2000, pp. 112–131.

———. *Exile in Mid-Qing China: Banishment to Xinjiang, 1758–1820*. New Haven: Yale Univ. Press, 1991.

———. *The Sextants of Beijing: Global Currents in Chinese History*. New York: W. W. Norton & Co., 1999.

Wang, Fei-ling. *Organizing Through Division and Exclusion: China's Hukou System*. Stanford: Stanford Univ. Press, 2005.

Wang Xiaotian. "Freeing Up of Rates Not on Agenda for this Year." *China Daily*, 7 February 2012, see: "http://news.xinhuanet.com/english/business/2012-02/07/c_131395812.htm" (accessed 26 March 2014).

Ward, Geoffrey C. *A First-Class Temperament: The Emergence of Franklin Roosevelt*. New York: Harper & Row, 1989.

Ward, Thomas W. "Remarks on the Canton Trade and the Manner of Transacting Business." *Essex Institute Historical Collections*, Vol. 73 (1937).

Watson, Alan. *Legal Transplants: An Approach to Comparative Law*. Athens, Ga.: Univ. of Georgia Press, 2d ed., 1993.

Weatherford, Jack. *Genghis Khan and the Making of the Modern World*. New York: Three Rivers Press, 2004.

Whelan, T. S. *The Pawnshop in China*. Ann Arbor, Mich.: Center for Chinese Studies, Univ. of Michigan, 1979.

White, Ann Bolbach. *The Hong Merchants of Canton*. Ph.D. dissertation. Philadelphia: Univ. of Pennsylvania, 1967.

Wills, John E., Jr. *Embassies and Illusions: Dutch and Portuguese Envoys to K'ang-hsi, 1666–1687*. Cambridge, Mass.: Harvard Univ. Press, 1984.

———. "Maritime Europe and the Ming," in Wills, John E., Jr., ed., *China and Maritime Europe, 1500–1800: Trade, Settlement, Diplomacy, and Missions*. Cambridge: Cambridge Univ. Press, 2011.

———. *Pepper, Guns and Parleys: The Dutch East India Company and China 1622–1681*. Cambridge, Mass.: Harvard Univ. Press, 1974.

Woellert, Lorraine and Gittelsohn, John. "Fannie-Freddie Fix at $160 Billion With $1 Trillion Worst Case." *Bloomberg News*, 13 June 2010 7:00PM ET, see: "http://www.bloomberg.com/news/2010-06-13/fannie-freddie-fix-expands-to-160-billion-with-worst-case-at-1-trillion.html" (accessed 26 March 2014).

Wong, J. Y. *Yeh Ming-ch'en, Viceroy of Liang Kuang*. Cambridge: Cambridge Univ. Press, 1976.

Wood, Herbert J. "England, China, and the Napoleonic Wars." *Pacific Historical Review*, Vol. 9, pp. 139–56 (1940).

Wright, Conrad E. "Merchants and Mandarins: New York and the Early China Trade," in David S. Howard, *New York and the China Trade* (New York: The New-York Historical Society, 1984), pp. 17–54.

Wright, Robert E. "The First Phase of the Empire State's 'Triple Transition': Banks' Influence on the Market, Democracy, and Federalism in New York, 1776–1838." *Social Science History*, Vol. 21, pp. 521–58 (1997).

Yang, Lien-sheng. "Government Control of Urban Merchants in Traditional China." *Tsing Hua Journal of Chinese Studies*, Vol. 8, new series, pp. 186–206 (1970).

———. *Money and Credit in China: A Short History*. Cambridge, Mass.: Harvard Univ. Press, 1952.

Zelin, Madeleine. "A Critique of Rights of Property in Prewar China," in Zelin, Madeleine, Ocko, Jonathan K. and Gardella, Robert, eds., *Contract and Property in Early Modern China*. Stanford: Stanford Univ. Press, 2004, pp. 17–36.

———. *The Magistrate's Tael: Rationalizing Fiscal Reform in Eighteenth-Century Qing China*. Berkeley: Univ. of California Press, 1984.

Zhao, Gang. *The Qing Opening to the Ocean: Chinese Maritime Policies, 1684–1757*. Honolulu: University of Hawai'I Press, 2013.

Zhao, Gang. *Shaping the Asian Trade Network: The Conception and Implementation of the Chinese Open Trade Policy, 1684–1840*. Ph.D. dissertation. Baltimore: The Johns Hopkins University, 2007.

Zhuang Guotu. "The Impact of the International Tea Trade on the Social Economy of Northwest Fujian in the Eighteenth Century," in Blussé, Leonard and Gaastra, Femme, eds., *On the Eighteenth Century as a Category of Asian History: Van Leur in Retrospect*. Aldershot, England: Ashgate Publishing Ltd., 1998, pp. 193–216.

2.2 *Dictionary and Encyclopedia*

Craigie, William A. and Hulbert, James R., eds. *A Dictionary of American English*. Chicago: Univ. of Chicago Press, 1944, Vol 4.

Davids, Lewis E. *Dictionary of Insurance*. Totowa, N.J.: Rowman & Allanheld, 1983, 6th rev. ed.

Funk, Isaac K., ed. *A Standard Dictionary of the English Language*. New York: Funk & Wagnalls Co., 1935, Vol. 2.

Hafer, Rik W. *The Federal Reserve System: An Encyclopedia*. Westport, Conn.: Greenwood Press, 2005.

Hayden, H. R., ed. *The Annual Cyclopedia of Insurance of the United States 1894–1895*. Hartford: H. R. Hayden, 1895.

Johnson, Allen and Malone, Dumas, eds., *Dictionary of American Biography*. New York: Charles Scribner's Sons, 1931, Vol. 6, pp. 525–526 (biography of Joshua Forman by H. T.).

Mathews, Mitford M. ed. *A Dictionary of Americanisms*. Chicago: Univ. of Chicago Press, 1951, Vol. 2.

Powell, William S., ed. *Dictionary of North Carolina Biography*. Chapel Hill: Univ. of North Carolina Press, 1986, Vol. 2, pp. 220–1 (biography of Joshua Forman by C. Sylvester Green).

Webster's New International Dictionary (1925).

Index

Abrami, Regina IX
Acapulco 28
Africa 259
Agriculture 19, 26, 202, 240, 245
Ahoy 159
Aisin Gioro clan 18
Alabama 242, 245,
Albany 191, 218, 223
Albany Argus 224 n.12
Aldridge, A. Owen 13
Alford, William P. IX
Algonac 243
Altree, Wayne X
America See "United States of America"
American Bankers Association 245
Americans See "United States of America"
Amoy XV, 26, 32 (See also "Xiamen")
Amsterdam 177
Anchang hong 201
Annam See "Vietnam"
Anqua 26 n.38
Anson, Commodore 28
Antibanker views 245
Antidebtor views 143–144, 190
Antwerp 177
Armenian merchants See "Merchants, Armenian"
Ashing 108, 160–162
Asia 2, 146, 154, 259–260
Asian financial crisis See "Financial crisis"
Astor, John Jacob 179 n.43, 225
Attendant See "Servant"
Australia 260
Austrian Emperor 38
Automaton XII, 69

Baboom, Gregory 174
Bailing 158, 161
Bangka Straits 28
Banishment,
  of Chinese XVII, 29, 75, 104, 107–108, 114, 117, 143–144, 158, 162, 188, 190, 198
  of Europeans (deportation) 73, 75 n.95, 117
Bank deposit insurance IX, XVI, 3–5, 12, 14, 17, 218, 220, 230–262, 272–280
  Ability to pay claims 250
  Accounting 254
  Benefits of 265
  Chinese origin 3, 5, 17, 185, 191, 218, 233–234
  Contemporary 4, 252–253
  Coverage 247–250, 254, 258–259
  Evasions of 158–159, 276
  Europe 257
  First statute 12, 14–15, 17, 185, 191, 218, 220, 230–237
  History 5, 14–15, 17, 191, 218, 220, 230–240, 243–262
  Insolvency 275
  International 3, 5, 12, 252–253, 257–262, 272–273
    History 252–253, 257–262, 272
  Public good 265
  True insurance 274
  United States IX, 3–5, 17, 191, 220, 234, 239–257, 262, 272, 278–279
    History 4–5, 17, 185, 191, 220, 239–257, 262, 272, 278–279
    National 5, 12, 17, 220, 234, 239–257, 272
    No depositor loss objective 254
    Popularity 234, 240–242, 247, 253–254
    Solvency 257
    State statutes 5, 12, 17, 185, 191, 220, 237–240
    Too big to fail 254–255, 276
Bank holidays 241
Bank of Credit and Commerce International 258
Bank of England 172
Bankers 218
Banking Act of 1863 238
Banking Act of 1933 XIII, 239, 241, 246–249, 248 (**Illustration**) (**Plate 22**), 253, 278
Banking Act of 16 June 1934 247
Banking Act of 1935 247–249
Banknotes See "Currency", "United States of America, Banknotes"

Bankruptcy 102, 113–114, 124, 184
Banks and banking 1, 5, 185, 219–221, 223, 234–246, 259 (See "New York, State of, Banks and Banking" and "United States of America, Banks and Banking")
Banking regulation 18, 234–246
Depositors 237, 239, 246, 248, 252, 254–255, 259, 261
Flight by, concern 252, 259–260
Employment by 275
Failures 228–229, 235–236
Loose credit 246
Stability 223, 230
Taxpayers 246, 278–280
Baojia system See "Collective responsibility"
Bastinado 143
Basu, Dilip Kumar x, 10, 58, 215 n.100
Batavia 26 n.38, 32, 35, 62
Massacre of Chinese in 1740 62
Beau Khequa (Li Guanghua) 56, 63, 65 n.55, 72, 87–88, 90 n.158, 119
Debts 72, 87–88, 119
Beijing xviii, 9, 12, 18–20, 39, 42, 45, 55, 57–58, 62, 65, 72, 76, 102, 111, 113, 122, 147, 153, 189, 209, 211, 263
Bengal 272
Bentham, Jeremy 272
Bently, Mr. 178
Bills of exchange 155
Bingham, Ship 177
Bird seller 200
Blue Sapphire Button 57
Blussé van Oud-Alblas, Dr. Johan Leonard bix, bx, 8
Bocca Tigris forts 210
Bodde, Derk 2 n.5
Bogue forts 28
Bol, Peter K. ix
Board of Punishments See "China, Government, Qing Dynasty, Board of Punishments"
Board of Revenue (*Hu Bu*) See "China, Government, Qing Dynasty, Board of Revenue"
Board of War See "China, Government, Qing Dynasty, Board of War"
Bodenhorn, Howard 227, 236–237
Bombay 139
Bonds See "Promissory notes"
Bookkeepers 109
Boston 174, 179 n.43, 228
Boston College Law School ix
Bowen, J. Ray, II 267
Bribes 72 n.72, 89, 110–111, 114, 119, 137, 170
Brink, Robert A. x
Britain See "Great Britain"
British East India Company xvi, xviii, 8, 17, 29, 32–34, 37–38, 64, 70–72, 74, 78, 86–87, 89–93, 100, 102, 110–118, 121, 123–124, 126, 130–135, 140–142, 147, 149–153, 158–164, 170, 173–175, 185–188, 192–193, 195–197, 202–203, 211–212, 266, 268–269, 276, 278–279
Advances to buy tea 185
Assignment of ships 64, 70
Bills on London 111–112
Bribes paid by 89–90, 110, 170
Charter 192
China Agency 202
Communications with Chinese officials 71–72, 91–93
Contracts with hong merchants 17, 192–193, 202–203, 268
Court of Directors 113
Creditor 87, 89, 91–93, 101, 107, 130, 134, 140–142, 150–153, 158–165, 170, 175, 185–187, 212
Debtor 134
Embargo of 1829–1830 192, 195–197, 211, 271, 274
EIC funds 140, 164, 202–203
Information gathering by 86, 102, 112, 152–154
Lender 34–35, 164, 185, 192, 212
Lender of last resort 35, 164, 192
Opium licenses 135
Petitioning by 71–72, 74, 114, 130, 188
Private venture cargo 70
Records 8, 86, 115, 142, 152, 209, 266, 269
Select Committee 117, 142, 161, 187
Shares of business 161, 164, 186–188, 192–193, 202–203, 268
Strategy of 159–160, 186, 195–197, 278
Supercargoes 28, 112–116, 118, 123, 163
Surgeons 116, 163

Trademark 187 n.63
Truck 134
Use of Chinese legal process 93, 130
Withdrawal from trade 17, 192–193, 195–197, 202–203, 209, 212, 279
Broken Hong Merchant XIII, 215, 216 **(Illustration) (Plate 17)**
Brokers 51, 172
Brooks, Jayson X
Browne, Henry 142–143
Bucksport 228
Buddhist priest X, 20
Business goodwill 101
Business records 6–7, 143, 144 n.66, 269
Dutch 8
Biases of 143, 144 n.66
British 8, 89 n.156, 143
Chinese 7, 9, 143
Dutch 8
French 8
Western traders 6–7
Business school graduate 269

Cai, Madame 144
Cai Zhaofu (Seunqua III) See "Seunqua III"
Calcutta 10, 135
Calicoes 123
Calomiris, Charles 241, 253
Camel 270
Canals 221
Canal companies 234
Cannon See "Weapons"
Canton (Guangzhou) XI, XIII, XV, XVIII, 4–5, 10, 13, 15–17, 20–21, 26, 28–29, 31–32, 35–36, 39, 43, 46–47, 55, 57, 60, 62–63, 72–75, 77–78, 110–113, 124, 131–132, 145, 147, 151, 155, 159, 171–173, 177–178, 183, 189–191, 197, 205, 209, 215–216, 225, 234, 243, 250, 252, 263, 268, 271–272, 274–275
Guilds at 37
Western side 35, 83
Canton Guaranty System IX, XVI, 3–5, 8, 10, 12, 14–15, 18, 31, 41, 46–47, 49, 53–54, 60–61, 76, 93, 101, 103–104, 107–109, 119–130, 138–147, 157–166, 169, 173, 182, 184–191, 193, 195, 201, 206–220, 224, 250–252, 262, 265, 270–279
Avoidance of system 103, 130, 145–146
Benefits of 265–266
Collective guaranty 3–5, 18, 61, 93, 101, 103–104, 107–109, 113, 119–130, 138–147, 157–166, 169, 182, 184–191, 195, 201, 206–217, 219–220, 234, 265, 270–271, 273–279
Coerced negotiation 101, 117, 119–122, 157–158, 189
Cornerstone of Canton System 77, 265–266
Means to placate foreigners 77, 216
Resistance to include new hongs 127
Collective liability 46–47, 51, 61, 64–71, 74, 90, 93, 101, 104, 109, 119–123, 126–127, 139, 143, 146–147, 157–166, 169, 182, 184–191, 195, 201, 206–217, 220, 234, 265, 270–271, 273–279
Annual liability burden XIV, 157, 166, 184, 195, 206–209, 270–271
Assumptions of hong debt 122, 126–127, 140, 146, 157–158, 206–209, 212, 265, 270–271
For customs duties 64–65, 74, 88, 119, 139, 169, 186, 212
For singsongs 60, 64, 65, 64–70
Of shopkeepers 70–71
Total liability burden XIV, 126, 146, 157–158, 166, 184, 195, 206–209, 216, 265, 270–271
Confucian ideal 120, 265
Development 46–47, 64–65, 119–125, 169
Evasions of 158–165, 173, 276
Final payment in 1843 17, 216–217, 277, 279
Frailty 145, 205, 266, 274
Funding assumptions 192
Government as implicit guarantor of system 17, 113, 160, 193–194, 215–217, 279
Guaranty fund 120 (See also, "Consoo Fund")
History 46–47, 64–65, 119–127, 157–166, 169, 173, 193, 205–207, 216, 251–252, 265, 274–279
Indirect costs of system 130, 145–146, 151, 159–160, 182, 195, 278
Initiated in 1780 47, 101, 104, 119–125, 184, 279

Canton Guaranty System (*cont.*)
- Native ports hong 123
- Western opinion of 145–146, 160, 173, 192, 218–220, 265
- Written agreement 120, 127, 169, 201

Canton Customs See "China, Canton Maritime Customs"

Canton System XVI, 3–5, 15–18, 26, 31, 35–37, 49, 53–125, 146–148, 192, 194, 209, 217–218, 224–226, 233–234, 262, 265, 269, 271, 273, 276
- Changes sought 72–74, 192, 195–197
- Chief merchants 36
- Chinese officials 32, 35–36, 57–60, 71–74, 148
  - Communication with 71–73
  - Investigation by 73–74, 82, 131, 148, 170
  - Petitions 71–73, 200
- Debt collection 4, 100–107, 215
  - Disclosure of assets 140–141, 153
  - Secret or extralegal 103
- Economic concerns 72
- Economic sanctions 62
- Evolution 62
- Foreign goods firms (yanghuo hang) 31
- History 16, 31–37, 62, 147–148, 209, 217
- Hong merchant duties 57, 62–64, 147
  - Collection of customs taxes 15, 62, 64–65, 146, 273
  - Maintain order (security) 61, 64, 146, 196, 273
  - Punishment for breach of duty 64, 108, 270
  - Reporting to officials 64, 147, 201
  - Secure ships 138, 146, 196, 200
  - Supervision of foreigners 15, 62, 64, 196
- Hong merchant licensing 15, 61–2, 86, 127, 131, 140, 148, 150, 158, 163, 169, 174, 188, 195–201, 205, 212, 219
  - Admission 61–2, 86, 127, 131, 150, 174, 188, 195–201, 205
  - Decline in strength 195, 198–201, 205
  - Licensing fees 61, 131, 150, 163, 195–196, 199, 205, 212
  - Operation without a license 158, 161, 164, 174
  - Provisional licenses 198
  - Retirement 148, 169
  - Revocation of license 200–201
  - Surrender of licenses 119
  - Transfer or assignment 61, 140, 163, 212
  - Wealthy and respectable men 62, 86, 131
- Law and regulations 4, 10, 15–16, 37, 57–58, 62, 64, 71, 74–84, 116, 170, 196–197, 201, 218, 224–226, 233–234, 262, 265, 269, 271
  - Foreign view of 185, 192, 194–197
  - Foreign violence 16, 28–30
  - Foreigners confined to waterfront enclave 78–79, 83, 185
  - Foreigners permitted only limited outings 83
  - Foreigners required to leave Canton in off-season 78
  - Foreigners required to reside in hong merchant properties 78–79
  - Jurisdiction 57–58, 60, 63
  - Penalties for violation 74–75, 82, 90
  - Personal conduct rules 81, 83–84
- Avoidance of system 103, 130, 145–146
- Prohibitions 71
  - Foreigners not allowed to learn Chinese 73, 82, 116
  - Foreigners not allowed to enter Canton 83
  - Mortgaging hong properies to foreigners 33, 79
  - Of communications with interior of China 77–78
  - Of determining inland commodity prices 77, 82
  - Of direct hong merchant contact with European firms 78
  - Of direct hong merchant contact with inland suppliers 77
  - Of hong merchant debt to foreigners 33, 49, 74–77, 79, 82–83, 89, 90, 105, 109–111, 115, 117–118, 126, 145, 157–158, 185, 201, 275
    - Ban violated 111, 126, 157
    - Claimed ignorance 117

Certification of no debt 108, 201
Illegal loans enforced 77, 109–110, 126, 145, 157, 185, 275
Lesson provided by failure to enforce 81, 109
Penalties for illegal loans 74, 82, 90, 109, 115, 201
Banishment 108–109, 115, 117
Confiscation 74–75, 109
Forfeiture 75–76, 109, 115, 117
Of firing ships' guns 28
Of loans to hong merchants 74–77, 79, 82–83, 105, 109–111, 115, 117–118, 126, 145, 157–158, 185, 201, 275
Of sedan chair use by foreigners 84
Of trading opium 110–111, 172
Of warships 28
Restrictions on hiring servants 77, 84, 161
Weapons not allowed in Canton factories 81
Women not allowed in Canton factories 81, 84, 199, 270
River travel closely monitored 83–84
Settlement of accounts 74–75
Ships required to surrender cannons 28
Some rules ignored 28, 81–82, 84, 110–111, 185, 201
Some rules thought meaningless 110–111
Trade regulations 18, 33, 53, 62–64, 71, 74–84, 170, 196–197, 201, 224–226, 233–4
Circulation and posting 80–81
Comparison of versions 82–83
Edicts of 1755–8 62–64, 71, 83 n.120, 86
Eight Regulations 79–84, 109, 185
Number of regulations 83
Provisions cumulative 82–83
Restatements 81–83
Summarization or abridgement 81
Trade regulations, abridged (Hunter) 81 (Abridged translation reproduced in full text as Appendix 5 312–314)
Trade regulations of 1760 33, 74–82, 84, 87, 89, 93, 105, 107, 109 (Modern translation reproduced in full text as Appendix 1 283–285; Contemporary translation reproduced in full text as Appendix 2 286–290)
Trade regulations of 1810 82
Trade regulations of 1831 81–82, 86 (Translation reproduced in full text as Appendix 3 291–300)
Trade regulations of 1835 81–83 (Translation reproduced in full text as Appendix 4 301–311)
Translations 82
Monopoly trading rights XVII, 5, 36–37, 56, 60, 62–63, 71, 86–87, 89, 137–138, 147, 158, 161, 195, 219, 234, 262
Monopoly authorized 1755 62–63, 71, 86, 262
Monopoly ignored 89, 137–138, 147, 158, 161
Official connections 32, 35–36
Official merchants 31, 32, 36, 54
First licensed 31
Purpose 49
Quasi diplomats 15, 64
Security concerns 18, 50, 53, 62, 72, 92, 105, 108, 133
Military defense 78–79, 82, 105, 133
Security merchants (baoshang) XVIII, 52, 60–62, 65, 89, 138 (See also "Hong merchants")
Assignment of ships 60, 63–65, 89, 138, 146
Exclusivity in trading 146
Wealthy and respectable men 62, 110
Security merchant system (baoshang zhidu) 52, 60–62
Imperial approval 1745 62
Senior or capital merchants 63–64, 89, 90 n.158
Social order concerns 77, 92, 111, 132–133, 171
Tax collection 15–16, 18, 26, 41–43, 62, 151, 170–171, 208–211
Deferral 171, 190–191, 208–211
Canton trade 15, 18, 31–33, 35–39, 54, 57–58, 60, 62–65, 111–130, 132–147, 151, 154–173, 193, 195, 199, 202–205, 209, 225, 263, 265–266, 276
Assaults or fights involving Chinese 29,

- Canton Trade (*cont.*)
  - Chinese side disadvantaged 78
  - Chinese dependence on 110
  - Debt cases 29, 87–88, 93–130, 140–141, 147, 157–165, 194, 200
    - Assumed debt contributes to failure of successor 87–88, 91
    - Chinese debts crisis of 1779–80 90, 111–125
    - Debt assumed rather than paid 87–88, 91, 140, 146
    - Debt assumed in return for new business 87–88, 91, 146
    - Flight by debtors 159, 162–163, 189, 211–212
    - Management by other hongs 141
    - Social duty to pay debt 120
  - Efficiency 265
  - Fighting between sailors 28–29, 104 **(Illustration of trial) (Plate 9)**
  - Foreign factories xii, xiii, xvii, 35, 81, 117 **(Illustration) (Plate 10)**, 155, 133 **(Illustration) (Plate 11)**, 193 **(Illustration) (Plate 15)**
  - Importance of 110, 146
  - Increase in trade 15, 33, 41, 43, 126, 130, 134–135, 193, 199, 202
  - Loans by foreigners 33, 79, 111–125, 157–165, 185
    - Unsecured 33, 79
  - Official participation 73, 86
  - Suspension or stoppage of trade 171, 192
    - by Chinese authorities 29, 43, 62, 89, 110
    - by Chinese merchants 63, 65, 70
    - by European traders 77, 87, 110, 149, 192, 195–197
  - Trade with Britain 132–135, 155–156, 266
  - Trade with Europe 32, 35–36, 39, 54–55, 60, 110, 155–156, 266
  - Trade with the United States 155–156, 169, 266
  - Western experience 35, 84, 185, 195
    - Trade generally well managed 84, 195, 263, 265
- Cao Yin 40
- Capurso, Richard x
- Carpenter 116
- Carrington, Edward 137, 155–156, 178
- Cash See "Currency, silver" and "Silver"
- Cawsanqua (Cudgin) 35
- Ce Leng 62
- *Centurion*, HMS 28
- Chai Hunqua 63, 90 n.158
- Chai Suequa 63, 90 n.158
- Chang Te-ch'ang 6
- Changlu salt monopoly See "Salt administration, Changlu salt monopoly"
- Changxian 158
- Chariot xii, 67, 69
- Château Margaux 224
- Checks 241
- Cheequa 169
- Ch'en, Kuo-tung Anthony x, 10–11, 131, 266–270
- Chen, Lydia ix
- Cheong, Weng Eang 10–11, 36, 60, 63–64, 83 n.120, 85, 127, 130
- Cherry trees 242
- Chetqua 63, 90 n.158, 128 n.14
- Chiang Ting-fu 210
- Chicken seller 200
- Children 52
- China ix, 3–4, 18, 44, 66, 193, 225, 259, 273
  - Canton Maritime Customs xvi, xvii, 6, 12, 16, 18, 26–27, 29, 39, 41–43, 47, 58–60, 71, 108, 137, 139, 146–147, 263
    - Administration 27, 40, 58–59, 74
    - Collective responsibility for debt 46, 51, 61, 64, 70–71, 74, 90, 123, 127, 129–130, 143, 146, 186, 220, 271
    - Commissioner 58–59, 108 (See also "China, Government, Qing Dynasty, Officials, Hoppo")
    - Customs funds 139
    - Customs House 29, 119
    - Customs table 41, 146
    - Customs tax collection 15–16, 18, 26, 28, 41–43, 60, 64–65, 71, 88, 90, 101, 137, 146, 170
    - Customs tax revenues 27, 39, 41, 43, 263
      - Compared to salt merchants 45
    - Fiscal year 42
    - Reporting 139, 147, 268

Chinese traditions 12, 18, 47, 53, 83
Customs (National)
  Administration 40, 63, 137, 139
  Taxes 39, 41–43, 55, 60, 132, 140, 156, 186
    Due date for payment 42–43, 140, 156, 159
    Emperor's present 42
    Export duties 41–42, 60, 71–72, 146
    Import duties 41–42, 60, 71–72, 146
    Measurement fees 41, 60, 146, 200
    Native tribute 42, 130, 153–154, 210
    Port charges 41
    Purchase privilege of payment 42–43, 151
    Recovered from hong debtors 90, 101, 186
    Rice cargo discount 42
    Surtaxes 42, 170
Emperor XVII, 28, 39–40, 42, 51, 57, 59, 65–69, 71–73, 82, 87, 91–93, 104–105, 107, 113, 115, 123, 130, 139, 141–142, 153–154, 161, 188, 190, 197, 209, 263
  Birthday 154
  Budget of imperial court 41
  Memorials 59, 82, 170
Foreign relations 105
Fujian Maritime Customs 35
Government, Qing Dynasty 3, 43, 215
  Board of Punishments 91–92, 104
  Board of Revenue 41, 58, 89 n.156, 95
  Board of War 106
  Civil Office 122
  Fees for public purposes 123, 129–130, 137, 162, 170–171, 190, 210–211, 267–268, 270–271, 276–277
  Government boatyards 109
  Government funds 33
  Grand Council 73
  Justice Office 122
  Monopolization of business 3, 6, 11–12, 39, 47–48, 56, 62, 262 (See also, "Ginseng trade," "Imperial Household Department" and "Salt trade")
Officials 28–29, 32, 36, 41, 43, 45, 52, 54–61, 63–66, 71, 76, 81–82, 92–94, 96–97, 102–103, 107–108, 110–111, 116, 120, 122, 125–127, 130–133, 137, 147–148, 151, 169–170, 185, 189, 199, 209, 252, 266 (See also, "Hong merchants, official rank, purchased")
  Administration 63
  Canton posting, reputation 43, 46, 130, 263
  Censors 170
  Confiscation of property 73
  Corruption 73, 131, 133, 137, 151–152, 170
  District (*xian*) magistrates 57–58, 90, 96–98, 100–102, 105, 119
    Nanhai district (Canton) 57–58, 70, 79, 87, 88 n.147, 100, 118, 142–143, 161, 170, 189, 210
    Panyu district (including Whampoa) 57–58, 79, 87, 88 n.147
    Xiangshan district (including Macao) 58
  Exactions or fees 51, 59, 61, 65–66, 71, 79, 97, 111, 122–123, 129–133, 142, 145, 151–153, 167, 170–171, 190, 210–211, 213, 267–268, 270–271, 276–277
  Gifts sent to Beijing 64–70, 123, 130, 153–154
  Governor (fuyuan) XVII, 28, 49, 57, 59, 61–63, 91–92, 102, 107, 114, 116–118, 122, 147, 158
  Governor–General (zongdu) (also called the "Viceroy") XVII, XVIII, 28–29, 49, 57, 59, 61–63, 72, 74, 86, 90, 92, 107, 114–115, 124, 143, 147, 158–159, 161–162, 170, 186, 188 190, 195–198, 200–201, 208, 213–214
  Hoppo XVI, XVII, XVIII, 6, 12, 28, 36, 40–41, 43–44, 46–47, 57–65, 73–74, 86–87, 89, 100, 102, 107, 114, 116–119, 122, 127, 131–132, 139–141, 143, 147–148, 153, 158, 161, 163–164, 170, 186, 188–190, 195–197, 199–201, 205, 208, 212
    Access to 63
    Ginseng sales 42, 44, 210
    Hong firm licensing 61–62, 127, 169, 198–201, 205, 212, 219
    Supervision of 147

China (*cont.*)
- Impeachment 73
- Indebted to government 43, 61, 131–132, 263
- Joint edicts 63, 102, 117
- Local officials 72
- Personal financial ruin 76–77
- Removal from office 73
- Retribution by 153
- Review of decisions 101, 103–105, 147, 161
- Viceroy See "Governor-General"
- Wealth 130–131
- Weiyuan XVIII, 57, 73, 119, 122
- Records 7, 9, 209
- Tax collection 41–43, 51, 76, 151, 171, 208–209
  - Performance 43, 51
    - Penalty for shortfall 43, 51, 76–77
  - Quotum system 41, 43, 51, 76
  - Regular quotum 41
  - Surplus quotum 41, 263
- Venality 15, 51, 56 n.11, 131, 133, 145, 151–152

History, Early 47
History, Han Dynasty 31, 92
History, Ming Dynasty 19, 23, 30–31, 35, 50, 92, 105, 109–110
- Illicit maritime trade 30
- Japanese pirates 30, 105, 109–110
- Trade policy 23, 26, 30, 109
- Tribute system 26, 109

History, Qing Dynasty 19–30, 52
- Manchu conquest X, 18–22, 25, 54
  - Anti-Manchu sentiment 27
  - Cavalry 20
  - Removal of coastal population 21–22
  - Feudal princes 20, 23, 54–56
  - Local rebellions 20, 27
  - Pacification 23, 25–28, 54
  - Siege of Canton 20–21
- Maritime foreign trade 18, 25–31, 35, 38–39, 54–55, 60, 109–110
  - Aggressive Western actions 28–30, 72 n.70, 103
  - Banned 21, 27–28, 32
  - Importance of 110
  - Early specialists in Western trade 32, 35
  - Early trade with the West 32, 35, 38–39, 54
  - Official concern with practices of Chinese 30, 70, 107–110
  - Regional junk trade 27–28, 32, 37
  - Seasonality of trade 32, 176–177
  - Security concerns 25–30, 50, 92, 105, 109–110
  - Trade with Japan 26, 28, 30, 32, 50
- Open trade policy of 1683 XII, 24–28, 54
  - Competition among ports 26
  - Security concerns 25–30, 54
  - Economic conditions 25–26
  - Trade ban reimposed 27–28, 32
  - Trade revival 26
- Trade policy 26, 31
- Tribute system 26, 73 n.83, 92

History, People's Republic
- Economic revival 26

History, Song Dynasty 31, 35, 92
History, Tang Dynasty 31, 92
Law, Qing Dynasty 73, 75, 81–82, 90, 93–95, 97, 102–110, 122, 183, 185, 212
- Bankruptcy 102
- Code (*Da Qing Lu Li*) 75–76, 94–97, 102–106
- Communication with Emperor 73
- Commercial law 95–96
- Confucian view of law 98–99, 120
- Criminal matters 29, 48–49, 103, 143
- Debt collection 4, 17
  - from foreign debtors 99, 183
  - property held in common 120–121
  - Self help barred 17, 96
- Foreign view of 185, 213, 215
- Guaranty 51–53
- Interest rate cap (*yi ben yi li*) XVIII, 93, 102–103, 114, 117–118, 122, 124
- Joint liability (*lianzuo*) 51
- Judicial process in debt cases 90, 93–111, 130, 142–144, 146–147, 158, 161–162, 186, 188, 201
  - Self help barred 17, 96

Banishment of debtor 92, 104, 107–108, 117, 143–144, 158, 162, 188, 190
Beating the debtor 91–92, 97, 100–101, 104–106, 143–144, 203–204, 212, 214
Death of debtor in custody 92, 108 n.239, 143–144, 162, 203–204, 212
Debt cases involving Chinese creditors 93–101, 161
Debt cases involving foreign creditors 4, 90, 93–94, 100–111, 122, 126, 130, 138–140, 142–144, 146–147, 157–158, 160–162, 186, 188, 190, 203, 212–214
  Allowance or payment of claims 101–106, 122, 126, 138, 140, 146, 157–158, 185–186, 188, 190, 201, 206, 212–214
  Chinese creditors involved 101–102, 140–141, 143, 161, 186, 188, 212
  Coerced negotiation 101, 117–119, 140, 157–158, 186, 188–190
  Creditor claims 100–103, 114, 122, 126, 140, 142, 157–158, 161, 185–186, 188, 190, 212, 214
  Debtors coopted (potential traitors) 107–108
  Determination of viability of firm 90, 101, 186, 214–215
  Disclosure and investigation 140–141, 161, 170, 188, 213
  Failure to enforce foreign loan ban 81, 109–111, 157, 185, 275
  Foreign avoidance of system 103, 130, 159–165, 173
  Lesson provided by nonenforcement 110
  Payment over time without interest 90, 101–102, 105–106, 126, 138–139, 142, 146–147, 152, 157–160, 161–162, 166, 186–187, 190, 206, 212–214
  Payment over time with interest 188, 214
  Priority of claim payment 90, 101, 186
  Recovery of assets 141, 143–144, 188
  Treated as a special class 107–110
  Trustees continue business 141, 158–165
  Waiver of rights by failing to participate 90–91, 93, 122, 138
Imprisonment of parties 91–92, 97, 104–106, 139, 142–144, 162, 186, 188, 203–204, 210, 212, 214
Neck yoke (cangue) penalty 105, 162
Offenses chargeable in debt cases 91, 103–109, 158, 162
  Deciding correct offense 103–109
  Bad debt 91, 104–109
  Cheating foreigners substatute 91, 105–109, 158, 162
Petition or claim 100, 103, 114–115, 117–118, 126, 139–140, 157–158, 160, 161–162, 185–186, 188, 190, 200–201, 205, 213
  Detailed statement 114, 117–118, 201, 213
Prohibition of opium trade 110, 172
Public and private process 94
Revocation of official title 57, 104, 106, 139, 158, 162, 188
Jurisdiction 57–58, 60, 63, 96, 183
Justice 73, 92, 98, 116
Litigation 93, 98
Notice, posted XII, 80–81, 80 **(Illustrations) (Plates 7–8)**, 102, 115–116
Perspective of the state 82, 93
Property rights 34
Punishment 93, 97–98, 101, 103–109, 138, 158, 162, 188, 212, 270
  Of the accuser (fan zuo) 98, 100
Sources of law 81, 75–76, 94–97, 102, 105–110

China (*cont.*)
Trial XII, 97, 100, 104 **(Illustration) (Plate 9)**
Military forces 29, 78–79, 82, 155
People's Republic 259–262
Banks and banking 261–262
Implicit deposit insurance 261–262
Republic of China 259
China Business Seminar IX
Chinaware See "Porcelain"
Chinese debts crisis of 1779–80 17, 90, 111–125, 127
Allowance of claims 122
British creditors 112–114, 118–119, 122
Danish creditors 115, 118
Disallowance of claims 122
Dutch creditors 115, 118
French creditors 112–113, 115, 118
Madras creditors 112–114, 118
Swedish creditors 115, 118
Chinese debts crisis of 1836–39 17, 193, 203, 205, 214–216, 279
Chinese government See "China, Government"
Chinese language 52–53, 56, 58 n.19, 72–73, 82, 86, 102, 106, 116, 156 n.35, 183
Chinese characters 66, 183, 187 n.63
Pinyin romanization XV, 52
Romanization 156 n.35
Chinese law See "China, Law"
Chingqua (Lin Yingkui) 198, 200, 210
Chinnery, George XII, 80
Chongzhen Emperor 19
Chop XVI, 120 n.279, 137
Chowqua I 87, 119, 127
Chowqua II See "Loqua"
Chu Dajun 31, 83 n.120, 263
Chufeng hong 90 n.158
Chunqua I (Liu Dezhang) 148–149, 156, 161, 169, 211
Creditor 156
Chunqua II (Liu Chengshu) 211–212
Debts 211–212
Chunqua III (Liu Dong) 194, 198, 206–207, 211–212
Debts 194, 206–207, 211–212
Citigroup 279
Civil Office (*Li Bu*) See "China, Government, Qing Dynasty, Civil Office"
Civil War, USA 238, 253
Civilization 17
Climate 202
Clive, Robert 112 n.248
Clocks XII, XVIII, 65–69, 141
Coal Hill 19
Coastal defense works 129
Coffee 173
Cohen, Jerome Alan IX
Cohong See "Hong merchants, Cohong"
Cold country 198
Collective financial responsibility 3–4, 6, 12, 47, 51 (See also, "Collective responsibility," "Canton Guaranty System," "Ginseng administration" and "Salt administration")
Collective responsibility 2 n.5, 3–4, 12, 18, 39, 47–51, 61, 64, 88 n.147, 109, 115, 123, 220, 262, 273
Among foreigners 103, 115–117
Baojia system 48–50, 52
Purpose 49
Criminal cases 48–49
Government officials 51
Household unit registration 47–49
Hukou system 48
Licensed brokers (*yahang*) 51
Lijia system 49–50
Military 47
Pledges of mutual responsibility 50
Ship registration 50
Urban merchants
Hangyi payments 48
Tax collection 43, 48, 51
Commerce See "Trade"
Commercial finance See "Credit in China"
Communications 1
Commutation Act 132
Compradors XVI, 62, 64, 77, 84
Computers 1
Confidential See "Secrecy"
Conflict of interest 145
Conner, Patrick X
Conqua (Chen Shiji) 100
Conseequa (Pan Changyao) 99, 146–147, 150, 156, 163–164, 166, 168, 173–188, 207

Assets attached in Philadelphia 179–180
Creditor 147, 150, 156, 173–175, 178, 181–184, 187
Debts 163–164, 166, 175, 178, 185–188, 207
Opium transaction 174
Petition of 183–184
Trustees for 163–164, 186
Consoo Fund XIV, XVI, XVII, 15, 42, 46, 88, 120, 122–126, 129–130, 137, 144–145, 151–154, 157, 159–160, 170–171, 182, 186, 190–191, 201, 205–206, 209, 212–213, 216 n.102, 216, 250–251, 265–266, 270–271, 274, 278–279
Bengang hang fund 123
Cash in chests 123–124, 126, 129, 137, 145
Contribution exposure 182
Creditor concerns 152, 159–160, 186, 205, 213, 278
Expenses of fund 129–130, 145, 151–154, 157, 265
Government fees 123, 129–130, 132, 137, 145, 151–154, 170–171, 190, 210–211, 250, 265, 267–268, 270–271, 276–277
Guarantee beneficiaries 145, 159–160, 213, 278
Hangyong tax XVII, 15, 42, 118, 120, 123, 125–126, 129, 137, 140, 145, 152, 209, 216, 265, 270
Payments refused 186, 217
Payments into fund 129, 152, 201, 217, 267
Payments from fund XIV, 129–130, 137, 144–145, 151–154, 157, 190–191, 206, 212, 216 n.102, 217, 265, 270–271, 274
Prior *ad hoc* surcharge on the trade 88
Records 129 n.16, 152–154
Risk assessment 152, 209, 217, 274
Supervisors 145, 217, 265
Surplus 145
Consoo House See "Hong merchants, Guild, Guild hall"
Continental Illinois National Bank 255
Cooks 64
Coolies See "Laborers"
Coolidge, Joseph 201
Copper 223
Coqua 90–91, 116–118, 122
Cordier, Henri 9
Corporations 234, 267
Corporations, Trading See "Merchants, Western, Corporations"
Cotton 89, 134–135, 138, 147, 158, 172, 190, 202, 212, 267
Cotton dealers 205
Levy on 157
Country traders XVI, 29, 92, 110, 112, 132, 134, 139, 151, 157–158, 173, 186, 190
Court of Common Pleas 179
Cowlo 32
Cowqua 156
Cox, James XII
Credit in China 33–34, 52, 99, 107, 110, 127, 137, 156–157, 171, 173–174, 176–177, 182–185, 193, 202–203, 205, 267, 269
Collateral 34, 79
Lack of 33, 99, 156, 269
Pledges 34, 50, 171, 210–211
Credit in the USA 223, 255
Creditor view 144 n.66
Crichton, John 114
Crossman, Carl X
Cultural Revolution 26
Currency, paper 3, 13, 218–219, 226–231, 236–238, 276
Convertability 14, 228–229
Soundness 219, 221, 227, 229, 231
Currency, silver 8, 13, 136, 155, 226 (See "Silver")
Cushing, John Perkins 189

Dacheng hong 148, 151, 158–162
Dadoloy, ship 28
Dagger 119
Dancing 246, 278–279
Danes Island 28
Danish East India Company 38, 115
Danish privateers 146
Dasan 188
Davidson, W.S. 192
De Grammont, Jean-Baptiste-Joseph 113
Debauchee 214
Debt 4
Legal release from debt IX, 187
Debt collection 4, 93–103, 112, 146, 178, 215
Deeds to property 142, 211
Delano, Catherine 243
Delano, Edward 6
Delano, Frederic A. 238 n.59, 244 n.73
Delano, Warren II XIII, 136, 168, 243 **(Illustration) (Plate 21)**, 250

Deng Dingjin 208, 213–214
Dengzhou 25
Depression See "Financial crisis"
Deregulation 255
Dermigny, Louis 8
Deposit insurance See "Bank deposit insurance"
Detroit 228
Development, scientific 1
Development, technological See "Development, scientific"
Devil 212
Dexter, Andrew, Jr. 228–229
Dexter, B. 178
Disease 211
Dobell, Peter 179 n.43, 182
Dogs 116, 196
Dollar, Spanish XII, XVIII, 8, 136 **(Illustration) (Plate 12)**
Dongchang hong 201
Dongsheng hong 148, 198, 206, 211–212
Dongyu hong 34, 150, 168–169
Dorabjee, Hormajee 157, 159
Dormer, Mr. 29
Downs, Jacques M. X, 8, 64
Driving 265
Drought and famine relief 129
Drugs See "Opium"
Drummey, Peter X
Ducks 107
Ducôté, A. 216
Duke of Sussex 215, 216 **(Illustration) (Plate 17)**
Dundas, Henry 225
Dutch East India Company 8, 26 n.38, 29, 38, 62, 78, 115
Dutch Embassy of 1655–57 22
Dutch Hong 138
Dutch language 54
Dutchess County 221
Dzengseo 20 n.13

East Asian Legal Studies Program IX
Eberhard, Wolfram 128 n.14
Economic development 13
Economic theory 252
Edwards, R. Randle 82, 103
Eequa (Wu Zhaoping) 57, 108, 126, 130, 135, 138–139, 143, 206
  Debts 139, 206
Eight Regulations See "Canton System, Law and regulations"
Elite 224
Elliot, Charles 193–194
Elliott, Mark IX, 6, 20
Embargo of 1807–1809 154, 156, 180, 225 n.14, 227–228
Embargo of 1829–1830 192, 211, 271, 274
Emden Company See "Prussian Company"
Emlen, George 179 n.43
Emperor's Merchants 36, 55–56
Empty Tea Chest XIII
England See "Great Britain"
Entertainment 1
Equity contribution 144
Erie Canal 14, 221
Eryi hong XIV, 42, 76, 129 n.16, 140–142, 144
Eshing 156, 177
Euro 252
Europe 146, 154, 221, 252, 257, 260
  Banks and banking 252, 257, 260
  Public finance 252, 260
European Union 257, 259–260
Ever-Normal Granary 2 n.5
Exchange Coffee House 228
Exchin I 150 n.11
Exchin II See "Loqua"
Exchin III See "Pacqua"

Factoor 54
Factories See "Canton Trade, Foreign Factories"
Fairbank, John King 151
Falk, Robert A. X
Famine relief 154, 202
Fang Guangcheng 73
Fannie Mae 256–257
  Explicit government guarantee 257
Farmers 230
Farmers' Exchange Bank 228
Fatqua (a/k/a Manhop II) 163 n.54
Fatqua I (Li Xiefa) 150, 169, 212
Fatqua II (Li Yinggui) 194, 207, 210, 212
  Debts 194, 207, 210, 212
Faure, David X
Federal Deposit Insurance Corporation 246, 249–250, 253–255

Federal Home Loan Mortgage Association See "Freddie Mac"
Federal National Mortgage Association See "Fannie Mae"
Federal Reserve Act 239
Federal Reserve banks 238
Federal Reserve System 238, 249
Fengjin hong 57, 91, 104
Fengtai hong 57, 138–139
Fengyuan hong 91
Fiadors See "Canton System, Security merchants" and "Hong merchants"
Fichter, James R. IX
Fiddler 246, 278–279
Fidelity and Deposit Company of Maryland 243–244
Financial Corporation of America 255
Financial crisis
  of 1819, international 172, 181, 227, 229, 269
  of 1825–26, international 172–173, 223, 269
  of 1829, New York State 4, 13–16, 226–230, 271
  of 1837, international 16–17, 193, 205, 213, 217, 235–236, 269
  of 1907, USA 220, 238–239
  of 1929–1933, international 220, 240–242, 252, 254
  of 1997, Asian 2
  of 2007–8, international 2, 252–253, 256–257, 259–261, 275–276, 279
Fires 29, 172
Fireworks 147
Firms, Western See "Merchants, Western"
First Anglo-Chinese War See "Opium War"
Fisher, Redwood 187 n.63
Fishing 19
Flags 116
Flint, James 72–74, 93
Flood, Mark 245, 247
Flood relief 129, 137, 153–154, 171, 210
Fonqua (Mu Shifang) 108, 150, 157–158, 206
  Debts 206
Foods 1, 202
Footae (Yi Yuanchang) 200
Forbes, H. A. Crosby X
Forbes, Robert Bennet 84
Forbidden City 19, 65
Foreign factories See "Canton Trade, Foreign Factories"
Foreign traders See "Merchants"
Forman, Joshua XIII, 3, 14, 218–226, 222 **(Illustration) (Plate 18)** 230–237, 265, 272–274
  Knowledge of 224–226, 272
Forman, Margaret 223
Fort St. George See "Madras"
France 8, 112, 132, 260
  French traders See "Merchants, French" and "Chinese debts crisis of 1779–80"
  Government 113
  Navy 29
Fraud 211, 228–229, 237
Freddie Mac 256–257
  Explicit government guarantee 257
French East India Company 38, 114
French Island 28
Fu Kangan 131
Fu Lo-shu 74
Fujian Province 25–27, 32, 37, 54, 86, 130, 188
Fuksune See "Tungqua"
Fulbright, J. William 254
Fulong hong 163, 166, 188–190
Fuquan hong 200
Futai hong 200
Furs 19, 135–136

Gang Zhao 50
Ganges, Ship 176
Gardella, Robert X
Gardens 122, 141, 263
Garner, John Nance 242, 249
Genoa 38
General Grave 20
George III, King 215
Geowqua (Wu Guozhao) 65 n.55, 127–128, 141
Germany 112, 260
Gibson, John 160, 225 n.14
Ginnie Mae 256
Ginseng administration 39, 44–45, 47
  Ginseng 44–45, 47
    Decline of harvest 45
    Overharvesting 44

Ginseng administration (*cont.*)
Production quotum 44–45
Penalties for shortfall 44–45
Merchants penalized 44–45
Officials penalized 44–45
Ginseng merchants 12, 44–45, 47
Collective responsibility for debt 12, 39, 44–47
Guaranties of collection 44–45,
Ginseng trade XVII, 11–12, 19, 39, 44, 135, 271–272
American imported 135
Cultivated ginseng 45
Monopolized 39, 44, 47
Import licenses 19
Wild ginseng 19, 44
Girard, Stephen XIII, 176–177, 264
Glass, Carter 242, 246–247, 249
Gloucester 228
Gnewqua II (Zheng Chongqian) 108, 148, 151, 154, 157–163, 164, 207, 276
Debts 207
God of Wealth, Chinese 49
Goede Hoop, ship 28
Golembe, Carter 239, 241
Gold 28, 131, 142, 144, 199–200
Goldstein, Jonathan IX, 2 n.5, 264
Golembe, Carter IX, 253
Gonqua (Shi Zhonghe) 42, 76, 119, 126–127, 129 n.16, 130, 140–144, 206
Death 143–144
Debts 141–142, 206
Statement of financial condition 140–141
Trustees for 141–142,
Goqua I (Xie Jiawu) 150, 163–164, 168–169
Debts 163–164
Goqua II (Xie Yuren) 34, 194
Debts 194
Goods, movement of 1–3
Goodwill See "Business goodwill"
Gordon, Robert 100
Government 25
Government National Mortgage Association See "Ginnie Mae"
Governor See "China, Government, Qing Dynasty, Officials"
Governor-General See "China, Government, Qing Dynasty, Officials"
Grand Council See "China, Government, Qing Dynasty"
Grant, Catherine D. 243
Grant, Eva Taylor X
Grant, Frederic D., Sr. X
Grant, James 255
Grant, Madeleine X
Great Enterprise 18–19
Great Britain 27 n.45, 28–29, 33, 66–69, 73, 84, 132–134, 155, 183, 187, 215, 225–226, 260
Banks and banking 260
British goods 134
British soldiers 29, 183
British subjects 116
British warships 29, 60, 113, 124
Consuls 215
Customs regulations 84, 132–133
Government 215
Missions to China 162, 199, 225
Fleet 113
House of Lords 192
Law 272
Manufacturers 192, 202
Parliament 192, 202
Private merchants See "Merchants, British," and "Country traders," and "Chinese debts crisis of 1779–80"
Great Depression See "Financial crisis of 1929–1933"
Greece 260
Greenberg, Michael 135, 212
Gregory, Martyn X
Grist mills 223
Guangdong and Fujian hong (*fuchao hang*) See "Junk trade merchants"
Guangdong Province XVII, 22, 25–27, 31, 37, 45, 54, 57–59, 107, 137, 155, 183, 202, 210
Coastal defenses 78–79, 82, 129, 137
Provincial treasury 139, 209
Guangli hong 140, 148, 203, 214–215
Guangshun hong 90
Guangxi Province XVII
Guangzhou See "Canton"
Guarantors 51–53, 60–61, 87, 101, 103, 113, 120, 244, 246, 256, 279
Guaranty of debt 4, 29, 46–47, 51–53, 60–61, 87–88, 101, 120, 123, 126–127, 139, 219, 234, 244, 246, 256, 265, 279

  Collective 4, 39, 46–47, 61, 70–71, 88 n.147, 90, 101, 103–104, 107–109, 113, 119–120, 123, 126–127, 139, 143, 146, 157–166, 182, 184–191, 195, 201, 206–209, 217, 219–220, 234, 246, 265, 270–271, 277 (See also, "Collective responsibility")
  Individual 4, 60, 62, 123, 256
  Unlimited XVI, 4–5, 15, 17, 46–47, 60–61, 70–71, 217, 220, 247, 250–251, 265, 277, 279
Guaranty funds 4, 219–220, 234, 237–246, 265
Guaranty system or process at Canton See "Canton Guaranty System"
Guards 64
Guns See "Weapons"
Gurkhas 130
Gypsum 223

Hainan hong 37 n.94
Hair See "Queue"
Hammond, Bray 5, 253
Han Chinese (ethnicity) 27, 53, 60
Han Dynasty See "China, History, Han Dynasty
Hangyong tax See "Consoo Fund"
Hangzhou 51
Hanser, Jessica 112 n.248
Harkins, Brian X
Harmony 265
Harvard Law School IX
Harvard University IX
Head merchants See "Merchants, Chinese"
Heaven XI, 20
Helen of Troy 156
Hell 243, 278
Hidden assets 143–144
Hingtae hong 107, 194 n.4, 198–199, 205–207, 212–215, 270, 278
  Debts 203, 205–207, 212–214, 216, 270
Ho, Ping-ti 45, 47
Holland 177
Holmes, Oliver Wendell 240
Honan 141
Hong Kong 260
Hong merchants XII, XIII, XVII, XVIII, 3–5, 7–11, 13, 15–16, 31–37, 39, 42, 46–47, 56–70, 75, 81, 83–93, 101–217, **149 (Illustration) (Plate 13)**, 250, 263–278, **264 (Illustration) (Plate 23)** (See also "Canton System" and subheadings including "Security merchants")
  Advances to buy tea 185
  Alliances among 11, 36, 88 n.147, 140, 167, 269–270
  As creditors
    Foreign debtors 99–101, 117, 121, 137, 140, 146–147, 150, 156, 164, 173–175, 178, 182–184, 187
    Debtor hong merchants 99–100, 151, 209, 212.
  Advances to buy tea 185
  Assets 101, 103, 139–140, 142, 144, 158, 167, 203, 211–212, 217, 263, 278
  Assignment of vessel 60, 63–64, 89, 146
  Banishment 75, 104, 107–108, 114, 117, 143–144, 158, 162, 188, 190
  Bankruptcy See "Hong merchants, Insolvency"
  Bookkeepers 109
  Brand identity 56, 263, 265–266
  Capitalization 33–34, 89, 127, 137, 145, 150, 167, 172–173, 175, 183, 194, 198–199, 209–214, 266–271
  Chief merchant 35, 85, 90 n.158, 127, 139, 148, 169, 196, 217
  Claims against foreign debtors 99, 121, 146, 178, 182–184
  Cohong (*gonghang*) XVI, 36–37, 64, 84–89, 195
    Cohong of 1720 XVI, 36–37
    Cohong of 1760 XVI, 84–91, 114
      Dissolved 1771 89–91
      Foreign protests 87
  Competition between 11
  Competitors 70
  Contracts 60–61, 88 n.147, 89, 140, 147–148, 176, 192–193, 197, 202, 266, 268,
  Costume 56, 143, 215–216, 263
  Credit 14, 33–34, 42–43, 107–108, 110, 127, 137, 185, 198, 214, 263, 265–266, 271, 274
  Creditors of
    Chinese creditors 101, 107–108, 143, 151, 161
    Knowledge of 101

- Hong merchants (*cont.*)
  - Creditworthiness 3, 14, 185, 198, 205, 219, 263, 265–266, 274
  - Debt XVII, 32–33, 49, 60, 70–72, 76, 87–93, 101–102, 104–108, 111–127, 140, 146, 155–170, 175, 189, 192, 194–196, 201, 205, 209–211, 214, 265–266, 271, 277
    - Discounted 151
    - Secret 211
  - Early hong merchants 32, 35–37, 55–56, 264
    - Indebted 32
  - Essential hongs See "Hong merchants, Too big to fail"
  - Expenses 7, 32–33, 112, 132, 140, 151–154, 156, 199–200, 212, 214, 263, 266–270
    - Household expenses 33, 156, 212, 263, 266, 270
  - Failures 4, 17, 88, 90–91, 104, 114, 119–121, 126–127, 138–143, 146, 158–166, 169, 185, 190, 193–196, 198, 201, 205–206, 209–215, 266, 269, 277, 279
  - Families 11, 33–34, 91–92, 101, 132, 138, 144, 148, 151, 158–165, 167–169, 173, 188–189, 196–199, 212–213, 263, 267, 269–270
    - Social duty to pay debt 120, 138, 148, 151
  - Finances 32, 34, 42–43, 88, 90, 107–108, 119, 146, 148, 156, 158–165, 169–171, 185, 191–192, 194, 205, 209–211, 216–217, 266, 269
  - Financial demands on 33, 57, 70, 123, 133, 137, 151–154, 167, 170–171, 208–211, 213, 217, 263, 266
    - Exactions 33, 123, 129–133, 137, 151–153, 167, 170–171, 190, 213, 267–268, 270–271, 276–277
    - Limits of 171, 190–191, 208–211, 217, 276
    - Military campaign contributions 57, 130, 133, 137, 153–154, 171, 210
  - Fines 64, 175, 270
  - Front for others 137, 140, 201
  - Generosity 180–182, 263
  - Ginseng sales 42, 44, 210
  - Goods 110, 112, 135–137, 144, 172
    - Prices of goods 85, 87–90, 108, 122, 126, 130, 135, 137, 145, 149, 192, 195, 202–203
    - Truck goods 134
  - Guaranty of debt 29, 60–62, 87, 107–108, 113, 120, 123, 126–127, 157–166, 169, 182, 184–191, 195, 201, 206–209, 217, 219, 234, 265–266, 277
  - Joint guaranty 61, 87, 113, 123, 126–127, 157–166, 169, 182, 184–191, 195, 201, 206–209, 217, 219, 234, 265–266, 270–271, 277
  - Guaranty of tea quality 121, 265
  - Guild (outer seas merchants) XVII, 16, 36–37, 63–64, 85, 88–90, 103, 120, 123, 126–127, 137, 139–140, 144–146, 148, 153, 157, 166–169, 190–192, 194–201, 205, 209–211, 213, 217, 265
    - Guild hall (*gongsuo*) XVI, 122–123, 213
    - Meetings 122
    - Membership 37, 127, 137, 148, 150, 166, 169, 192, 194–201, 205, 265
    - Records 213, 268
    - Tiered structure 36–37, 63–64, 167, 190
  - Head merchant See "Hong merchants, Chief merchant"
  - History 9–11, 33, 35–36, 144–145, 166–169, 209–211
    - Condition in 1829 13, 15–16
    - Decade of the 1720s 35–36
    - Decade of the 1730s 60
    - Decade of the 1750s 62, 64–70
    - Decade of the 1760s 85–90, 111
    - Decade of the 1770s 89–92, 111–124
    - Decade of the 1780s 126–127, 134, 139
    - Decade of the 1790s 126–127, 130, 134, 140, 155
    - Decade of the 1800s 148–154, 155–156
    - Decade of the 1810s 107–108, 130, 145, 148–156, 166–171
    - Decade of the 1820s 172–173, 186, 195–197, 211
    - Decade of the 1830s 193–206
    - Decade of the 1840s 216–217
  - Hong seal or chop 137, 140, 161, 164, 187 n.63
  - Hong premises 116–117
  - Hope of success 196
  - Imprisonment 64, 162, 199–200, 203–204, 210, 212, 215

Insolvency 10, 15–16, 32, 42, 72, 90, 101, 107–108, 115–117, 124, 126, 145–146, 148, 151, 156–165, 170, 191–193, 201, 205, 209–215, 266, 268–271, 277
Joint ventures 11, 87, 88 n.147, 120, 167, 269–270
Junior hong merchants 16, 63–64, 150, 153–154, 158–159, 163–166, 168–170, 185–186, 190
  Receivership of 158, 163–166, 168–169, 185–186, 190
Knowledge 15
Licensing 16, 61–2, 127, 140, 158, 169, 195–201, 205, 212, 219
  Wealthy and respectable 62
Lifestyles 132, 190, 203, 263, 266–267, 270
Litigation 99, 121, 150, 156, 176, 179–180, 182–184
Loans
  Collateral 33–34
  Loans to hong merchants 33–34, 76, 145, 151, 175, 189, 192, 194, 266, 267
  Lending by hong merchants 34, 151, 156, 174–175, 178, 182–184, 187, 212
Luxuries 132, 190, 203, 214, 263, 266–267
Management ability 268–269
Marketing 56, 266
Mortgages 33–34, 79, 87
Official rank, purchased 51, 56–57, 158, 162, 188
Official supervision 122, 145, 153, 201, 209–211, 268
Other business activities 32, 37, 137
Participation in business 86, 140
Partnerships 11, 159, 167, 188, 190, 200, 211, 214, 269–270
Path to riches 169, 195–197
Patrons 54–56
Portraits 56, 263, 266
Prefix "Mandarin" 56
Pricing See "Hong merchants, Goods, Price of goods"
Profits 7, 33, 107, 130, 144, 175, 266–268, 271
Punishment 64, 91, 101, 108, 158, 199–201, 212, 266, 270
Receivership of 150, 158–166, 168–169, 185
Records 7, 9, 122, 143, 209, 213, 268
Regulation See "Canton System"
Relations among 60, 64, 120, 140, 269–270
Reputation 3, 14, 107–108, 174, 198, 205, 224, 263, 265–266
Requirements for success 15
Residences 83, 132, 263
Retirement 16, 61, 148, 169, 196–197, 201, 212, 266
Return on investment 16, 270
Revenues 126, 192, 209–211, 269
Salt merchants, compared 11, 39, 45
Savings 144, 217, 270
Senior merchant See "Hong merchants, Chief merchant"
Seniority 63–64, 127, 139
Skills 15, 268–269
Social background 62, 120, 127, 198–201, 205
Social standing 57, 198–201
Sole proprietorships 11
Solvency 16, 70, 90, 101, 107–108, 119, 146, 148, 156, 194, 205, 209–211, 217, 266
Status group 56
Success 199, 217, 263
Suffix "qua" 56
Suicide 140, 212
Support among 186, 215, 269–270
Thirteen hongs XVIII, 9, 16, 31, 35, 83, 199, 263
  Origin of term 83
Too big to fail 168, 171, 276–277, 279
Trade
  Monopoly of 15, 36, 47–48, 56, 60, 62–63, 70–71, 86, 89, 123, 137–138, 147, 158, 161, 195, 219, 234, 262
  Volume of 15, 33, 37, 39, 133–134, 194, 266, 269
Trading names 56
Trustees for 141–142, 158–165, 169, 185–186
Wealth 31–32, 88–89, 107–108, 156, 169, 174, 263, 266
Withdrawal of capital 16, 61, 90, 148, 196–197, 266
Honian 62
Honohan, Patrick 261

Hoover, Herbert 241–242, 244
Hoppo See "China, Government, Qing Dynasty, Officials"
Hostages 29
Houqua See "Howqua"
Howqua I (Lin Shimao) 28, 128 n.14, 139
Howqua II (Wu Bingjian) XII, XIII, 56, 57, 61, 128, 146–149, 156, 164, 167–168, **168 (Illustration) (Plate 14)**, 171, 180–182, 205, 214, 217, 243, 263–264
  Creditor 156, 164, 180–182, 186, 194
  Death 217
  Wealth 167–168
Howqua III (Wu Yuanhua) 128 n.14
Howqua IV (Wu Chongyue) 128 n.14
Hsiao, Kung-chuan 49
Huaian Customs 132
Hubei 52
Hudson River 221
Huguang 130
Hughes, Admiral Sir Edward 124
Hughes, William XII, 67
Huilong hong 148, 159–162
Hukou system See "Collective responsibility"
Hunsunquin 35
Hunter, William C. 81, 180–181
Hunting 19

Iceland 260
Ideas
  Economic value 1
  Movement of 1–2, 221, 223–226, 231, 237–240, 250
Ideas, Chinese 2 n.5, 3–4, 12, 25, 27, 53, 220, 224–226, 252, 271, 273
  Transfers of 3–4, 12, 224–226, 250, 252, 271–273
Ideas, legal 13, 224–226, 237–240, 252, 271–273 (See also, "Legal transplants")
Ili XVII, 75, 104, 107–109, 143–144, 158, 162, 188, 190, 198
Immigration 44
Imperial Company See "Ostend Company"
Imperial Factory 29
Imperial Household Department (*neiwufu*) XVII, 6, 11–12, 39–41, 44–47, 58, 60–61, 131–132, 147, 263
  Death 217
  Bondservants 12, 39–41, 44, 46, 58
  Indebted officials 43, 61, 131–132, 263
    Origin of term 83
    Posted to Canton 43, 61, 131–132, 263
  Financial function 39–40
  Ginseng sales 42, 44–45, 47, 210
  Secret status 6, 41
Imperial Textile Factories 44, 51
Imperialism 2
Inaba Iwakichi 19
Inauguration Day 241
India XVI, 29, 112–113, 115, 132, 134–135, 147, 155, 157, 172, 190, 202, 257, 259
Indiana 237
Individualism 220, 273
Inflation 8, 254
Ingersoll, Charles Jared 179, 182
Inn 223
Innes, James 29
Innovation 1, 47
Inqua (Deng Zhaoxiang) 150, 163, 189, 211
  Debt 163
  Son of 189
Inqua (tea merchant) 211–212
Insurance 4, 143, 219, 245–246, 252, 254, 259, 275, 280
Insurance companies 230, 234
Intellectual property 1
Interest rates 33–34, 43, 89, 92–93, 103, 111, 116, 164, 212, 214, 256, 267, 275
International Monetary Fund 259
Iowa 237
Ireland 260
Iron 123
Israel 259
Italian city states 27 n.45
Italy 260

Jackson, Andrew 234
Japan 26, 28, 30, 32, 50, 259
  Japanese copper 32
  Japanese pirates 30, 105, 109–110
Jardine, William 197 199, 205, 212, 278
Jardine, Matheson & Co. 212
  Creditor 212
Jefferson, Thomas 228
Jesuits 113

Jiansheng title 57, 91
Jieshan 153
John King Fairbank Center for Chinese Studies IX
Joint liability See "Collective responsibility"
Jones, William C. 95, 104
Junk trade merchants 32, 37, 86, 91, 123
Bengang hong merchants 37, 50, 86, 91, 123
Fuchao hong merchants 37, 86
Law and regulation 37
Junks See "Ships"
Jurchen Mongols 18–19
Just, Mr. 200
Justice Office (*Xing Bu*) See "China, Government, Qing Dynasty, Justice Office"

Kadlick, James BX
Kamensky, Jane 228
Kangxi Emperor XII, 18, 23, 24 **(Illustration) (Plate 1)**, 25–26, 32, 36, 40, 53, 98
Kashgar 171, 209–210
Kaske, Elisabeth IX
Keene 228
Keetshing 156
Kejuan zashui 267–268, 276
Kemmerer, Edwin W. 246, 278–279
Kewshaw (Zhang Tianqiu) 57, 65 n.55, 108, 117–119, 122, 124, 126–127, 206
Debts 206
Kiang, Nelson Y.S. IX
Kickbacks 78
Kingling 156
King's Merchants 54
Kingqua See "Kinqua"
Kinqua I (Liang Jingguo) 11, 39, 151, 163–164, 169, 194 n.4, 195, 205–207, 210–211
Debts 163–164, 205–207
Kinqua II (Liang Zhenxi) 210–211, 214, 216
Debts 210–211, 213–215
Kirby, William C. IX, 267
Kirby Puzzle 267
Kirin 44
Kluz, Linda IX
Köll, Elisabeth IX
Koops, Egbert X
Koxinga See "Zheng Chenggong"
Kuhn, Philip A. IX
Kuiper, Koos X, 58 n.19
Kumin, Max IX

Laborers 64 (See also, "Servants")
Lach, Donald 12
Ladrones XVII, 155 (See also "Piracy")
Lajoie, Jeff X
Lake Erie 221
Lamqua (Guan Qiaochang) (painter) XII, XIII, 168, 204
Lamqua (Luo Futai) 200–201
Lanterns 116
Lascars 116
Law 1, 17
British 17, 272
Common law 17
Chinese See "China, Law"
United States 183, 221
Violence, seeks to reduce 17, 96
Law, Geoffrey Suess IX
Lawsuits See "Litigation"
Lawune (Luo Yuan) 200
Lawyers 179
Legal transplants 12–13, 220, 252, 272
Leiden University IX, X, 2 n.5
Lemperly, Bertha X
Lemperly Grant, Barbara X
Lenin, Vladimir 19
Leslie, Abraham 116–117
Lewis, Michael 260
Li Hongbin 16, 196
Li Hu 117
Li Shiyao 73, 74 n.86, 85 n.130, 86, 89–90, 92, 105, 107
Li Shizhen 31
Li Yongbiao 12, 47, 62, 65, 73
Li Zhiying 60, 91–92, 104, 114–115, 118, 122–123, 131
Li Zicheng 19–20, 91–92
Liability, collective See "Collective responsibility"
Liang See "Tael"
Liang Jiabin 9, 11, 39
Lianghuai 45
Lianghuai salt monopoly See "Salt administration, Lianghuai salt monopoly"
Liao Valley 18
Lijia system See "Collective responsibility"

Limitation of liability 277
Lin Zexu 50, 111, 201
Lind, Abram 58 n.19
Lineage property 270
Linguists 62–64, 77–78, 81, 84, 118
Lintin Island 42, 111, 172
Liquan hong 148, 173–188
Litigation 146, 156, 176, 179–180, 182–184
Liu Yabian 73
Loans See "Credit in China"
Lobbying 215
London 65, 84, 112, 155, 172, 193–194, 212, 215–216, 225–226, 278
Long, Huey 247
Loqua (Exchin II) 141, 150, 156, 163–164, 169, 185
  Creditor 156
  Debts 163–164, 169
Loss 279
Lu Kun 201
Lum, Raymond IX
Lunshaw 127
Lyqua (Zhou Xinzhao) 150 n.10

Macao IX, XV, 21, 25–26, 29, 55, 58, 60, 62–63, 73, 78, 113, 117–118, 142, 198
Macartney, George 162
Madison, James 99, 155, 183–184
Madras 60, 112–116, 118, 124
  Council 124
  Governor 124
  Madras traders See "Merchants, Madras" and "Chinese debts crisis of 1779–80"
Magniac, Hollingsworth 164, 212, 278
Magniac & Co. 190
Maine 228
Manchu XVII, 6, 12, 18–22, 27, 40, 44, 53–54, 58–60, 62, 252 (See also "China, History, Qing Dynasty")
  Banner system 19, 40, 60
  Manchu language 19
  Manchu traditions 18, 53
  Military power 19–20
  Soldiers 19–22
  Regional trade 19, 23, 53
    Ginseng trade 19, 44
Manchuria 12, 44
Mandarins See "China, Government, Qing Dynasty, Officials"
Manhop I 150, 163–164, 166, 185–186, 189, 207
  Debts 163–164, 166, 186, 189, 207
Manhop II 108, 150, 163–164, 166, 168, 185–186, 188–190, 194, 207
  Debts 163–164, 166, 186, 188–190, 207
Manila 28, 35, 39, 86, 155
Manufacturing 1, 14, 192, 234
Manufacturing companies 234
Maosheng hong 200, 210
Markets 25, 51, 130, 192–193, 202
Martyn Gregory Gallery X, 80, 104, 133, 149, 193, 204
Massachusetts 228
Mathematics 280
McClary, Captain John 28–29
McClay, Mary X
McElderry, Andrea 50
McKinney, Stewart 255
McLean, T.M. 216
Mechanical toys XVIII, 65
Medicine 1
Mercantilism 219
Merchant bureaucrats 127
Merchants
  Armenian 28, 174
  British XVI, 29, 38, 50, 92, 110, 137, 147, 163, 192, 194, 202, 214–216
  Chinese 21, 32, 35–36, 48, 50, 54–56, 58, 73, 146, 215
    Head merchants 46–47, 50–51, 86, 139
  Danish 118
  Dutch 118
  French 8, 28, 112, 118, 174, 263
  Japanese 30
  Madras 112
  Manchu 19, 53
  Parsi 157, 159, 186, 214
  Portuguese 63
  Spanish 39, 63
  Swedish 118
  United States 6–8, 132, 135–137, 139, 147, 155–156, 160, 169, 172–175, 183–184, 190, 214, 224, 264

Western 6, 10, 15, 26, 28, 32–33, 35–36, 38–39, 41–42, 49, 52, 54, 58, 60, 70–71, 76–78, 85, 87, 89, 91, 114, 118, 132, 135, 213
Corporations 36–39, 54, 78, 81, 87, 114, 127, 132, 134, 145, 147
Head merchants 114–115, 118
Mexico 136, 171
Michigan 228, 237, 245
Middle East 4
Milhender, Diane Charipar x
Milhender, Richard x
Military taxes 129–130, 133, 137, 153–154, 171, 210–211, 270
Ming Dynasty See "China, History, Ming Dynasty
Mingqua (Pan Wentao) 198–199
Mingqua's hong xii, 80
Minqua See "Mingqua"
Missionaries 113
Mok, Maria 133
Moley, Raymond 249
Molony, James 163
Monackjee, Dosabhae 157
Money See "Currency"
Money, issuance of 219
Mongols 2 n.5, 12 n.30, 18–19 (See also "Jurchen Mongols")
Monisov, Leonard x
Monopolies 15, 19, 36, 38–39, 47–48, 56, 60, 62–63, 71, 89, 123, 137–138, 195, 202, 219
Monsoons 32
Moral hazard xvii, 217, 237, 242, 246, 275, 278
Morse, Hosea Ballou 8, 86, 151
Mortgage-backed securities 256
Mortgages 33–34, 79, 87, 252, 255–256
Moss, David A. x, 218, 229, 253
Mouqua See "Mowqua"
Mowqua i (Lu Guanheng) 140–141, 148, 151, 156, 158, 164, 214–215
Creditor 164
Mowqua ii (Lu Wenjin) xiii, 57, 169, 186, 194–195, 203, **204 (Illustration) (Plate 16)**, 212, 215
Creditor 212
Debts 203, 215–216
Mowqua iii (Lu Jiguang) 214–215
Debts 214–215
Munqua (Cai Shiwen) 91, 119, 127, 139–141, 143
Attacks Puankhequa 119
Debts 119, 139
Suicide 140
Murders 29
Music 279
Musical boxes xviii, 65, 67–68
Mutual liability See "Collective responsibility"
Mutual responsibility See "Collective responsibility"

Namshing 156
Nanjing 21, 51
Nankeen cloth 141, 144
Napier, Lord 199
National Banking Act of 1863 See "Banking Act of 1863"
National Banking Act of 1933 See "Banking Act of 1933"
Native ports hong (*bengang hang*) See "Junk trade merchants"
Neptune sailors xii, **104 (Illustration) (Plate 9)**
Netherlands 132, 250, 259
New Bedford 223
New Deal 241
New Brunswick 223
New England 135
New Hampshire 228
New Jersey 223
New Year, Chinese 190, 197
New York City 173, 179 n.43, 182, 218, 221, 225
Trade with China 225
New York, State of 3, 12–17, 68, 191, 217–218, 220–221, 223, 226–227, 229–237, 241, 243, 250, 252, 271–272
Banks and Banking 13–17, 219–220, 227–231, 236–237
Charters 230, 235, 237
Condition in 1829 13–16, 230–231, 241, 271
Corruption 229–230
Crisis of 1820s 223, 226, 229–231, 271
Failures 229, 235–236
Free banking 236, 238
History 13–17, 227, 241
Business community 219, 221, 224

New York, State of (*cont.*)
  Competitive position 231
  Development of 221, 231
  Legislature XIII, 3–6, 185, 191, 217, 220, 223–224, 230–231, 234–235, 252, 272–274
    Assembly 221, 230, 234
    Senate 230, 234
  Safety Fund 3, 13–17, 220, 234–238, 252
    Administration 220, 235
    Creditors of 236–237
    Failure of 220, 236–237
    Payment of claims 220
  Safety Fund Act of 1829 3, 5, 12–17, 185, 191, 217–218, 220, 223, 230–237, 271
    Amendment 1842 217, 236–237
    Criticism of 231
    Inspiration XIII, 14, 16, 185, 191, 217, 224, 233–234, 262, 271
New York Times 249
New Zealand 260
Newburgh 243
Newspapers 224 n.12, 274
Ningbo 25–26, 63 n.41, 71–72, 89 n.156
Nonack, Stephen Z. X
North Carolina 223
Norway 257, 259
Notices, posted XII, **80 (Illustrations) (Plates 7–8)**
Nottingham, ship 29
Nuestra Señora de Covadonga, galleon 28
Numbers, auspicious 83
Nurhaci 18

Ohio 237
Okinawa 28
Oklahoma 240
Old Canton 11
Old China Street XII, 80
Old Tuckee 156
Onondaga County 221
Opium 19, 42, 50, 110–111, 134–136, 140, 147, 173–174, 202, 208, 215
  Opium dealers 50, 62, 111, 198
  Opium trade 42, 50, 110–111, 135–136, 147, 172–174, 198, 202, 208
  Opium suppression 50, 111, 172, 208
Opium War XIII, 17, 111, 194, 215–217, 243, 277, 279
  Pro-war propaganda 194, 215–216
Ostend Company 38
Outside shopmen XVII, 16, 29, 36, 70–71, 86, 137–138, 147, 151, 156, 169, 175, 188, 200–201, 214
  American traders 137, 169
  Creditors 156
  Goods sold by 137–138
  Registration 61, 70–71
  Reputation 137, 169
  Tax collection 151
Overpricing 78

Pacific Northwest coast 136
Pacqua (Li Guangyuan) 108, 156, 166, 169, 185–186, 188–189, 207
  Creditor 156
  Debts 166, 186, 188, 207
  Trustees for 186
Paine, Lincoln P. X
Palace Museum, Beijing 65–69
Palmerston, Lord 193–194
Pamphlets 215, 231–234
Pan Changyao See "Conseequa"
Pan Ruiqing 188
Panic See "Financial crisis"
Panton, Captain John Alexander 17, 60, 113–116, 124
Paper 187
Paper currency See "Currency, paper"
Parsis 139, 157–159, 186, 214
Pawnshops 33–34
Peacock feathers (*hualing*) 57
Pearl River XVIII, 28, 172
Pearls 28
Pearson, Alexander 163, 182
Peking XV (See also "Beijing")
Pennsylvania 231
Pension programs 145
People's Bank of China 261
Perjury 98
Perkins, Thomas Handasyd 174
Peru 1, 171
Petitions 63, 71–74, 92, 97, 100, 114, 139, 157–158, 160, 186, 188, 200

Philadelphia xiii, 156 n.35, 160, 172–173, 175–176, 178–179, 181–182, 264
Philippines 27, 32, 35, 86, 155
Philosophy See "Ideas"
Pidgin English 65, 78, 181–182
Pinqua 127, 138
Pinyin romanization xv
Piracy 50, 132, 137, 145–146, 153–154
Pittsfield 228
Plagues 146
Plassey 112 n.248
Plaster 223
Pledge of mutual responsibility See "Collective responsibility"
Pledges See "Credit in China"
Plowden, William H.C. 170
Poem 31
Ponqua (Ni Bingfa) 108, 148, 151, 157–162, 164, 207, 276
  Debts 207
Poonequa (Mai Jinting) 150, 163–164, 166, 168, 185, 188–189, 207
  Debts 163–164, 166, 188–189, 207
Porcelain xii, xvii, 1, 36, 86, 136, 147, 150 n.11
Portugal 63, 260
  Portuguese traders See "Merchants, Portuguese"
Postal Savings banks 242
Potato 1
Poughkeepsie 221
Pozen, Robert 257, 260
Preston, David 1
Preston, Douglas 214
Preston, Richard M. 211
Prices 192, 202–203, 246
Prince Augustus See "Duke of Sussex"
Prince, Chuck 279
Princeton University 246, 278
Principal 103
Prisoner 196
Pritchard, Earl 90, 112, 124, 133
Privatization of profit 17
Promissory notes 100, 112, 141, 155, 156 n.35, 171, 178, 180–181
Proprietary See "Secrecy"
Proto-insurance 4
Providence, R.I. 182
Prussia 2 n.5
Prussian Company 38
Puankhequa i (Pan Zhencheng) 35, 56, 63, 85–86, 89, 90 n.158, 100, 117, 119, 122 n.286, 123, 127, 139, 143, 173
  Debts 86, 119, 127
  Ties to Li Shiyao 86, 89, 292 n.1
Puankhequa ii (Pan Zhixiang) 61, 139, 141, 148–149, 169–170, 196 n.14
Puankhequa iii 57, 194, 203, 205
Pu'er tea 224
Puiqua 128, 141, 146, 148–149 (See also "Howqua ii")
Puk Wing-kin x
Punhoyqua See "Pwanhoyqua"
Pwanhoyqua (Pan Wenhai) 198

Qianlong Emperor 25, 30–31, 45, 49, 62, 72–74, 92, 108, 113, 117, 122, 139
Qin Shi Huang Di 47
Qing Dynasty See "China, History, Qing Dynasty
Qing government See "Government, Chinese"
Quanzhou 32, 39, 86
Queue 20

Rabinel, Mr. 177
Railroad companies 234
Rank See "Hong merchants, official rank, purchased"
Rattan mats 147
Read, William 175, 177
Real estate development 221, 223–224, 227–228
Real estate lending 255, 261
Real estate speculators 235
Records See "Business records"
Reform 192, 195
Regulations at Canton See "Canton System, Law and Regulations, Trade Regulations"
Regulated business 15
Reischauer Lectures ix
Releases 187
Renhe hong 198 n.26 and n.28
Renting property 116
Reorganization value 101
Republican National Committee 249

Republican Party 249
Revolt of the Three Feudatories 22, 25
Revolving door 275
Rhode Island 178, 228
Rice 42, 147
Rights or privileges 219
Risk 166, 240, 245–246, 273, 277
Robot 66
Rockets 29
Rome 4
 Roman law 13
Roosevelt, Franklin D. XIII, 238 n.59, 241–251, 243 **(Illustration) (Plate 21)**, 248 **(Illustration) (Plate 22)** 279
 Opposed to deposit insurance 242–244, 247, 250–251, 279
Rose, David C. 267
Rossiter, Arabella 83
Rossiter, Charlotte 83
Rossiter, Lindsay 83
Rossiter, Winton X
Rousseau, Ship 177
Royal Society 215
Ruan Yuan 186, 188
Russell & Company 6, 9, 81, 201
Russell, Samuel 137
Russia 2 n.5, 271
Rutherfordston 223
Ryukyu Islands 28

Safety Fund Act of 1829 See "New York, State of, Safety Fund Act of 1829"
Sailors XII, 104 **(Illustration)**
Salem 174
Salt administration, China XVII, 39–40, 44–47
 Administration 40, 45–47
 Changlu salt monopoly 44, 132
 Lianghuai salt monopoly 44,
 Salt merchants 11, 36, 39, 45–46
  Collective responsibility for debt 39, 46–47
  Guaranty system 46
  Factory merchants 46
  Lianghuai salt merchants 45–46
  Transport merchants 46
  Wealth 45–46
 Tax revenues 45–46
  Quotum system 46
Salt production, USA 221, 223
Salt trade, China 47, 271
 Lianghuai salt merchants 45–46
 Monopolized 39, 46–47
 Monopoly abolished 46
 Salt merchants 169
Saltworks 223
Samqua (Wu Tianyuan) 57 n.14, 200
Sanyizhu 131
Saoqua (Ma Zuoliang) 198–199
Satins 31
Satirical print 215–216
Savings Bank Association of Massachusetts 246
Saying 52
Schrecker, John IX
Science 1, 11
Scientific development See "Development, scientific"
Scriptures 212
Sea Horse, frigate 60, 113, 124
Sea otters 136
Second Bank of the United States 238
Secrecy 6, 225, 274
Securitization 252, 256
Security merchants See "Canton System, Security merchants" and "Hong merchants"
See Samyee (Shi Sanyo) 159
Seequa 127, 140
Servants 62, 69, 77, 84, 190
Seunqua II 90–91, 112, 119, 126, 138, 206
 Debts 206
Seunqua III 91, 118–119, 126, 138
Shandong Province 25, 154
Shang Kexi X, XII, 20–21, 55, 55 **(Illustration) (Plate 2)**
 Official merchants 55
Shanghai 9
Shanhai Pass (Shanhaiguan) 19, 44
Shattuck, Elizabeth X
Shattuck, Peter X
Shaw, Samuel 113 n.255, 114–115
Shengjing 45
Shenxi 130
Shi Lang 22
Shinqua (Pan Zhengheng) 196 n.14

Shizimen 31
Ships
  Chinese 21, 26, 28–29, 31, 50, 153
    Warships 28–29, 153
  Western 27, 32, 42, 60, 62–63, 65, 70, 72, 75, 79, 83, 87, 108, 114, 135, 146–147, 149, 156, 172, 174, 176, 197
    Storeships 172
    Warships 28, 60, 113, 124
Shopkeepers See "Outside shopmen"
Shroffs XVIII, 27 n.45, 64, 170, 199
Shuer 131
Shuntai hong 198 n.27
Shuxi 140
Shy Kinqua I (Shi Mengjing) 140
Shy Kinqua II See "Gonqua"
Sichuan Province 73, 130
Signed documents 52
Silks 31, 86, 203 (See also, "Imperial Textile Factories")
  Silk merchants 197, 200, 203
Silver XVIII, 8, 27 n.45, 31, 132, 135, 155, 170–171, 173, 227–228, 263, 276
  Inferior 205
  Silver coins 13, 132, 135–136, 155, 170–171, 173, 227–228, 276
Sinqua 127, 138
Singsongs XII, XVIII, 42, 60, 65–70, **66–69 (Illustrations) (Plates 3–6)**, 123, 130, 141, 153
  Gifts to Beijing 42, 65–70, 123, 130, 153
  Tax on trade for purchases 42, 65, 70, 153
Singyquan (Wang Shengyi) 57 n.14
Sinn, Elizabeth IX
Slaves 196
Smith, Joanna F. Handlin IX
Smith, Shawn J. X
Smith, Thomas H. 173
Smith, Vincent X
Smuggling 16, 42, 71, 134, 137, 147, 172, 175, 201
Snow, Peter 155
Snow, Samuel 178
Socialization of risk 17
Song Dynasty See "China, History, Song Dynasty"
Songyun 162
Souchong tea 177
South China Sea 27
Sovereignty 219
Spain 28, 63, 86, 155, 171, 260
  Spanish dollar See "Dollar, Spanish"
  Spanish galleons 28
  Spanish traders See "Merchants, Spanish"
Spanish America 155
Spears See "Weapons"
Specie See "Silver"
Spence, Jonathan 40
Spices 135
Spies 113 n.255
Spoilum XII, 149
Squeeze See "China, Government, Qing Dynasty, Officials, Exactions or Fees" and "Hong merchants, Financial demands on, Exactions"
Staunton, George 34, 98, 162
Steagall, Henry 242, 245
Stephenson, Rome 245
Stone, Cathleen Douglas X
Stone, James M. X
Subprime mortgages 256–258, 260, 279
Success, ship 72
Suleski, Ronald IX
Sullivan, Christine X
Sullivan, William 179 n.43
Sun Shiyi 131
Sunshing 199
Suqua (Cumshaw) 32, 35, 88 n.147
Supercargoes 28, 147, 176
Surety bonds 243
Suzhou 51
Swedish East India Company 38, 115
Sweetia 63, 87–88, 90 n.158, 119
Sy Anqua (Seunqua II) See "Seunqua II"
Symons, Van Jay 45
Syracuse 14, 221, 223
Szonyi, Michael IX

Tael XVII, XVIII, 8, 27 n.45
Taihe hong 57, 87–88, 90 n.158, 116, 118
Taiwan 3, 21–22, 25, 27, 130
Takqua (Rung Yuguang) 201
Tam Hoanfun 200
Tan Hunqua (Chen Fangguan) 78
Tang Dynasty See "China, History, Tang Dynasty

Tartar-General's Merchant 55
Tavern 223
Taxpayers 246, 254, 256–257, 278–280
Tea XVIII, 36, 89, 121, 133–135, 137, 141, 144, 146, 150 n.12, 167, 173, 176–177, 185, 197, 201–203, 215, 224, 265–267, 270
  Consumer demand 133, 202
  Credit purchase 176–177, 203
  Export quantity 134–135, 202
  Prices 133–134, 177, 185, 192, 202
  Quality 176–177
  Return guaranty 121, 178, 265
  Security required 203
  Selection or tasting 150 n.12, 176–177
  Tea contracts 89, 121, 140, 176, 185, 197, 203, 267, 270
  Tea merchants 89, 140–143, 159, 161, 185–186, 189, 197–198, 202–203, 211, 267, 270
    Contracting directly with foreigners 89
Technological development. See "Development, scientific"
Telecommunications 1
Temperance 223
Terrill, Ross IX
Teunqua I (Tehanqua) 79 n.110
Teunqua II 79 n.110
Teyuan hong See "Tuckune"
Thirteen hongs See "Hong merchants, Thirteen hongs"
Thomson, Edward 173
Thomson, Richard R. 187 n.63
Thonching 156
Thought See "Ideas"
Throop, Enos T. 234
Tianbao hong 151, 205, 213–214
Tianjin 25, 72
Tien, Wen-hao IX
Tinqua I (Tehanqua) 79 n.110
Title See "Hong merchants, official rank, purchased"
Title deeds See "Deeds to property"
Tommy Birdman 200
Ton Anqua 86, 88 n.147
Tongshun hong 57 n.14, 200
Tongtai hong 150 n.12, 189
Tongwen hong 35, 56, 90 n.158, 148, 169, 173
Too big to fail XII, 168, 171, 217, 254–255, 260, 276–277, 279
Torbert, Preston 6
Trade, generally 1, 26–27
Trade regulations See "Canton System, Law and Regulations, Trade Regulations"
Traders See "Merchants"
Tranquility 263
Transcultural effects 1
Transplants See "Legal transplants"
Travel 1
Treaty of Nanking 16, 211, 215–217
Tree 144
Tribute System See "China, History, Ming Dynasty, and Qing Dynasty"
Truck XVIII, 134
Tsai Suequa 70
Tu-ming-a 114, 118–119
Tuckune hong 198, 200
Tungqua (Wang Datong) 200
Turkey 147
Turnaround management consultant 269
Turnpike companies 234
Tuscany 38

Ukraine 259
Union College 221
United States of America 3–5, 13–14, 17, 99–100, 112, 132, 135–136, 146, 155–156, 171–173, 178, 183–184, 220, 225–228, 234, 238–242, 244–257, 272
  Banks and banking (See also "Bank deposit insurance")
    History 3–5, 13–14, 17, 220, 227–257, 272
    Failures 13–14, 228, 235–236, 255
    Insolvency 256
    Solvency 257
    State licensing 13–14, 227
  Banknotes 13–14, 227, 238, 253
    National banknotes 13, 227, 238, 253
  China traders See "Merchants, United States"
  Colonial era 219
  Congress 238–239, 247, 254–255
  Constitution 227, 240
  Consumer demand 173
  Comptroller of the Currency 255

Customs 173
Embargo of 1807–1809 155–156, 180
Federal agencies 256
House of Representatives 239, 242, 245, 247, 255
Law, Impartiality of 183
Litigation in 146, 150, 176, 179–180, 183–184
Money supply 226
Mortgages 252
National Archives 183
President 183–184, 241, 247–251
Savings and loan crisis 253, 255–256, 258
Senate 239, 242, 245–247, 249, 254
Ships from 146
State guaranty funds 12, 17, 220, 237–240
Subprime mortgages 256–258, 260
Supreme Court 240
Trade with China 147, 173, 225
Treasury 238, 242, 244, 256–257, 279
Implicit guarantor 256
University of California, Berkeley 10
University of Macao IX
University of Pennsylvania 9
Urmston, James Brabazon 187
Debtor 187
Usury 124

Valuation 1
Van Buren, Martin 14, 218, 223, 229–231, 234, 250
Van der Hoop bankiers N.V. 259
Van der Sprenkel, Sybille 52–53, 95, 98
Van Dyke, Paul A. X, 11, 78, 133, 269
Van Kley, Edwin 12
Van Wissen-van Staden, Marijke X
Vandenberg, Arthur H. 245–246, 249
Varnham, Warner XII, 80
Vermont 237
Vernon, Rear Admiral Sir Edward 113, 124
Vessels See "Ships"
Viceroy's Merchant 55
Vietnam 28, 32

Wagner, Rudolf IX
Waley-Cohen, Joanna 105
Wallace, Henry A. 2 n.5
Waln, William 181
Wancheng hong 150, 157–158
Wanhe hong 139–140
Wanyuan hong 150, 210, 212
War of 1812 155, 169, 183, 227
Wars 132, 146, 154, 169, 171, 188, 210–211, 215–217, 269
Ward, Thomas W. 174
Washington, D.C. 238, 241–242, 272
Watches XVIII, 65, 141, 200
Watson, Alan 13, 272
Wayqua (Ni Hongwen) 50, 57, 91–92, 104–108, 113
Weapons 28, 81
Wedell, Captain John 28
Wenlian 189
Western financial model 2
Whampoa XVIII, 28, 58–59, 79
White, Ann Bolbach 9, 56
White House 183
Wilcocks, Benjamin C. 178–182, 187
Debtor 180–181, 187
Wilcocks, R.H. 178
Williams, Jeffrey R. IX
Williamson, Timothy XII, 66, 68
Willing & Francis 174
Willow palisade 44
Wills, John E., Jr. (Jack) 8
Wines 224
Wokou See China, History, Ming Dynasty, Japanese pirates"
Written agreements 52, 61, 70, 72, 169
Wong, Winnie IX
Woolens XVIII, 123, 134–135, 137, 159, 266
Women 81, 199, 270
World Bank 259
World War II 254
Wright, Conrad E. X
Wu, Silas IX
Wu Xiongguang 29
Wu Yuanhua 61
Wuyi Hills 167
Wyequa (Shi Huailian) 108, 141–144

Xiamen 26, 32, 36, 39, 63
Xiangshao 43 n.140, 132, 170
Xicheng hong 169, 186, 188
Xinjiang Province XVII, 29, 75, 104, 107–109, 144
Xingtai hong See "Hingtae hong"

Yale University 10
Yales, Captain 200
Yalu River 44
Yamen XVIII
Yan Qiqang 199, 212
Yan Qixiang 199, 212, 270
Yang Jingsu 60
Yang, Lien-sheng 52–53
Yang Yingzhu 62
Yangzi River 30
Yanlong 190
Yanqua (Ye Shanglin) 61, 148
Yao rebellion 57
Yellow River works 129, 137, 153–154, 171, 209
Yi ben yi li, rule See "China, Law, Qing Dynasty"
Yicheng hong 148
Yifeng hong 90 n.158, 118, 138
Yihe hong (Howqua) 56, 128, 148, 167, 171
Yihe hong (Teunqua) 79 n.110
Yngshaw (Yan Shiying) 57, 65 n.55, 88, 108, 116–119, 122, 124, 126–127, 206
Debts 206
Yokqua 90 n.158
Yongzheng Emperor 36, 55
Yoshimune, Shogun 32
Youngqua 28
Youqua 150 n.12, 156
Yu Bashi 86–87, 93
Yuanchuan hong 141
Yuanlai hong 100
Yugun 208
Yuntaishan 25
Yuyuan hong 57, 118

Zhangzhou 25
Zheng Chenggong 21–22
Zhili Province 25, 72
Zhonghe hong 198 n.26 and n.28
Zhongxiang 199
Zhufeng hong 90, 119
Ziyuan hong 56, 72, 87–88, 90 n.158
Zombie banks 235–236, 256